Camping & Caravanning
Great Britain & Ireland 1999

Trossachs Holiday Park, Aberfoyle, Scotland

Finlake Leisure Park, Chudleigh, Devon

Fishguard Bay Caravan Park, Fishguard, Wales

West One Publishing • London

© West One (Trade) Publishing Ltd. 1998

This book is sold subject to the condition that it shall not, by way of trade, or otherwise, be lent, re-sold, hired out or otherwise circulated without the publisher's prior consent in any form of binding or cover other than that in which it is published.

All rights reserved. No parts of this work may be reproduced, stored in a retrieval system or transmitted by any means without permission. Whilst every effort has been made to ensure that the information contained in this publication is accurate and up to date, the publisher does not accept any responsibility for any error, omission, or misrepresentation. All liability for loss, disappointment, negligence or other damage caused by reliance on the information contained in this guide, or in the event of bankruptcy, or liquidation, or cessation of trade of any company, individual or firm mentioned is hereby excluded.

ISBN 1-900327-22-8 paperback

A CIP catalogue record for this book is available from the British Library.

Printed and bound in Spain by Artes Graficas ELKAR S Co op., 48012 Bilbao.

Pictures reproduced with the kind permission of: Robert Harding (p.239 a typical French road, John Miller); The Stock Market (pp.224-225 Co.Galway, Republic of Ireland); Tony Stone Images (p.21 Gold Hill in Shaftesbury, Dorset, England, p.167 The fishing town of Tobermory, Isle of Mull, Scotland, pp.198-199 Dolbadarn Castle, ruins at the entrance to Llanberis Pass, Gwynedd, Wales, p.237 Gorey Castle, Jersey, Channel Islands).

Cover photograph: The Camping & Caravanning Club, Keswick Club Site, overlooking Derwent Water, Cumbria.

Published by
West One (Trade) Publishing Ltd
Portland House
4 Great Portland Street
London W1N 5AA

Telephone: 0171 580 6886
Fax: 0171 580 9788
Email: sales@west-one.com

Publisher	Alan Wakeford
Managing Editor	Stan Dover
Production Manager	Ted Timberlake
Production Team	John Jones
	Graeme Kay
	Elaine Pate
	Sara Foster
Director Corporate and Retail Sales	Marcia Smythe
Director Media Sales	Michael Clancy
Telesales Manager	Virginie Bellivier
Sales Executives	Xavier de Greef
	Yeside Akiwowo
	Miguel Pagan
	Supriya Tiwari
Finance and Administration Team	Sarah Browne
	Friederike Brexendorff
	Emma Keens
	Katya Skaff
Chief Executive Officer	Martin Coleman

Contents

Introduction	4
How to use the guide	5
An entry explained	6
Symbols and abbreviations	7
Caravan security	8
Caravan safety	12
Caravans, trailers and the law	14
Useful addresses	16

Directory of Hotels

England	21
Scotland	167
Wales	198
Northern Ireland	224
Republic of Ireland	227
Channel Islands	237
Isle of Man	237
France and the Benelux countries	239
Great Britain & Ireland Maps	265

4

Introduction

For 1999, RAC Camping & Caravanning is again fully revised and features 1,000 campsites in Great Britain and Ireland.

This guide provides an extensive selection of sites that individually cater for the interests of all camping enthusiasts. Whether you seek sporting activities, wildlife reserves, on-site entertainment or just wish to get away from it all, we believe that the variety of sites in this guide will accommodate all your needs, enabling you to enjoy the perfect camping or caravanning break.

New for 1999, is a supplementary directory of European campsites. The popularity of Continental camping holidays has steadily increased during recent years and has undoubtedly been assisted by competitive ferry rates and the advent of the Le Shuttle rail service. Within this guide, we have provided a selection of quality sites in France and the Benelux countries and current information necessary for booking a Channel crossing.

All of the establishments in this guide have been selected from our Camping & Caravanning site database and are included on the basis of a 'paid-for' listing and have not been inspected by the RAC.

How to use the guide

This book is divided into clear sections: useful information, directory of sites and maps. The 19-page map section at the back of the book plots the locations of sites. The front section of the guide provides essential information for campers, including guidelines for towing a caravan, security tips, and an explanation of how to use the directory. For easy reference, the guide is arranged in alphabetical order by town.

Choosing your site
The type of site you choose to visit will depend on the holiday you have in mind. For those who want peace and quiet, to get away from the crowds and noise of everyday life, there are sites with only the most basic facilities, where a friendly nod to a fellow camper may be all the human contact you have. Others may prefer somewhere more lively, with every modern facility, play areas for children, and evening entertainment laid on. We hope we have provided all the information you need to choose your site, but if you are unsure about anything at all, check with the site before you book.

Size
The total area of the site is given in acres; not all this area may be used for touring pitches. We give the number of pitches for touring visitors in caravans, motor caravans and tents, and how many of these pitches are level, and how many have electric hook-ups. We also give the number of static caravans on the site. Please note that these are not necessarily for hire. Where caravans and chalets are available for hire, it is shown under rental. We next list the number of hot showers, WCs and chemical waste disposal points (CWPs) on the site.

Disabled facilities
Sites shown with this symbol have some facilities for the disabled, but it is essential to ask the site in advance whether they cater for your personal requirements.

Dogs
Most sites accept dogs, but owners are expected to keep their pets under control (often on a lead while on the site) and to exercise them with consideration for other campers. Some sites will permit only one dog per camping unit, while others will not accommodate certain breeds – it is advisable to check when booking.

Prices
The prices are those quoted to us by the site management and show the price for two people plus car/caravan, car/tent or motorhome. It is always advisable to confirm charges before your arrival at a site. Prices quoted for Camping & Caravanning Club Sites are for non-members only. Members will pay a different rate.

Booking
As a general rule, it is necessary to book during high season on all sites. Out of high season, it is advisable to book if you want to stay at one specific site, or in an area with few sites. It is sensible to telephone ahead to check on the space available and to time your arrival so that if a site is full you have time to find space on another site.

Complaints
Should you have any cause for complaint at any site featured in this guide, speak to the site owners as soon as the problem arises. This gives them an opportunity to put it right and you the chance to enjoy your stay.

Credit cards
Where a site accepts credit cards, the cards accepted are shown after the price information.

Description and directions
The short description of the site gives an idea of what sort of site it is, what amenities it has and what the surroundings are like. The directions should enable you to locate the site from the nearest main road.

Caravan storage
'WS' shows a site which has winter storage for caravans. Please contact the site direct (not the RAC) if you wish to store a caravan.

6

An entry explained

1 Town, county and map reference —— CIRENCESTER Gloucestershire   7F4

2 Campsite or caravan park name with address and telephone number —— Cotswold Hoburne

Broadway Lane, South Cerney, Cirencester GL7 5UQ

☏ 01285-860216   Fax 01285-862106

3 Months open —— **Open** Easter-31 October ▲ 🚐 🚏

4 Short description with a picture of the caravan park or campsite

Set in the Cotswold Water Park, this quality site has fish-stocked lakes, a magnificent indoor pool and a licensed lakeside lounge with seasonal entertainment.

5 Size of site —— **Size** 70 acres, 302 touring pitches, 302 with electric hookup, 302 level pitches, 158 static caravans, 18 ❨, 54 WCs, 6 CWPs

6 Details of prices and credit cards accepted —— **£** car/tent £8.50-£21, car/caravan £8.50-£21, motorhome £8.50-£21

Rental 🚐 Chalet.

CC MasterCard Visa

7 Site amenities —— ♨ ✕ 🍽 🛒 📞 📺 ♿ 🎮 🚿 🧺 🎯 GR 🔍 TV 🎣 ⛰ Calor Gaz ♿

Last arrival time: 21:00

8 Directions to site —— ➡ The park is signposted from A419, 4 miles S of Cirencester.

Symbols and abbreviations

English

- Licensed bar
- Cold storage
- Launderette
- Telephone on site or within ¼ mile
- Dogs allowed
- Suitable for disabled
- Restaurant on site
- Restaurant within ¼ mile
- Shop on site
- Shop within ¼ mile
- Snacks on site
- Snacks within ¼ mile
- Motorhome
- Caravan
- Tent
- Credit cards
- Children's playground
- TV room

Sporting facilities

- Indoor swimming pool
- Outdoor swimming pool
- Table tennis
- Snooker/billiards
- Horse riding
- Gym
- Fishing
- Golf
- Sauna
- Tennis
- Squash
- Games room

Français

- Bar avec licence
- Emplacements frigorifiques
- Laverie
- Cabines téléphoniques sur le terrain ou près du camping
- Chiens acceptés
- Aménagements pour handicapés
- Restaurant sur le terrain
- Restaurant dans un périmètre de 500m
- Epicerie sur le terrain
- Epicerie dans un périmètre de 500m
- Plat cuisinés à emporter sur le terrain
- Plat cuisinés à emporter dans un périmètre de 500m
- Camping-car
- Caravanes
- Tente
- Cartes de crédit
- Aire de jeux pour enfants
- Salle de télévision

- Piscine couverte
- Piscine en plein air
- Tennis de table
- Billard
- Equitation
- Gymnase
- Pêche
- Terrain de Golf
- Sauna
- Tennis
- Squash
- Salle de jeux

Deutsch

- Bar
- Kühllagerungsmöglichkeiten
- Waschsalon/Reinigung
- Telefon am Platz oder innerhalb von 500m
- Hunde erlaubt
- Einrichtungen für Behinderte
- Restaurant am Platz
- Restaurant innerhalb von 500m
- Lebensmittelgeschäft am Platz
- Lebensmittelgeschäft innerhalb von 500m
- Imbiss am Platz
- Imbiss innerhalb von 500m
- Wohnmobil
- Wohnwagen
- Zelt
- Kreditkarten
- Spielplatz
- Fernsehraum

- Hallenbad
- Freibad
- Tischtennis
- Billard
- Reiten
- Sporthalle
- Angeln
- Golfplatz
- Sauna
- Tennis
- Squash
- Spieleraum

Caravan security

Good security is absolutely essential if you want to protect your caravan from theft. Much of the advice given below applies to trailer tents and motor caravans as well as to caravans. It will show you:
- how to deter theft by using security devices and by taking sensible precautions
- how to make it less likely that your caravan will be broken into
- what you can do to get your caravan back if it's been stolen.

Finally, do remember that caravan theft is relatively rare. By taking sensible precautions you can make sure that it doesn't happen to you.

Security Devices

Some of the many security devices you can buy are better than others. None will prevent your caravan from being stolen but all will make it less likely. Devices vary in quality so you should buy the best you can afford. Make sure the thief knows it's there; use bright paint on wheel clamps and display the security stickers that manufacturers usually supply with their equipment.

Don't assume that your caravan is safe if it's parked on your driveway or in your garden.
After storage compounds, private driveways are the most popular target area for theft.

Security systems

A reliable alarm, properly fitted, can deter thieves but don't forget that an alarm that goes off when there is no security risk can make you the most unpopular person in the road or on the campsite and may deter neighbours from raising the alarm if there is a real emergency.

If you keep your van at home, you may want to consider linking it into your home security system, if you have one. Talk to your security consultants... it may be a simple task.

Hitch locks

Hitch locks provide a reasonable degree of protection. A good lock is necessary so buy the best you can afford (preferably in heavy gauge steel) and ensure it covers the tow socket fixing bolts. Some hitch locks will lock the caravan to the car so you need to ensure it is unlocked before you commence towing. Hitch locks are useful on site or for short stays but do not generally offer adequate security when the caravan is in storage.

Wheel clamps

As a rule, the easier a wheel clamp is to put on, the easier it will be for the thief to remove it. Remember that some wheel clamps can be bypassed if they allow the thief to remove the entire wheel. Buy a good one and check that it fits your caravan before you do.

Wheel stands

Putting your caravan on wheel stands can be a useful deterrent but removing the wheels won't stop the tenacious thief. You should check with your insurer before fitting wheel stands as some policies require that wheel clamps are fitted at all times. Check your handbook too: some manufacturers recommend wheel stands for winter storage.

Security posts

Security posts cemented into a drive or hard surface will physically prevent your van from being moved off site. Lockable, some are detachable or fold down to allow access. Others have a towball fitted to the top of the post so that your caravan can be fitted to it with a hitch lock.

Caravan Watch

Early in 1995 Essex Police launched a crime prevention initiative called Caravan Watch with a view to raising public awareness of caravan theft in the Essex area. The aim of the scheme is to encourage owners to make their caravans as secure as possible, more identifiable and therefore less attractive to a thief.

The scheme has generated wide interest already and has spread to other areas of the country such as Lincolnshire, Yorkshire, Cheshire, and Sussex. You can register all the details of your caravan with the scheme. The more details a caravanner can supply, the better the chance of recovering a stolen vehicle. If you change your vehicle the Essex police will supply a new sticker for free.

A sticker displayed on the caravan identifies the make and registration number of the usual towing vehicle. With the sticker displayed, a thief risks either a caravan with an unmatched tow vehicle, or breaking into the caravan to try and remove the sticker.

For more information on Essex Police Caravan Watch Scheme, please contact Wickford police station Tel: 01268 561312.

Security Precautions
If you follow the advice below in addition to using security devices, it is even less likely that your caravan will be stolen and more likely that it will be recovered if it is. Act now.

Records
Take photographs of your caravan showing distinctive features, including scratches and dents, if any. Keep a note of your chassis number. If your van has been CRIS registered, do not keep those documents, or any others that the thief may find useful, in it.

CRIS
Under the Caravan Registration and Identification Scheme, almost all British manufactured caravans (there are some exceptions) should, since 1992 have a 17 digit number stamped into their A frame and etched into at least three windows. The owner is issued with a registration document like a car log book. If you are buying a CRIS registered van, you can phone CRIS with the 17 digit number and the name and address of the owner and they will be able to tell you if it has been lost or stolen or if there is outstanding finance on it.
Ring 01722 411430 between 8.00 am-8.00 pm Monday to Saturday and 10.00 am-5.00 pm on Sunday.

Vehicle Watch
Vehicle Watch is a scheme designed to significantly increase the chances of a stolen vehicle being spotted by the police. Register and you will be issued with a sticker. The police regularly stop vans displaying this sticker, particularly between midnight and 5.00 am when there is a greater chance of the van being a stolen vehicle. If you belong to the scheme, always carry proof of your ownership, in case you are stopped.

Etching
Etch your caravan chassis number or your postcode on all windows and mark them in hidden places inside the van, such as inside a cupboard or under a bed. Ultra violet pens are useful for this as the results are very difficult to detect in non-UV light. A simple spirit-based felt-tip pen used on raw plywood is almost impossible to remove.

Roof marking
Many police forces recommend marking the roof of your van with (for example) a number of your choice in large stick-on letters which can be recognised by a police helicopter. You can do it yourself or use a commercially available kit.

Microchip
Several companies will embed into your caravan structure a microchip that can be detected by a scanner. Be warned that there is, as yet, no central network of scanners for tracing stolen vans. From 1998 new British caravans will have a microchip inserted into their structure at the time of manufacture. This chip will carry a CRIS 17 digit number.

Tracker
Under this scheme, Tracker will fit a hidden transmitter into your van. If your caravan is reported stolen, the transmitter may be activated to emit a signal which can be picked up by a homing device, allowing the police to locate it. Tracker has scored some notable successes but be aware that it is a battery operated system that's only activated when your van is reported stolen. This can be a problem if your van is in long-term storage and is checked only occasionally.

Storage
If you can't store your van at home, local planning officers may supply details of landowners who have areas where planning permission for caravan storage has been granted. Don't choose a storage area on price alone. Storage areas are particularly popular with thieves: there's plenty of choice and sometimes little chance of being disturbed. Some are high security sites with security guards, floodlighting and sophisticated security systems. Others are not. If you take seat cushions home when your van is in winter storage, you will make it a less attractive prospect for the casual thief. Similarly, removing all personal items and leaving the curtains open and cupboard doors open will encourage the opportunist thief to look elsewhere.

Holidays
Don't relax your guard when you're on holiday. Remember: thieves will steal caravans from picnic sites, motorway service areas and lay-bys and at times of the year when both demand and supply may be high.

Buying a caravan
Don't buy caravans in the dark, in pub car parks or motorway service areas. Always try to visit a seller's home. Make sure it is the seller's home. Unscrupulous sellers have been known to use the drive of an empty house.

Check that the number plate is the same on the van as on the tow car. Temporary and handwritten number plates should be regarded with suspicion.

If you contact a seller and are asked to ring only at certain times, make sure you aren't ringing a public phone box... a sure sign that something is adrift.

Ring 100 and ask the operator to check the status of a line.

Check the caravan chassis number. Has it been removed or altered? If so, contact the police.

Both the major caravan organisations keep lists of stolen caravans. Check with them to see if the van you are interested in has been listed as stolen.
Camping and Caravanning Club Tel: 01203 694995,
Caravan Club Tel: 01342 326944.

Selling a caravan
Never part with your caravan until the buyer's cheque has been cleared. This includes building society cheques and bankers drafts. They could be forgeries or stolen.

Crime prevention
If you have any information about caravan theft or disposal of stolen caravans, use the confidential free phone Crime Stopper line 0800 555111. You don't have to give your name if you don't want to and you may be entitled to a reward.

This section has been written with the kind assistance of the Camping and Caravanning Club.

Hints & Tips

Don't neglect the servicing of your caravan. An on-the-spot police caravan check at the M5 service area in Exeter, reported in *Practical Caravan*, revealed more faults than expected. Out of 118 caravans inspected, only 33 were in a satisfactory condition, so make sure your caravan is in good repair and working order before setting out on a journey.

The survey revealed that:

- 32 tyres in the spot check were perished.
- The brakes of many of the caravans had been neglected.
- 15 caravans had defective lighting.
- 37 vans had too much downward pressure exerted on the towbar – in some cases by more than 100 per cent above the factory recommendations – and most vans had at least 80 kg on the hitch.

You should also make sure the van has registration plates on the back, and that the jockey wheel braces are not worn.

WHO ELSE CAN OFFER ALL THIS?

FANTASTIC
TOURING VALUE
from only
£4 PER NIGHT

The Freedom TRAIL
BRITISH HOLIDAYS

14 FANTASTIC LOCATIONS IN SOME OF THE MOST SOUGHT AFTER DESTINATIONS

- ◆ **NORTH AND SOUTH WALES**
- ◆ **SOMERSET AND DORSET**
- ◆ **LAKE DISTRICT**
- ◆ **NORTHUMBERLAND**
- ◆ **SCOTLAND**

- ◆ Indoor/Outdoor Swimming Pools
- ◆ Indoor/Outdoor Play Area
- ◆ Sports/Leisure Facilities
- ◆ Entertainment/Cabaret
- ◆ The Bradley Bear Club
- ◆ Teen Challenge Club
- ◆ Takeaways/Restaurant
- ◆ FREE Awning Spaces
- ◆ Modern Upto Date Facilities
- ◆ Fully Serviced Premier, Super & Euro Pitches

JOIN THE FREEDOM TRAIL AND
SAVE 10%
ON ALL YOUR BOOKINGS
CALL TO FIND OUT HOW

CALL US NOW FOR THE LATEST AVAILABILITY AND PRICES ON

LO-CALL **0990 134 402**

BRILLIANT FAMILY HOLIDAYS

Caravan safety

Safety on the road is vital, so you should ensure that your caravan or trailer is serviced and maintained by skilled professionals at regular intervals. You will also need to make sure that you carry out key checks before every trip. Some of these checks are simple and you may feel that you can carry them out yourself, many are best left to the professionals. Caravan accidents are extremely rare and their number has decreased in recent years but make sure you take all necessary precautions before you set out. Above all, drive safely.

Tow bar
A well-fitted and maintained tow bar is vital for safety as it is the means by which car and trailer are connected. Make sure all bolts are tightened to the recommended torque figure and that there is no cracking or rusting around the mounting points. From August 1st 1998, all type approved cars must have a type approved tow bar and tow ball fitted.

Tyres
Your tyres are all that's between you and the road, so look after them: proper maintenance will improve performance and road safety. Never mix radial and cross-ply tyres. Before every trip, check the pressure and condition of your tyres and make sure that your caravan wheel nuts are tight and that wheel trims are securely attached. Always carry a spare wheel.

Brakes
Good brakes can save lives so brake maintenance is best left to qualified professionals. But do keep an eye on brake cables and mechanisms: get them checked if you have any doubts. Always connect the breakaway cable or secondary coupling to a separate mounting point and not to the tow ball. Its purpose is not to keep caravan and car together in the event of a tow bar failure.

Electrics
Road lights on your caravan or trailer are operated from the tow vehicle through a 12N socket and plug. Check indicators and lights are in working order before setting off. A visual or audible device must be fitted inside the car to show that the traffic indicators are working.

Suspension
Check the condition of both car and trailer suspension regularly. It's important for safety as well as comfort. When your caravan is attached to its vehicle, it should tow level or slightly nose down, never nose up. If you find that the rear of your car sags, you may need to review your suspension arrangements. Get advice from your dealer or a specialist.

Mirrors
An adequate rear view mirror that gives a good view of the road, both behind and along both sides of your caravan, is essential. Generally, this means that you will need special towing mirrors as well as making sure those you already have are properly adjusted.

Coupling
Before every journey, make sure that the jockey wheel and all steadies are raised and secured and that the coupling head on the trailer is fully engaged with the tow bar of the towing vehicle.

Trailer weight
Responsible bodies recommend that the loaded weight of your caravan should not exceed 85% of the kerb weight of your car. Experienced towers may sometimes exceed this recommended limit but the loaded weight of your trailer should never exceed the kerb weight of the towing vehicle, or the car manufacturer's towing limit.

Nose weight
This is the weight you put on the tow ball of your vehicle and is typically between 50 kg and 100 kg. For best stability, the nose weight should not exceed 7% of the actual laden weight of the caravan. Adjust the loading around the caravan's axle as necessary to ensure that your trailers nose weight does not exceed this limit.

Payload
Also known as the gross weight, this is the weight of the items that you are allowed to carry in your van for personal use. You will find this figure in the manufacturer's handbook. Check before every trip to make sure you don't exceed the total weight allowed. It is important when loading your van to keep weight low down and over its axle.

Corners
Remember when negotiating roundabouts and corners that your van will not follow exactly the same path as its towing vehicle. To avoid hitting the kerb, you will need to take a wider path so that the rear of your trailer clears the kerb line. Remember too, that when turning right at junctions, you will have to turn later and then more sharply than if you were driving solo.

Reversing round corners can be difficult and needs practice. Always use a helper to keep an eye on the back of the van if you can. Unhitching and manhandling the van may sometimes be necessary.

Hill starts
With a trailer in tow, you need more throttle to get you going on a hill start. Delicate clutch avoids stalling.

Speed and overtaking
Watch your speed. Exceeding legal speed limits for caravans is dangerous and may cause you to lose control. Remember that your van/car combination is heavier and wider than a solo vehicle and you will therefore need to allow yourself plenty of time and space for overtaking.

If traffic builds up behind you, pull over at a convenient spot to allow other vehicles to pass.

Braking
When towing, it will take you an average of 20% more distance to stop. ABS systems may improve braking performance but they are no substitute for proper anticipation, so remember to leave more space between you and the car in front and to allow plenty of time for braking.

Instability
Lateral instability (snaking) is the most common form and is usually the result of bad loading, excessive speed, or both. But it can be caused by air displaced as heavy vehicles pass you. Vertical instability (pitching) can occur if you hit a pothole. In neither case should you apply your brakes hard as you may make matters worse. Instead, slow down gradually by easing off the accelerator. A stabiliser will help but proper weight distribution and a good car/van match is essential.

Tiredness
Tiredness can kill, so if you're planning a long journey make sure you allow enough time for breaks.

This section has been written with the kind assistance of the Camping and Caravanning Club.

General Advice
Roadside camping
Camping or siting a caravan on verges or lay-bys is not allowed. However, permission to camp on land near by can often be obtained from the farmer or landowner. If an outbreak of foot and mouth or swine vesicular disease occurs, campers must be very careful to follow all necessary precautions.

London
If you are visiting London with a caravan on tow, try to avoid travelling across the centre of London, particularly during the rush hours Monday to Friday 0800-1000 and 1600-1800 hours, and if you are unfamiliar with the route.

Parking of car/caravan outfits at meter bays is not permitted. It is best to leave a caravan at the site and visit central London solo, or by public transport. If it is essential to park an outfit in London, find a suitable car park. Underground and multi-storey car parks often have a height limit which will not permit access for caravans or motor caravans.

Motorway service areas
Caravans are permitted to park at motorway service areas for the purpose of utilising the facilities. Parking for the purpose of cooking meals etc., is not usually permitted, and at some service areas it is forbidden to lower the corner legs of a caravan for any reason. Charges for overnight stops are available on application to the individual service areas.

14

Caravans, trailers and the law

This is a brief summary of some of the more important things you should know:

- Caravans and their towing vehicles should be in such a condition that they cause no danger to other road users.

- You are allowed to drive up to 60 mph on motorways and dual carriageways. On all other roads, the speed limit is 50 mph unless lower limits are in force.

- Normally, cars can tow a trailer up to a maximum of 7 metres long, excluding the A frame. Trailers should usually be no more than 2.3 metres wide.

- No special driving licence is needed to tow a caravan. If they have passed their car test after 1st January 1997, some new drivers may need to take an additional test if they want to tow a very large caravan.

- Your trailer must carry a number plate displaying the number of the tow vehicle and red reflecting triangles.

- Passengers are not allowed to travel in any trailer while it is being towed.

- You must have a full driving licence before you attempt to tow.

- Towing vehicles must not use the outside lane of a three (or more) lane motorway, even when overtaking.

- Trailer tyres must be capable of carrying the gross load of the trailer and have a tread depth of no less than 1.6 mm across the central three-quarters of the breadth of the tyre and around the entire circumference.

- Trailer caravan outfits must not park at parking meters.

- Stopping in a lay-by is considered an obstruction. You may be moved on.

- If you park your caravan in the street overnight you must display lights all round.

- Make sure your motor insurance policy covers you for towing.

Forest Holidays

Come to the heart of Britain's wonderful woodlands

for a holiday or short break. The Forestry Commission has almost 30 touring caravan and camping sites in scenic forest locations throughout the UK. From Glenmore in the Cairngorms to the New Forest, with a network of sites in between.

Brochure hotline 0131 334 0066
Quote ref: RAC

Forestry Commission

Useful addresses

British Holiday & Home Parks Association
Chichester House
6 Pullman Court, Great Western Road
Gloucester GL1 3ND
Tel: 01452 526911

The Camping and Caravanning Club
Greenfields House
Westwood Way
Coventry
West Midlands CV4 8JH
Tel: 01203 694995

The Caravan Club
East Grinstead House
East Grinstead
West Sussex RH19 1UA
Tel: 01342 326944

The Motor Caravanners' Club
22 Evelyn Close
Twickenham
Middlesex TW2 7BN
Tel: 0181 893 3883

National Caravan Council Limited
Catherine House
Victoria Road
Aldershot
Hampshire GU11 1SS
Tel: 01252 318251
(comprehensive list of members includes manufacturers, dealers, parks and traders).

Society of Motor Manufacturers & Traders Ltd
Motor Caravan Section
Forbes House
Halkin Street
London SW1X 7DS
Tel: 0171 235 7000
(listing of members available)

UK Towing bracket suppliers

Towing brackets should be made to British Standard BSAU 114b or the 28th July 1993 equivalent international standard ISO 3853.

Anchor Towbars Ltd
Orchard House
Appleby Hill
Austrey, Atherstone
Warwicks CV9 3ER
Tel: 01827 830039

B. Dixon-Bate Ltd
Unit 45
First Avenue
Deeside Industrial Park
Deeside
Flintshire CH5 2LG
Tel: 01244-288925

Exhaust Ejector Co
11 Wade House Road
Shelf
Halifax
West Yorkshire HX3 7PE
Tel: 01274 679524/5/6

PCT Leisure Ltd
Holbrook Industrial Estate
New Street
Holbrook
Halfway
Sheffield S20 3GH
Tel: 0114 2510210

Peter J. Lea Co Ltd
Shaw Road South
off Shaw Heath
Stockport
Cheshire SK3 8JG
Tel: 0161 480 2377

Tanfield Ltd
Blatchford Road
Roffey
Horsham
West Sussex RH13 5QR
Tel: 01403 269100

Towsure Products Ltd
151-183 Holme Lane
Sheffield S6 4JR
Tel: 01142 503000

Watling Engineers Ltd
88 Parkstreet Village
St. Albans
Hertfordshire AL2 2LR
Tel: 01727 873661

Witter Towbars Ltd
18 Canal Side
Chester CH1 3LL
Tel: 01244 341166

Inspected Hotels 1999

Inspected Hotels
Great Britain & Ireland 1999

RAC

A superb, full colour guide to over 4,500 establishments (over 1250 illustrated) – all inspected by the RAC's rigorous team of hotel inspectors.

Choice, quality, value – a place to stay for everyone, regardless of budget.

Recommended for the business traveller or independent leisure traveller – an essential short break planner.

Special feature on fourposter beds. Every hotel with a fourposter bed is flagged with a unique symbol – the ideal indicator for booking that special weekend away.

Information on the RAC's Blue Ribbon hotels – the crème de la crème of establishments.

Announcing the RAC's Small Hotels of the Year Awards.

Full colour mapping for hotel location and journey planning.

£13.99 – Available from your local bookshop

Or contact:

Trade Sales Department
West One Publishing
Portland House
4 Great Portland Street
London W1N 5AA

Telephone: 0171 580 6886, Fax: 0171 580 9788
e-mail: sales@west-one.com

British Tourist Authority

Tourist Information Centres are located in cities and towns throughout Great Britain with information on places of interest for tourists. These Information Centres are indicated by distinctive 'i' signs placed in their vicinity. The addresses of the National Tourist Boards are as follows:

English Tourist Board
Head Office:
Thames Tower
Black's Road
Hammersmith
London W6 9EL
(written enquiries only)

Scottish Tourist Board
Head Office:
23 Ravelston Terrace
Edinburgh EH4 3EU
Tel: 0131 332 2433

London Office:
19 Cockspur Street
London SW1Y 5BL
Tel: 0171 930 8661

Wales Tourist Board
Head Office:
Brunel House
2 Fitzalan Road
Cardiff CF2 1UY
Tel: 01222 499909

Northern Ireland Tourist Board
Head Office:
St Anne's Court
59 North Street
Belfast BT1 1NB
Tel: 01232 231221

London Office:
24 Haymarket
London SW1Y 4DG
Tel: 0171 766 9920

Irish Tourist Board (Bord Failte)
Head Office:
Baggot St. Bridge
Dublin 2
Tel: 00 353 1 602 4000

London Office:
150 New Bond Street
London W1Y 0AQ
Tel: 0171 493 3201

Channel Islands
Guernsey Tourist Board
PO Box 23
North Plantation
St Peter Port
Guernsey GY1 3AN
Tel: 01481 723552

Jersey Tourist Board
Liberation Square
St Helier
Jersey JE1 1BB
Tel: 01534 500777

National Parks

The most beautiful, spectacular and dramatic expanses of country in England and Wales have been given the status of National Parks under the National Parks and Access to the Countryside Act, 1949, in recognition of their national importance. Ten *National Parks* were established during the 1950s: *Brecon Beacons, Exmoor, Dartmoor, the Lake District, Northumberland, North York Moors, the Peak District, the Pembrokeshire Coast, Snowdonia* and the *Yorkshire Dales*. In addition, the Norfolk and Suffolk Broads, *The Broads*, were established in 1989, although not a National Park by name, it has equal status to the Parks. *The New Forest* is also considered by many to be of comparable quality to a National Park and legislation that will provide it with similar protection is currently being drafted.

The essence of each of these areas is in the striking quality and remoteness of much of their scenery, the harmony between activity and nature that they display and the opportunities they offer for suitable forms of recreation. National Parks are 'national' in the vital sense that they are of special value to the whole nation. But designation of an area as a National Park does not affect the ownership of the land. It does not remove from local communities the right to live their own lives, nor does it give the public any right of access.

The 1949 Act also created *Areas of Outstanding Natural Beauty*. The landscape in these areas is no less beautiful but the opportunities for extensive outdoor recreation are lacking. The following 39 Areas of Outstanding Natural Beauty have been designated:
Anglesey, Arnside and Silverdale, Blackdown Hills,

Just rewards
Join the RAC today and take out Standard Cover.

If you don't call us out during your membership year, we'll reward you with a £25 discount when you renew at the same level of cover.

Call us on 0800 029 029
quoting ref GUIDE 1

rac

movement drives us

www.rac.co.uk

Cannock Chase, Chichester Harbour, Chilterns, Clwydian Range, Cornwall, Cotswolds, Cranborne Chase & West Wiltshire Downs, Dedham Vale, Dorset, East Devon, East Hampshire, Forest of Bowland, Gower Peninsula, High Weald, Howardian Hills, Isles of Scilly, Isle of Wight, Kent Downs, Lincolnshire Wolds, Lleyn, Malvern Hills, Mendip Hills, Norfolk Coast, North Devon, North Pennines, Northumberland Coast, North Wessex Downs, Quantock Hills, Shropshire Hills, South Devon, South Hampshire Coast, Suffolk Coast and Heaths, Surrey Hills, Sussex Hills, Sussex Downs, Solway Coast, Wye Valley.

Although there are no National Parks or Areas of outstanding Natural Beauty in Scotland, there are 40 National Scenic Areas (NSAs), designated in 1980 under the 1972 Town and Country Planning (Scotland) Act, which are given a measure of protection through special development control procedures. Protection of the NSAs is the duty of Scottish Natural Heritage (formed from the merger of the Countryside Commission for Scotland and the Nature Conservancy Council for Scotland in 1992).

Countryside Commission
John Dower House,
Crescent Place,
Cheltenham,
Gloucestershire GL50 3RA
Tel: 01242 521381

The Countryside Council for Wales
Plas Penrhos,
Penrhos Road,
Bangor,
Gwynedd LL57 2LQ
Tel: 01248 370444

Forest Parks
The Forestry Commission
231 Corstorphine Road,
Edinburgh EH12 7AT
General enquiries Tel: 0131 334 0303
Campsite brochure requests Tel: 0131 334 0066

The Forestry Commission is one of Britain's largest providers of tourist and recreation facilities, attracting over 50 million day-visitors every year and encouraging the public to enjoy the publicly-owned forests in its care through its freedom to roam policy. It also provides for many activities including walking, picnics, mountain biking, orienteering, skiing, field sports, water sports and nature study.

The National Trust
The National Trust is an independent charity responsible for the preservation of many historic houses, industrial monuments, formal and romantic gardens, nature reserves, open countryside and hundreds of miles of Britain's coastline. Details of the various National Trust activities can be obtained from:

The National Trust
36 Queen Anne's Gate,
London SW1H 9AS
Tel: 0171 222 9251

The National Trust, North Wales Office
Trinity Square,
Llandudno,
Gwynedd LL30 2DE
Tel: 01492 860123

The National Trust, South Wales Office
The King's Head,
Bridge Street,
Llandeilo,
Carmarthenshire SA19 6BB
Tel: 01558 822800

The National Trust, Northern Ireland
Rowallane House
Saintfield
Ballynahinch
Co. Down BT24 7LH
Tel: 01238 510721

The National Trust for Scotland
5 Charlotte Square
Edinburgh EH2 4DU
Tel: 0131 226 5922

English Heritage
Over 350 ancient monuments, buildings and other sites are looked after by English Heritage (formerly known as the Historic Buildings and Monuments Commission). Further details can be obtained from:

English Heritage
23 Savile Row
London W1X 1AB
Tel: 0171 973 3000

22   Acle

ACLE Norfolk   9F3

Reedham Ferry Camping & Caravan Park
Ferry Road, Reedham, Acle NR13 3HA
📞 01493-700429 Fax 01493-700429
Open March-end October ⚜ 🚐 🚛

A well-kept site with children's play area located next to the River Yare and the charming 17th century Ferry Inn. Boating, fishing and birdwatching with a free slipway. Well behaved dogs free of charge.
Size 4 acres, 20 touring pitches, 20 with electric hookup, 20 level pitches, 4 ⚐, 8 WCs, 1 CWP
£ car/tent £6.50-£11, car/caravan £6.50-£11, motorhome £6.50-£11, motorbike/tent £6.50-£11
((MasterCard Visa
✗ 🍴 📞 📂 🍽 & 🐕
Last arrival time: 22:00
➡ Off A47, 7 miles S of Acle on B1140, situated on the N bank of River Yare.

ALNWICK Northumberland   13F3

Camping & Caravanning Club Site
Dunstan Hill, Dunstan, Alnwick NE66 3TQ
📞 01665-576310
Open March-November ⚜ 🚐 🚛
Size 12 acres, 150 touring pitches, 78 with electric hookup, 12 ⚐, 18 WCs, 1 CWP
£ car/tent £11.50-£14.60, car/caravan £11.50-£14.60, motorhome £11.50-£14.60, motorbike/tent £11.50-£14.60, children £1.60, ((MasterCard Visa
🚿 🚿¼ ✗¼ 🍴 🍽¼ 🗄 📞 📂 🏪 📺 🛒 🔲 ⛽ Calor &
🐕 WS
Last arrival time: 23:00
➡ From A1 travelling N take B1340 signposted Seahouses, follow to T junction at Christon Bank, turn right. Take next signposted Embleton.
Turn right at crossroads then first left signposted Craster.

Proctors Steads Caravan & Camping Park
Procters Steads, Craster, Alnwick NE66 3TF
📞 01665-576613
Open March-October ⚜ 🚐 🚛

A good sheltered, level site covering 3½ acres, one mile from the sea, Dunstanburgh Castle and Craster. Excellent for beaches, golf courses and coastal walks.
Size 3.5 acres, 70 touring pitches, 40 with electric hookup, 70 level pitches, 20 static caravans, 8 ⚐, 10 WCs, 1 CWP
£ car/tent £8, car/caravan £8, motorhome £8, motorbike/tent £8, children £1
Rental 🚐 From £150
🚿 ✗ 🍴 🗄 📞 📂 Calor Gaz & 🐕 WS
Last arrival time: 22:00
➡ From A1 take B1340 for 2 miles. Follow signs.

ALWINTON Northumberland   13F3

Clennell Hall
Alwinton NE65 7BG
📞 01669-650341
Open February-December ⚜ 🚐 🚛

A caravan site situated in the Border country of the Cheviot Hills and set in the grounds of Clennell Hall, a 16th century, Grade II Listed building. The caravan site provides an ideal base for many outdoor pursuits, which are available within a short distance, such as: fishing, bird watching, orienteering, mountain biking, walking, trail riding, golf and pony trekking.
Size 14.5 acres, 50 touring pitches, 44 with electric hookup, 50 level pitches, 18 static caravans, 8 ⚐, 10 WCs, 1 CWP
£ car/tent £6-£8.50, car/caravan £8.50-£11, motorhome £8.50-£11, motorbike/tent £6
Rental 🚐 Cabins. £85-£225
🚿 ✗ 🍴 🗄 📞 📂 🛒 🔲 📺 ⛽ ⛽ Calor Gaz & 🐕 WS
Last arrival time: 23:00
➡ From Rothbury follow B6341 for 4 miles, turn right signed Harbottle and Alwinton. Go through

Andover

23

Harbottle village and follow sign for Alwinton, continue for 2 miles and after second bridge turn right signed Clennell Hall. From Otterburn take B6341 to Elsdon.

→ From Ambleside take B5286 to Hawkshead. Site is one mile on the right.

ANDOVER Hampshire   4B3

AMBLESIDE Cumbria   10B2

Wyke Down Caravan & Camping Park
Picket Piece, Andover SP11 6LX
☎ 01264-352048 Fax 01264-324661
Open all year ▲ ⌂ ⛺

Camping & Caravanning Club Site
Grizedale Hall, Grizedale, Ambleside LA22 0GL
☎ 01229-860257
Open March-September ▲ ⌂ ⛺
Size 4 acres, 60 touring pitches, 11 with electric hookup, 2 ⚿, 5 WCs, 1 CWP
£ car/tent £9.60-£12.10, car/caravan £9.60-£12.10, motorhome £9.60-£12.10, motorbike/tent £9.60-£12.10, children £1.50
℠ MasterCard Visa
⚏ ⚏¼ ✕¼ ⚐¼ ⊡ ☏ ▶ ♪ GR ◉ TV ⌂ Calor ♿ ✈ WS
Last arrival time: 23:00
→ From A5092 take minor road signed Colton, Oxon Park, stay on this road for about 5 miles, do not deviate to Grizedale, look for Caravan & Camping sign, then next entrance on right.

A family-owned park with country pub and golf driving range. Ample space for caravans and tents. A relaxing, peaceful setting with scenic views.
Size 7 acres, 150 touring pitches, 31 with electric hookup, 150 level pitches, 4 ⚿, 14 WCs, 1 CWP
£ car/tent £9, car/caravan £9, motorhome £9, motorbike/tent £8, children £1
℠ MasterCard Visa
⚏ ✕ ⚐ ⊡ ☏ ⊡ ⚒ GR ◉ TV ⌂ ⌂ Gaz ♿ ✈
→ Follow International Camping signs from A303, Andover Ring Road, then through village. Picket Piece signposted two miles ahead.

Low Wray Camp Site
Low Wray, Ambleside LA22 0JA
☎ 01539-432810
Open Easter-end October ▲
Size 10 acres, 200 touring pitches, 200 level pitches, 13 ⚿, 30 WCs
℠ MasterCard Visa
⚏ ⊡ ☏ ⌂ Gaz ♿ ✈
Last arrival time: 23:00

ENGLAND

Friendly park in beautiful Eden Valley, twixt Lakes and Dales.

Superb facilities include:
– Heated Outdoor Pools – Play areas –
– Indoor TV and games room –
– Mini-market & licensed restaurant –

Seasonal and monthly rates, also luxury holiday homes for sale.
Sorry, no letting, no bar, no club.

Brochure with pleasure:

Ormside, Appleby-in-Westmorland, Cumbria CA16 6EJ
Tel: 017683 51077
E.mail: **broch@wildrose.co.uk**
or visit our website at **www.wildrose.co.uk**

24

Appleby-In-Westmorland

APPLEBY-IN-WESTMORLAND Cumbria   10B2

Wild Rose Park
Ormside, Appleby-in-Westmorland CA16 6EJ
017683-51077   Fax 017683-52551
Open all year
Size 40 acres, 240 touring pitches, 200 with electric hookup, 110 level pitches, 240 static caravans, 20 , 60 WCs, 3 CWPs
£ car/tent £7.30-£11.60, car/caravan £7.30-£11.60, motorhome £7.30-£11.60, motorbike/tent £3, children £1.50
cc MasterCard Visa
Calor Gaz WS
Last arrival time: 22:00
➜ From B6260 take road marked to Ormside and Soulby at village of Burrells. After 1½ miles take left turn to Ormside. Take first right and right again into park.
See advert on previous page

ARUNDEL West Sussex   4C4

Camping & Caravanning Club Site
Slindon Park, Slindon, Arundel BN18 0RG
01243-814387
Open March-September
Size 2 acres, 46 touring pitches, 12 with electric hookup, 1 CWP
£ car/tent £8.40-£9.40, car/caravan £8.40-£9.40, motorhome £8.40-£9.40, motorbike/tent £8.40-£9.10, children £1.10
cc MasterCard Visa
Calor WS
Last arrival time: 23:00
➜ From A27 to Eartham at Britton's Lane and then second right to Slindon, the site is on this road.

Maynard's Caravan & Camping Park
Crossbush, Arundel BN18 9PQ
01903-882075
Open all year
Size 2.5 acres, 70 touring pitches, 62 with electric hookup, 70 level pitches, 4 , 9 WCs, 1 CWP
£ car/tent £8, car/caravan £8, motorhome £8, motorbike/tent £8, children £0.50-£1
Calor Gaz WS
➜ From Arundel ¾ mile on A27 to Worthing. Turn left into car park at Beefeater pub and restaurant.

Hints & Tips
When braking it will take you an average of 20% more distance to stop. Always avoid violent braking.

ASHBOURNE Derbyshire   8A2

Callow Top Holiday Park
Buxton Road, Ashbourne DE6 2AQ
01335-344020   Fax 01335-343726
Open March-November

Select holiday park situated in beautiful Derbyshire countryside. Ideal base for Alton Towers, Tissington Trail cycle path and Carsington Reservoir.
Size 9 acres, 160 touring pitches, 80 with electric hookup, 160 level pitches, 17 static caravans, 6 , 16 WCs, 1 CWP
£ car/tent £8.50, car/caravan £8.50, motorhome £8.50, motorbike/tent £8.50, children £0.75
Calor Gaz
Last arrival time: 22:00
➜ ½ mile from Ashbourne on the A515 Buxton Road. The entrance is opposite Sandybrook Garage. Follow the private road for ½ mile (past Haywood Farm). Please report to reception on arrival.

Sandybrook Hall Holiday Centre
Buxton Road, Ashbourne DE6 2AQ
01335-342679
Open 1 April-1 November

A long established family site in picturesque setting. An ideal base for walking the dales and cycling (Tissington Trail 500m away). Cycle hire. 20 minutes to Alton Towers, American Adventure and Gulliver's Kingdom.
Size 20 acres, 70 touring pitches, 28 with electric hookup, 15 level pitches, 20 static caravans, 9 , 13 WCs, 1 CWP
Calor Gaz
➜ 1 mile N of Ashbourne on A515. Opposite Dovedale turn-off.

Ashburton

ASHBURTON Devon 3D3

Ashburton Caravan Park
Waterleat, Ashburton TQ13 7HU
☎ 01364-652552 Fax 01364-652552
Open Easter-October

Secluded, south-facing wooded river valley within Dartmoor National Park. A haven of peace, centrally located for easy access to the moors, coast or the historic cities of Exeter and Plymouth.
Size 4 acres, 35 touring pitches, 8 with electric hookup, 35 level pitches, 9 static caravans, 6 🚿, 7 WCs, 1 CWP
£ car/tent £7.50-£10, motorhome £7.50-£10, motorbike/tent £7.50-£10, children £1.50-£2.25
Rental £110-£280
Calor Gaz
Last arrival time: 22:30

Parkers Farm Holiday Park
Ashburton TQ13 7LJ
☎ 01364-652598 Fax 01364-654004
Open Easter-October

A large working farm with beautifully terraced marked pitches overlooking Dartmoor. 12 miles from Torbay. Family run, very clean and friendly. Free showers. Children's and pets paradise. Also cottages and caravans.
Size 10 acres, 80 touring pitches, 80 with electric hookup, 80 level pitches, 25 static caravans, 10 🚿, 12 WCs, 3 CWPs
£ car/tent £4.50-£9, car/caravan £4.50-£9, motorhome £4.50-£9, motorbike/tent £4.50-£9, children £1
Rental Cottage £90-£400
CC MasterCard Visa
Calor Gaz WS
➜ Take A38 Exeter to Plymouth. When you see sign

PARKERS FARM HOLIDAY PARK

Site situated on a 300 acre working farm, lots of animals. Beautifully terraced level campsite, large pitches, overlooks Dartmoor, 12 miles Torbay. Very clean, fully tiled shower block and new block for 1997 – also cottages and caravans, some new.

**HIGHER MEAD FARM,
ASHBURTON, NEWTON ABBOT,
SOUTH DEVON TQ13 7LJ
Tel: 01364-652598 Fax: 01364-654004**

26 miles to Plymouth, take second left at Alston Cross, marked Woodland and Denburt. 400 yards down road.
See advert on this page

RIVER DART
Country Park

Our magnificent 90 acre Park was once part of a Victorian Country Estate. The camping area is set along the fringes of woodland in gently sloping parkland with spacious individual pitches. Our outdoor heated swimming pool is available all season plus a fun environment for children to enjoy non-stop activity in the woodland adventure playgrounds. Dartmoor is only a few minutes away offering marvellous walks and car tours.
Phone for our colour brochure.
**The River Dart Country Park,
Holne Park, Ashburton, Devon TQ13 7NP
Tel/Fax: 01364 652511**

26

Ashburton

River Dart Country Park
Holne Park, Ashburton TQ13 7NP
01364-652511 Fax 01364-652020
Open 1 April-mid September
Size 90 acres, 120 touring pitches, 86 with electric hookup, 120 level pitches, 16, 16 WCs, 1 CWP
£ car/tent £9.50-£13.10, car/caravan £9.50-£13.10, motorhome £9.50-£13.10, motorbike/tent £9.50-£13.10, children £3.95-£5.20
CC MasterCard Visa

Last arrival time: 22:00
→ From M5 at Exeter, take A38 Expressway towards Plymouth. Exit at Peartree Cross junction. Follow brown signs.
See advert on previous page

ASHFORD Kent   5E3

Broad Hembury Farm Caravan & Camping
Steeds Lane, Kingsnorth, Ashford TN26 1NQ
01233-620859 Fax 01233-620859
Open all year

Surrounded by quiet Kentish countryside. Park graded 'excellent' by E.T.B, offering every modern facility. Convenient for channel crossings and hundreds of interesting places to visit. Open all year.
Size 5 acres, 60 touring pitches, 48 with electric hookup, 60 level pitches, 25 static caravans, 6, 16 WCs, 1 CWP
£ car/tent £8-£13, car/caravan £8-£13, motorhome £8-£13, motorbike/tent £8-£11, children £1.50
Rental
CC MasterCard Visa

→ From J10 on M20 take A2070 for 2 miles, then continue on A2042 following signs for Kingsnorth. Left at second cross roads in village.

ASHURST Hampshire   4B4

Forestry Commission Ashurst Campsite
Lyndhurst Road, Ashurst SO4 2AA
01703-283771

Open end March-end September
Size 25 acres, 280 touring pitches, 200 level pitches, 12, 30 WCs, 3 CWPs
£ car/tent £6.50-£10.40, car/caravan £6.50-£10.40, motorhome £6.50-£10.40, motorbike/tent £6.50-£10.40
CC MasterCard Visa

Last arrival time: 22:00
→ 5 miles SW of Southampton on A35.

AXMINSTER Devon   3E3

Andrewshayes Caravan Park
Dalwood, Axminster EX13 7DY
01404-831225 Fax 01404-831893
Open 1 March-31 January

A family park overlooking the Axe Valley. Luxury 'Rose Award' caravans set amongst maturing trees. Excellent facilities for touring/camping. Heated outdoor pool.
Size 12 acres, 90 touring pitches, 80 with electric hookup, 40 level pitches, 80 static caravans, 12, 18 WCs, 2 CWPs
£ car/tent £8, car/caravan £8-£9.50, motorhome £8-£9.50, motorbike/tent £5, children £1
Rental £85-£360
CC MasterCard Visa

WS
Last arrival time: 22:00
→ Turn N at Taunton Cross on A35, 3 miles from Axminster, 6 miles from Honiton, signposted to Dalwood and Stockland.

AYSGARTH North Yorkshire   10C2

Westholme Caravan Park
Aysgarth DL8 3SP
01969-663268
Open 1 March-31 October

Banbury

Set in the Yorkshire Dales National Park, enjoying striking views amidst splendid walking and touring country.
Size 22 acres, 69 touring pitches, 44 with electric hookup, 69 level pitches, 42 static caravans, 8 ⚒, 16 WCs, 2 CWPs
£ car/tent £6.75-£9.25, car/caravan £6.75-£9.25, motorhome £6.75-£9.25, motorbike/tent £6.20-£7.30, children £1.10
⚒ ✕ ⚒ ⚒ ⚒ ⚒ ⚒ ⚒ ⚒ ⚒ ⚒ Calor Gaz ⚒
➔ 7 miles W of Leyburn turn left off A684, ¾ mile after junction with B6160. 1 mile E of Aysgarth.

Beautiful park amidst stunning Northumbrian scenery. Shop, restaurant, solarium, games room, heated outdoor pool, laundry.
Size 99 acres, 175 touring pitches, 100 with electric hookup, 140 level pitches, 300 static caravans, 32 ⚒, 16 WCs, 2 CWPs
£ car/tent £7.75-£11.50, car/caravan £7.75-£15, motorhome £7.75-£11.50, motorbike/tent £7.75-£11.50, children £1
Rental ⚒
㏄ MasterCard Visa
⚒ ✕ ⚒ ⚒ ⚒ ⚒ ⚒ ⚒ ⚒ Calor Gaz ⚒ ⚒
Last arrival time: 22:00
➔ At ¼ mile S of Belford on A1 turn E on B1342. Site in 2½ miles.

BAKEWELL Derbyshire   8A2

Camping & Caravanning Club Site

Hopping Farm, Youlgreave, Bakewell DE45 1NA
📞 01629-636555
Open March-September ⚒ ⚒ ⚒
Size 11.9 acres, 100 touring pitches, 60 with electric hookup, 1 CWP
£ car/tent £8.40-£9.40, car/caravan £8.40-£9.40, motorhome £8.40-£9.40, motorbike/tent £8.40-£9.40, children £1.10
㏄ MasterCard Visa
⚒ ⚒¼ ✕¼ ⚒ ⚒¼ ⚒ ⚒ ⚒ ⚒ ⚒ ⚒ ⚒ ⚒ Calor ⚒ ⚒ WS
Last arrival time: 23:00
➔ Take the B5056 Ashbourne Road off the A6 Bakewell to Matlock section. After ½ mile take right hand branch to Youlgreave. Turn sharp left after church down Bradford Lane and opposite The George Hotel. Continue ½ mile to club sign then turn right for ¼ mile up Farmers Lane.

BAMBURGH Northumberland   13F3

Waren Caravan Park

Waren Mill, Bamburgh NE70 7EE
📞 01668-214366 **Fax** 01668-214224
Open 27 March-31 October ⚒ ⚒ ⚒

BANBURY Oxfordshire   4B1

Barnstones Caravan & Camping Site

Great Bourton, Banbury OX7 2BB
📞 01295-750289
Open all year ⚒ ⚒ ⚒

Beautiful award winning park situated on the edge of a pretty village close to the Cotswolds. Delightfully landscaped with trees and flower beds. Immaculate toilet block, free showers, laundry room and children's play area.
Size 2.5 acres, 49 touring pitches, 49 with electric hookup, 49 level pitches, 3 ⚒, 5 WCs, 1 CWP
£ car/tent £5, car/caravan £5, motorhome £5, motorbike/tent £5, children £0.50
⚒¼ ✕¼ ⚒¼ ⚒ ⚒ ⚒ Calor Gaz ⚒ ⚒
➔ From junction 11 of M40 (Chipping Norton) continue to third roundabout and take A423 to Southam. After 3 miles turn right to Great Bourton. Site is 100 yards on right.

Banbury

Bo Peep Farm Caravan Park
Aynho Road, Adderbury, Banbury OX17 3NP
☎ 01295-810605 Fax 01295-810605
Open March-November

Beautiful six acre site with 56 all-electric pitches, surrounded by farmland. Excellent campsite facilities. Central for Oxford, Blenheim, Stratford-on-Avon and Warwick Castle. Access M40 junctions 10 and 11.
Size 6 acres, 88 touring pitches, 88 with electric hookup, 70 level pitches, 12, 13 WCs, 3 CWPs
£ car/tent £6.50-£7.50, car/caravan £7.50-£10.50, motorhome £7.50-£10.50, motorbike/tent £6.50-£7.50, children £1.10
Calor Gaz WS
Last arrival time: 20:00
➜ Site is on the B4100 just east of Adderbury near Banbury. From Banbury (M40 Jn 11) follow signs for Adderbury A4260. From S (Jn 10) or Oxford follow signs to Adderbury. At Adderbury traffic lights take B4100, look for caravan sign, approx half mile.

FARM MEADOW
Caravan & Camping Park

Enjoy the very best of East Anglia or just relax in our beautiful Norfolk countryside.

Whatever your choice of holiday, Farm Meadow Touring Caravan and Camping Park, adjacent to Banham Zoo, Norfolk has to be the ideal venue for you. Just check out our list of on site facilities, consider the attraction of the staggering Norfolk coastline, sleepy Suffolk villages, the beauty of the Norfolk Broads, and you'll know you've made the right choice.

- 8 acre countryside site
- Awnings FREE of charge
- Shower & toilet block
- Full disabled facilities
- Electric hookups & made up roads
- Choice of catering facilities
- Licensed farm shop and bakery
- Appleyard Shopping Court & Cidery
- Hairdressing
- Over 25 acres of spectacular wildlife

BANHAM ZOO, THE GROVE, BANHAM, NORFOLK
Tel: 01953 887771

Mollington Touring Caravan Park
The Yews, Mollington, Banbury OX17 1AZ
☎ 01295-750731
Open March-November

Spacious pitches, well lit with new toilet facilities, free showers etc. Large field to play ball games etc.
Size 2 acres, 24 touring pitches, 24 with electric hookup, 20 level pitches, 4, 4 WCs, 1 CWP
£ car/tent £5, car/caravan £5-£6, motorhome £5-£6, motorbike/tent £5
Last arrival time: 23:00
➜ Site is directly off A423 Banbury to Southam road, 200 yards past Mollington, turn left from Banbury direction. Signposted close to site.

BANHAM Norfolk   9E3

Farm Meadow Caravan & Camping Park
The Grove, Banham Zoo, Banham NR16 2HB
☎ 01953-888370 Fax 01953-887445
Open all year
Size 13 acres, 123 touring pitches, 123 with electric hookup, 123 level pitches, 6, 12 WCs, 1 CWP
£ car/tent £5-£7, car/caravan £6.50-£9, motorhome £6.50-£9, motorbike/tent £7
℅ MasterCard Visa
➜ Banham is situated on B1113 Norwich to Bury St Edmunds road, halfway between Attleborough and Diss.
See advert on this page

BARNARD CASTLE Co. Durham   10C2

Camping & Caravanning Club Site
Dockenflatts Lane, Lartington, Barnard Castle DL12 9DG
☎ 01833-630228
Open March-November
Size 10 acres, 90 touring pitches, 39 with electric hookup, 90 level pitches, 8, 10 WCs, 1 CWP
£ car/tent £11.50-£14.60, car/caravan £11.50-£14.60, motorhome £11.50-£14.60, motorbike/tent £11.50-£14.60, children £1.60
℅ MasterCard Visa

Bath

29

Last arrival time: 23:00
➜ On approach from Scotch Corner take second right for Middleton in Teesdale and Barnard Castle. On approach from Penrith take B6277 to Middleton in Teesdale. In 1 mile take turn on left, signposted 'Raygill Riding Stables'. The site is 500 yards on left.

Thorpe Hall
Barnard Castle DL12 9TW
☎ 01833-627230 Fax 01833-627471
Open March-October ▲ ⚐ ⛺
Size 2 acres, 12 touring pitches, 8 with electric hookup, 12 level pitches, 16 static caravans, 4 ☂, 6 WCs, 1 CWP
£ car/tent £7-£7.50, car/caravan £7-£7.50, motorhome £7-£7.50, children £1
🅿 ☎ 🅿 Calor ⚐ WS
➜ 1½ miles N off A66 near Greta Bridge. Take the turn to Wycliffe and continue for 1½ miles to site on right.

BARNSTAPLE Devon	2C2

Midland Caravan Park
Braunton Road, Ashford, Barnstaple EX31 4AU
☎ 01271-343691 Fax 01271-326355
Open April-October ▲ ⚐ ⛺

Level, well protected grass park overlooking the River Taw Estuary. Ideally situated to enjoy all of North Devon's beaches and attractions, and Exmoor.
Size 8.5 acres, 35 touring pitches, 35 with electric hookup, 35 level pitches, 62 static caravans, 8 ☂, 24 WCs, 1 CWP
£ car/tent £6-£12, car/caravan £8-£14, motorhome £8-£14, motorbike/tent £6-£12, children £1.50
Rental ⚐ £90-£349
㏄ MasterCard Visa
🅿 ✕ ⚑ 🅿 ☎ 🅿 📺 ⚐ ⚑ Calor Gaz ⚐ WS
Last arrival time: 21:00
➜ Take A361 through Barnstaple and follow Braunton and Ilfracombe signs. Park is 2 miles W of Barnstaple on right of dual carriageway.

BARTON-ON-HUMBER Lincolnshire	11E4

Silver Birches Tourist Park
Waterside Road, Barton-on-Humber DN18 5BA
☎ 01652-632509
Open 1 April-October ▲ ⚐ ⛺
Size 1.5 acres, 24 touring pitches, 24 with electric hookup, 24 level pitches, 4 ☂, 6 WCs, 1 CWP
£ car/tent £5.50, car/caravan £5.50, motorhome £5.50, motorbike/tent £5.50, children £0.50
🅿¼ ✕¼ ⚑¼ ☎ 🅿 ⚑ Calor Gaz ⚐ ⚑
Last arrival time: 23:00
➜ From A15 or A107, follow signs for Humber Bridge viewing area, just past The Sloop public house.

BATH Somerset	3F1

Bath Marina & Caravan Park
Brassmill Lane, Bath BA1 3JT
☎ 01225-428778 Fax 01225-428778
Open all year ⚐ ⛺
Size 4 acres, 88 touring pitches, 88 with electric hookup, 88 level pitches, 9 ☂, 23 WCs, 2 CWPs
£ car/caravan £12, motorhome £12, children £0.75
㏄ MasterCard Visa
🅿 ✕¼ 🅿 ☎ ⚑ Calor Gaz ⚐ ⚑
Last arrival time: 00:00
➜ Two miles W of Bath on A4 at Newbridge.
See advert on this page.

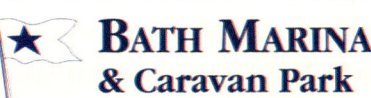

As one of the West of England's premier touring caravan and motor home parks, we provide our guests with 88 all-weather hard standings on a level, well drained site close to the River Avon.

Every site has been individually created within this carefully landscaped park to maximise privacy. We also take pride in providing excellent facilities which have achieved ETB grade 5 standard.

OPEN ALL YEAR.

BRASSMILL LANE, BATH, AVON BA1 3JT
Tel/Fax: 01225 424301/428778

30

Bath

Newton Mill Touring Centre
Newton St Loe, Bath BA2 9JF
☎ 01225-333909
Open all year

Somerset's leading park, situated in Bath, Britain's most elegant city. 43 acres of beauty with own trout stream, away from road noise with superb facilities.
Size 43 acres, 195 touring pitches, 90 with electric hookup, 195 level pitches, 18, 32 WCs, 1 CWP
cc Visa

➜ SE from junction of A4 and A39 on B3110 to site on left.

BEACONSFIELD Buckinghamshire   4C2

Highclere Farm Country Touring Park
Newbarn Lane, Seer Green, Beaconsfield HP9 2QZ
☎ 01494-874505 Fax 01494-875238
Open 1 March-31 January

A quiet meadowland site, one mile from the railway station. Cheap travel cards for London. Legoland 11 miles. Pub food ¼ mile, swimming 1½ miles.
Size 2 acres, 45 touring pitches, 45 with electric hookup, 45 level pitches, 6, 8 WCs, 2 CWPs
£ car/tent £8.50-£10, car/caravan £8.50-£10.50, motorhome £8.50-£10.50, motorbike/tent £8.50-£9.50
Rental Chalet. B & B - £35 single, £50 double.
cc MasterCard Visa

Last arrival time: 22:00

➜ Leave M40 at junction 2 onto A40 to Gerrards Cross. Turn left after ¼ mile to Seer Green and follow tourist signs.

BEADNELL Northumberland   13F3

Camping & Caravanning Club Site
Anstead, Beadnell NE67 5BX
☎ 01665-720586
Open March-September
Size 12 acres, 150 touring pitches, 150 level pitches, 7, 17 WCs, 1 CWP
£ car/tent £10.40-£13.60, car/caravan £10.40-£13.60, motorhome £10.40-£13.60, motorbike/tent £10.40-£13.60, children £1.50
cc MasterCard Visa

Calor WS
Last arrival time: 23:00

➜ From the south, leave A1 and follow B1430, signposted Seahouse. At Beadnell ignore the signs for Beadnell village. The site is on the left after the village, just beyond the left hand bend. From the north, leave A1 and follow B1342 via Bamburgh and Seahouse. The site is on the right before Beadnell village.

BELLINGHAM Northumberland   13E3

Brown Rigg Caravan & Camping Park
Bellingham NE48 2JY
☎ 01434-220175 Fax 01434-220175
Open Easter-31 October

A family run site within the Northumberland National Park. ½ mile south of Bellingham on B6320. Walking, golf, fishing nearby. Hadrian's Wall and Kielder Water 9 miles.
Size 6 acres, 60 touring pitches, 26 with electric hookup, 60 level pitches, 6, 10 WCs, 1 CWP
£ car/tent £6-£7.50, car/caravan £7-£8.50, motorhome £7-£8.50, motorbike/tent £6-£7.50, children £1

Calor Gaz
Last arrival time: 20:30

➜ From A69 ½ mile W of Hexham to Chollerford/Bellingham. At Chollerford take B6318, left over N Tyne River to roundabout signposted B6320 Bellingham.

Hints & Tips

Make sure your mirrors are adjusted correctly before moving off.

Berwick-upon-Tweed

31

| BERKELEY Gloucestershire | 7E4 |

Hogsdown Farm
Lower Wick, Dursley GL11 6DS
☎ 01453-810224
Open all year ⛺ 🚐 🚚

Ideal base for exploring the beauty of Cotswold Edge country, visiting historic market towns, picturesque villages, riverside meadows of Berkeley Vale and Severn Estuary.
Size 4 acres, 40 touring pitches, 25 with electric hookup, 40 level pitches, 2 ⚿, 7 WCs, 2 CWPs
£ car/tent £5.50, car/caravan £7, motorhome £7, children £0.50
Rental 🚐
⚑ ⚑¼ ⊡ 🔋 ⊡ ⚠ Calor ✱ WS
Last arrival time: 22:30
➡ Between junctions 13 and 14 on A38. One mile off A38 opposite Berkeley turning.

| BERWICK-UPON-TWEED Northumberland | 13F2 |

Beachcomber Campsite
Goswick, Berwick-upon-Tweed
☎ 01289-381217
⛺ 🚐
Size 4 acres
⚑ ✕ ⊡ ⊠ ⊡
➡ 4 miles S of Berwick take road signposted Goswick and Cheswick. Follow signs for 4 miles.

Berwick Holiday Centre
Magdalene Fields, Berwick-upon-Tweed TD15 1NE
☎ 01289-307113 **Fax** 01289-306276
Open March-October 🚐 🚚

A family holiday park close to excellent beaches and with indoor and outdoor heated pools, leisure facilities, kids clubs, live entertainment, bars and food. A 'British Holidays Park'.
Size 58 acres, 35 touring pitches, 35 with electric hookup, 35 level pitches, 819 static caravans, 1 CWP
£ car/caravan £8-£14, motorhome £8-£14
Rental 🚐
⟪ Visa
⚑ ✕ 💷 ⊡ 🔋 ⊡ ⚿ ⚑ ⊞ ⊡ ⚠ Calor ♿ ✱
➡ Signposted on A1 from both N and S, signs directing you to Berwick Holiday Centre in town.

Haggerston Castle Caravan Park
Boal, Berwick-upon-Tweed TD15 2RA
☎ 01289-381333
Open 20 March-1 November 🚐 🚚

'Toweringly' different family holiday park set around lakes and trees with heated indoor and outdoor pools, kids clubs, tennis and bowling included in the wide range of leisure facilities, restaurants and bars, excellent cabaret entertainment. A 'British Holidays Park'.
Size 220 acres, 159 touring pitches, 153 with electric hookup, 159 level pitches, 800 static caravans, 16 ⚿, 16 WCs, 2 CWPs
£ car/caravan £7-£17.50, motorhome £7-£20
Rental 🚐
⟪ MasterCard Visa
⚑ ✕ 💷 ⊡ 🔋 ⊡ ⚿ ⚑ 🔲 ⊞ ⊡ ⚑ ⚑ ⊠ ⊞ ⊡ 📺 ⊡ ⚠
Calor ♿ ✱ WS
➡ 7½ miles S of Berwick on A1.

Ord House Caravan Park
East Ord, Berwick-upon-Tweed TD15 2NS
☎ 01289-305288 **Fax** 01289-330832
Open 1 March-9 January ⛺ 🚐 🚚

ENGLAND

➡

32

Berwick-upon-Tweed

← Ord House Caravan Park

40 acre tree-lined estate dominated by an 18th century mansion containing a licensed club. Luxury toilet and shower facilities. Recreation and play area. Practice golf.
Size 41 acres, 70 touring pitches, 60 with electric hookup, 34 level pitches, 220 static caravans, 8 ⌂, 16 WCs, 1 CWP
£ car/tent £5.50-£12, car/caravan £7.50-£12, motorhome £7.50-£12
Rental 🚐 £150-£395 p.w.
℃ MasterCard Visa
🛁 🛁¼ ✕ ⛽ 🍴 🛒 🎮 ⚡ ⚠ Calor Gaz ♿ 🐕
Last arrival time: 23:00
➡ On A1 Berwick bypass. Turn off at second roundabout at East Ord and follow caravan symbol.

| BEXHILL-ON-SEA East Sussex | 5E4 |

Kloofs Caravan Park
Sandhurst Lane, Whydown, Bexhill-on-Sea TN39 4RG
📞 01424-842839
Open March-January ⛺ 🚐 🚚

Family run camp site set in tranquil and secluded surroundings with sheltered, level open grass or shaded pitches. Within easy reach of Bexhill, Hastings and Eastbourne.
Size 22 acres, 50 touring pitches, 16 with electric hookup, 40 level pitches, 75 static caravans, 6 ⌂, 9 WCs, 1 CWP
£ car/tent £6, car/caravan £6, motorhome £6, motorbike/tent £6, children £0.80
Rental 🚐
🛁 🛒 Calor Gaz 🐕 WS
➡ On A259 from Hastings.

| BICESTER Oxfordshire | 4B1 |

Heyford Leys Farm
Camp Road, Upper Heyford, Bicester OX6 3LU
📞 01869-232048 Fax 01869-232048
Open 1 April-31 October ⛺ 🚐 🚚

Quiet family run park in rural area. Ideal base for Oxfordshire, Cherwell Valley, central Midlands, Bicester Retail Village. Great for weekend breaks and journey stop-overs.
Size 10 acres, 22 touring pitches, 10 with electric hookup, 22 level pitches, 47 static caravans, 2 ⌂, 4 WCs, 1 CWP
£ car/tent £5-£9, car/caravan £6.50-£8.50, motorhome £6.50-£8.50, motorbike/tent £5
℃ MasterCard Visa
🛁 🛒 🍴 🎮 ⚠ Calor Gaz ♿ 🐕
➡ From junction 10 M40 follow B430 for 1½ miles.

| BILLINGSHURST West Sussex | 4C3 |

Limeburner Arms Site
Newbridge, Billingshurst RH14 9JA
📞 01403-782311
Open 1 April-end October ⛺ 🚐 🚚
Size 2.75 acres, 42 touring pitches, 21 with electric hookup, 42 level pitches, 6 ⌂, 6 WCs, 1 CWP
£ car/tent £7, car/caravan £7, motorhome £7, motorbike/tent £7
🛁 ✕ ⛽ 🍴 🛒 ⚡ ⚠ Calor Gaz ♿ 🐕 WS
Last arrival time: 22:00
➡ 1½ miles W of Billingshurst on A272, turn left on B2133. Site 400 yards on left.

| BIRCHINGTON Kent | 5F2 |

Two Chimneys Caravan Park
Five Acres, Shottendane Road, Birchington CT7 0HD
📞 01843-841068 Fax 01843-848099
Open Easter-end October ⛺ 🚐 🚚
Size 10 acres, 90 touring pitches, 60 with electric hookup, 140 level pitches, 50 static caravans, 13 ⌂, 22 WCs, 1 CWP
£ car/tent £7-£14, car/caravan £7-£14, motorhome £7-£14, motorbike/tent £7-£14
Rental 🚐 Chalet. £130-£400
℃ MasterCard Visa
🛁 ✕¼ ⛽ 🍴 🛒 🏊 🎮 🎯 🎮 🎮 ⚡ ⚠ Calor Gaz ♿ 🐕 WS
Last arrival time: 22:00
➡ From the A299 follow A28 to Birchington Square, turn right at church into Park Lane (B2048). Left at Manston Road (B2050), first left into Shottendane Road. Site is 300 yards on right.

Blackpool

BISHOP'S CASTLE Shropshire 7D3

Bacheldre Watermill
Churchstoke, Montgomery SY15 6TE
☎ 01588-620489 Fax 01588-620489
Open Easter-October

A quiet, secluded, 4 tick site set in the peaceful grounds of a watermill. Ideally situated for exploring the Shropshire/Welsh borders. Self catering accommodation available.
Size 2 acres, 25 touring pitches, 18 with electric hookup, 18 level pitches, 2, 8 WCs, 1 CWP
£ car/tent £6, car/caravan £6, motorhome £6, motorbike/tent £6, children £1
Last arrival time: 22:30
➡ 2 miles west of Churchstoke, turn left off A489, signposted Bacheldre Watermill.

High Compley Park

Relax in 17 acres of secluded country park, one mile from Blackpool.

Within walking distance of the ancient market town of Poulton-le-Fylde, with its fine restaurants and shopping malls.

Fishing, riding, golf and boating nearby. Open for 10½ months.

Luxury holiday homes for sale and hire with central heating. Excellent facilities for tourers.

GARSTANG ROAD WEST, POULTON-LE-FYLDE, LANCASHIRE FY6 8AR
Tel: 01253 890831 Fax: 01253 892832

BLACKPOOL Lancashire 10B3

High Compley Park
Garstang Road West, Poulton-le-Fylde FY6 8AR
☎ 01253-890831 Fax 01253-892832
Open 1 March-4 January
Size 14 acres, 50 touring pitches, 50 with electric hookup, 50 level pitches, 150 static caravans, 8, 10 WCs, 1 CWP
£ car/tent £8.50-£12, car/caravan £8.50-£12, motorhome £8.50-£12, motorbike/tent £8.50-£12, children £1.50
Rental £50 - £305 weekly.
Calor Gaz
Last arrival time: 22:00
➡ From M55 turn right onto A585 to Fleetwood and fork left at traffic lights. Follow Blackpool sign onto A586, park on left.
See advert on this page

Kneps Farm Holiday Park
River Road, Thornton Cleveleys, Blackpool FY5 5LR
☎ 01253-823632 Fax 01253-863967
Open 1 March-15 November
Size 10 acres, 70 touring pitches, 60 with electric hookup, 70 level pitches, 80 static caravans, 11, 17 WCs, 1 CWP
£ car/tent £8.50-£11, car/caravan £8.50-£11, motorhome £8.50-£11, motorbike/tent £8.50-£11, children £1-£1.50
Rental £150-£300 per week
CC MasterCard Visa
Calor Gaz
Last arrival time: 20:00
➡ Leave M55 at junction 3 and follow A585 for Fleetwood. At the first roundabout turn right onto B5412. After 1 mile, turn right after the school into Stanah Road, which leads to River Road.

Maaruig Caravan Park
71 Pilling Lane, Preesall, Blackpool FY6 0HB
☎ 01253-810404
Open 1 March-4 January

We can offer the enjoyment of a peaceful holiday on a quiet, friendly, small site. Pleasant local walks along the sea wall with views around Morecambe Bay.
Size 1 acre, 28 touring pitches, 28 with electric hookup, 28 level pitches, 4, 6 WCs, 1 CWP
£ car/tent £8.50, car/caravan £8.50, motorhome £8.50, children £0.50

ENGLAND

34

Blackpool

← Maaruig Caravan Park

👥¼ 🚐¼ 🏠 🐕
Last arrival time: 21:30
➜ M6 (jn 32) join M55 (jn 3) exit onto A585 for Fleetwood. At third set of traffic lights turn right onto A588 for Lancaster. 5 miles to Ford garage on left. Follow signs for Knott-End onto B5377 up to T-junction. Turn left then first right onto Pilling Lane. Round the corner, second caravan park on left.

Marton Mere Holiday Park

Mythope Road, Blackpool FY4 4XN
📞 01253-767544   Fax 01253-698419
Open March-end of illuminations ⛺ 🚐 🚗

A family holiday park set in 93 acres just three miles from Blackpool. Heated indoor pool, kids clubs, tennis and bowling included in the wide range of leisure facilities, restaurants and bars, excellent cabaret entertainment. A 'British Holidays Park'.
Size 93 acres, 420 touring pitches, 420 with electric hookup, 400 level pitches, 900 static caravans, 36 🚿, 40 WCs, 20 CWPs
£ car/tent £9-£12, car/caravan £14-£16, motorhome £14-£16, motorbike/tent £12
Rental 🚐 £90 upwards
cc MasterCard Visa
👥 ✕ 🛒 🍴 🎮 🏊 🎣 🎾 🎯 🎰 🎳 📺 🍺 🔥 Calor Gaz ♿ 🐕 WS
Last arrival time: 22:00
➜ Take junction 4 off M55 (A583) towards Blackpool. At second set of traffic lights turn right into Mythope Road. Site is 100 yards on left.

Pipers Height Camping & Caravan Site

Peel Road, Peel, Blackpool FY4 OEJ
📞 01253-63767
Open March-October ⛺ 🚐 🚗

Family owned and run in a pleasant rural area, yet within 4 miles of the extensive beaches and entertainment of Blackpool and Lytham St Annes. Entertainment mid to high season, new toilet and shower block, and facilities for the disabled.
Size 10 acres, 140 touring pitches, 140 with electric hookup, 140 level pitches, 22 static caravans, 15 WCs, 1 CWP
£ car/tent £6-£11, car/caravan £6-£11, motorhome £6-£11
Rental Chalet. £315 weekly, including gas, water, electric & VAT.
👥 ✕ 🛒 🍴 🎮 🍺 🔥 Calor Gaz ♿ 🐕
Last arrival time: 22:00

Stanah House Caravan Park

River Road, Thornton, Blackpool FY5 5LW
📞 01253-824000   Fax 01253-863060
Open March-October ⛺ 🚐 🚗
Size 6 acres, 55 touring pitches, 50 with electric hookup, 55 level pitches, 4 🚿, 6 WCs, 1 CWP
£ car/tent £8.50, car/caravan £8.50, motorhome £8.50, motorbike/tent £8.50
cc MasterCard Visa
👥 👥¼ ✕¼ 🚐¼ 🏠 🍴 🔥 Calor Gaz ♿ 🐕 WS
➜ Leave M55 junction 3 onto A585. After 6 miles at roundabout by River Wyre Hotel, turn right onto B5415 signposted Little Thornton and Stanah picnic area. Follow picnic area signs and continue to very end of River Road, turn right into caravan site nearest river.
See advert on this page

Stanah House
CARAVAN PARK

A small select touring site, overlooking the River Wyre with good views of the Fells and Lake District mountains. Close access to a slipway for sailing and water-skiing.

Open March – October

**River Road, Thornton,
Blackpool FY5 5LR
Tel: 01253-824000
Fax: 01253-863060**

Bodmin

35

BLANDFORD FORUM Dorset   3F2

Inside Park Caravan & Camping
Blandford Forum DT11 9AP
☎ 01258-453719 Fax 01258-459921
Open Easter-31 October
Size 13 acres, 120 touring pitches, 90 with electric hookup, 12 ⚿, 14 WCs, 1 CWP
£ car/tent £7-£12, car/caravan £7-£12, motorhome £7-£12, motorbike/tent £7-£12, children £1.25
℅ MasterCard Visa
Calor Gaz WS
Last arrival time: 22:00
➜ From junction of A354 and A350, take Blandford St Mary exit and follow signs to park.
See advert on this page

Lady Baily Holiday Park
Winterbourne Whitechurch, Blandford Forum DT11 0HS
☎ 01258-880829 Fax 01929-471636
Open March-October
Peaceful, grassy site set in lovely countryside. Has a children's play area.
Size 4 acres, 140 touring pitches, 16 with electric hookup, 140 level pitches, 4 ⚿, 10 WCs, 1 CWP
£ car/tent £5-£8.50, car/caravan £5-£8.50, motorhome £5-£8.50, motorbike/tent £5-£8.50
Calor Gaz WS
➜ Five miles SW of Blandford on A354.

BODIAM East Sussex   5E3

Bodiam Caravan and Camping Park
Park Farm, Bodiam TN32 5XA
☎ 01580-830514 Fax 01580-830519
Open April-October

A quiet rural site in a beautiful setting with a riverside walk to Bodiam Castle. Childrens play area and free fishing in River Rother.
Size 7 acres, 50 touring pitches, 50 level pitches, 5 ⚿, 7 WCs, 1 CWP
£ car/tent £5-£6, car/caravan £6, motorhome £6, motorbike/tent £6, children £1
WS
Last arrival time: 22:00
➜ 3 miles S of Hawkhurst on B2244 and 3 miles N of Sedlescombe.

THE INSIDE PARK
Touring Caravan & Camping Park

One of Dorset's Premier Touring Parks

Surrounded by farm and woodland rich in wildlife, this peaceful and beautiful setting is an ideal central location from which to explore Dorset's varied and fascinating countryside. Comfortable and fully equipped modern facilities are housed in 18th Century coach and stable building.

Brochure & Information
BLANDFORD FORUM, DORSET
Tel: 01258 453719 Fax: 01258 454026

Park Farm Caravan & Camp Site
Park Farm, Bodiam TN32 5XA
☎ 01580-830155 Fax 01580-830514
Open 1 April-30 October
Size 15 acres, 50 touring pitches, 50 level pitches, 5 ⚿, 7 WCs, 1 CWP
£ car/tent £6, car/caravan £6, motorhome £6, motorbike/tent £6, children £1
WS
➜ Three miles S of Hawkhurst on B2244. Three miles N of Sedlescombe on B2244.

BODMIN Cornwall   2B3

Camping & Caravanning Club Site
Old Callywith Road, Bodmin PL31 2DZ
☎ 01208-73834
Open March-November
Size 10.5 acres, 175 touring pitches, 54 with electric hookup, 8 ⚿, 18 WCs, 1 CWP
£ car/tent £9.60-£12.10, car/caravan £9.60-£12.10, motorhome £9.60-£12.10, motorbike/tent £9.60-£12.10, children £1.50
℅ MasterCard Visa
Calor WS
Last arrival time: 23:00
➜ From N, turn right off A30 at Bodmin signpost, crossing over dual carriageway in front of industrial estate, then immediately left at international sign. The site is on left down Old Callywith Road. From A38 (Liskeard) follow signpost to Bodmin until roundabout (ignore no-entry road). Take second exit and right in ½ mile following signs to Crooklands Industrial Estate.

ENGLAND

36

Bognor Regis

BOGNOR REGIS West Sussex	4C4

Lillies Nursery & Caravan Park
Yapton Road, Barnham, Bognor Regis PO22 0AY
☎ 01243-552081
Open March-October ⚐

Stay at the Lillies for a quiet and relaxing holiday set in 3 acres of secluded countryside. Leisure facilities. ETB Graded.
Size 1 acre, 10 touring pitches, 10 with electric hookup, 10 level pitches, 4 static caravans, 3 ☂, 3 WCs, 1 CWP
£ car/tent £8, car/caravan £8, motorhome £8, motorbike/tent £8
Rental £120-£180
⚐ ×¼ ●¼ ▫ ▫ ▫ Calor Gaz ⚐ ⚐ WS
Last arrival time: 24 hours

BOROUGHBRIDGE North Yorkshire	11D3

Camping & Caravanning Club Site
Bar Lane, Roecliffe, Boroughbridge YO51 9LS
☎ 01423-322683
Open January-December ⚐
Size 6 acres, 80 touring pitches, 55 with electric hookup, 6 ☂, 14 WCs,
£ car/tent £10.40-£13.60, car/caravan £10.40-£13.60, motorhome £10.40-£13.60, motorbike/tent £10.40-£13.60, children £1.50
⚐ MasterCard Visa
⚐ ⚐¼ ×¼ ●¼ ▫ ▫ ▫ ▫ ▫ ▫ Calor ⚐ ⚐ WS
Last arrival time: 23:00
➡ From A1 jn48, follow the signs for Bar Lane Industrial Estate and Roecliffe Village. The site entrance is ¼ mile from the roundabout.

BOSTON Lincolnshire	9D2

White Cat Park
Shaw Lane, Old Leake PE22 9LQ
☎ 01205-870121
Open March-November ⚐
Size 2.5 acres, 40 touring pitches, 36 with electric hookup, 40 level pitches, 5 static caravans, 2 ☂, 6 WCs, 1 CWP
£ car/caravan £5.50-£6.50, motorhome £5.50-£6.50, motorbike/tent £5.50-£6.50
Rental £145-£175
⚐ ⚐¼ ×¼ ●¼ ▫ ▫ ▫ Calor Gaz ⚐ WS
Last arrival time: 22:00
➡ Take A52 Skegness Road as far as the Old Leake crossroads, turn right opposite B1184 Sibsey Road. Park is 300 yards on left.

BOURNEMOUTH & BOSCOMBE Dorset	3F3

Cara Touring Park
Old Bridge Road, Iford, Bournemouth BH6 5RQ
☎ 01202-482121 Fax 0118-945 2063
Open all year ⚐
Size 3 acres, 36 touring pitches, 36 with electric hookup, 36 level pitches, 6 ☂, 6 WCs,
£ car/caravan £6.50-£11.25, motorhome £6.50-£11.25
Rental £90-£270
⚐ MasterCard Visa
⚐ ×¼ ●¼ ▫ ▫ ▫ Calor
➡ A35 between Christchurch and Boscombe. One mile from Christchurch and 1½ miles from Boscombe.

St Leonards Farm Camping & Caravan Park
West Moors, Bournemouth BH22 0AQ
☎ 01202-872637 Fax 01202-872637
Open Easter-30 September ⚐

BOURNEMOUTH
St Leonards Farm
Caravan & Camping Park
West Moors, Ferndown, Dorset BH22 0AQ

Quiet level site near Bournemouth, Poole Cross Channel Ferries and New Forest. Electric hook-ups, modern shower and toilet block, private room for disabled, launderette, play area with picnic tables.
Shops, bars, restaurants, takeaways, swimming, golf, riding, water sports all nearby.

Bookings: W. E. Love & Son
Ferndown
Telephone: 01202 872637

Bransgore

Quiet, level site near Bournemouth, Poole, cross channel ferries and the New Forest. Easy access off A31. Electric hook-ups, modern facilities including those for disabled, launderette.
Size 8 acres, 110 touring pitches, 40 with electric hookup, 110 level pitches, 12, 33 WCs, 2 CWPs
£ car/tent £8-£12, car/caravan £8-£12, motorhome £8-£12, motorbike/tent £8-£12, children £1
¼ ¼ ¼ Calor Gaz WS
➜ On A31 4 miles W of Ringwood, opposite West Moors garage.
See advert on opposite page

BRAMPTON Cumbria 10B1

Irthing Vale Caravan Park
Old Church Lane, Brampton CA8 2AA
016977-3600
Open March-October
Size 4.5 acres, 20 touring pitches, 8 with electric hookup, 20 level pitches, 25 static caravans, 6, 8 WCs, 1 CWP
£ car/tent £7.50, car/caravan £7.50, motorhome £7.50, motorbike/tent £6.80, children £2-£2.50
Rental
Calor
➜ Site is on A6071, 1½ mile to N of Brampton village.

BRANDS HATCH Kent 5D3

Thriftwood Camping & Caravanning Park
Plaxdale Green Road, Stansted, Brands Hatch TN15 7PB
01732-822261 Fax 01732-822261

Set in both secluded and open areas. Near stately homes and castles, and only 35 minutes to London by train.
Size 22 acres, 160 touring pitches, 102 with electric hookup, 160 level pitches, 10 static caravans, 9, 18 WCs, 1 CWP
£ car/tent £8-£10.75, car/caravan £8-£10.75, motorhome £8-£10.75, motorbike/tent £6-£8, children £1.50
Rental £125-£320
cc MasterCard Visa
¼ ¼ ¼ Calor Gaz WS
Last arrival time: 22:00
➜ M26 junction 2A and M20 junction 2. Follow caravan & camping signs N on A20.

BRANSGORE Hampshire 4A4

Harrow Wood Farm Caravan Park
Poplar Lane, Bransgore
01425-672487 Fax 01425-672487
Open 1 March-6 January

Situated in a pleasant village right on the edge of the New Forest, this six acre site offers the perfect centre from which to explore the surrounding area. Christchurch, Highcliffe and the market town of Ringwood are but a short drive away.
Size 6 acres, 60 touring pitches, 60 with electric hookup, 60 level pitches, 6, 12 WCs, 3 CWPs
£ car/caravan £9-£12.75, motorhome £9-£12.75
cc MasterCard Visa
¼ ¼ ¼ Calor Gaz WS
➜ Take Ringwood Road into Bransgore. Follow signs to site, between Three Tuns Pub and the Crown Inn.

Hints & Tips
If you have any information concerning caravan theft contact the confidential freephone Crimestoppers Line on 0800 555111. You may be entitled to a reward and there is no need to give your name if you don't want to.

ENGLAND

Braunton

BRAUNTON Devon　　　　　　　　　　2C2

Chivenor Caravan Park
Chivenor, Braunton EX31 4BN
01271-812217

A well maintained level site with all facilities, ideal for touring North Devon. Nicely laid out site.
Size 1.5 acres, 30 touring pitches, 4 ☔, 6 WCs
➜ 3½ miles from Barnstaple on A361 to Ilfracombe. Entrance off the only roundabout.

Lobb Fields Caravan & Camping Park
Saunton Road, Braunton EX33 1EB
01271-812090　Fax 01271-812090
Open Easter-October

A large, level, grassy park facing south with panoramic views across to the Taw/Torridge Estuary. One mile from Saunton Golf Club and 1½ miles from a large beach. Dishwashing facilities are available, as are hairdryer and razor points.
Size 14 acres, 180 touring pitches, 43 with electric hookup, 100 level pitches, 18 ☔, 50 WCs, 2 CWPs
£ car/tent £4-£7, car/caravan £5.50-£8.50, motorhome £4-£7, motorbike/tent £4-£7, children £0.50

Calor Gaz
Last arrival time: 22:00
➜ In Braunton at traffic lights, turn W off A361 to B3231, towards Saunton and Croyde. The site is one mile on the right.

BRENTWOOD Essex　　　　　　　　　　5D2

Camping & Caravanning Club Site
Warren Lane, Frog Street, Kelvedon Hatch, Brentwood CM15 0JG
01277-372773

Open March-November
Size 12 acres, 90 touring pitches, 60 with electric hookup, 6 ☔, 13 WCs, 1 CWP
£ car/tent £10.40-£13.60, car/caravan £10.40-£13.60, motorhome £10.40-£13.60, motorbike/tent £10.40-£13.60, children £1.50
℄ MasterCard Visa

Calor WS
Last arrival time: 23:00
➜ A12 N at junction 28 of M25, join A1023 then turn right onto A128 and site is on right.

BRIDGWATER Somerset　　　　　　　　3E2

Mill Farm Caravan & Camping Park
Fiddington, Bridgwater TA5 1JQ
01278-732286
Open all year

MILL FARM
Caravan & Camping Park
• OPEN ALL YEAR •

SWIMMING • RIDING • BOATING
FISHING • FARM PETS

Three heated swimming pools, licensed Riding Centre, free rowing boats, recreation rooms, off licence.

FIDDINGTON, BRIDGWATER, SOMERSET TA5 1JQ
Tel: 01278 732286

Bristol

Inland family holiday park situated in a picturesque valley between the beautiful Quantock Hills and the sea. Children's paradise, new luxury indoor heated pools with whirlpool and waterslides, boating, riding, large sandpit, games and TV rooms, trampolines, holiday cottage.
Size 10 acres, 125 touring pitches, 125 with electric hookup, 125 level pitches, 18 ⓘ, 56 WCs, 3 CWPs
£ car/tent £6-£8, car/caravan £6-£8, motorhome £6-£8, motorbike/tent £6-£8, children £0.50
🛁 🍴 🔌 🏪 ♿ 🚿 📺 ⚠ Calor Gaz 🐕 WS
➡ Leave M5 at Bridgwater, junction 23 or 24. Go through Bridgwater and take A39 in Minehead direction for 6 miles. Turn right to Fiddington, then follow camping signs for 1 mile.
See advert on opposite page

BRIDPORT Dorset   3E3

Freshwater Beach Holiday Park
Burton Bradstock, Bridport DT6 4PT
📞 01308-897317 Fax 01308-897336
Open 19 March-7 November ⛺ 🚐 🚚

Situated at the mouth of the River Bride with its own private beach, and nightly entertainment in the high season. A golf course adjoins the site.
Size 40 acres, 425 touring pitches, 171 with electric hookup, 425 level pitches, 250 static caravans, 34 ⓘ, 171 WCs, 4 CWPs
£ car/tent £8.50-£18, car/caravan £8.50-£18, motorhome £8.50-£18, motorbike/tent £8.50-£18
Rental 🚐
CC MasterCard Visa
🛁 ✂ 🍴 🔌 🏪 ♿ 🚿 📺 ⚡ ⚠ Calor Gaz ♿ 🐕
Last arrival time: 23:30
➡ At Bridport take B3157 Weymouth road. Site entrance 1½ miles on right from Crown roundabout.

Golden Cap Caravan Park
Seatown, Chideock, Bridport DT6 6JX
📞 01308-422139 Fax 01308-425672
Open 23 March-3 November ⛺ 🚐 🚚

ENGLAND

Unique location on the West Dorset Heritage coastline. Entrance is 100m from the beach and the surrounding National Trust Golden Cap Estate.
Size 28 acres, 108 touring pitches, 108 with electric hookup, 70 level pitches, 200 static caravans, 12 ⓘ, 29 WCs, 3 CWPs
£ car/tent £7.50-£12, car/caravan £7.50-£12, motorhome £7.50-£12, motorbike/tent £7.50-£12, children £1.25-£1.50
Rental 🚐
CC MasterCard Visa
🛁 🍴 🔌 🏪 🚿 📺 ⚠ Calor Gaz ♿ 🐕
Last arrival time: 22:00
➡ In the village of Chideock, two miles W of Bridport, turn S for Seatown.

Highlands End Farm Holiday Park
Eype, Bridport DT6 6AR
📞 01308-422139 Fax 01308-425672
Open March-October ⛺ 🚐 🚚
Size 28 acres, 120 touring pitches, 120 with electric hookup, 120 level pitches, 160 static caravans, 15 ⓘ, 24 WCs, 2 CWPs
£ car/tent £7.50-£11.75, car/caravan £7.50-£11.75, motorhome £7.50-£11.75, motorbike/tent £7.50-£11.75, children £1.25-£1.40
Rental 🚐 Chalet. £119-£400
CC MasterCard Visa
🛁 ✂ ✂¼ 🍴 🔌¼ 🏪 ♿ 🚿 📺 🏊 🎾 🏓 📺 GR ⚡ ⚠ Calor Gaz ♿ 🐕
Last arrival time: 23:00
➡ One mile W of Bridport on A35. Turn S for village of Eype at picnic area.

BRISTOL   3E1

Brook Lodge Farm Touring C & C Park
Cowslip Green, Redhill, Bristol BS40 5RD
📞 01934-862311
Open 1 March-31 October ⛺ 🚐 🚚
Size 3.2 acres, 29 touring pitches, 25 with electric hookup, 29 level pitches, 4 ⓘ, 8 WCs, 1 CWP
£ car/tent £8.50-£10.50, car/caravan £8.50-£10.50, motorhome £8.50-£9.50, motorbike/tent £7.50
Rental 🚐 Chalet.
🛁¼ 🍴 🔌 🏪 ♿ ⚠ Calor WS
Last arrival time: 23:00   ➡

40   Bristol

← Brook Lodge Farm Touring C & C Park

➜ From Bristol take A38 SW for 7 miles, park signposted on left. From Bath take A4 to Bristol and turn left at Southern Ring Road onto A38. From M5 S junction 19 take A369/B3129/B3130 to A38, turn right, park is 4 miles on left. From A358 at Churchill take A38 north 3½ miles, site is on the right.

Oak Farm Touring Park
Weston Road, Congresbury, Weston-super-Mare BS19 5EB
☎ 01934-833246
Open April-October ▲ ⏏ ⛺
Size 2 acres, 27 touring pitches, 32 with electric hookup, 12 level pitches, 4 ⌂, 6 WCs, 1 CWP
£ car/tent £7.50-£8.50, car/caravan £7.50-£10.50, motorhome £7.50-£8.50, motorbike/tent £7.50, children £1.50
♨¼ ✕¼ ⚑¼ ⌂ ☐ ✈ WS
Last arrival time: 23:00
➜ On A370, midway between Weston-super-Mare and Bristol, 4 miles from M5 junction 21.

BRIXHAM Devon   3D4

Galmpton Touring Park
Greenway Road, Galmpton, Brixham TQ5 0EP.
☎ 01803-842066   **Fax** 01803-844405
Open Easter-end of September ▲ ⏏ ⛺

An award winning family park, terraced to provide superior pitches enjoying spectaucular views over the River Dart, from the heart of Torbay.
Size 10 acres, 120 touring pitches, 60 with electric hookup, 10 ⌂, 18 WCs, 1 CWP
Rental Chalet. 2 holiday cottages available to rent.
Œ MasterCard Visa
♨ ✕¼ ⛽ ⌂ ☐ ⚠ Calor Gaz ♿
Last arrival time: 22:00
➜ A380 Torbay ring road to junction A379/A3022 Paignton-Brixham coast road. Turn right towards Brixham then second right into Manor Vale Road. Stay on this road, the site is on the right, 500 yards past the school.

Hillhead Camp
Brixham TQ5 0HH
☎ 01803-853204
Open Easter-October ▲ ⏏ ⛺

The Gateway to the Cotswolds

Leedons Park BROADWAY

Leedons Park is in the village of Broadway at the gateway to the Cotswolds with the towns of Cheltenham, Evesham and Stratford-upon-Avon nearby.

The park itself has 40 acres of lawns with gardens and duck ponds as a welcoming feature. You and your family could explore the endless lanes through unspoilt Cotswold scenery, to eat and drink in village pubs which abound in character.

We cater for caravanner and camper alike, with Pet and Pet free areas, Vidange Disposal point, electric Hook-up (10 amps) and childrens play area.

Our Modern Caravan Holiday Home Hire Fleet is available for your main holiday or just a few days break. Also Luxury Caravan Holiday Homes For Sale on the park.

Whether your stay is a couple of days or longer you will be assured a warm welcome.

For booking and colour brochure write, phone or call.

OPEN ALL YEAR

LEEDONS PARK BROADWAY
CHILDSWICKHAM ROAD
BROADWAY, WORCS WR12 7HB
Tel: 01386 852423

Bromyard

41

Centrally situated family site with live nightly entertainment plus separate childrens entertainment. Individual pitches and terraced areas, many with sea views. Colour brochure available.
Size 20 acres, 300 touring pitches, 200 with electric hookup, 260 level pitches, 37, 49 WCs, 2 CWPs
£ car/tent £6.50-£10, car/caravan £6.50-£11.50, motorhome £6.50-£10, motorbike/tent £6.50-£10, children £1.30
Calor Gaz
Last arrival time: 21:00
→ From A380 towards Brixham, turn onto A379 (Dartmouth) at Prouts Garage, avoiding Brixham town centre. After the BP garage, take the left fork (Kingswear) and the camp is 200 yards ahead.

BROADWAY Worcestershire 7F4

Leedons Park
Childswickham Road, Broadway WR12 7HB
☎ 01905-795999 Fax 01905-794012
Open all year
Size 40 acres, 400 touring pitches, 200 with electric hookup, 400 level pitches, 13 static caravans, 22, 22 WCs, 1 CWP
Calor Gaz
→ Signposted off A44 Broadway to Evesham road. 1 mile from Broadway village
See advert on opposite page

BROCKENHURST Hampshire 4B4

Forestry Commission Aldridge Hill
Aldrige Hill, Brockenhurst SO42 7QD
☎ 01703-283771 Fax 01703-283929
Open 22 May-1 September
Size 22 acres, 200 touring pitches, 200 level pitches, 1 CWP
£ car/tent £6.50, car/caravan £6.50, motorhome £6.50, motorbike/tent £6.50
CC MasterCard Visa
→ At the ford in Brockenhurst turn right. Site is one mile on the right.

Forestry Commission Hollands Wood
Lyndhurst Road, Brockenhurst SO42 7QH
☎ 01703-283771 Fax 01703-283929
Open end March-end September
Size 44 acres, 600 touring pitches, 600 level pitches, 26, 67 WCs, 4 CWPs
£ car/tent £7.50-£11.50, car/caravan £7.50-£11.50, motorhome £7.50-£11.50, motorbike/tent £7.50-£11.50
CC MasterCard Visa
Last arrival time: 22:00
→ Off A337 Lyndhurst to Brockenhurst road, 3 miles S of Lyndhurst

Forestry Commission Roundhill C & C
Beaulieu Road, Brockenhurst SO42 7QL
☎ 01703-283771
Open end March-end September
Size 67 acres, 500 touring pitches, 500 level pitches, 61 WCs, 2 CWPs
£ car/tent £6-£9.30, car/caravan £6-£9.30, motorhome £6-£9.30, motorbike/tent £6-£9.30
CC MasterCard Visa
Last arrival time: 22:00
→ Off B3055 Brockenhurst to Beaulieu road, 2 miles E of Brockenhurst

BROMYARD Worcestershire 7E3

Boyce Caravan Park
Stanford Bishop, Bringsty, Nr Worcester WR6 5UB
☎ 01885-483439
Open March-December

A peaceful, family run, top grade farm park ideal for exploring the Heart of England and the Welsh Border Country. Coarse fishing available.
Size 10 acres, 24 touring pitches, 10 with electric hookup, 24 level pitches, 70 static caravans, 6, 12 WCs, 1 CWP
£ car/tent £7.50, car/caravan £7.50, motorhome £7.50, motorbike/tent £7.50
Calor Gaz
Last arrival time: 18:00
→ Take B4220 (Bromyard to Malvern). After 1¾ miles turn sharp left at Linley Green signpost, then turn right and follow the signs.

ENGLAND

Bruton

BRUTON Somerset 3E2

Batcombe Vale Caravan Park
Batcombe, Shepton Mallet BA4 6BW
☎ 01749-830246
Open 1 May-30 September ⚠ ⛺ 🚐

Small, peaceful site in a secluded valley of lakes and wild gardens. Close to Longleat, Stourhead, Wells and Glastonbury.
Size 5 acres, 32 touring pitches, 16 with electric hookup, 32 level pitches, 4 🚿, 4 WCs, 1 CWP
£ car/tent £8-£9, car/caravan £8-£9, motorhome £8-£9, motorbike/tent £8, children £2
🔌 🍴 🛒 Calor Gaz 🐕 WS
➜ Off B3081 between Bruton and Evercreech, from where it is well signed.

BUDE Cornwall 2B3

Budemeadows Touring Holiday Park
Poundstock, Bude EX23 0NA
☎ 01288-361646 Fax 01288-361646
Open all year ⚠ ⛺ 🚐
Size 10 acres, 145 touring pitches, 80 with electric hookup, 70 level pitches, 13 🚿, 22 WCs, 1 CWP
£ car/tent £8-£11, car/caravan £8-£11, motorhome £8-£11, motorbike/tent £8-£11, children £2-£2.75
Rental Chalet. £200-£350
CC MasterCard Visa
🔌 🍴 🛒 🛁 ♿ GR 🔍 📺 ⚠ Calor Gaz ♿ 🐕 WS
Last arrival time: 21:00
➜ 3 miles S of Bude on A39.
See advert on this page.

Camping & Caravanning Club Site
Gillards Moor, St Gennys, Bude EX23 0BG
☎ 01840-230650
Open March-September ⚠ ⛺ 🚐
Size 6 acres, 105 touring pitches, 33 with electric hookup, 8 🚿, 11 WCs, 1 CWP
£ car/tent £11.50-£14.60, car/caravan £11.50-£14.60, motorhome £11.50-£14.60, motorbike/tent £11.50-£14.60, children £1.60
CC MasterCard Visa
🔌 🛒¼ ✖¼ 🍴¼ 🛁 🛒 P 🔑 GR 🔍 📺 ⚠ Calor ♿ 🐕 WS
Last arrival time: 23:00
➜ Going S on A39, site is on right in lay-by, 9 miles from Bude. Going N on A39, site is on left in lay-by 9 miles from Camelford. There are brown camping signs ½ mile either side of site, and also on both ends of lay-by.

BUDEMEADOWS
Touring Holiday Park

100 pitches in 9½ acres of landscaped grounds. NO OVERCROWDING. One mile from renowned, surfing beach of Widemouth Bay. Heated outdoor pool and separate heated toddler pool, TV lounge and games room. Giant chess, barbecues, logland playground. Award winning loos. Dishwashing, shop, laundry. We charge per person – no additional charges for what you bring. No charge for hot water, showers, hairdryers, swimming pool. The spectacular coastal scenery within easy reach is also free.

Please write or phone for a free brochure.

BUDE, CORNWALL   TEL: 01288 361646

Bude

Cornish Coasts Caravan Park
Middle Penlean, Poundstock, Widemouth Bay,
Bude EX23 0EE
☎ 01288-361380
Open Easter-31 October

Peaceful family park, with no club or bar, just beautiful views and beaches nearby. Great touring/walking location. 2-6 berth caravans for hire.
Size 4 acres, 67 touring pitches, 25 with electric hookup, 50 level pitches, 3 static caravans, 4 🚿, 5 WCs, 1 CWP
£ car/tent £5.50-£7, car/caravan £5.50-£7, motorhome £5.50-£7, motorbike/tent £5.50-£7, children £0.80-£1
Rental £70-£240
Calor Gaz
Last arrival time: 21:00
➡ On coastal side of A39, 5½ miles S of Bude. ½ mile S of Treskinnick Cross. Good access from layby.

Hedley Wood Caravan & Camping Park
Bridgerule, Holsworthy EX22 7ED
☎ 01288-381404   Fax 01288-381404
Open all year
Size 16.5 acres, 120 touring pitches, 110 with electric hookup, 60 level pitches, 12 static caravans, 12 🚿, 14 WCs, 2 CWPs
£ car/tent £5.50-£7.50, car/caravan £5.50-£7.50, motorhome £5.50-£7.50, motorbike/tent £5.50-£7.50, children £1-£1.25
Rental from £85-£285
Calor Gaz WS
Last arrival time: 24 hours
➡ From A3072 (midway between Holsworthy and Bude), at red post and roads, turn S on B3254 for 2½ miles, turn right, the site is in 500 yards.
See advert on this page

Sandymouth Bay Holiday Park
Bude EX23 9HW
☎ 01288-352563   Fax 01288-352563
Open April-October

ENGLAND

Hedley Wood
Caravan & Camping Park

16 acre woodland family run site with outstanding views, where you can enjoy a totally relaxing holiday with a "laid-back" atmosphere, sheltered and open camping areas. Just 10 minutes drive from the beaches etc.
All amenities, Bar, Dog walk/nature trail etc.
Daily Kennelling, Caravan Storage, Static van hire.
OPEN ALL YEAR.

**Bridgerule, (Nr. Bude),
Holsworthy, Devon EX22 7ED
Tel/Fax: 01288 381404**

SANDYMOUTH BAY HOLIDAY PARK

Friendly family park, 14 acres of level or terraced meadowland, overlooking beautiful heritage coastline and countryside. 3 miles from Bude, ¾ mile from award winning beach. 6-8 berth caravans, lodges and bungalows, tents and tourers welcome. Hook-ups, club, entertainment etc. New indoor heated pool, sauna and solarium.

**BUDE, CORNWALL EX23 9HW
TEL: 01288-352563
FAX: 01288-352563**

Bude

← Sandymouth Bay Holiday Park

Family park set in 14 acres overlooking beautiful heritage coastline and award winning sandy beaches. 3 miles from Bude. 6-8 berth caravans, lodges and bungalows.
Size 14 acres, 55 touring pitches, 40 with electric hookup, 120 static caravans, 14 ⌂, 15 WCs, 1 CWP
£ car/tent £7-£12, car/caravan £7-£12, motorhome £7-£12, motorbike/tent £7-£12, children £1.20-£1.80
Rental £99-£450.
₢ MasterCard Visa
Calor Gaz WS
Last arrival time: 22:00
➜ A39 from Kilkampton to Bude. Turn right immediately after Penstone turning through Stibb. 3 miles from Bude.
See advert on previous page

Widemouth Bay Caravan Park
Widemouth Bay, Bude
☎ 01288-361208 Fax 01271-866791
Open March-October
Size 56 acres, 80 with electric hookup, 140 static caravans,
£ car/tent £4-£8, car/caravan £5-£10.50, motorhome £5-£10.50, motorbike/tent £8
Rental
₢ MasterCard Visa
Calor WS
Last arrival time: 22:00
➜ Take A39 past Bude and turn right to Widemouth Bay. Turning to Millook in Widemouth Bay.
See advert on this page

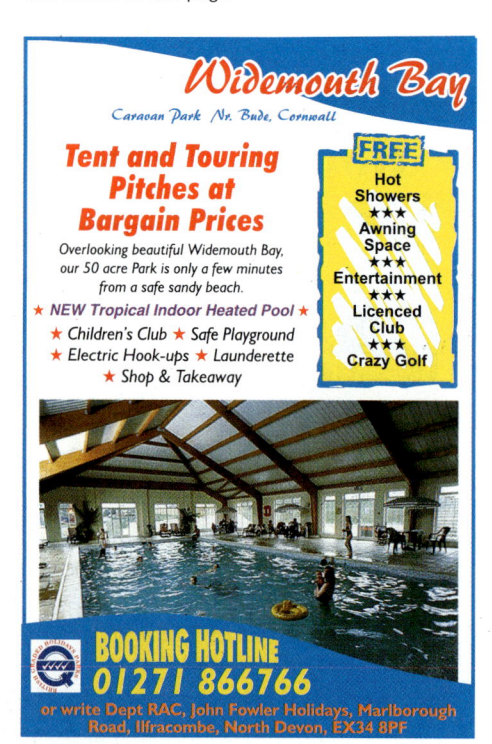

Wooda Farm Caravan & Camping Park
Wooda Farm, Poughill, Bude EX23 9HJ
☎ 01288-352069 Fax 01288-355258
Open April-October

A quiet, family run farm park, overlooking Bude Bay and the countryside. Excellent for touring and camping. Luxury holiday homes for hire. Sandy beaches one and a half miles. 'Splash' indoor pool nearby.
Size 15 acres, 200 touring pitches, 122 with electric hookup, 100 level pitches, 54 static caravans, 22 ⌂, 36 WCs, 2 CWPs
£ car/tent £6.50-£10.50, car/caravan £6.50-£10.50, motorhome £6.50-£10.50, motorbike/tent £6.50-£10.50, children £1-£1.75
Rental £99-£450
₢ MasterCard Visa
Calor Gaz WS
Last arrival time: 21:00
➜ From A39 at Stratton take road to Poughill/Coombe Valley. Drive 1 mile through crossroads. Wooda is 200 yards on right.

BUNGAY Suffolk   9F3

Outney Meadow Caravan Park
Bungay NR35 1HG
☎ 01986-892338
Open March-October
Size 8 acres, 45 touring pitches, 45 with electric hookup, 45 level pitches, 30 static caravans, 4 ⌂, 10 WCs, 1 CWP
£ car/tent £6.50-£10.50, car/caravan £6.50-£10.50, motorhome £6.50-£10.50, motorbike/tent £6.50-£10.50, children £1
Calor Gaz WS
Last arrival time: 22:00
➜ Park is signposted from roundabout of junction A144/A143.

BURNHAM-ON-SEA Somerset   3E2

Widemouth Bay
Caravan Park Nr. Bude, Cornwall

Tent and Touring Pitches at Bargain Prices
Overlooking beautiful Widemouth Bay, our 50 acre Park is only a few minutes from a safe sandy beach.
★ NEW Tropical Indoor Heated Pool ★
★ Children's Club ★ Safe Playground
★ Electric Hook-ups ★ Launderette
★ Shop & Takeaway

FREE
★★★ Hot Showers ★★★
★★★ Awning Space ★★★
★★★ Entertainment ★★★
★★★ Licenced Club ★★★
★★★ Crazy Golf ★★★

BOOKING HOTLINE 01271 866766
or write Dept RAC, John Fowler Holidays, Marlborough Road, Ilfracombe, North Devon, EX34 8PF

Just rewards
Join the RAC today
and take out Standard Cover.
If you don't call us out during your membership year, we'll reward you with a £25 discount when you renew at the same level of cover.

Call us on **0800 029 029**
quoting ref GUIDE 1

rac
movement drives us

www.rac.co.uk

Burnham-on-Sea

Burnham on Sea Holiday Village
Marine Drive, Burnham-on-Sea TA8 1LA
☎ 01278-783391
Open mid March-mid November

Burnham Holiday Village is situated near the town centre, with access onto the esplanade and beach and offers superb facilities for the perfect family holiday. A 'British Holidays Park'.
Size 95 acres, 52 touring pitches, 29 with electric hookup, 52 level pitches, 500 static caravans,
£ car/tent £7-£16, car/caravan £7-£16, motorhome £7-£16, motorbike/tent £7-£16, children £1.50
Rental Chalet.
ℂℂ MasterCard Visa

Last arrival time: 22:00
➔ Off M5 jn 22, A38 to Highbridge, B3139 to Burnham. Signposted from there.

Diamond Farm Caravan & Touring Park
Weston Road, Brean, Burnham-on-Sea
☎ 01278-751041
Open March-October

Size 5 acres, 100 touring pitches, 100 with electric hookup, 120 level pitches, 12, 28 WCs, 1 CWP
£ car/tent £4-£8, car/caravan £4-£8, motorhome £4-£8, motorbike/tent £4-£8
Rental Chalet. From £130

Calor Gaz WS

Last arrival time: 23:00
➔ From M5 junction 22 take B3139 to Brean. Through village for 2 miles down coast road. Turn at Weston Road, site is ½ mile on the left.

Home Farm Holidays
Burnham-on-Sea TA9 4HD
☎ 01278-788888 Fax 01278-792365
Open open all year

Size 40 acres, 850 touring pitches, 750 with electric hookup, 850 level pitches, 34, 48 WCs, 4 CWPs
£ car/tent £6.50-£16.50, car/caravan £6.50-£16.50, motorhome £6.50-£16.50, motorbike/tent £6.50-£16.50, children £1-£2
ℂℂ MasterCard Visa

Calor Gaz

Last arrival time: 22:00
➔ ½ mile from M5 junction 22.
See advert on previous page

BURTON-UPON-TRENT Staffordshire 7F2

THE BASS MUSEUM
Horninglow St., Burton upon Trent, Staffs DE14
Tel: 01283 511000

Museum of the history of Bass, Brewing and Beer. Features include a working 'N' Gauge model of Burton upon Trent dated 1921. An Edwardian Bar, "The Story of Brewing", historical fleet of horse drawn and motorised vehicles. Also the home of the famous "Bass Shire Horses". Fully licensed bars, restaurant and souvenir shop.

Open everyday except Christmas, Boxing and New Years day from 4pm-5pm (last admission 4pm).

BUXTON Derbyshire 8A1

Cottage Farm Caravan Park
Blackwell In The Peak, Taddington, Buxton SK17 9TQ
☎ 01298-85330
Open 1 March-31 October

Size 3 acres, 29 touring pitches, 30 with electric hookup, 24 level pitches, 5, 5 WCs, 1 CWP
£ car/tent £6, car/caravan £6, motorhome £5.50, children £0.50

Calor Gaz

➔ Six miles from Buxton on A6 to Bakewell. Turn left on unclassified road. Signposted.

Pomeroy Caravan & Camping Park
Street House Farm, Pomeroy, Flagg, Buxton SK17 9QG
☎ 01298-83259
Open Easter/April-October

A well maintained level park adjoining the High Peak Trail with a large rally field available. Good access from the A515.
Size 2 acres, 30 touring pitches, 24 with electric hookup, 30 level pitches, 4, 6 WCs, 1 CWP
£ car/tent £4.50-£6.50, car/caravan £6-£6.50, motorhome £5.50-£6, motorbike/tent £4.50-£5, children £0.50
Rental

Calor Gaz

Cambridge

Last arrival time: 22:00
➜ On A515 Buxton/Ashbourne road. Five miles from Buxton, 16 miles from Ashbourne. Entrance over double cattle grid with 100 yards of tarmac drive to site.

CAISTER-ON-SEA Norfolk 9F3

Scratby Hall Caravan Park
Scratby, Caister-on-Sea NR29 3PH
☎ 01493-730283
Open Easter-mid October
Size 4.5 acres, 108 touring pitches, 64 with electric hookup, 108 level pitches, 10, 18 WCs, 1 CWP
£ car/tent £4.50-£9.90, car/caravan £4.50-£9.90, motorhome £4.50-£9.90, motorbike/tent £4.50-£9.90
Calor Gaz
Last arrival time: 22:00
➜ At roundabout, junction of A149 and B1159, 1½ miles N of Caister, turn N along B1159 for 1 mile to site on the left.

CALNE Wiltshire 4A2

Blackland Lakes Holiday & Leisure Centre
Stockley Lane, Calne SN11 0NQ
☎ 01249-813672 Fax 01249-811346
Open all year

An interesting family run site, scenic, beautiful area with walking, riding, K & A canal. Ideal family holiday. Bikes, covered swimming pool. Open all year. 15 superpitches. Colour brochure available with site plan, tariff and booking form on request.
Size 17 acres, 180 touring pitches, 120 with electric hookup, 100 level pitches, 13, 23 WCs, 2 CWPs
Calor Gaz WS
Last arrival time: 23:00
➜ Signposted from A4 E of Calne.

CAMBRIDGE Cambridgeshire 9D4

Apple Acre Park
London Road, Fowlmere, Royston SG8 7RU
☎ 01763-208354
Open all year

Size 3.5 acres, 20 touring pitches, 20 with electric hookup, 20 level pitches, 12 static caravans, 2, 4 WCs, 1 CWP
£ car/tent £4-£6, car/caravan £7-£7.50, motorhome £6-£7, motorbike/tent £5
Last arrival time: 22:00
➜ From Cambridge, A10 to Harston, turn left onto B1368 to site through village of Fowlmere on left. From Royston, A505 to Flint Cross Road, turn left onto B1358, site is on right after Fowlmere village sign.

Camping & Caravanning Club Site
Behind 19 Cabbage Moor, Great Shelford, Cambridge CB2 5NB
☎ 01223-841185
Open March-November
Size 12 acres, 120 touring pitches, 70 with electric hookup, 8, 11 WCs, 1 CWP
£ car/tent £11.50-£14.60, car/caravan £11.50-£14.60, motorhome £11.50-£14.60, motorbike/tent £11.50-£14.60, children £1.60
㏄ MasterCard Visa
Calor WS
Last arrival time: 23:00
➜ M11 (Jn 11) onto B1309, signposted Cambridge. At the first set of traffic lights turn right. In ½ mile see site sign on left pointing down lane.

Highfield Farm Camping Park
Long Road, Comberton, Cambridge CB3 7DG
☎ 01223-262308 Fax 01223-262308
Open 1 April-31 October

A popular award winning park with an exellent grading, close to the historic university city of Cambridge. Other nearby attractions include the Imperial War Museum at Duxford and Wimpole Hall.
Size 8 acres, 120 touring pitches, 100 with electric hookup, 80 level pitches, 16, 23 WCs, 3 CWPs
£ car/tent £7-£8.25, car/caravan £7.25-£8.75, motorhome £7-£8.25, motorbike/tent £5.75-£6.75, children £1-£1.50
Calor Gaz
Last arrival time: 22:00
➜ From M11 junction 12 take A603 to Sandy for ½ mile, then turn right on B1046 to Comberton. From A428 leave at Hardwick roundabout and follow signs to Comberton.

ENGLAND

Stanford Park Camping and Caravanning
Weirs Road, Burwell, Cambridge CB5 OBP
01638-741547 Fax 01638-743508
Open all year

Family run site, excellently landscaped. Conveniently situated for visiting Cambridge, Newmarket and Ely. Lovely countryside for walking, cycling and fishing.
Size 20 acres, 120 touring pitches, 40 with electric hookup, 120 level pitches, 3 static caravans, 5, 13 WCs, 1 CWP
£ car/tent £7.50-£9, car/caravan £7.50-£9.50, motorhome £7.50-£9.50, motorbike/tent £7.50
Rental £100-£120
¼ ¼ ¼ Calor Gaz WS
Last arrival time: 22:00
➜ From Cambridge at Stow Cum Quy roundabout take B1102 to Burwell. From Newmarket turn off A14 onto A142 following signs to Burwell via Exning.
See advert on this page

Stanford Park
CAMBRIDGE
Telephone: 01638 741547 or 0802 439997

Quiet, family-run park, offering excellent facilities including a children's playground, in an attractive country setting.

Situated on the edge of the Fens, ideal for picturesque walks and cycling. Local rivers offer the opportunity for boating and fishing.

Superb modern toilet block and launderette, including facilities for the disabled.

Close to the university city of Cambridge and also Newmarket racing.

**OPEN 52 WEEKS OF THE YEAR.
DISCOUNTED RATES FOR SEASONAL AND LONG TERM PITCHES.**

CANTERBURY Kent 5E3

Ashfield Farm Camping & Caravanning Site
Waddenhall, Petham, Nr. Canterbury CT4 5PX
01227-700624
Open April-October

Quiet family touring park situated in an area of outstanding natural beauty with views over open countryside. Easy reach of Canterbury and Kent coastline.
Size 4 acres, 20 touring pitches, 16 with electric hookup, 20 level pitches, 3, 5 WCs, 1 CWP
£ car/tent £6-£7, car/caravan £6-£9.50, motorhome £6-£9.50, motorbike/tent £6-£7
Calor Gaz WS
Last arrival time: 22:00

Camping & Caravanning Club Site
Bekesbourne Lane, Canterbury CT3 4AB
01227-463216
Open all year
Size 20 acres, 210 touring pitches, 85 with electric hookup, 19, 22 WCs,
£ car/tent £13.60-£14.60, car/caravan £13.60-£14.60, motorhome £13.60-£14.60, motorbike/tent £13.60-£14.60, children £1.60
€ MasterCard Visa
¼ ¼ ¼ Calor WS
Last arrival time: 23:00
➜ From Canterbury follow A257 signs (Sandwich), turn right opposite the golf course.

Red Lion Caravan Park
Old London Road, Dunkirk, Canterbury ME13 9LL
01227-750661
Open all year
Size 1 acre, 15 touring pitches, 12 with electric hookup, 11 level pitches, 2, 5 WCs, 1 CWP
£ car/caravan £7, motorhome £7, children £1
¼ ¼ WS
Last arrival time: 23:00
➜ From A2 London bound follow signs. Turn off ½ mile at Dunkirk. From A2 Dover bound take Dunkirk turning immediately after joining from M2 junction 7. Follow signs. Car park 3 miles.

Castle Donington

CARLISLE Cumbria — 10B1

Dalston Hall Caravan Park
Dalston Road, Carlisle CA5 7J
☎ 01228-710165
Open 1 March-31 October
Size 4.5 acres, 40 touring pitches, 40 with electric hookup, 40 level pitches, 17 static caravans, 4 🚿, 15 WCs, 1 CWP
£ car/tent £6-£6.50, car/caravan £7-£7.50, motorhome £7-£7.50, motorbike/tent £6-£6.50, children £0.75
Calor Gaz WS
Last arrival time: 21:00
➡ Leave M6 at junction 42 and follow sign for Dalston. Turn right for Carlisle and site is on right after 1½ miles.

Dandy Dinmont Caravan & Camping Park
Blackford, Carlisle CA6 4EA
☎ 01228-674611
Open 1 March-31 October

A quiet rural park yet only 1½ miles north of the M6 (44). A good overnight halt or a base for a longer stay to visit the Lake District, historic Carlisle, Roman Wall or romantic Scottish Border.
Size 4.5 acres, 27 touring pitches, 20 with electric hookup, 27 level pitches, 4 🚿, 14 WCs, 1 CWP
£ car/tent £5.75-£6.25, car/caravan £7-£7.25, motorhome £7-£7.25, motorbike/tent £5.75-£6
Calor
Last arrival time: 00:00
➡ Just N of Carlisle leave M6 junction 44 and take A7 Galashiels road. From here park is 1½ miles on right. After Blackford village sign, follow road directional signs to park.

Orton Grange Caravan Park
Wigton Road, Carlisle CA5 6LA
☎ 01228-710252 Fax 01228-710252
Open all year
Size 7 acres, 50 touring pitches, 30 with electric hookup, 50 level pitches, 22 static caravans, 6 🚿, 11 WCs, 1 CWP
£ car/tent £6.90-£8.60, car/caravan £7-£9, motorhome £6.90-£8.60, motorbike/tent £4.40-£5, children £0.60-£0.80
Rental £99-£185

CC MasterCard Visa
Calor Gaz WS
Last arrival time: 22:00
➡ 4 miles W of Carlisle on A595.

CARNFORTH Lancashire — 10B3

Detron Gate Caravan Site
Bolton-le-Sands, Carnforth LA5 9TN
☎ 01524-732842
Open 1 March-30 September
Size 10 acres, 150 touring pitches, 98 with electric hookup, 50 level pitches, 42 static caravans, 12 🚿, 18 WCs, 2 CWPs
£ car/tent £4, car/caravan £6, motorhome £6, children £0.75
Calor Gaz
Last arrival time: 22:00
➡ 1½ miles S of Carnforth on A6. Once you pass a large lay by on left, site is next turning on right off A6.

CASTLE DONINGTON Leicestershire — 7F2

Donington Park Farmhouse
Melbourne Road, Isley Walton, Castle Donington DE74 2RN
☎ 01332-862409 Fax 01332-862364
Open March-December

Well screened grassland site adjacent mature woods in farmhouse hotel grounds. Perfect base for touring southern Derbyshire.
Size 8 acres, 60 touring pitches, 45 with electric hookup, 45 level pitches, 3 🚿, 10 WCs, 2 CWPs
£ car/tent £8-£12, car/caravan £8-£12, motorhome £8-£12, motorbike/tent £7, children £1
CC MasterCard Visa
Calor WS
Last arrival time: 21:00
➡ Take the Melbourne turn at Isley Walton on the A453 and the site is ½ mile on the right.

Don't forget to mention the guide
When booking, please remember to tell the site that you chose it from RAC Camping & Caravanning 1999

50

Chard

CHARD Somerset	3E2

Alpine Grove Touring Park
Forton, Chard TA20 4HD
☎ 01460-63479
Open Easter-30 September
Size 7.5 acres, 40 touring pitches, 20 with electric hookup, 40 level pitches, 2, 5 WCs, 1 CWP
£ car/tent £5.50-£7, car/caravan £5-£7, motorhome £6-£8, motorbike/tent £5.50-£7, children £1
Rental
Calor Gaz
Last arrival time: 23:00
➜ Leave M5 at junction 25 and follow signs for Cricket St Thomas. Turn right immediately before Crinkley Bottom entrance onto B3167. Turn right at second signpost for Forton. Site on right.

CHARLBURY Oxfordshire	4B1

Cotswold View Caravan & Camping Site
Enstone Road, Charlbury OX7 3JH
☎ 01608-810314 Fax 01608-811891
Open 1 April-30 October
Size 7 acres, 90 touring pitches, 75 with electric hookup, 70 level pitches, 9, 10 WCs, 1 CWP
Calor Gaz
➜ From A44 Oxford to Stratford-upon-Avon road, take B4022 road to Charlbury, just S of Enstone. Site is 2 miles on left. (O.S. SP 365210).

CHARMOUTH Dorset	3E3

Manor Farm Holiday Centre
Charmouth DT6 6QL
☎ 01297-560226 Fax 01297-560429
Open all year

A large, open site in an area of outstanding natural beauty at Charmouth. A 10 minute level walk to a beach famous for its fossils and safe for bathing.
Size 32 acres, 302 touring pitches, 30 with electric hookup, 100 level pitches, 15 static caravans, 30, 42 WCs, 2 CWPs
£ car/tent £7-£10, car/caravan £7-£10, motorhome £7-£10, motorbike/tent £7-£10, children £1-£1.50
Rental £100-£380, houses - £150-£420
CC MasterCard Visa

¼ X X¼ ¼ Calor Gaz WS
Last arrival time: 23:00
➜ On main A35 from Bridport travelling W, Charmouth is 6 miles. Enter Charmouth from A35, Manor Farm Holiday Centre is ¾ mile on right in Charmouth.

Monkton Wylde Farm Caravan Park
Charmouth DT6 6DB
☎ 01297-34525 Fax 01297-33594
Open Easter-end October
Size 6 acres, 60 touring pitches, 40 with electric hookup, 50 level pitches, 5, 7 WCs, 1 CWP
£ car/tent £6.25-£10.50, car/caravan £6.25-£10.50, motorhome £6.25-£10.50, motorbike/tent £6.25-£10.50, children £1
¼ Calor Gaz WS
Last arrival time: 22:00
➜ Take A35 E towards Charmouth. 100 yards inside Dorset boundary turn left down unmarked lane. Brown tourism sign is on junction.

CHEADLE Staffordshire	7E1

Hales Hall Caravan & Camping Park
Oakamoor Road, Cheadle ST10 1BU
☎ 01538-753305 Fax 01782-202316
Open 1 March-30 October
Size 8 acres, 48 touring pitches, 30 with electric hookup, 10 level pitches, 4, 8 WCs, 3 CWPs
£ car/tent £6-£7, car/caravan £6-£7, motorhome £6-£7, motorbike/tent £6-£7, children £1
X Calor Gaz WS
Last arrival time: 23:30
➜ From Cheadle take the B5417 signposted Oakamoor. The site is ½ mile on the left.

CHEDDAR Somerset	3E1

Broadway House Caravan & Camping Park
Axbridge Road, Cheddar BS27 3DB
☎ 01934-742610 Fax 01934-744950
Open March-November
Size 30 acres, 200 touring pitches, 190 with electric hookup, 200 level pitches, 35 static caravans, 29, 64 WCs, 2 CWPs
£ car/tent £5-£13.50, car/caravan £5-£13.50, motorhome £5-£10.50, motorbike/tent £5-£13.50, children £1-£2
Rental £110-£485
CC MasterCard Visa
Calor Gaz
Last arrival time: 00:00
➜ Leave M5 at junction 22, and continue for 8 miles to park, following brown tourist signs to Cheddar Gorge and Caves. Midway between Cheddar and Axbridge on A371
See advert on opposite page

Chester

Froglands Farm
Cheddar BS27 3RH
☎ 01934-742058
Open Easter-October

A small, family site situated in an area of outstanding natural beauty, within walking distance of village shops, pubs, restaurants, swimming pool, leisure centre, gorge and caves.
Size 3 acres, 60 touring pitches, 30 with electric hookup, 50 level pitches, 6 ⚲, 12 WCs, 1 CWP
£ car/tent £6.50-£7.50, car/caravan £7.50-£8.50, motorhome £6.50-£7.50
Calor Gaz
Last arrival time: 22:30
→ On the main A371 Wells/Cheddar road, 100 yards past Cheddar Church.

CHERTSEY Surrey 4C2

Camping & Caravanning Club Site
Bridge Road, Chertsey KT16 8JX
☎ 01932-562405
Open all year
Size 12 acres, 200 touring pitches, 95 with electric hookup, 14 ⚲, 22 WCs, 1 CWP
£ car/tent £13.60-£14.60, car/caravan £13.60-£14.60, motorhome £13.60-£14.60, motorbike/tent £13.60-£14.60, children £1.60
⚀ MasterCard Visa
Calor WS
Last arrival time: 23:00
→ Off M25 (jn 11), follow A317 to Chertsey, at roundabout take first exit to traffic lights, straight across to next set of traffic lights, turn right up road, 400 yards, turn left into site.

CHESTER Cheshire 7D1

Chester Southerly Caravan Park
Balderton Lane, Marlston-cum-Lache, Chester CH4 9LF
☎ 0976-743888
Open 1 March-30 November
Size 8 acres, 90 touring pitches, 65 with electric hookup, 90 level pitches, 8 ⚲, 12 WCs, 1 CWP
£ car/tent £6.20-£9.30, car/caravan £6.20-£9.30, motorhome £6.20-£9.30, motorbike/tent £6.20-£9.30, children £1.10-£1.20

ENGLAND

Taste The Real Cheddar! at BROADWAY HOUSE
Holiday Touring Caravan & Camping Park

CHEDDAR SOMERSET: LAND OF THE SUMMER PEOPLE

- HOLIDAY CARAVANS FOR HIRE
- PREMIER TOURING AND CAMPING PITCHES
- FREE HEATED SWIMMING POOL
- FREE MARVELLOUS ADVENTURE PLAYGROUND/PIXIE AREA
- DISABLED AND BABIES ROOM
- CORNER SHOP WITH THE FRIENDLY SERVICE
- FREE CUDDLE WITH THE LLAMAS
- FREE ENTRANCE TO "ENGLISH PUB"& FAMILY ROOM
- BARBEQUES FOR YOUR OWN USE
- LAUNDERETTE, SUNBED, AMUSEMENTS, CRAZY GOLF, BOULES, SKATEBOARD RAMP, INDOOR TABLE TENNIS, MOUNTAIN BIKE/CYCLE TANDEM HIRE
- ACTIVITY PROGRAMME ARCHERY, RIFLE SHOOTING, ABSEILING, CAVING, CANOEING, NATURE TRAILS, PLUS PRIVATE THREE ACRE FISHING LAKE

ROSE AWARD | AA | SILVER

BROADWAY HOUSE, CHEDDAR, SOMERSET. BS27 3DB
TEL:01934 742610 FAX:01934 744950
E-MAIL: broadway.house@btinternet.com www.btinternet.com/~broadway.house

52

← **Chester Southerly Caravan Park**

🏕 🚿¼ ✕¼ 🚻¼ 🔌 📞 🚿 ⚠ Calor Gaz ♿ 🐕
Last arrival time: 21:00
➔ Leave A55 at A483 junction towards Wrexham. After 300 yards at roundabout double back to Balderton Lane.

CHESTER ZOO – *it's always new! The UK's largest zoo, with 5,000 animals from 500 species. Spacious animal enclosures set in award winning gardens. Open all year from 10am. Last entry and closing times vary with the seasons.*

UPTON-BY-CHESTER, CHESTER CH2 1LH
Tel: 01244 380280 Fax: 01244 371273

CHICHESTER West Sussex	4C4

Camping & Caravanning Club Site

343 Main Road, Southbourne PO10 8JH
📞 01243-373202
Open all year ⛺ 🚐 🚍
Size 3 acres, 58 touring pitches, 58 with electric hookup, 10 🚿, 8 WCs, 1 CWP
£ car/tent £13.60-£14.60, car/caravan £13.60-£14.60, motorhome £13.60-£14.60, motorbike/tent £13.60-£14.60, children £1.60
⚡ MasterCard Visa
🏕 🚿¼ ✕¼ 🍴 🚿¼ 🔌 📞 🅿 ♿ 📺 ⚠ Calor ♿ 🐕 WS
Last arrival time: 23:00
➔ From Chichester take the A259 to Southampton, the site is on the right, past Inlands Road.

Red House Farm

Earnley, Chichester PO20 7JG
📞 01243-514216 Fax 01243-514216
Open April-October ⛺ 🚐 🚍
Size 4 acres, 100 touring pitches, 100 level pitches, 4 🚿, 12 WCs, 1 CWP
£ car/tent £7-£8, car/caravan £7-£8, motorhome £7-£8, motorbike/tent £7-£8
🏕¼ ✕¼ 📞 🚿 ⚠ Gaz ♿ 🐕 WS
Last arrival time: 22:00
➔ Take A286 from Chichester to Witterings. Turn left at Birdham garage onto B2198 to Bracklesham Bay. After ½ mile turn left again to Earnley on sharp right hand bend. Site is 500 yards on left.

Chester

Southern Leisure Centre

Vinnetrow Road, Chichester PO20 6LB
📞 01243-787715 Fax 01243-533643
Open March-October ⛺ 🚐 🚍

A family holiday park set in 220 acres and amongst 12 lakes, excellent for watersports, heated outdoor pool, kids clubs, tennis and bowling included in the wide range of leisure facilities, restaurants and bars, entertainment. A 'British Holidays Park.'
Size 220 acres, 1,500 touring pitches, 420 with electric hookup, 1500 level pitches, 900 static caravans, 32 🚿, 66 WCs, 5 CWPs
£ car/tent £5, car/caravan £6.50-£12.50, motorhome £6.50-£12.50, motorbike/tent £5, children £1.50
⚡ MasterCard Visa
🏕 🍴 🔌 📞 🏊 🎮 🍽 ⚠ Calor Gaz ♿ 🐕 WS
➔ At roundabout junction of A27 (Chichester by-pass) and A259, 1 mile SE of Chichester, turn into Vinnetrow Lane and it's ¼ mile to the park.

CHIPPENHAM Wiltshire	3F1

Plough Lane Caravan Site

Kington Langley, Chippenham SN15 5PS
📞 01249-750795 Fax 01249-750795
Open March-October ⛺ 🚐 🚍
Size 2.5 acres, 35 touring pitches, 35 with electric hookup, 35 level pitches, 5 🚿, 8 WCs, 1 CWP
£ car/tent £10, car/caravan £10, motorhome £10, motorbike/tent £10
🏕¼ ✕¼ 🚿¼ 🔌 📞 🚿 ♿ 🐕
➔ Signposted off A350 N of Chippenham. Approximately five minutes from M4 (jn 17). Adults only site.

CHIPPING NORTON Oxfordshire	4B1

Camping & Caravanning Club Site

Chipping Norton Road, Chadlington, Chipping Norton OX7 3PE
📞 01608-641993
Open March-November ⛺ 🚐 🚍
Size 4 acres, 75 touring pitches, 50 with electric hookup, 6 🚿, 9 WCs, 1 CWP
£ car/tent £11.50-£14.60, car/caravan £11.50-£14.60, motorhome £11.50-£14.60, motorbike/tent £11.50-£14.60, children £1.60

Chudleigh

cc MasterCard Visa
♨ ♨¼ ✕¼ 🚿 🚿¼ 🔌 📞 ▶ 📂 GR 🔍 TV ⚠ Calor ♿ 🐕
WS
Last arrival time: 23:00

CHRISTCHURCH Dorset 3F3

Forestry Commission Holmsley Campsite
Holmsley, Christchurch BH23 7EQ
📞 01703-283771
Open end March-end October ⛺ 🚐 🚚
Size 35 acres, 755 touring pitches, 120 with electric hookup, 600 level pitches, 30 🚿, 71 WCs, 3 CWPs
£ car/tent £6.50-£10.40, car/caravan £6.50-£10.40, motorhome £6.50-£10.40, motorbike/tent £6.50-£10.40
cc MasterCard Visa
♨ 🚿 🔌 📞 📂 ⚠ Calor Gaz ♿ 🐕
Last arrival time: 22:00
➜ Off A35 Lyndhurst to Christchurch road, 8 miles S of Lyndhurst

Hoburne Park
Christchurch BH23 4HU
📞 01425-273379 Fax 01425-270705
Open March-October 🚐 🚚

A family holiday park with an extensive range of quality family and sporting entertainment facilities. Close to the beach, New Forest and Bournemouth.
Size 40 acres, 285 touring pitches, 285 with electric hookup, 285 level pitches, 287 static caravans, 23 🚿, 38 WCs, 4 CWPs
£ car/caravan £9.50-£23, motorhome £9.50-£23
cc MasterCard Visa
♨ ✕ 🚿 🔌 📞 📂 🏊 🎾 🔍 🗞 GR TV ⚽ ⚠ Calor ♿
Last arrival time: 21:00
➜ From Lyndhurst, take A35 signed Bournemouth for 13 miles to roundabout. Take first exit left onto A337, then take first left at roundabout. The site is 100 yards on left.

CHUDLEIGH Devon 3D3

Finlake Leisure Park
Chudleigh TQ13 0EJ
📞 01626-853833 Fax 01626-854031
Open all year ⛺ 🚐 🚚

Situated in a 130 acre park, encompassing hills, valleys, woodland and lakes. Facilities include indoor and outdoor pools with waterslide, tennis, bar, restaurant and entertainment.
Size 130 acres, 409 touring pitches, 319 with electric hookup, 409 level pitches, 41 static caravans, 61 🚿, 107 WCs, 7 CWPs
£ car/tent £4.50-£11.25, car/caravan £6.25-£14.50, motorhome £6.25-£14.50, motorbike/tent £4.50-£11.25, children £1.25-£2
Rental 🚐 £150-£550, lodge £180-£630
cc MasterCard Visa
♨ ✕ 🚿 🔌 📞 📂 🏊 🎾 ▶ 🔍 🗞 📂 GR ⚽ ⚠ Calor Gaz 🐕 WS
Last arrival time: 22:00
➜ From A38 take Chudleigh/Knighton exit (B3344). Site is ½ mile on right.

Holmans Wood Caravan Park
Chudleigh TQ13 0DZ
📞 01626-853785 Fax 01626-854707
Open March-end October ⛺ 🚐 🚚

Set amongst beautiful Devon countryside with breathtaking views on all sides, Holmans Wood is an immaculately well kept site. Peaceful and relaxing for all the family. Graded excellent. Winner of 1996 Calor award.
Size 20 acres, 125 touring pitches, 110 with electric hookup, 125 level pitches, 10 static caravans, 10 🚿, 15 WCs, 3 CWPs
£ car/tent £6-£8.35, car/caravan £6-£9.75, motorhome £6-£9.75, motorbike/tent £6-£8.35, children £1.50
Rental 🚐
cc MasterCard Visa
♨ ✕¼ 🚿¼ 🔌 📞 📂 🔍 Calor Gaz ♿ 🐕 WS
Last arrival time: 22:00 ➜

ENGLAND

53

54

Chudleigh

← Holmans Wood Caravan Park

➜ Follow M5 to Exeter and take A38 towards Plymouth. After the racecourse (about ½ mile on the left) is an exit signposted to Chudleigh. Site entrance is 300 yards on the left.

CHURCH STRETTON Shropshire	7D3

Small Batch Site

Ashes Valley, Little Stretton, Church Stretton SY6 6PW
📞 01694-723358
Open 17 April-30 September
Size 1.5 acres, 32 touring pitches, 17 level pitches, 2 ⚲, 5 WCs, 1 CWP
£ car/tent £8, car/caravan £8, motorhome £8, motorbike/tent £8

➜ Off A49 into Little Stretton, onto B4370. Left at Ragleth Inn and site is ¼ mile on right.

CIRENCESTER Gloucestershire	7F4

Cotswold Hoburne

Broadway Lane, South Cerney, Cirencester GL7 5UQ
📞 01285-860216 Fax 01285-862106
Open Easter-31 October

Set in the Cotswold Water Park, this quality site has fish-stocked lakes, a magnificent indoor pool and a licensed lakeside lounge with seasonal entertainment.
Size 70 acres, 302 touring pitches, 302 with electric hookup, 302 level pitches, 158 static caravans, 18 ⚲, 54 WCs, 6 CWPs
£ car/tent £8.50-£21, car/caravan £8.50-£21, motorhome £8.50-£21
Rental Chalet.
cc MasterCard Visa
Calor Gaz
Last arrival time: 21:00
➜ The park is signposted from A419, 4 miles S of Cirencester.

Mayfield Touring Park

Cheltenham Road, Perrotts Brook, Cirencester GL7 7BH
📞 01285-831301 Fax 01285-831301
Open all year
Size 12 acres, 72 touring pitches, 42 with electric hookup, 20 level pitches, 2 static caravans, 4 ⚲, 5 WCs, 1 CWP
£ car/tent £5.40-£9.40, car/caravan £6.80-£9.40, motorhome £5.80-£9.40, children £1.50
Rental £65-£155
cc MasterCard Visa
Calor Gaz WS
Last arrival time: 22:30
➜ Immediately off main A435 Cirencester to Cheltenham road, 2 miles N of Cirencester.

CLACTON-ON-SEA Essex	5E1

Orchards Holiday Park

Point Clear, St. Osyth, Clacton-on-Sea CO16 8LJ
📞 01255-820651
Open March-October

A family holiday park surrounded on three sides by water, ideal for watersports and the active family. New indoor heated pool, outdoor pool, kids club, tennis and bowling included in the wide range of leisure facilities, restaurants and bars, excellent cabaret entertainment. A 'British Holidays Park'.
Size 120 acres, 22 touring pitches, 22 with electric hookup, 22 level pitches, 1,400 static caravans, 14 ⚲, 10 WCs, 1 CWP
Calor Gaz
➜ From Clacton on Sea, take the B1027 out of Clacton (signposted Colchester). Turn left after Pump Hill petrol station, then over crossroads in St Osyth to park entrance.

CLEETHORPES Lincolnshire	11F4

Thorpe Park Holiday Centre

Humberton, Cleethorpes DN36 4HG
📞 01472-813395
Open March-October

Clitheroe

55

A family holiday park close to excellent beaches with a new indoor heated pool, kids clubs, coarse fishing lake, kids pets corner - a wide range of leisure facilities, hot food, bars and cabarets. A 'British Holidays Park'.
Size 279 acres, 115 touring pitches, 115 with electric hookup, 80 static caravans, 78 ⌂, 22 WCs, 19 CWPs
cc MasterCard Visa
⚡ ♿ 🔲 📞 🔲 ❄ 🔲 GR ⛰ Calor 🐕
➡ Follow A180 from M180, following signs for Grimsby and Cleethorpes. In Cleethorpes town centre, with seafront on left, follow signs for 'Fitties'. At the mini roundabout you will see Thorpe Park's entrance straight ahead.

CLIPPESBY Norfolk　　　　　　　　　9F3

Clippesby Holidays
Clippesby, Great Yarmouth NR29 3BL
📞 01493-367800　Fax 01493-3667809
Open May-September & Easter week ⚡ ♿ 🚐

At Clippesby you can choose between sunny lawns or leafy glades, and you will never be far from one of our 3 shower blocks.
Size 34 acres, 100 touring pitches, 70 with electric hookup, 70 level pitches, 10 ⌂, 20 WCs, 3 CWPs
£ car/tent £8.50-£15, car/caravan £8.50-£15, motorhome £8.50-£15, motorbike/tent £8.50-£13, children £0.50-£0.75
Rental Chalet. £159-£499
cc MasterCard Visa
⚡ ✖ ♿ 🔲 📞 🔲 ❄ 🔲 GR 🔲 ⛳ ⛰ Calor Gaz ⚓
Last arrival time: 17:30
➡ Take A47 to Acle, then A1064 for 3 miles and turn left at Clippesby. After ½ mile, turn left again and then first right after 200 yards.
See advert on this page

CLIPPESBY HOLIDAYS

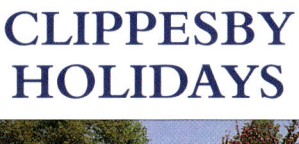

Family-run Touring Park Camping and Holiday Cottages in the beautiful wooded grounds of Clippesby Hall, with lots of family things to do.

"DAVID BELLAMY CONSERVATION AWARD"

"BEST PARK IN ENGLAND"
1996 CALOR AWARD

"BEST FAMILY PARK"
2 years running, Practical Caravan

Clippesby, Nr Gt. Yarmouth NR29 3BJ
Tel: 01493 369367 Fax: 01493 368181

ENGLAND

CLITHEROE Lancashire　　　　　　　　10C3

Camping & Caravanning Club Site
Edisford Bridge, Edisford Road, Clitheroe BB7 3LA
📞 01200-425294
Open March-November ⚡ ♿ 🚐
Size 6 acres, 80 touring pitches, 32 with electric hookup, 6 ⌂, 14 WCs, 1 CWP
£ car/tent £9.60-£12.10, car/caravan £9.60-£12.10, motorhome £9.60-£12.10, motorbike/tent £9.60-£12.10, children £1.50
cc MasterCard Visa
⚡ ⚡¼ ✖¼ ♿ ♿¼ 🔲 📞 🔲 ▶ 🔲 GR 🔲 ⛰ Gaz ♿ 🐕 WS
Last arrival time: 23:00
➡ From A59 take A671 into Clitheroe. Look for the signpost indicating left turn to Longridge/Sports Centre. Turn into Greenacre Road approximately 25 metres beyond pelican crossing. Continue forward until T junction at Edisford Road, turn left and continue past church on right. Look for Sports Centre on right and car park oppposite. The site access road is 50 metres past car park, entrance is on left.

Hints & Tips

In winter take your seat cushions home. Not only will they keep dry but a caravan without cushions is a less attractive prospect to thieves.

56

Cockermouth

COCKERMOUTH Cumbria 10A1

Inglenook Caravan Park
Lamplugh CA14 4SH
☎ 01946-861240
Open all year
Size 3.5 acres, 36 touring pitches, 20 with electric hookup, 32 level pitches, 24 static caravans, 4 🚿, 8 WCs, 1 CWP
£ car/tent £6.50-£8.50, car/caravan £7.50-£8.50, motorhome £7.50-£8.50, motorbike/tent £6.25-£7.25, children £1.25
Rental £150-£260
Calor Gaz WS
Last arrival time: 20:00
➜ Leave A5086 at sign for Lamplugh Green. Site ½ mile on right-hand corner.

Wyndham Hall Caravan Park
Old Keswick Road, Cockermouth CA13 9SF
☎ 01900-822571
Open 1 March-15 November

A family site. Short walk into the market town (Cockermouth), and quarter of an hour drive to Keswick.
Size 12.5 acres, 32 touring pitches, 24 with electric hookup, 32 level pitches, 105 static caravans, 9 🚿, 21 WCs, 2 CWPs
£ car/tent £8, car/caravan £8, motorhome £8, motorbike/tent £8, children £0.75
Rental Chalet.
Calor Gaz WS
➜ Off A66 on Old Keswick Road.

COLEFORD Gloucestershire 7E4

Forestry Commission Bracelands C & C
Bracelands Drive, Christchurch, Coleford GL16 7NN
☎ 01594-833376
Open start March-end October
Size 30 acres, 520 touring pitches, 72 with electric hookup, 200 level pitches, 30 🚿, 48 WCs, 3 CWPs
£ car/tent £5.40-£9.40, car/caravan £5.40-£9.40, motorhome £5.40-£9.40, motorbike/tent £5.40-£9.40, children £1.30-£2.40
℄ MasterCard Visa
Calor Gaz WS
Last arrival time: 22:00

➜ 1 mile N of Coleford on A4136, at crossroads at Pike House Inn, go N for ½ mile, reception signposted on left.

Forestry Commission Christchurch C & C
Bracelands Drive, Christchurch, Coleford GL16 7NN
☎ 01594-833376
Open start March-end December
Size 14 acres, 280 touring pitches, 87 with electric hookup, 50 level pitches, 18 🚿, 32 WCs, 3 CWPs
£ car/tent £5.40-£9.40, car/caravan £5.40-£9.40, motorhome £5.40-£9.40, motorbike/tent £5.40-£9.40, children £1.30-£2.40
℄ MasterCard Visa
WS
Last arrival time: 22:00
➜ 1 mile N of Coleford on A4136, at crossroads at Pike House Inn, go N for ½ mile, reception signposted on left.

Forestry Commission Woodland C & C
Bracelands Drive, Christchurch, Coleford GL16 7NN
☎ 01594-833376
Open start March-end October
Size 22 acres, 90 touring pitches, 28 with electric hookup, 60 level pitches, 1 CWP
£ car/tent £5.40-£9.40, car/caravan £5.40-£9.40, motorhome £5.40-£9.40, motorbike/tent £5.40-£9.40, children £1.30-£2.40
℄ MasterCard Visa
Calor Gaz
Last arrival time: 22:00
➜ 1 mile N of Coleford on A4136, at crossroads at Pike House Inn, go N for ½ mile, reception signposted on left.

COMBE MARTIN Devon 2C2

Napps Camp Site
Old Coast Road, Berrynarbor, Ilfracombe EX34 9SW
☎ 01271-882557 Fax 01271-882557
Open 1 April-31 October

A high quality family site in a peaceful setting right on the beautiful North Devon coast, with woodland and coastal walks to the beach. Breathtaking views and excellent facilities and amenities.
Size 15 acres, 200 touring pitches, 90 with electric hookup, 200 level pitches, 10 🚿, 20 WCs, 1 CWP
£ car/tent £5-£9, car/caravan £5-£9, motorhome £5-£9, motorbike/tent £5-£9

Combe Martin

Rental 🔊

MasterCard Visa

[icons] Calor Gaz WS

➜ Take A399 1½ miles W of Combe Martin. Site is signposted on right, 300 yards along old coast road.
See advert on this page

Stowford Farm Meadows

Combe Martin, Ilfracombe EX34 0PW
☎ 01271-882476 Fax 01271-883053
Open Easter-31 October
Size 500 acres, 570 touring pitches, 550 with electric hookup, 250 level pitches, 60, 110 WCs, 10 CWPs
£ car/tent £4.40-£9.30, car/caravan £4.40-£9.30, motorhome £4.40-£9.30, motorbike/tent £4.40-£9.30, children £2

MasterCard Visa

[icons] Calor Gaz WS

Last arrival time: 20:00

➜ M5 junction 27, follow North Devon Link to Barnstaple, then A39 (for Lynton) through Barnstaple town centre. One mile from Barnstaple turn left onto B3230. Turn right at garage onto A3123. Site is 1½ miles on right.
See advert on this page

Napps CARAVAN SITE

Friendly and popular, well kept family site in probably the most beautiful coastal setting you will see, offering terrific value for money and superb modern facilities.

"Impressive not only for its setting but also for its state of cleanliness" Buccaneer Owners Club
"One of North Devon's top six sites" Practical Caravan Mag.
"What a view" Camping & Trailer Magazine
"Simply the best" Owners, Staff and Regulars

For colour brochure and full site details please phone or write:

OLD COAST ROAD, BERRY NARBOR, ILFRACOMBE, NORTH DEVON EX34 9SW
Tel/Fax: 01271 882557

WELCOME TO STOWFORD Farm Meadows

Where Fun meets the countryside

AA PREMIER PARK
TOP TOURING PARKS
CARAVAN LIFE 1997 STOWFORD FARM MEADOWS
CAMPING & CARAVANNING BRITAIN'S BEST PARKS 1998
BRITISH GRADED HOLIDAY PARKS ✓✓✓✓
PRACTICAL CARAVAN REGIONAL CHOICE

Touring Caravan & Camping Park

Berry Down, Combe Martin, North Devon EX34 0PW
Telephone 01271 882476 Fax 01271 883053

- 500 acres of Glorious Devon Countryside
- Superb choice of 5 local beaches
- Renowned as a high quality park offering outstanding value

Great Facilities

Shop • Take - Away & Carvery • Bars • Swimming Pool •
Pitch & Putt • Snooker • Games Room • Crazy Golf •
• Horse Riding • Kiddies Kars • Mini - Zoo Petorama •
Sports Field • Nature Walks in mature Woodland •

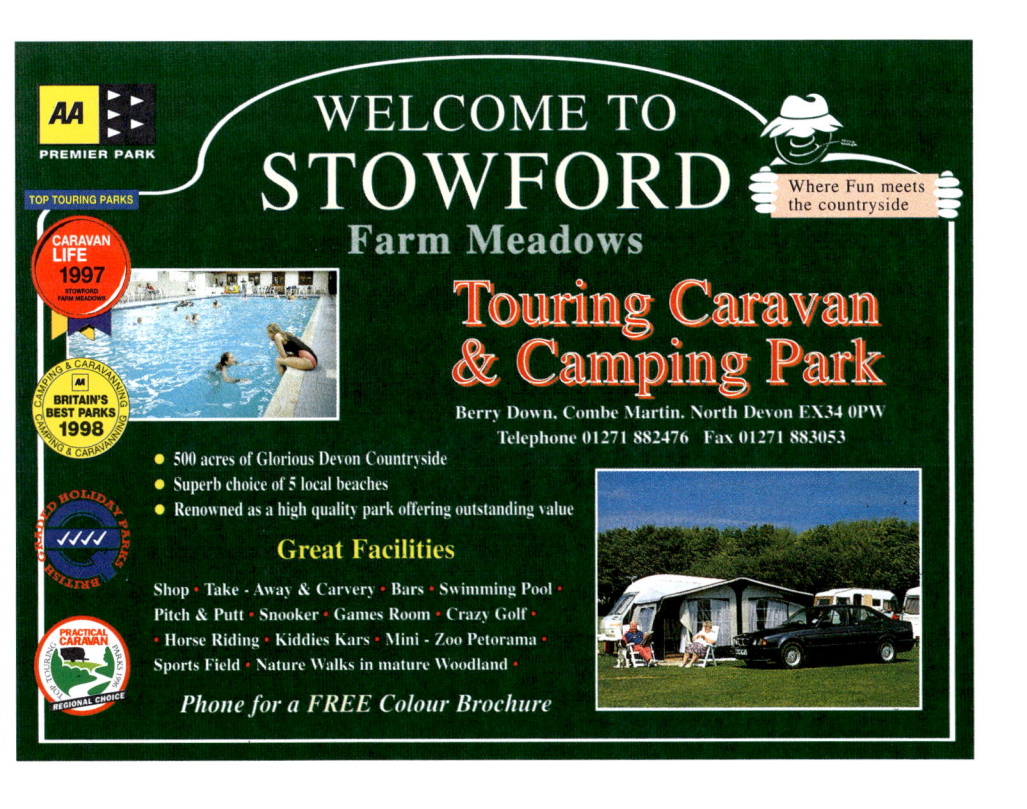

Phone for a FREE Colour Brochure

58

Coverack

COVERACK Cornwall　　　　　　　　　2A4

Little Trevothan Caravan Park
Coverack, Helston TR12 6SD
☎ 01326-280260
Open Easter-October ▲ ⚲ ⛺

Near the picturesque fishing village of Coverack, this spacious level site provides the perfect location for a peaceful holiday in this unspoilt corner of England.
Size 10.5 acres, 48 touring pitches, 18 with electric hookup, 48 level pitches, 26 static caravans, 8 ☗, 14 WCs, 1 CWP
£ car/tent £5-£6.50, car/caravan £5-£6.50, motorhome £5-£6.50, motorbike/tent £4.50-£5, children £1
Rental ⚲ £95-£295
℃ MasterCard Visa
⛲ ☕ 🅱 🔌 🅿 GR ⚠ Calor Gaz ✴ WS
Last arrival time: 22:00
➜ From A30 take A39 through Truro, then A394 to Helston. Join A3083 to The Lizard and proceed past Culdrose air base. Turn left at roundabout onto B3293 signposted to Coverack. Follow road past Goonhilly Downs satellite dishes and after 2 miles turn right just before garage following sign to 'Little Trevothan Caravan Park and Fox Club'. Take third turning on left and site is 300 yards on right.

CRANTOCK Cornwall　　　　　　　　　2A4

Quarryfield
Crantock
☎ 01637-872792
Open March 31st-October ▲ ⚲ ⛺
Size 15 acres, 20 touring pitches, 20 with electric hookup, 125 level pitches, 40 static caravans, 18 ☗, 20 WCs, 2 CWPs
£ car/caravan £4.30-£5.50, motorhome £4.30-£5.50, children £0.50-£1.25
Rental ⚲ Chalet. Apply for free brochure
⛲ ☕ 🅱 🔌 🚿 🅿 GR ⚠ 🍴 Calor ✴
Last arrival time: 21:30
➜ Off A3075 Redruth road to Crantock to bottom of village. There is a red telephone kiosk, a road up on right of kiosk. The site is at top.

CREDITON Devon　　　　　　　　　3D3

Yeatheridge Farm Caravan Park
East Worlington, Crediton EX17 4TN
☎ 01884-860330　Fax 01884-860330
Open Easter-30 September ▲ ⚲ ⛺

A genuine working family farm, plenty of animals and panoramic views from a spacious park. Coarse fishing, lakes and horse riding. Two indoor heated swimming pools and 20 acres of woodland.
Size 9 acres, 85 touring pitches, 75 with electric hookup, 2 static caravans, 12 ☗, 17 WCs, 1 CWP
£ car/tent £6.50-£8.20, car/caravan £6.50-£8.20, motorhome £6.50-£8.20, motorbike/tent £6.50-£8.20, children £1.50
℃ MasterCard Visa
⛲ ☕¼ 🅱 🔌 🚿 🅿 🎣 🍴 GR 🎱 TV ⚠ 🍴 Calor Gaz ✴ WS
Last arrival time: 22:00
➜ Leave M5 at junction 27 onto B3137 out of Finerton. Take B3042 before Witheridge. The site is 3½ miles on the left.

CROMER Norfolk　　　　　　　　　9F2

Camping & Caravanning Club Site
Holgate Lane, West Runton, Cromer NR27 9NW
☎ 01263-837544
Open March-November ▲ ⚲ ⛺
Size 11.5 acres, 225 touring pitches, 111 with electric hookup, 10 ☗, 30 WCs, 1 CWP
£ car/tent £13.60-£14.60, car/caravan £13.60-£14.60, motorhome £13.60-£14.60, motorbike/tent £13.60-£14.60, children £1.60
℃ MasterCard Visa
⛲ ☕¼ ✖¼ ☕¼ 🅱 🔌 🅿 🚿 🎣 GR 🎱 TV ⚠ Gaz ♿ ✴ WS
Last arrival time: 23:00
➜ On A148 from King's Lynn, approaching West Runton turn left at Roman Camp Inn, site entry track ½ mile long is right at crest of hill, opposite National Trust sign.

Croyde Bay

Manor Farm Caravan & Camp Site
East Runton, Cromer NR27 9PR
☎ 01263-512858 Fax 01263-512858
Open Easter-October ▲ 🚐 🚍

Peaceful family run site with glorious sea and woodland views. Well equiped toilet facilites. Separate field for dog owners. Ideal for families. Tents welcome. Beach one mile.
Size 20 acres, 200 touring pitches, 128 with electric hookup, 200 level pitches, 20 ☗, 55 WCs, 5 CWPs
£ car/tent £6.60-£8.20, children £0.75
♨¼ ✕¼ ●¼ ▣ ◨ ▭ ⚠ Calor Gaz ⊁
Last arrival time: 22:00
➜ 1½ miles W of Cromer turn off A148 at signpost Manor Farm.

Seacroft Camping & Caravan Park
Runton Road, Cromer NR27 9JN
☎ 01263-511722 Fax 01263-511512
Open 20 March-30 October ▲ 🚐 🚍

The pitches are individually marked with shrubs forming boundaries. Within easy walking distance from Cromer.
Size 7 acres, 120 touring pitches, 110 with electric hookup, 120 level pitches, 15 ☗, 30 WCs, 1 CWP
£ car/tent £7-£11.50, car/caravan £7-£11.50, motorhome £7-£11.50, motorbike/tent £7-£11.50, children £0.50-£1.50
℅ MasterCard Visa
♨ ✕ ● ▣ ◨ ⌂ ⚐ ℝ ℹ ▭ ⚠ ⚙ Calor Gaz ♿ ⊁
Last arrival time: 23:00
➜ 1 mile W of Cromer on A149 coast road.

CROWBOROUGH East Sussex 5D3

Camping & Caravanning Club Site
Goldsmith Recreation Ground, Crowborough TN6 2TN
☎ 01892-664827
Open February-December ▲ 🚐 🚍
Size 13 acres, 88 touring pitches, 46 with electric hookup, 8 ☗, 11 WCs, 2 CWPs
£ car/tent £11.50-£14.60, car/caravan £11.50-£14.60, motorhome £11.50-£14.60, motorbike/tent £11.50-£14.60, children £1.60
℅ MasterCard Visa
♨ ♨¼ ✕¼ ● ●¼ ▣ ◨ ⚐ ℝ ℹ ℝ ℹ ▭ ⚠ Calor ♿ ⊁ WS
Last arrival time: 23:00
➜ From N turn right, from S turn left off A26 into entrance to "Goldsmiths Ground" signposted leisure centre, A top of road turn right onto site.

CROYDE BAY Devon 2C2

Bay View Farm
Braunton, Croyde Bay EX33 1PN
☎ 01271-890501
Open March-October ▲ 🚐 🚍
Size 10 acres, 70 touring pitches, 30 with electric hookup, 70 level pitches, 3 static caravans, 16 ☗, 18 WCs,
Rental 🚐
♨ ● ▣ ◨ ⚠ Calor Gaz ♿ ⊁
Last arrival time: 22:00
➜ From Braunton take B3231. Site on right.

Deer Park
Holiday Estate

Set admidst outstanding natural coastal beauty our level site with panoramic views includes heated swimming pool, modern toilet block, childrens playground, pub and restaurant, shop, laundry, telephone and electric hook ups. Close to beaches. Dogs allowed.

**DARTMOUTH ROAD,
STOKE FLEMING, S. DEVON
Tel: 01803 770253
Fax: 01803 770320**

ENGLAND

59

Dartmouth

DARTMOUTH Devon   3D4

Deer Park Holiday Estate
Stoke Fleming, Dartmouth TQ6 0RF
☎ 01803-770253   Fax 01803-770320
Open March-November

Family site with excellent facilities: adventure playground, pub with family room, games room, swimming pool and sunbathing area. All facilities are free on site. Four caravans and four flats for hire.
Size 12 acres, 160 touring pitches, 100 with electric hookup, 160 level pitches, 12, 18 WCs, 1 CWP
£ car/tent £7.25-£9.25, car/caravan £7.95-£9.95, motorhome £7.95-£9.95, motorbike/tent £7.25-£9.25, children £0.80
Rental Flat
CC MasterCard Visa
Calor Gaz
Last arrival time: 22:00
→ Situated 2 miles S of Dartmouth on A379. Observe bus stop at site entrance.
See advert on previous page

Woodland Leisure Park
Blackawton, Dartmouth TQ9 7DQ
☎ 01803-712598   Fax 01803-712680
Open 15 March-15 November

1998 Practical Caravan Award 'Top Family Park' for superb facilities combined with fantastic leisure park. Sixty glorious acres with three water-coasters, fourteen action zones and animals.
Size 65 acres, 80 touring pitches, 65 with electric hookup, 80 level pitches, 12, 11 WCs, 1 CWP

CC MasterCard Visa
Calor Gaz WS
→ Direct access from main Dartmouth A3122 (formerly B3207) road. 4 miles W of Dartmouth.

DAWLISH Devon   3D3

Cofton Country Holiday Park
Starcross, Dawlish EX6 8RP
☎ 01626-890111   Fax 01626-891572
Open Easter-31 October
Size 16 acres, 450 touring pitches, 300 with electric hookup, 62 static caravans, 46, 97 WCs, 2 CWPs
£ car/tent £6-£10.50, car/caravan £6-£10.50, motorhome £6-£10.50, motorbike/tent £6-£10.50, children £1-£2
Rental £90-£420, cottages £190-£525.
CC MasterCard Visa
Calor Gaz WS
Last arrival time: 22:00
→ From M5 junction 30 take A379 to Dawlish. Park is on left, ½ mile after small harbour at Cockwood Village.
See advert on opposite page

Lady's Mile Touring & Camping Park
Exeter Road, Dawlish EX7 0LX
☎ 01626-863411   Fax 01626-888689
Open mid March-end October
Size 20 acres, 300 touring pitches, 300 with electric hookup, 300 level pitches, 40, 80 WCs, 3 CWPs
£ car/tent £8-£11.50, car/caravan £8-£11.50, motorhome £8-£11.50, motorbike/tent £11.50, children £1.50-£2.30
Rental Chalet.
CC MasterCard Visa
Calor Gaz WS
Last arrival time: 22:00
→ 1 mile N of Dawlish on A379.
See advert on next page

Leadstone Camping
Warren Road, Dawlish EX7 0NG
☎ 01626-872239   Fax 01626-873833
Open 18 June-4 September

Seven acres of rolling grassland in a natural secluded bowl within ½ mile of Dawlish Warren Beach and nature reserve. Ideally situated for →

Dawlish

TOURING & CAMPING HOLIDAYS IN SOUTH DEVON

EVERY YEAR PRACTICAL CARAVAN TOP 100 FAMILY PARKS

Cofton Country
HOLIDAY PARK

This is the heart of Cofton Country. A family-owned park in beautiful landscaped grounds. Dotted with bright flowerbeds, surrounded with green meadows and rolling woodland. Yet in easy reach of the beaches and attractions of South Devon.

TOURING & CAMPING PITCHES. 2/7 BERTH HOLIDAY HOMES. DELIGHTFUL COTTAGES

Heated Swimming Pool • Pub & Family Lounges • Woodland Trails & Play Areas
Licensed Mini-Market • Games Room • Takeaway • Coarse Fishing Lakes
Electric Hook-ups • Launderettes • Free Hot Water & Showers

Free colour brochure: Mrs U Jeffery, Cofton Country Holiday Park, Starcross, Nr. Dawlish, S. Devon EX6 8RP.

DEVON Swan HOLIDAYS
The firm family favourite

APPROVED

EXCELLENT

Cofton Country – 20 mins from J30 M5 Exeter   **01626 890111**

Dawlish

← Leadstone Camping

exploring Devon.
Size 8 acres, 15 touring pitches, 45 with electric hookup, 100 level pitches, 8 🚿, 12 WCs, 1 CWP
£ car/tent £7.60-£8.90, car/caravan £9.85-£11.70, motorhome £7.60-£8.90, motorbike/tent £7.60-£8.90, children £1.20-£1.40
🛒 ✕¼ 🍴¼ 🛁 🛒 Calor Gaz 🐕

→ From M5 junction 30 take A379 to Dawlish. As you approach Dawlish, turn left on the brow of hill signposted Dawlish Warren. Site is ½ mile on right.

Peppermint Park
Warren Road, Dawlish Warren EX7 0PQ
📞 01626-863436
Open Easter-October ⛺ 🚐 🚌

Grassland park with some level terraces, all sheltered by mature trees. Nearest touring park to Dawlish Warren beach (600 yards). Free family entertainment nightly in licensed club.

Size 26 acres, 300 touring pitches, 190 with electric hookup, 250 level pitches, 35 static caravans, 39 🚿, 37 WCs, 2 CWPs
£ car/tent £5-£11, car/caravan £5-£11, motorhome £5-£11, motorbike/tent £5, children £1-£1.75
Rental 🏠 holiday homes £55-£435
CC MasterCard Visa
🛒 ✕ 🍴 🛁 🛒 🛒 🛁 🔲 🔲 🔲 🔲 🔲 Calor Gaz ♿ 🐕

→ From M5 (jn 30) take A379 to Dawlish. Turn left to Dawlish Warren, 7 miles on, just before entering Dawlish. Park is on left at bottom of hill.

DEAL Kent   5F3

Sutton Vale Caravan Club
Sutton-by-Dover, Deal CT15 5DH
📞 01304-374155   **Fax** 01304-381132
Open March-January ⛺ 🚐 🚌

Luxury full facility homes in a beautiful rural park, surrounded by countryside and within easy reach of ferry to France. Heated swimming pool, clubhouse,

---

*L*ADY'S MILE
Miles more family fun!
Camping & Caravanning at its best!

- **TWO** Swimming Pools ● **TWO** Waterslides
- "The Mile" family bar ● **TWO** Launderettes
- Licensed Shop ● Electric Hook-ups
- Adventure Fort & Play Area
- Families & Rallies welcome
- Takeaway ● Multi Sports
- 9-hole Golf Course
- Games room/Pool room
- Free hot water & showers
- Luxury Self-Catering Flats
- **PLUS NEW FOR 1999 AJ'S FAMILY DISCO**

AA AWARDED DE-LUXE SITE 1998

Send for our FREE colour brochure: MRS R. A. JEFFERY LADY'S MILE TOURING & CAMPING PARK, FREEPOST DAWLISH SOUTH DEVON EX7 9YZ

TEL: (01626) 863411   FAX: (01626) 888689

Dorchester

restaurant and sports field.
Size 6 acres, 14 touring pitches, 14 with electric hookup, 100 level pitches, 100 static caravans, 8 🚿, 8 WCs, 1 CWP
£ car/caravan £9.50-£13.50, motorhome £9.50-£13.50
Rental Chalet. £105-£335
✻ MasterCard Visa
🛁¼ ✗ 🍴 🛒 📞 🎯 🅿 GR ⚡ ♨ Calor Gaz ♿ 🐕 WS
Last arrival time: 23:00
➡ From A2, 5 miles from Dover, exit Whitfield roundabout old A256, then after 20 yards turn right opposite McDonalds, signposted Cornilo Partners. Site is 4 miles on left.

DEVIZES Wiltshire 4A3

Bell Caravan & Camp Site

Andover Road, Lydeway, Devizes SN10 3PS
📞 01380-840230 Fax 01380-840137
Open Easter-1 October 🏕 🚐 🚚
Size 3 acres, 30 touring pitches, 24 with electric hookup, 30 level pitches, 5 🚿, 6 WCs, 1 CWP
£ car/tent £7.50-£9, car/caravan £7.50-£9, motorhome £7.50-£9, motorbike/tent £7.50-£9, children £1.50-£2
Rental 🚐
✻ MasterCard Visa
🛁 🍴 🛒 📞 🎯 ⛳ GR 🎮 📺 ⚡ ♨ Calor Gaz 🐕 WS
➡ 3 miles SE of Devizes on A342.

Lower Foxhangers Farm

Rowde, Devizes
📞 01380-828254 Fax 01380-828254
Open Easter-October 🏕 🚐 🚚

Quietly located working farm alongside canal flight of 29 locks. Fishing, boating, walking and cycling. Self catering in 4 holiday homes.
Size 2 acres, 10 touring pitches, 8 with electric hookup, 10 level pitches, 4 static caravans, 1 🚿, 2 WCs, 1 CWP
£ car/tent £6, car/caravan £6, motorhome £6, motorbike/tent £6
Rental Self catering holiday homes £160-220 per week.
📞 🛒 Calor Gaz 🐕
➡ 2 miles W of Devizes on A361. ½ mile E of junction of A361/A365.

DISS Norfolk 9E3

Willows Camping & Caravan Park

Diss Road, Scole IP21 4DH
📞 01379-740271
Open May-September 🏕 🚐 🚚
Size 4 acres, 32 touring pitches, 18 with electric hookup, 32 level pitches, 2 🚿, 7 WCs, 2 CWPs
£ car/tent £6.50, car/caravan £6.50, motorhome £6.50, motorbike/tent £6.50, children £0.25
🛁¼ ✗¼ 🍴¼ 🛒 📞 🎯 ⚡ Calor Gaz 🐕
Last arrival time: 23:00
➡ 200 yards off the A140 roundabout at Scole, in the direction of Diss on A1066.

DORCHESTER Dorset 3E3

Giant's Head Caravan & Camping Park

Old Sherborne Road, Dorchester DT2 7TR
📞 01300-341242
Open 17 April-31 October 🏕 🚐 🚚
Size 3.5 acres, 50 touring pitches, 20 with electric hookup, 50 level pitches, 2 🚿, 8 WCs, 1 CWP
£ car/tent £5.50-£7, car/caravan £5.50-£7, motorhome £5.50-£7, motorbike/tent £5.50-£7, children £1
Rental Chalet.
🛒 📞 🎯 Calor Gaz 🐕 WS
➡ Into Dorchester, avoiding bypass, at Top o' Town roundabout take Sherborne road. After 500 yards take right fork at Loders (BP) Garage and follow signs.

Home Farm Camping & Caravan Site

Puncknowle, Dorchester DT2 9BW
📞 01308-897258
Open April-October 🏕 🚐 🚚

Small secluded site in beautiful area. Good food at village inn. Sea fishing nearby.
Size 5 acres, 27 touring pitches, 22 level pitches, 14 static caravans, 4 🚿, 8 WCs, 1 CWP
£ car/tent £4-£5, car/caravan £5-£6, motorhome £4-£5, motorbike/tent £4-£5
Rental 🚐
🛁¼ 🛒 📞 🎯 ⚡ Calor Gaz 🐕
Last arrival time: 21:00
➡ From Dorchester take A35 towards Bridport. Drive through Winterbourne Abbas and turn left just before the dual carriageway to Litton Cheney. Follow signs to Puncknowle.

ENGLAND

Dunwich

DUNWICH Suffolk   9F4

Cliff House
Minsmere Road, Dunwich IP17 3DQ
☎ 01728-648282 Fax 01728-648282
Open 1 April-October ▲ ⚑ ⚐
Size 30 acres, 87 touring pitches, 83 with electric hookup, 7 level pitches, 90 static caravans, 8 🚿, 12 WCs, 3 CWPs
£ car/tent £8-£12, car/caravan £8-£12, motorhome £8-£12, motorbike/tent £8-£12
Rental ⚑ Chalet. £120-£300
℅ MasterCard Visa
🛁 ✕ 🍽 🔲 🔆 🔲 🍴 GR 🔍 ⚒ ⚐ Calor Gaz 🐕 WS
Last arrival time: 21:00
➔ From A12, 5 miles N of Saxmundham, follow signs to Dunwich Heath. Site is on left.

EAST HORSLEY Surrey   4C3

Camping & Caravanning Club Site
Ockham Road North, East Horsley KT24 6PE
☎ 01483-283273
Open March-November ▲ ⚑ ⚐
Size 12 acres, 135 touring pitches, 61 with electric hookup, 10 🚿, 17 WCs, 1 CWP
£ car/tent £11.50-£14.60, car/caravan £11.50-£14.60, motorhome £11.50-£14.60, motorbike/tent £11.50-£14.60, children £1.60
℅ MasterCard Visa
🛁 🛁¼ ✕¼ 🍽 🍽¼ 🔲 🔆 🔲 P 🔲 GR 🔍 TV ⚒ Calor & 🐕 WS
Last arrival time: 23:00
➔ From junction 10 off M25 go S and take first major turning off, signposted Ockham. Then take left turn and site is 2½ miles on right. From S take A3 past Guildford and turn off towards Ripley (B2215). Continue over roundabout and through Ripley village. At roundabout turn right and take B2039 to Horsley (2½ miles). The site is on right.

ELY Cambridgeshire   9D3

Two Acres Caravan & Camping
Ely Road, Little Thetford, Ely CB6 3HH
☎ 01353-648870
▲ ⚑ ⚐

Family run grassy park, set on level ground 2 miles south of the historic cathedral town of Ely, 12 miles north of Cambridge. Also bordering the Fens.
Size 2 acres, 36 touring pitches, 20 with electric hookup, 36 level pitches, 2 🚿, 5 WCs, 1 CWP
£ car/tent £5.50-£6.50, car/caravan £6.50-£7.50, motorhome £6.50-£7.50, motorbike/tent £4.50-£5.50, children £0.50
🔆 🔲 & 🐕 WS
Last arrival time: 00:00
➔ On the A10 Cambridge to Ely road, watch for Little Thetford sign, site at junction.

ESKDALE GREEN Cumbria   10A2

Fisherground Farm
Eskdale Green CA19 1TF
☎ 01946-723319
Open mid March-mid November ▲ ⚐

Peaceful family site in a beautiful location. Adventure playground, children's raft pool, 7 mile miniature railway, (station on site). Brand new toilet block. Camp fires allowed. Brochure on request.
Size 3 acres, 30 touring pitches, 4 with electric hookup, 30 level pitches, 8 🚿, 10 WCs, 1 CWP
£ car/tent £7-£8, motorhome £7-£8, motorbike/tent £7-£8, children £2
Rental Chalet.
✕¼ 🍽 🔆 🔲 ⚒ & 🐕
➔ At King George IV inn, turn up valley towards Hard Knott pass. Fisherground is 400 yards on left.

EVESHAM Worcestershire   7F4

Ranch Caravan Park
Honeybourne, Evesham WR11 5QG
☎ 01386-830744 Fax 01386-833503
Open March-November ⚑ ⚐
Size 48 acres, 120 touring pitches, 95 with electric hookup, 120 level pitches, 180 static caravans, 10 🚿, 20 WCs, 2 CWPs
£ car/caravan £6-£16, motorhome £6-£16, children £1.25
Rental ⚑ £180-£350
🛁 ✕ 🍽 🔲 🔆 🔲 ⚓ ⚒ ⚐ Calor Gaz 🐕 WS
Last arrival time: 22:00
➔ From Evesham travel E on A44, turn left onto B4035 to Bretforton, then left to Honeybourne, turn left, site on left ¼ mile.

Exmouth

EXETER Devon   3D3

Haldon Lodge Farm Caravan & Camping Park
Kennford, Near Exeter EX6 7YG
01392-832312
Open all year
Size 7.5 acres, 40 touring pitches, 80 with electric hookup, 60 level pitches, 4 static caravans, 8 🚿, 14 WCs, 2 CWPs
£ car/tent £5-£7.50, car/caravan £5-£7.50, motorhome £5-£8, motorbike/tent £5-£7.50
Rental Chalet. £70-£195
Calor Gaz WS
Last arrival time: 22:00
→ Off A38 at Kennford services, follow signs to Haldon Lodge turning left into village. Proceed passing post office and over motor bridge turning left. 1¼ miles to site.

Springfield Holiday Park
Tedburn Road, Tedburn St Mary, Exeter EX6 6EW
01647-24242   **Fax** 01647-24131
Open 15 March-15 November

A quiet family owned park set in nine acres of beautiful countryside on the fringe of Dartmoor National Park. Eight miles west of Exeter and approximately 30 minutes drive to the beaches.
Size 9 acres, 88 touring pitches, 50 with electric hookup, 88 level pitches, 13 static caravans, 8 🚿, 16 WCs, 2 CWPs
£ car/tent £6-£7.50, car/caravan £5.50-£8.50, motorhome £5.50-£9.50, motorbike/tent £6-£7, children £1.50
Rental £100-£260
¼ Calor Gaz WS
Last arrival time: 21:30
→ From M5 (jn 31) take A30 to Okehampton. Leave A30 at second exit, signposted Tedburn St Mary. Turn left at roundabout and drive through village to site on right, 1¾ miles from village.

EXFORD Somerset   3D2

Westermill Farm
Exford, Minehead TA24 7NJ
01643-831238   **Fax** 01643-831660
Open all year

Beautiful secluded site for tents by shallow river. Heart of Exmoor National Park. Four waymarked walks over 500 acre working farm. Natural and uncommercialised. Quality Scandinavian log cottages for hire. Free hot showers. Gold David Bellamy award for conservation.
Size 6 acres, 60 touring pitches, 60 level pitches, 6 🚿, 14 WCs, 1 CWP
£ car/tent £8, motorhome £8, motorbike/tent £8, children £1
Rental Cottages £140-£399
Calor Gaz
→ Leave Exford on Porlock road, after ¼ mile fork left. Continue 2 miles past another campsite until 'Westermill' seen on tree, then fork left.

EXMOUTH Devon   3D3

St John's Camping & Caravan Park
St. Johns Road, Withycombe, Exmouth EX8 5EG
01395-263170   **Fax** 01395-568247

Set in six acres of pasture, the site adjoins lovely walking country, moorlands, woods and the sea. Excellent bathing from two miles of sandy beach at Exmouth. Many activities and historical places to visit. Brochure available.
Size 50 touring pitches, 12 with electric hookup, 50 level pitches, 2 🚿, 10 WCs, 1 CWP
£ car/tent £3.50-£8, car/caravan £3.50-£8, motorhome £3.50-£8, motorbike/tent £3.50-£8
Calor

Webbers Farm Caravan Park
Castle Lane, Woodbury, Exeter EX5 1EA
☎ 01395-232276 Fax 01395-233389
Open Easter-end September
Size 7.5 acres, 100 touring pitches, 100 with electric hookup, 20 level pitches, 14, 17 WCs, 6 CWPs
£ car/tent £7-£9.50, car/caravan £7-£9.50, motorhome £7-£9.50, children £1.75
CC MasterCard Visa
Calor Gaz WS
Last arrival time: 22:00

➜ From M5 junction 30 take A376 to Exmouth. At second roundabout take B3179 to Woodbury and follow signs from village centre.

EYE Suffolk   9E3

Honeypot Camp & Caravan Park
Wortham, Eye IP22 1PW
☎ 01379-783312 Fax 01379-783293
Open April-September

A quiet, well organised landscaped country site, part of which surrounds two lakes, on well grassed, level, free draining land, facing due south. Under the personal supervision of the owners for over 20 years.
Size 6.5 acres, 35 touring pitches, 22 with electric hookup, 35 level pitches, 4, 4 WCs, 1 CWP
£ car/tent £6.50-£7.50, car/caravan £7.50, motorhome £7.50, motorbike/tent £6.50, children £1
Calor Gaz WS
Last arrival time: 23:00

➜ South side of A143, 4 miles W of Diss, 17 miles E of Bury St Edmunds. Main 'A' road entrance opposite the tea pot sign.

FALMOUTH Cornwall   2A4

Calamankey Farm
Longdowns, Penryn TR10 9DL
☎ 01209-860314
Open April-end October
Size 4 static caravans, 3, 14 WCs, 1 CWP
£ car/tent £5, motorhome £5, motorbike/tent £5, children £1.25

Rental £80-£150
Last arrival time: 22:00

➜ From Truro, take A39 to Treluswell roundabout and go straight across onto A394 towards Helston. Calamankey Farm is in Longdowns village, opposite Murco filling station.

Menallack Farm Caravan & Camping Site
Treverva, Penryn, Falmouth TR10 9BP
☎ 01326-340333 Fax 01326-340333
Open April-October
Size 1.5 acres, 30 touring pitches, 4 with electric hookup, 30 level pitches, 2, 6 WCs, 1 CWP
£ car/tent £5-£5.50, car/caravan £5-£5.50, motorhome £5-£5.50, motorbike/tent £5-£5.50, children £0.70-£0.80
Calor Gaz
Last arrival time: 21:00

➜ From Truro go towards Falmouth for 10 miles. Follow A39 over double mini roundabouts. At next roundabouts go straight across first roundabout and take second exit from second roundabout. Do not take the Helston road. In Mabe Burnthouse go straight over crossroads. 2 miles further on at next crossroads turn right towards Gweek. Go through Lamanva and Treverva. Farm is ¾ mile beyond Trevera on left going towards Gweek.

FAREHAM Hampshire   4B4

Ellerslie Camping & Caravan Park
Down End Road, Fareham PO16 8TS
☎ 01329-822248 Fax 01329-822248
Open March-October

A small, attractive wooded site on the southern slopes of Portsdown Hill with space for approximately 40 caravans and cars. Positioned close to the M27.
Size 4 acres, 40 touring pitches, 30 with electric hookup, 4 level pitches, 8, 2 WCs, 1 CWP
£ car/tent £6, car/caravan £6.50, motorhome £6.50, motorbike/tent £5.50, children £0.50
CC MasterCard Visa
WS
Last arrival time: 22:00

➜ From M27 junction 11 take A27 to Portsmouth. After ½ mile turn left at traffic lights into Down End Road. Site ½ mile on right.

Folkestone

FARNHAM Surrey 4C3

Tilford Touring
Tilford, Farnham GU10 2DF
01252-792199 Fax 01252-781027
Open all year
Size 4 acres, 75 touring pitches, 50 with electric hookup, 75 level pitches, 3, 4 WCs, 1 CWP
£ car/tent £6-£7.50, car/caravan £8
Rental

➜ From Farnham railway station, head S over level crossing and immediately turn right. Then 3 miles to Tilford village, site beside Hankley Pub & Restaurant.

FENSTANTON Cambridgeshire 9D4

Crystal Lakes Caravan Park
Low Road, Fenstanton PE18 9W
01480-497728 Fax 01480-497728
Open 1 March-31 October
Size 40 acres, 50 touring pitches, 45 with electric hookup, 72 level pitches, 16, 16 WCs, 1 CWP
Calor Gaz WS
Last arrival time: 24 hours

➜ Halfway between Cambridge and Huntingdon, off A14. Signposted in village.
See advert on this page

CRYSTAL LAKES TOURING CARAVAN AND COARSE FISHING CENTRE

- Excellent Fishing - fully stocked lakes, Carp in excess of 20lb and all types of coarse fish. (3 star rating in Angling Times).
- Picturesque, secluded site with beautiful mature lakes.
- Top showers and toilets, Laundry, Washing-up sinks.
- Big tourist area, Cambridge 8 miles, St Ives 1½ miles.
- Lakeside café for full English breakfast and afternoon tea.
- Popular for both weekends and holiday breaks.
- Children's playhouse and playground.
- Local Sunday car boot sale and market.
- Caravan and family tent up to 3 people - £8.50/night.
- Electric hook-up £1.50 per night.
- Designated lakes offer free fishing for residents.
- Cycle paths and footpaths to St Ives and Fenstanton, plus lots of cross country walks.
- Brillian local pubs and restaurants.
- Seasonal pitches available - 8 months plus winter storage.
- Very, very warm welcome - telephone or write for a brochure.

LOW ROAD, FENSTANTON, CAMBRIDGESHIRE PE18 9HU
TELEPHONE: 01480 497728

FILEY North Yorkshire 11E2

Blue Dolphin Holiday Centre
Gristhorpe Bay, Filey YO14 9PU
01723-515155 Fax 01723-512059
Open Easter-end October
Size 87 acres, 416 touring pitches, 210 with electric hookup, 116 level pitches, 380 static caravans, 34, 101 WCs, 3 CWPs
Rental Chalet.
cc MasterCard Visa
Calor Gaz

➜ Off A165 1½ miles N of Filey. Turn right at roundabout signposted to Blue Dolphin.

Reighton Sands Holiday Village
Reighton Gap, Filey YO14 9SJ
01723-890476 Fax 01723-891043
Open March-October
Size 110 acres, 150 touring pitches, 150 with electric hookup, 150 level pitches, 12, 30 WCs, 4 CWPs
Rental Chalet.
cc MasterCard Visa
Calor Gaz
Last arrival time: 23:00

➜ One mile off main A165 Filey to Bridlington road. Signposted opposite a garage.

FOLKESTONE Kent 5F3

Camping & Caravanning Club Site
The Warren, Folkestone CT19 6PT
01303-255093
Open March-September
Size 4 acres, 82 touring pitches, 6, 17 WCs, 1 CWP
£ car/tent £9.60-£12.10, car/caravan £9.60-£12.10, motorhome £9.60-£12.10, motorbike/tent £9.60-£12.10, children £1.50
cc MasterCard Visa
Calor WS
Last arrival time: 23:00

➜ From M2 and Canterbury on A260, turn left at the island into Folkestone, Hill Road, straight on over crossroads, into Wear Bay Road, and second left turn past Martello Tower, site is ½ mile on right.

Little Switzerland Caravan Site
Wear Bay Road, Folkestone CT19 6PS
01303-252168
Open 1 March-31 October
Size 2 acres, 18 touring pitches, 12 with electric hookup, 13 static caravans, 4, 12 WCs, 1 CWP
£ car/tent £8.85, car/caravan £9.50, motorhome £9.50, motorbike/tent £8.50
Calor Gaz

➜ On A20 over first two roundabouts. At third roundabout at foot of Folkestone Hill turn right along A2033 (Hill Road), then ½ mile further continue ahead into Wear Bay Road for ¼ mile, site on left.

ENGLAND

FOLKINGHAM Lincolnshire	8C2

Low Farm Touring Park
Spring Lane, Folkingham, Sleaford NG34 0SJ
☎ 01529-497322
Open Easter-end October
Size 2.5 acres, 36 touring pitches, 25 with electric hookup, 36 level pitches, 4, 6 WCs, 1 CWP
£ car/tent £6.50-£7.50, car/caravan £6.50-£7.50, motorhome £6.50-£7.50, motorbike/tent £6.50-£7.50, children £1
WS
→ Signposted from A15. Folkingham is midway between towns of Bourne and Sleaford. Turn opposite petrol station.

FORDINGBRIDGE Hampshire	4A4

Sandy Balls Holiday Centre
Godshill, Fordingbridge SP6 2JY
☎ 01425 653042 Fax 01425-653067
Open all year
Size 120 acres, 350 touring pitches, 340 with electric hookup, 350 level pitches, 250 static caravans, 40, 50 WCs, 9 CWPs
£ car/tent £10.50-£21.75, car/caravan £12-£21.75, motorhome £12-£21.75, motorbike/tent £10.50-£19.75, children £1
Rental £110-£545, lodge £120-£630
℄ MasterCard Visa
Calor Gaz
Last arrival time: 21:00
→ From A338 take B3078 to Cadnam. 1½ miles from M27 take B3078 to Fordingbridge 9 miles. See advert on opposite page

FOWEY Cornwall	2B4

Yeate Farm Campsite
Bodinnick, Fowey PL23 1LZ
☎ 01726-870256
Open 1 April-31 October
Size 1 acre, 33 touring pitches, 12 with electric hookup, 33 level pitches, 2 static caravans, 2, 3 WCs, 1 CWP
£ car/tent £6-£8, car/caravan £6-£8, motorhome £6-£8, motorbike/tent £6-£8, children £1
Calor Gaz
Last arrival time: 21:00
→ From A38 Liskeard bypass fork left onto A390. Turn left on B3359 and follow signs to Bodinnick, signposted from there.

Hints & Tips
Make sure your mirrors are adjusted correctly before moving off.

GATESHEAD Tyne & Wear	13F4

Derwent Park Caravan and Camping Site
Gateshead
☎ 01207-543383
Open 1 April-30 September

This beautiful riverside park offers tennis, crazy golf, bowling green and adventure playground. Ideally placed for touring Northumbria and near to the Gateshead Metro Centre and Beamish museum.
Size 9 acres, 47 touring pitches, 35 with electric hookup, 25 static caravans, 12, 13 WCs, 1 CWP
£ car/tent £9-£10, car/caravan £9-£10, motorhome £9-£10, motorbike/tent £8, children £0.75
℄ MasterCard Visa
Calor Gaz
WS
Last arrival time: 23:30
→ Situated seven miles SW of Newcastle at the junction of A694 and B6314, 3 miles from A1.

GLASTONBURY Somerset	3E2

Old Oaks Touring Park
Wick Farm, Wick, Glastonbury BA6 0JS
☎ 01458-831437
Open 1 March-31 October

A family run park, set in delightfully tranquil and unspoilt countryside with lovely views and walks, offering excellent amenities in an outstanding environment.
Size 4 acres, 40 touring pitches, 40 with electric hookup, 40 level pitches, 6, 9 WCs, 2 CWPs

Glastonbury

Wish you were here?...

Sandy Balls ...the award winning Holiday Centre

bordering the New Forest, offering a wonderful woodland location, superbly equipped timber lodges, caravan holiday homes, all-weather super pitches for tourers and camping, a wide range of facilities and recreational facilities for all ages.

- *Luxurious Leisure Centre*
- *Indoor and outdoor pools*
- *Sauna and Solarium*
- *Thatched Restaurant and Bar*
- *Jacuzzi and Steam Room*
- *Toning Tables and Aerobics*
- *Woodland Walks and Nature Trail*
- *Adventure Playground*
- *Large Screen Video*
- *Spar Shop and Gift Shop*

Call to find out more
(01425) 653042

Sandy Balls Holiday Centre, Godshill, Fordingbridge, Hants SP6 2JY

On all correspondence please quote ref: RAC mag. 8/98

70

← Old Oaks Touring Park

£ car/tent £7-£9, car/caravan £7-£9, motorhome £7-£9, motorbike/tent £7-£9, children £1.50-£1.75
CC MasterCard Visa
Calor Gaz
Last arrival time: 21:00
➜ 1½ miles from Glastonbury on A361 Shepton Mallet road, turn left at sign for Wick. Park on left in 1 mile; or from A39 Wells Road, left off roundabout approaching Glastonbury, at sign for Wick park is 1½ miles on right.

GOATHLAND North Yorkshire	11E2

Brow House Farm
Goathland YO22 5NP
☏ 01947-896274
Open March-November

Excellent location for exploring the National Park and the Moors.
Size 3 acres, 50 touring pitches, 50 level pitches, 2 ⌂, 2 WCs, 1 CWP
£ car/tent £4-£5, car/caravan £4-£5, motorhome £4-£5, motorbike/tent £4-£5
Last arrival time: 23:00
➜ Turn W off A169 at ¼ mile N of Eller Beck Bridge. Site 1 mile S of Goathland.

GOONHAVERN Cornwall	2B4

Rose Hill Farm Tourist Park
Goonhavern TR4 9LA
☏ 01872-572448
Open Easter-September
Size 7 acres, 65 touring pitches, 40 with electric hookup, 65 level pitches, 7 ⌂, 9 WCs, 1 CWP
£ car/tent £5.25-£8.75, car/caravan £5.25-£8.75, motorhome £5.25-£8.75, motorbike/tent £5.25-£8.75, children £0.75
Calor Gaz
Last arrival time: dusk
➜ From A30 take B3285 signposted Perranporth to village of Goonhavern. Turn right at New Inn. Site is on right.

Glastonbury

Silverbow Park
Goonhaven, Truro TR4 9NA
Tel: 01872 572347

Situated in beautiful countryside near Perranporth. Swim in our beautiful heated pool, play tennis or short mat bowls on our all weather courts or just relax in our grounds. Large superior leisure homes and large individual touring pitches, many fully serviced. Families and couples only.
NOT commercialised.

1992 AA & 1997 CALOR GAS AWARDS "BEST IN BRITAIN"

Silverbow Park
Goonhavern TR4 9NX
☏ 01872-572347 Fax 01872-572347
Open May-mid October
Size 24 acres, 90 touring pitches, 54 with electric hookup, 80 level pitches, 12 ⌂, 15 WCs, 1 CWP
£ car/tent £6-£13.50, car/caravan £6-£13.50, motorhome £6-£13.50, motorbike/tent £6-£13.50, children £2-£3.20
Rental
Calor Gaz
Last arrival time: 22:30
➜ From A30 take B3285 Perranporth road. At T junction in Goonhavern village, turn left onto A3075 for ½ mile. Silverbow entrance is on the left.
See advert on this page

Hints & Tips
If you have any information concerning caravan theft contact the confidential freephone Crimestoppers Line on 0800 555111.
You may be entitled to a reward and there is no need to give your name if you don't want to.

Grassington

GOSFORTH Cumbria 10A2

Church Stile Camp Site

Wasdale, Seascale, Gosforth CA20 1ET
📞 01946-726388
Open March-October

Set on a working family farm within easy reach of Scafell and many other mountains. An ideal walking and climbing area.
Size 4 acres, 50 touring pitches, 50 level pitches, 30 static caravans, 4 ⚿, 9 WCs, 1 CWP
£ car/tent £5-£6, motorhome £5-£6, motorbike/tent £5-£6, children £1
✕¼ 🛒¼ WS
Last arrival time: 22:00
➡ Off A595, 4½ miles E of Gosforth to Nether Wasdale village.

GRANGE-OVER-SANDS Cumbria 10B3

Lakeland Leisure Park

Moor Lane, Flookburgh LA11 7LT
📞 015395-58556 Fax 015395-58559
Open March-October

A family holiday park, just a few minutes drive from picturesque Grange-over-Sands and within easy driving distance of the Lakes. Indoor/outdoor pools, kids clubs, tennis and bowling. Live family entertainment, bars, great food. A 'British Holidays Park'.
Size 105 acres, 100 touring pitches, 90 with electric hookup, 100 level pitches, 750 static caravans, 7 ⚿, 1 CWP
£ car/tent £8-£14, car/caravan £8-£14, motorhome £8-£14, motorbike/tent £8-£14, children £2
Rental
⊂⊂ MasterCard Visa

Calor Gaz
Last arrival time: 21:00
➡ From M6 junction 36 take A590 to Barrow-in-Furness. Then take B5277 through Grange-over-Sands and into Flookburgh. Turn left at the village square and travel 2 miles down this road to park.

Old Park Wood Caravan Park

Holker, Cark-in-Cartmel LA11 7PP
📞 015395-58266 Fax 015395-58101
Open March-October

Overlooking the estuary of the River Leven with exceptional view of the hills. Facilities are provided for both touring and motor caravans. No tents allowed.
Size 36 acres, 42 touring pitches, 42 with electric hookup, 32 level pitches, 325 static caravans, 8 ⚿, 12 WCs, 2 CWPs
£ car/caravan £13.50, motorhome £13.50
Calor
➡ At 4¾ miles W of Grange, or 1 mile N of Cark on B5277, turn W.

GRASSINGTON North Yorkshire 10B3

Hawkswick Cote Caravan Park

Arncliffe, Skipton BD23 5PX
📞 01756-770226 Fax 01756-770327
Open March-October
Size 2 acres, 50 touring pitches, 50 with electric hookup, 50 level pitches, 90 static caravans, 7 ⚿, 10 WCs, 1 CWP
£ car/tent £9, car/caravan £9-£12, motorhome £9-£12, motorbike/tent £9, children £1.50
Calor Gaz
➡ B6160 Threshfield to Grassington road. Half a mile N of Kilnsey take road to Arncliffe. Park is on left, 1½ miles.

Hints & Tips

Tyres are your only contact with the road. Look after them and you will improve the safety and behaviour of your unit. Never mix cross ply and radials on the same axis.

Halesowen

Ripley Caravan Park
Ripley, Harrogate HG3 3AU
Tel: 01423-770050

Luxury touring park in the countryside. First class facilities: Indoor heated swimming pool, sauna, sunbed, games room, nursery playroom, playground, tennis net, football pitch, shop, laundry and disabled unit. At a crossroads for the Yorkshire Dales, only three miles to Harrogate and the Yorkshire Dales. At junction of A61/B6165. Park 300 yards towards Knaresborough.

HALESOWEN West Midlands — 8A3

Camping & Caravanning Club Site
Fieldhouse Lane, Romsley, Halesowen B62 0NH
☎ 01562-710015
Open March-November
Size 6.5 acres, 120 touring pitches, 47 with electric hookup, 8 ☂, 13 WCs, 1 CWP
£ car/tent £11.50-£14.60, car/caravan £11.50-£14.60, motorhome £11.50-£14.60, motorbike/tent £11.50-£14.60, children £1.60
CC MasterCard Visa
Calor WS
Last arrival time: 23:00
➔ Leave M5 at junction 3, take A456, then turn left on B4551 to Romsley, turn right past Sun Hotel, take 5th left hand turn from Sun junction and next left for site, 330 yards on left

---

HALTWHISTLE Northumberland — 10B1

Camping & Caravanning Club Site
Burnfoot Park Village, Haltwhistle NE49 OJP
☎ 01434-320106
Open March-November
Size 3 acres, 60 touring pitches, 34 with electric hookup, 4 ☂, 9 WCs, 1 CWP
£ car/tent £9.60-£12.10, car/caravan £9.60-£12.10, motorhome £9.60-£12.10, motorbike/tent £9.60-£12.10, children £1.50

CC MasterCard Visa
Calor WS
Last arrival time: 23:00
➔ New Bypass opened end of May 1998. Follow signposts from there.

HARROGATE North Yorkshire — 11D3

Bilton Park
Village Farm, Bilton Lane, Harrogate HG1 4DH
☎ 01423-863121
Open April-October
Size 10 acres, 25 touring pitches, 25 with electric hookup, 25 level pitches, 4 ☂, 17 WCs, 1 CWP
£ car/tent £7-£9, car/caravan £7-£9, motorhome £7, motorbike/tent £7
Rental
Calor Gaz WS
➔ A59 in Harrogate between A661 and A61. Turn at Dragon Inn. Park 1 mile.

High Moor Farm Park
Skipton Road, Harrogate HG3 2LZ
☎ 01423-563637 Fax 01423-529449
Open 1 April-31 October
Size 22 acres, 250 touring pitches, 200 with electric hookup, 250 level pitches, 151 static caravans, 10 ☂, 25 WCs, 2 CWPs
£ car/tent £8.75-£9.25, car/caravan £8.75-£9.25, motorhome £8.75-£9.25, motorbike/tent £8.75-£9.25
Rental
CC MasterCard Visa
Calor Gaz WS
Last arrival time: 23:00
➔ On A59, 4 miles W of Harrogate.

Ripley Caravan Park
Ripley, Harrogate HG3 3AU
☎ 01423-770050 Fax 01423-770050
Open Easter-31 October
Size 18 acres, 100 touring pitches, 100 with electric hookup, 100 level pitches, 25 static caravans, 15 ☂, 18 WCs, 1 CWP
£ car/tent £6.75-£8, car/caravan £6.75-£8, motorhome £6.75-£8, motorbike/tent £6.75-£8, children £1
Calor Gaz WS
Last arrival time: 21:00
➔ About 3 miles N of Harrogate, access is 300 yards down B6165 Knaresborough road from roundabout junction with A61.
See advert on this page

Rudding Holiday Park
Follifoot, Harrogate HG3 1JH
☎ 01423-870439 Fax 01423-870859
Open March-October

Hayle

Size 50 acres, 141 touring pitches, 141 with electric hookup, 76 level pitches, 16, 24 WCs, 2 CWPs
£ car/tent £6.50-£12, car/caravan £9.50-£20.50, motorhome £9.50-£20.50, motorbike/tent £6.50-£12
Rental Cottages & lodges available from £150 p.w.
cc MasterCard Visa
Calor Gaz WS
Last arrival time: 22:00
➜ Between A61 and A661 on A658, 1½ miles SE of Harrogate, turn NW ½ mile on right.

Shaws Trailer Park

Knaresborough Road, Harrogate HG2 7NE
01423-884432
Open all year
Size 11 acres, 65 touring pitches, 30 with electric hookup, 65 level pitches, 120 static caravans, 4, 1 CWP
£ car/tent £7.50, car/caravan £8.50, motorhome £7.50, motorbike/tent £6
Calor Gaz WS
Last arrival time: 24 hours
➜ On A59 off Grand Hospital, 1 mile from centre of Harrogate, 3 miles from centre of Knaresborough.

HARTLEPOOL Cleveland   11D1

Ash Vale Holiday Homes Park

Easington Rd, Hartlepool TS24 9RF
01429-862111 Fax 01429-862900
Open 1 April-31 October
Size 22 acres, 25 touring pitches, 25 with electric hookup, 25 level pitches, 50 static caravans, 6, 10 WCs, 1 CWP
£ car/tent £5-£7.50
Rental £70-£200
Calor Gaz WS
Last arrival time: 24 hours
➜ From A19 take A179 towards Hartlepool, at the third roundabout turn left onto A1086 to Peterlee. Through next roundabout 300 yards on left.

HAWES North Yorkshire   10C2

Bainbridge Ings Farm

Hawes DL8 3NU
01969-667354 Fax 01822-613371
Open 1 April-31 October
Size 5 acres, 80 touring pitches, 25 with electric hookup, 15 static caravans, 6, 15 WCs, 1 CWP
£ car/tent £6-£8, car/caravan £6-£8, motorhome £6-£8, motorbike/tent £6-£8, children £1
Rental £125-£250
Calor Gaz
Last arrival time: 21:30
➜ Approaching Hawes from Bainbridge on A684, turn left at signpost marked Gayle 300 yards on left.

HAYFIELD Derbyshire   7F1

Camping & Caravanning Club Site

Kinder Road, Hayfield SK22 2LE
01663-745394
Open March-November
Size 7 acres, 90 touring pitches, 6, 12 WCs, 1 CWP
£ car/tent £7.25-£11.30, motorhome £7.25-£11.30, motorbike/tent £7.25-£11.30, children £1.50
cc MasterCard Visa
Calor WS
Last arrival time: 23:00
➜ On the A624, Glossop to Chapel en le Frith, is the Hayfield by-pass, well signed into the village, follow wooden carved signs to the site.

HAYLE Cornwall   2A4

Calloose Caravan & Camping Park

Leedstown, Hayle TR27 5ET
01736-850431 Fax 01736-850431
Open 15 April-30 October

Award winning secluded family park in suntrap valley offering, superb facilities for tourers.
Size 12.5 acres, 120 touring pitches, 99 with electric hookup, 120 level pitches, 17 static caravans, 15, 21 WCs, 2 CWPs
£ car/tent £6.50-£12.50, car/caravan £6.50-£12.50, motorhome £6.50-£12.50, motorbike/tent £6.50-£12.50, children £0.75-£1.75
Rental £100-£480
cc MasterCard Visa
Calor Gaz
Last arrival time: 22:00
➜ Take B3302 towards Helston. Turn left at approach to Leedstown opposite village hall.

Don't forget to mention the guide
When booking, please remember to tell the site that you chose it from RAC Camping & Caravanning 1999

ENGLAND

Hayle

Parbola Holiday Park
Wall, Gwinear, Nr Hayle TR27 5LE
☎ 01209-831503 Fax 01209-831503
Open Easter-September Å ⌂ ⛺

Secluded family woodland park. Rose Award caravans/pre-erected tents for hire. Large, spacious pitches for campers. Close to glorious beaches.
Size 17.5 acres, 115 touring pitches, 70 with electric hookup, 115 level pitches, 19 static caravans, 12 ♨, 16 WCs, 2 CWPs
£ car/tent £7.25-£12, car/caravan £7.25-£12, motorhome £7.25-£12, motorbike/tent £7.25-£12, children £1.60
Rental Å ⌂ Chalet. £99-£499
cc MasterCard Visa
🚿 🍴 🏪 🛒 ❄ ▶ 📞 📺 ⚠ Calor Gaz ♿ WS
Last arrival time: 22:00
➜ Take A30 to Hayle. At roundabout leave first exit to Connor Downs. At end of village turn right to Carnhell Green and turn right at T junction. Parbola is 1 mile on left.

St Ives Bay Holiday Park
73 Loggans Road, Upton Towans, Hayle TR27 5BH
☎ 01736-752274 Fax 01736-754523
Open 1 May-1 October Å ⌂ ⛺

Set in sand dunes with private access to a fabulous sandy beach. Two bars and a large indoor pool. Family and children oriented.
Size 75 acres, 250 touring pitches, 130 with electric hookup, 200 level pitches, 250 static caravans, 26 ♨, 38 WCs, 5 CWPs
£ car/tent £5-£18, car/caravan £5-£18, motorhome £5-£18, motorbike/tent £5-£18
Rental ⌂ Chalet. £99-£450
cc MasterCard Visa
🚿 🍴 🏪 🛒 🛍 🛒 📞 📺 ⚠ ⛽ Calor Gaz 🐕
➜ Exit A30 at Hayle and take B3301 coast road. Park entrance is 600 yards on left.

HAYLING ISLAND Hampshire 4B4

Lower Tye Farm Camp Site
Copse Lane, Hayling Island PO11 0RQ
☎ 01705-462479 Fax 01705-462479
Open 1 March-1 January Å ⌂ ⛺

Quiet family site near family pub. An excellent touring base for Portsmouth, Isle of Wight and the New Forest. Long term parking is available on site.
Size 5 acres, 150 touring pitches, 150 with electric hookup, 150 level pitches, 13 ♨, 18 WCs, 1 CWP
£ car/tent £8, car/caravan £8, motorhome £8, motorbike/tent £8, children £1
Rental ⌂
🚿 🚿¼ ✂ 🍴 🏪 🛒 ❄ 🛍 📞 ⚠ Calor Gaz ♿ 🐕 WS
Last arrival time: 00:00
➜ Exit M27 or A3M motorways at Havant. For Hayling Island follow A3023 from Havant. Lower Tye camp site is indicated to turn left in to Copse Lane approximately 1½ miles after crossing the bridge onto Hayling Island. The site is on the right in Copse Lane about ½ mile from the main road.

HELMSLEY North Yorkshire 11D2

Foxholme Touring Caravan Park
Harome, Helmsley YO6 5JG
☎ 01439-770416 Fax 01439-771744
Open 1 March-31 October Å ⌂ ⛺

Quiet, sheltered and level wooded site. All pitches attractively situated among evergreen trees and well spaced to ensure peace, quiet and privacy. Hard roads throughout the site give good all-weather access.
Size 6 acres, 60 touring pitches, 60 with electric hookup, 60 level pitches, 8 ♨, 16 WCs, 2 CWPs
£ car/tent £6.50-£7.50, car/caravan £6.50-£7.50, motorhome £6.50-£7.50, motorbike/tent £6.50-£7.50

Helston

🛁 🔌 📞 🚽 Calor Gaz ♿ 🐕 WS
➜ On A170 for ½ mile, turn right on road to Harome, 2 miles turn left at church, ½ mile further keep left, then take first turn on left to site in 350 yards.

Golden Square Caravan Park
Oswaldkirk, Helmsley YO62 5YQ
📞 01439-788269 Fax 01439-788236
Open 1 March-31 October ⛺ 🚐 🚍

A quiet secluded site with excellent facilities, hidden from the outside world. All service pitches. Storage and seasonal pitches available.
Size 12 acres, 129 touring pitches, 100 with electric hookup, 129 level pitches, 14 🚿, 18 WCs, 2 CWPs
£ car/tent £6-£7.90, car/caravan £6-£7.90, motorhome £6-£7.90, motorbike/tent £6-£7.90
Rental 🚐 Chalet. £90-£300
🛁 ✕¼ 🛒 🔌 📞 🚽 GR 📺 ⚠ Calor Gaz ♿ 🐕 WS
Last arrival time: 22:00
➜ 2 miles S of Helmsley off B1257 road to Ampleforth.

HELSTON Cornwall   2A4

Franchis Holiday Park
Cury Cross Lanes, Nr Mullion, Helston TR12 7AZ
📞 01326-240301
Open 1 March-31 October ⛺ 🚐 🚍

Rose award park in an area of outstanding natural beauty. Close mown grass and woodland. Excellent facilities.
Size 17 acres, 70 touring pitches, 37 with electric hookup, 65 level pitches, 7 static caravans, 11 🚿, 11 WCs, 1 CWP
£ car/tent £6-£7, car/caravan £6-£7, motorhome £6-£7, motorbike/tent £6-£7, children £0.50
Rental 🚐 £135-£400. Bungalows £115-£315.
🛁 📞 🚽 Calor Gaz 🐕
Last arrival time: 22:00
➜ 6 miles from Helston on A3083. Helston to Lizard road

Beautiful Spaces in Breathtaking Places
Mullion Holiday Park in Cornwall...

In an area of outstanding natural beauty close to glorious sandy beaches. Award winning park with all weather facilities including heated indoor & outdoor pools, free nightly entertainment & childrens' clubs, restaurant, supermarket & launderette, Super hook-ups with TV, electricity & water. Mullion Holiday Park - a very special place for family holidays.

WESTSTAR Holiday Parks
For our Latest Brochure & Friendly Service
Call (01326) 240 000 Quote: RC

Mullion Holiday Park
Ruan Minor, Helston TR12 7LJ
📞 01326-240000 Fax 01326-241141
Open Easter-September ⛺ 🚐 🚍

Level park with superb facilities. Indoor swimming pool, all-day pub with food. Close to outstanding beaches.
Size 49 acres, 159 touring pitches, 87 with electric hookup, 348 static caravans, 15 🚿, 15 WCs, 1 CWP
£ car/tent £7.50-£14.50, car/caravan £7.50-£14.50, motorhome £7.50-£14.50, motorbike/tent £7.50-£14.50
Rental 🚐 Chalet. £105-£599
⚆ MasterCard Visa
🛁 ✕ 🛒 🔌 📞 🚽 ⚲ 📻 GR 📺 ⚠ ⚐ Calor Gaz 🐕
Last arrival time: 21:00
➜ From A30, take A39 from Fraddon to Truro and continue on Falmouth road. Take A394 to Helston, then A3083 for Lizard. After 7 miles site is on left opposite Mullion turning.
See advert on this page

ENGLAND

Free yourself

RAC Hotel Reservations will find you a room in the UK or Ireland and if you're an RAC Member, the service is absolutely free.
Phone 0870 603 9109.

If you're travelling in Europe, RAC Motoring Assistance provides rapid help in the event of breakdown, fire, accident, theft or illness.
In addition, our **Personal Travel Insurance** covers you for lost luggage, theft of personal belongings, personal injury or cancellation.
Call us on 0800 550 055.

www.rac.co.uk

rac
movement drives us

Hinkley

HEREFORD Herefordshire 7D4

Hereford Racecourse Caravan Club Site
Roman Road, Hereford HR4 9QU
☎ 01432-272364
Open March-September
Size 5 acres, 60 touring pitches, 36 with electric hookup, 6, 18 WCs, 1 CWP
£ car/tent £9.60-£12.10, car/caravan £9.60-£12.10, motorhome £9.60-£12.10, motorbike/tent £9.60-£12.10, children £1.50
₡ MasterCard Visa
¼ ¼ ¼ Calor WS
Last arrival time: 23:00
➜ 1 mile N of Hereford (A49), turn W onto A4103. Site ½ mile.

Poston Mill Park
Golden Valley, Peterchurch HR2 0SF
☎ 01981-550225 Fax 01981-550885
Open all year

This is an outstanding park, beautifully maintained, offering excellent service and facilities. Nestling in the Golden Valley alongside the River Dore the picturesque surroundings allow you to relax and enjoy the countryside. Highly recommended.
Size 25 acres, 60 touring pitches, 60 with electric hookup, 60 level pitches, 60 static caravans, 8, 12 WCs, 2 CWPs
£ car/tent £6-£8.75, car/caravan £6.50-£7.75, motorhome £6.50-£7.75, motorbike/tent £6, children £0.50
Rental holiday home £130-£240
¼ ¼ ¼ Calor Gaz WS
Last arrival time: 22:00
➜ Site on B4348 Hereford to Hay-on-Wye road.

HERTFORD Hertfordshire 5D2

Camping & Caravanning Club Site
Mangrove Road, Hertford SG13 8QF
☎ 01992-586696
Open March-November
Size 32 acres, 250 touring pitches, 109 with electric hookup, 16, 21 WCs, 3 CWPs
£ car/tent £13.60-£14.60, car/caravan £13.60-£14.60, motorhome £13.60-£14.60, motorbike/tent £13.60-£14.60, children £1.60
₡ MasterCard Visa
¼ ¼ ¼ Calor WS
Last arrival time: 23:00
➜ From A10 follow A414 Hertford signs to next roundabout (Foxholes), go straight across, 200 yards along turn left (signposted Balls Park - Hertford University), turn left at T junction into Mangrove Road, go past Simon Balle School, University and cricket ground, the site is 400 yards on the left. From Hertford town, A414 to Stag House roundabout, turn right, first right through centre reservation, then follow same directions as from Hertford University.

HIGH BENTHAM Lancashire 10B3

Riverside Caravan Park
Wenning Avenue, High Bentham LA2 7HS
☎ 01524-261272
Open March-October
Size 12 acres, 30 touring pitches, 30 with electric hookup, 30 level pitches, 170 static caravans, 8, 7 WCs, 1 CWP
£ car/tent £6.80, car/caravan £7.80, motorhome £7.80
¼ ¼ ¼
Last arrival time: 21:00
➜ Turn S on B4680 at Black Bull Hotel in High Bentham. Site signposted.

HINKLEY Leicestershire 8B3

Wolvey Villa Farm Caravan & Camp Site
Wolvey, Hinkley LE10 3HF
☎ 01455-220493
Open all year
Size 7 acres, 55 with electric hookup, 110 level pitches, 8, 11 WCs, 1 CWP
£ car/tent £5.60-£5.80, car/caravan £5.70-£5.90, motorhome £5.50-£5.70, motorbike/tent £5.40, children £1
Calor Gaz WS
Last arrival time: 23:00
➜ M6 junction 2 to B4065 and follow Wolvey signs. M69 junction 1, then follow Wolvey signs.

Hints & Tips

Caravans are stolen from lay-bys and motorway service stations. Even if you are just stopping for a cup of tea or to stretch your legs make sure you secure your caravan.

ENGLAND

Holebeach

| HOLBEACH Lincolnshire | 9D2 |

Delph Bank Touring Park
Main Street, Fleet Hargate, Holbeach, Spalding PE12 8LL
☏ 01406-422910 Fax 01406-422910
Open 1 March-31 October ▲ 🚐 🚛
Size 3 acres, 45 touring pitches, 22 with electric hookup, 45 level pitches, 4 🚿, 5 WCs, 1 CWP
£ car/tent £6.50, car/caravan £6.50, motorhome £6.50, children £1
♿¼ ✗¼ ♿¼ 🅿 📞 🚾 Calor Gaz 🐕 WS
Last arrival time: 22:30
➡ From Spalding take A151 to Holbeach. Continue further 3 miles to Fleet Hargate. Turn right into village just before A151 joins A17.

| HOLMFIRTH West Yorkshire | 10C4 |

Holme Valley Camping & Caravan Park
Thongsbridge, Holmfirth HO7 2TD
☏ 01484-665819 Fax 01484-663870
Open all year ▲ 🚐 🚛

Picturesque setting in beautiful 'Summer Wine' country, bordering the Peak District. 16-amp hook-ups, well-stocked shop, licensed for alcohol sales. Rally fields available. Booking advisable.
Size 8.5 acres, 62 touring pitches, 62 with electric hookup, 56 level pitches, 4 static caravans, 4 🚿, 8 WCs, 1 CWP
£ car/tent £6-£7, car/caravan £7-£8, motorhome £6-£7, motorbike/tent £3-£6
Rental 🚐 £95-£180
⟪ MasterCard Visa
♿ ♿¼ ✗¼ ♿¼ 🅿 📞 🚾 🅐 Calor Gaz ♿ 🐕
Last arrival time: 22:00
➡ Entrance to private lane is off A6024, one mile N of Holmfirth.

Hints & Tips
In winter take your seat cushions home. Not only will they keep dry but a caravan without cushions is a less attractive prospect to thieves.

| HONITON Devon | 3D3 |

Camping & Caravanning Club Site
Otter Valley Park, Northcote, Honiton EX14 8ST
☏ 01404-44546
Open March-November ▲ 🚐 🚛
Size 6 acres, 89 touring pitches, 35 with electric hookup, 10 🚿, 15 WCs, 2 CWPs
£ car/tent £10.40-£13.60, car/caravan £10.40-£13.60, motorhome £10.40-£13.60, motorbike/tent £10.40-£13.60, children £1.50
⟪ MasterCard Visa
♿ ♿¼ ✗¼ ♿ ♿¼ 🅿 📞 🚾 🅿 🅖🅡 🅠 🆃🆅 🅐 Calor ♿ 🐕 WS
Last arrival time: 23:00
➡ Leave the first exit to Honiton from A30. Keep left off the slip road and keep coming left. (Road skirts perimeter of site).

| HOPE Derbyshire | 8A1 |

Laneside Caravan Site
Laneside Farm, Hope S30 2RR
☏ 01433-620215 Fax 01433-620214
Open 31 March-31 October ▲ 🚐 🚛

Breathtaking scenery, spotless, well equipped, manicured level valley site surrounded by hills. Adjoins Hope, so seven day late shopping, pubs, restaurants, etc are all within five minutes walk.
Size 7 acres, 100 touring pitches, 100 with electric hookup, 95 level pitches, 24 static caravans, 6 🚿, 14 WCs, 2 CWPs
£ car/tent £6.75-£7.75, car/caravan £6.75-£7.75, motorhome £6.75-£7.75, children £0.75
Rental Cottages from £60 w/e to £350 weekly.
♿ ♿¼ ✗¼ ♿¼ 🅿 📞 🚾 🅐 Calor Gaz 🐕
Last arrival time: 21:00
➡ Site on A625, ½ mile E of Hope village.

Hints & Tips
Make sure your mirrors are adjusted correctly before moving off.

Huntley

HORAM East Sussex　　　　　　　　5D4

Horam Manor Touring Park
Horam, Near Heathfield TN21 0YD
☎ 01435-813662
Open March-mid October

A tranquil rural site in an area of outstanding natural beauty. Plenty of space. Special mother and toddler room. Free hot water and showers.
Size 7 acres, 90 touring pitches, 52 with electric hookup, 75 level pitches, 7, 10 WCs, 1 CWP
£ car/tent £11, car/caravan £11, motorhome £11, motorbike/tent £11, children £0.85
¼ ¼ ¼ Calor Gaz
➡ Site is on A267, S of Horam village. 3 miles S of Heathfield, 13 miles N of Eastbourne.

HORSHAM West Sussex　　　　　　　4C3

Honeybridge Park
Dial Post, Horsham RH13 8NX
☎ 01403-710923 Fax 01403-710923
Open all year

A spacious park nestling in an area of outstanding natural beauty. Centralised for the south coast, ferry ports and only one hour from London. Free showers etc in a lovely heated amenity block.
Size 15 acres, 100 touring pitches, 62 with electric hookup, 100 level pitches, 7, 20 WCs, 1 CWP
£ car/tent £7.50-£9.50, car/caravan £9.50-£11.50, motorhome £9.50-£11.50, motorbike/tent £5.50-£7.50, children £1
℅ MasterCard Visa
¼ Calor Gaz WS
Last arrival time: 22:00
➡ 300 yards off A24. Follow international camping signs to Ashurst ¼ mile S of Dial Post village.

HUNTINGDON Cambridgeshire　　　　8C4

Park Lane Touring Park
Park Lane, Godmanchester, Huntingdon PE18 8AF
☎ 01480-453740 Fax 01480-453740
Open March-October
Size 2.5 acres, 50 touring pitches, 50 with electric hookup, 50 level pitches, 4, 8 WCs, 1 CWP
£ car/tent £8.50, car/caravan £8.50, motorhome £8.50, motorbike/tent £8.50, children £1
¼ ¼ ¼ Calor Gaz WS
Last arrival time: 22:30
➡ From A14 turn off to Godmanchester and pick up camp signs on lamp post. Turn right at Black Bull pub. Entrance on left.

Quiet Waters Caravan Park
Hemingford Abbots, Huntingdon PE18 9AJ
☎ 01480-463405
Open April-October
Size 5 acres, 20 touring pitches, 20 with electric hookup, 20 level pitches, 9 static caravans, 6, 6 WCs, 1 CWP
£ car/tent £8-£9, car/caravan £8-£9, motorhome £8-£9, motorbike/tent £8-£9
Rental
℅ Visa
¼ ¼ Calor Gaz
Last arrival time: 20:00
➡ From A14 turn off at Hemingford Abbotts. 1 mile into village follow signs.

HUNTLEY Gloucestershire　　　　　　7E4

Forest Gate Campsite
Huntley GL19 3EU
☎ 01452-831192 Fax 01452-831192
Open 1 March-31 October
Size 2.5 acres, 30 touring pitches, 24 with electric hookup, 30 level pitches, 2, 6 WCs, 1 CWP
£ car/tent £8.80, car/caravan £8.80, motorhome £8.80, motorbike/tent £8.80, children £2.20
℅ MasterCard Visa
¼ ¼ ¼ Calor Gaz
Last arrival time: 22:30
➡ On A40 at junction with A4136 (Monmouth Road), 7 miles from Gloucester, 9 miles from Ross-on-Wye.

Hints & Tips

Caravans are stolen from lay-bys and motorway service stations. Even if you are just stopping for a cup of tea or to stretch your legs make sure you secure your caravan.

80

Hyde

HYDE Cheshire   10C4

Camping & Caravanning Club Site
Crowden, Hadfield, Hyde SK14 7HZ
☎ 01457-866057
Open March-November
Size 2.5 acres, 45 touring pitches, 2 ⚲, 6 WCs, 1 CWP
£ car/tent £6.45-£9.80, car/caravan £6.45-£9.80, motorhome £6.45-£9.80, motorbike/tent £6.45-£9.80, children £1.50
cc MasterCard Visa
Last arrival time: 23:00
➜ From M67 (Hyde) take A628. Site is on left at Crowden.

IPSWICH Suffolk   5E1

Low House Touring Caravan Centre
Bucklesham Road, Foxhall, Ipswich IP10 0AU
☎ 01473-659437 Fax 01473-659880
Open all year
Size 3 acres, 30 touring pitches, 30 with electric hookup, 3 level pitches, 4 ⚲, 5 WCs, 1 CWP
£ car/tent £6.50
➜ Turn off A14 Ipswich ring road onto A1156 (signposted Ipswich East). Follow road over bridge which crosses A14 and almost immediately turn right (no sign). After ½ mile turn right again (signposted Bucklesham) and site is on left after ¼ mile.

Priory Park
Off Nacton Road, Ipswich IP10 0JT
☎ 01473-727393 Fax 01473-278372
Open all year

Set in 85 acres on the banks of the River Orwell, with woodland, a golf course, swimming pool, tennis and foreshore access for small boats. Bar with food. Open all year.
Size 85 acres, 75 touring pitches, 75 with electric hookup, 75 level pitches, 75 static caravans, 16 ⚲, 15 WCs, 2 CWPs

£ car/tent £13, car/caravan £13, motorhome £13, motorbike/tent £13
Rental Chalet. From £200 per week.
Last arrival time: 21:00
➜ Leave A14 Ipswich southern bypass at Nacton interchange (east of Orwell Bridge). Turn towards Ipswich, after 300 yards turn left, following signs to Priory Park.

ISLE OF WIGHT   4B4

Adgestone Camping Park
Lower Road, Adgestone, Sandown PO36 0HL
☎ 01983-403432 Fax 01983-404955
Open Easter-September

Superb award winning park in glorious countryside, 1½ miles from beach. Facilities include swimming pool, takeaway, adventure playground, river and pond fishing. Special ferry inclusive package holidays, plus park fee concessions for over 50's.
Size 15.5 acres, 200 touring pitches, 200 with electric hookup, 200 level pitches, 15 ⚲, 30 WCs, 2 CWPs
£ car/tent £7.60-£11, car/caravan £7.60-£11, motorhome £7.60-£11, motorbike/tent £7.60-£11, children £1.90-£3.25
cc MasterCard Visa
Last arrival time: dusk
➜ Turn off A3055 at Manor House pub in Lake. Go past golf club to T-junction and turn right. Site is 200 yards on right.

Appuldurcombe Gardens C&C Holiday Park
Wroxhall, Ventnor PO38 3EP
☎ 01983-852597 Fax 01983-856225
Open 1 March-31 October

Isle of Wight

Family site with country views, yet only ten minutes drive to the beaches of Shanklin/ Sandown and Ventnor. Ideal base for walkers and cyclists
Size 12 acres, 100 touring pitches, 46 with electric hookup, 75 level pitches, 40 static caravans, 12 ®, 12 WCs, 1 CWP
£ car/tent £5.30-£10.30, car/caravan £5.30-£10.30, motorhome £5.30-£10.30, motorbike/tent £5.30-£9.30, children £1.75-£2
Rental Chalet. 4 berth £130-£290, 8 berth £170-£330
CC MasterCard Visa
Last arrival time: 23:00
➜ From Newport take the A3020, turning off towards Shanklin. Through Godshill, turn right at Whiteley Bank roundabout towards Wroxall.

Comforts Farm
Pallance Road, Northwood, Cowes PO31 8LS
01983-293888
Open May-October

Set on a 60 acre working farm near the sea at Cowes, with excellent views and good amenities. No charge for children or dogs.
Size 9 acres, 50 touring pitches, 25 with electric hookup, 25 level pitches, 6 ®, 11 WCs, 1 CWP
£ car/tent £6-£6.80, car/caravan £6.80, motorhome £6.80, motorbike/tent £6
Calor Gaz
➜ From Cowes take A3020, turn right into Three Gates Road at Plessy Road and after ¼ mile, right into Pallance Road.

Heathfield Farm Camping Site
Heathfield Road, Freshwater PO40 9SH
01983-756756 Fax 01983-752480
Open May-end September

Peaceful family site with sea and downland views. High standard of cleanliness maintained in modern toilet block. Close to the beach, shops and buses. Ferry inclusive holidays.
Size 5 acres, 60 touring pitches, 16 with electric hookup, 60 level pitches, 5 ®, 7 WCs, 1 CWP
£ car/tent £6-£7, car/caravan £6-£7, motorhome £6-£7, motorbike/tent £6-£7, children £1.25-£1.75
Gaz
Last arrival time: 22:00
➜ Two miles W from Yarmouth ferry port on A3054 turn left into Heathfield Road. Site entrance is 200 yards on right.

Landguard Camping Park
Landguard Manor Road, Shanklin PO37 7PH
01983-867028 Fax 01983-865988
Open May-September

Countryside setting only ½ mile from town centre. Heated swimming pool. Licensed club with evening entertainment. Cafe. Horse riding. Marked pitches, all with electric hook-up.
Size 6 acres, 150 touring pitches, 150 with electric hookup, 140 level pitches, 10 ®, 16 WCs, 1 CWP
£ car/tent £6.50-£11, car/caravan £6.50-£11, motorhome £6.50-£11, motorbike/tent £6.50-£11, children £2-£3
CC MasterCard Visa
Calor Gaz
Last arrival time: 21:00
➜ From Newport take A3056 to Sandown. Do not turn off at A3020 to Shanklin. Continue on the Sandown road past Safeway and take next turning right into Whitecross Lane. Follow signs.

Hints & Tips

If you have any information concerning caravan theft contact the confidential freephone Crimestoppers Line on 0800 555111.
You may be entitled to a reward and there is no need to give your name if you don't want to.

ENGLAND

Isle of Wight

Ninham Country Holidays
Shanklin PO37 7PL
☎ 01983-864243 Fax 01983-868881
Open Easter-September

Country park setting overlooking a wooded valley and small lakes. Adjacent to the island's main resort of Shanklin.
Size 5 acres, 98 touring pitches, 40 with electric hookup, 90 level pitches, 4 static caravans, 8 ⌂, 12 WCs, 1 CWP
£ car/tent £7.30-£9.80, car/caravan £7.30-£9.80, motorhome £7.30-£9.80, motorbike/tent £7.30-£9.80, children £1.85-£2.65
Rental £190-£365
℃ MasterCard Visa

↳¼ ✗¼ ⬤¼ Calor Gaz WS
Last arrival time: 21:00
➜ Main site entrance is 1½ miles W of Lake on Newport-Sandown road (A3056). Private drive on left past mini-roundabout outside 'Safeway' superstore.

Orchards Holiday Caravan & Camping Park
Newbridge, Yarmouth PO41 0TS
☎ 01983-531331 Fax 01983-531666
Open late February to early January

The only park on the Isle of Wight to be appointed by the Caravan Club and to be a member of The Best of British Caravan parks. Indoor and outdoor swimming pools. Ferry inclusive packages throughout the season.
Size 15 acres, 175 touring pitches, 175 with electric hookup, 60 level pitches, 61 static caravans, 14 ⌂, 25 WCs, 3 CWPs
£ car/tent £7.35-£10.75, car/caravan £7.35-£10.75, motorhome £7.35-£10.75, motorbike/tent £7.35-£10.75, children £1.35-£3
Rental £105-£545
℃ MasterCard Visa

Calor Gaz
Last arrival time: 23:00
➜ 4 miles E of Yarmouth and 6 miles W of Newport on B3401. Entrance is opposite Newbridge village post office.

Pondwell Caravan & Camping Park
Pondwell Hill, Ryde
☎ 01983-612330 Fax 01983-613511
Open May-September
Size 8 acres, 150 touring pitches, 20 with electric hookup, 45 level pitches, 20 ⌂, 30 WCs, 2 CWPs
£ car/tent £4-£7, car/caravan £4-£7, motorhome £4-£7, children £1-£1.75
Rental Chalet. £73-£381
℃ MasterCard Visa

↳ ✗¼ ⬤¼ Calor Gaz
Last arrival time: 23:30
➜ Take A3054 to Ryde, then A3055 turning left along B3330 to Seaview. Park is next to Well pub.

Southland Camping Park
Newchurch, Sandown PO36 0LZ
☎ 01983-865385 Fax 01983-867663
Open Easter-end September

Award-winning, sheltered and flat family-run Park which provides an ideal base for exploring the Isle of Wight.
Size 6 acres, 100 touring pitches, 100 with electric hookup, 100 level pitches, 7 ⌂, 14 WCs, 1 CWP
£ car/tent £6.75-£9.30, car/caravan £6.75-£9.30, motorhome £6.75-£9.30, motorbike/tent £6.75-£9.30, children £1.40-£2
℃ MasterCard Visa

↳ ↳¼ ✗¼ Calor Gaz
Last arrival time: 22:30
➜ Park is signposted from A3055/6 Newport to Sandown road, SE of Arreton.

Isle of Wight

WAVERLEY PARK HOLIDAY CENTRE

A beautiful site offering ample space for a carefree holiday. Overlooking Cowes Harbour and the shipping lanes of the Solent, this family run site covers 12½ acres and includes a busy Club House, Shop, heated outdoor pool, children's play area, launderette etc., and offers entertainment nightly high season. Delicious home cooked food and a licensed bar complete the picture.
Holiday accommodation can be enjoyed in either your touring caravan, motor caravan or tent, or why not select one our our 2, 4, or 6 berth caravans or flats, complete with toilet & shower facilities, colour television etc. Special 'Bargain Break' offers are available early and late season. The Red Funnel ferry Terminal is within easy walking distance of the siSite.

Old Road, East Cowes, Isle of Wight
Tel: 01983 293452   Fax: 01983 200494
Internet: TBA

Waverley Park Holiday Centre
Old Road, East Cowes
01983-293452 Fax 01983-200494
Open Easter-October

Overlooking the Solent, this beautiful site has children's play area, heated pool and entertainment nightly in high season.
Size 12 acres, 45 touring pitches, 28 with electric hookup, 42 static caravans, 12, 15 WCs, 1 CWP
£ car/tent £6.80-£10, car/caravan £6.80-£10, motorhome £6.80-£10, motorbike/tent £10, children £1.70-£2.20
Rental £100-£380
CC MasterCard Visa
Calor WS
Last arrival time: 22:30
➡ Signposted from the Red Funnel terminal, East Cowes and also from York Avenue, coming from Newport or Ryde.
See advert on this page

Whitecliff Bay Holiday Park
Hillway, Bembridge PO35 5PL
01983-872671 Fax 01983-872941
Open March-31 October

Set in an area of outstanding natural beauty, and an ideal base for the family to explore the Isle of Wight. Facilities available close by include outdoor pools, shops, entertainment and snack bars.
Size 40 acres, 400 touring pitches, 130 with electric hookup, 200 level pitches, 14 static caravans, 38, 68 WCs, 15 CWPs
£ car/tent £6.60-£9.80, car/caravan £6.60-£9.80, motorhome £6.60-£9.80, motorbike/tent £6.60-£9.80, children £1.90-£2.60
Rental Chalet.
CC MasterCard Visa
Calor Gaz WS
Last arrival time: 22:00
➡ Take A3055, turn onto B3395 at Brading and follow signs to Whitecliff Bay
See advert on this page

WHITECLIFF BAY HOLIDAY PARK
DEPT RAC, BEMBRIDGE, ISLE OF WIGHT PO35 5PL
TEL: 01983-872671 FAX: 01983-872941

CELEBRATING OVER 50 YEARS OF GREAT VALUE HOLIDAYS
- FERRY & HOLIDAY PACKAGES AVAILABLE
- OUTDOOR & INDOOR POOLS
- CLUBS & ENTERTAINMENT
- ELECTRIC HOOK UPS
- SUPER PITCHES
- GREAT LOCATION

PHONE TODAY FOR YOUR BROCHURE 01983-872671

ENGLAND

Kendal

KENDAL Cumbria — 10B2

Camping & Caravanning Club Site
Millcrest, Shap Road, Kendal LA9 6NY
☎ 01539-741363
Open March-November
Size 3 acres, 53 touring pitches, 37 with electric hookup, 4 ⛺, 6 WCs, 1 CWP
£ car/tent £11.50-£14.60, car/caravan £11.50-£14.60, motorhome £11.50-£14.60, motorbike/tent £11.50-£14.60, children £1.60
cc MasterCard Visa
Calor WS
Last arrival time: 23:00
➡ On the A6, 1½ miles north of Kendal, the site entrance is 100 yards north of nameplate "Skelsmergh".

Millness Hill Park
Crooklands, Milnthorpe LA7 7NU
☎ 01539-567306 Fax 01539-567306
Open 1 March-mid November
Size 5 acres, 15 touring pitches, 15 with electric hookup, 15 level pitches, 15 static caravans, 2 ⛺, 5 WCs, 1 CWP
£ car/tent £6.50-£8, car/caravan £6.50-£8, motorhome £6.50-£8, motorbike/tent £6.50-£8
Rental £140-£350, chalets £205-£555
Calor Gaz
Last arrival time: 21:00
➡ Exit M6 junction 36 onto A65 to Kirkby Lonsdale. Turn left at next roundabout signposted Endmoor and Crooklands. Site is 100 yards on left.

Waters Edge Caravan Park
Crooklands, Kendal LA7 7NN
☎ 015395-67708 Fax 015395-67610
Open 1 March-14 November
Size 3 acres, 30 touring pitches, 30 with electric hookup, 30 level pitches, 5 ⛺, 8 WCs, 1 CWP
£ car/tent £6.50, car/caravan £9.95-£13.50, motorhome £9.95-£13.50, motorbike/tent £6.50
Rental £150-£230
cc MasterCard Visa
Calor Gaz WS
Last arrival time: 23:00
➡ Located at Crooklands, ¾ miles along A65, M6 junction 36.

Hints & Tips
Tyres are your only contact with the road. Look after them and you will improve the safety and behaviour of your unit. Never mix cross ply and radials on the same axis.

KENNACK SANDS Cornwall — 2A4

Silver Sands Holiday Park
Gwendreath, Kennack Sands, Helston TR12 7LZ
☎ 01326-290631 Fax 01326-290631
Open May-September

View towards Nature Reserve, through which footpath leads to award-winning beach.
Size 9 acres, 34 touring pitches, 18 with electric hookup, 34 level pitches, 16 static caravans, 4 ⛺, 8 WCs, 1 CWP
£ car/tent £6-£7.50, car/caravan £6-£7.50, motorhome £6-£7.50, motorbike/tent £6-£7.50, children £1.10-£1.50
Rental £90-£350
Calor Gaz
Last arrival time: 22:00
➡ Take A3083 "The Lizard" out of Helston. Past Naval Air Station Culdrose, turn left onto B3293 (St Keverne) past Goonhilly Satellite Station. Turn right at crossroads, after 1½ miles sign on left indicating "Gwendreath." Site is about 1 mile down lane on right.

KESSINGLAND Suffolk — 9F3

Heathland Beach Caravan Park
London Road, Kessingland NR33 7PJ
☎ 01502-740337 Fax 01502-742355
Open Easter-October

Flat, grassy park surrounded by farmland close to the beach.
Size 30 acres, 106 touring pitches, 65 with electric hookup, 106 level pitches, 168 static caravans, 25 ⛺, 44 WCs, 3 CWPs
£ car/tent £10-£12, car/caravan £10-£12, motorhome £10-£12, motorbike/tent £10-£12,

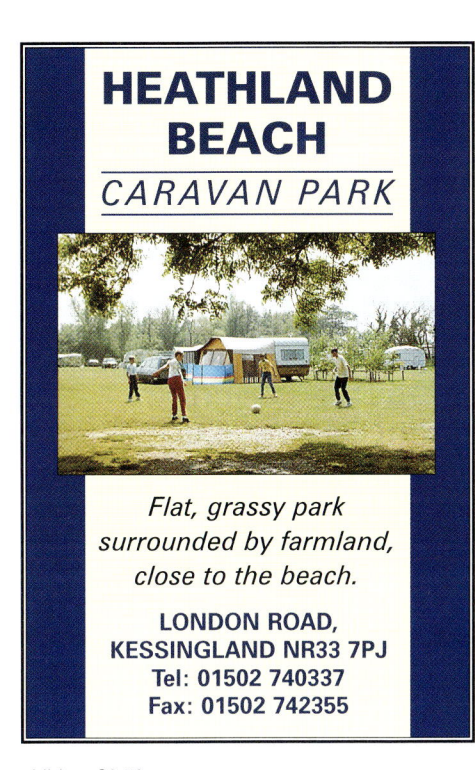

Keswick

HEATHLAND BEACH
CARAVAN PARK

Flat, grassy park surrounded by farmland, close to the beach.

LONDON ROAD, KESSINGLAND NR33 7PJ
Tel: 01502 740337
Fax: 01502 742355

children £0.50
Rental £195-£350
cc Visa
Last arrival time: 22:00
→ 1 mile N of Kessingland on B1437. 3 miles S of Lowestoft off A12.
See advert on this page

KESWICK Cumbria   10B2

Camping & Caravanning Club Site
Derwentwater, Keswick CA12 5EP
01768-772392
Open February-November
Size 14 acres, 250 touring pitches, 129 with electric hookup, 18, 26 WCs, 2 CWPs
£ car/tent £13.60-£14.60, car/caravan £13.60-£14.60, motorhome £13.60-£14.60, motorbike/tent £13.60-£14.60, children £1.60
cc MasterCard Visa
Calor WS
Last arrival time: 23:00
→ From Penrith take A66, ignore Keswick signs and follow road to roundabout, turn right onto A5271, take first right at bottom of road, site is adjacent to Rugby Club.
See picture of site on front cover.

Castlerigg Hall
Keswick
017687-72437 Fax 017687-72437
Open Easter-mid November

Castlerigg Hall Caravan & Camping Park overlooks Derwentwater with panoramic views of the surrounding fells. Fully serviced touring pitches available. Luxury holiday caravan for hire.
Size 15 acres, 53 touring pitches, 53 with electric hookup, 53 level pitches, 30 static caravans, 12, 26 WCs, 1 CWP
£ car/tent £6.20-£7.40, car/caravan £8.50-£10, motorhome £7-£8, motorbike/tent £5.70-£6.30, children £1.70-£2
Rental £150-£290
cc MasterCard Visa
Calor Gaz
Last arrival time: 21:00
→ 1½ miles SE of Keswick. Turn right off A591, 50 yards past Heights Hotel on the right.

Derwentwater Caravan Park
Crowe Park Road, Keswick CA12 5EN
017687-72579
Open 1 March-14 November

Situated on the shores of Derwentwater, with its own lake frontage and excellent views of the surrounding fells, yet convenient for the town.
Size 17.5 acres, 50 touring pitches, 50 with electric hookup, 50 level pitches, 160 static caravans, 10, 12 WCs, 2 CWPs
£ car/caravan £8.80-£9.60, motorhome £8.80-£9.60, children £2.20-£2.40
Calor Gaz
Last arrival time: 22:00
→ From M6 (jn 40) take A66 signposted Keswick for 13 miles and at roundabout signed Keswick turn left. At the T-junction turn left to Keswick town centre. At the mini roundabout turn right. In 200 yards bear right, and in 400 yards turn right. Park is right after the bend in the road.

ENGLAND

85

PENTNEY PARK
CARAVAN & CAMPING SITE

Best Placed for Beautiful Norfolk.

Our family run Park aims to provide high standards of cleanliness, service and a friendly welcome.

Areas for Family groups, and a quieter corner for others to relax.

Colour brochure available.

PENTNEY, KING'S LYNN, NORFOLK PE32 1HU
Tel: 01760 337479
Fax: 01760 338118

Gill Head Farm
Troutbeck, Keswick CA11 0ST
017687-79622
Open 1 April-10 November
Size 1.5 acres, 17 touring pitches, 17 with electric hookup, 17 level pitches, 17 static caravans, 4 ®, 8 WCs, 2 CWPs
£ car/tent £7-£10, car/caravan £7-£10, motorhome £7, motorbike/tent £7, children £3.50
Calor Gaz
Last arrival time: 22:00
➡ From A66 take A5091 for Ullswater. 100 yards through Troutbeck take right turn, then first right again.

KIDDERMINSTER Worcestershire   7E3

Camp Easy
The Old Vicarage Activity Centre, Stottesdon, Kidderminster DY14 8UH
01746-718436 Fax 01746-718420
Open March-October

Camp Easy is based in Ginny Hole Nature Reserve, situated on the outskirts of the village of Stottesdon. When you arrive a tent can be pitched and ready for you or use your own. Prices from £2.50.
Size 27 acres, 25 touring pitches, 25 level pitches, 4 ®, 4 WCs,
£ car/tent £6
Rental from £8-£10 per night, fully equipped
Calor
Last arrival time: 22:00
➡ B4194 from Budley, left on B4363, then first right signposted Stottesdon and follow signs.

Camping & Caravanning Club Site
Brown Westhead Park, Wolverley, Kidderminster DY10 3PX
01562-850909
Open March-November
Size 8.2 acres, 119 touring pitches, 72 with electric hookup, 6 ®, 12 WCs, 1 CWP
£ car/tent £10.40-£13.60, car/caravan £10.40-£13.60, motorhome £10.40-£13.60, motorbike/tent £10.40-£13.60, children £1.50
cc MasterCard Visa
Calor WS
Last arrival time: 23:00
➡ From Kidderminster A449 to Wolverhampton, turn left at traffic lights, B4189 signposted Wolverley. Look for brown camping sign, turn right, entrance on the left.

KIELDER Northumberland   13E3

Forestry Commission Kielder C & C Site
Kielder, Hexham NE48 1EP
01434-250291
Open end March-end September
Size 9 acres, 70 touring pitches, 32 with electric hookup, 50 level pitches, 6 ®, 9 WCs, 1 CWP
£ car/tent £7-£8.50, car/caravan £7-£8.50, motorhome £7-£8.50, motorbike/tent £7-£8.50
cc MasterCard Visa
Calor Gaz
Last arrival time: 22:00
➡ Site is 500 yards N of Kielder village, on right.

KING'S LYNN Norfolk   9D3

Pentney Park Caravan Site
Gayton Road, Narborough, King's Lynn PE32 1HU
01760-337479 Fax 01760-338118

Size 16 acres, 200 touring pitches, 156 with electric hookup, 190 level pitches, 16 ®, 44 WCs, 3 CWPs
£ car/tent £8-£10, car/caravan £8-£10, motorhome £8-£10, motorbike/tent £10, children £1.10-£1.40
Rental from £100
cc MasterCard Visa
Calor Gaz WS

Lacock

Last arrival time: 22:00
➜ On A47, midway between King's Lynn and Swaffham. Entrance on B1153, 150 yards from junction.
See advert on opposite page

Rickels Caravan Site

Bircham Road, Stanhoe, King's Lynn PE31 8PU
☎ 01485-518671 Fax 01485-518969
Open March-October ▲ ⌘ ⛟
Size 2 acres, 30 touring pitches, 26 with electric hookup, 20 level pitches, 4 ☗, 7 WCs, 1 CWP
£ car/tent £7.50-£8.50, car/caravan £7.50-£8.50, motorhome £7.50-£8.50, motorbike/tent £8.50, children £0.50
Rental ⌘
☏ ▯ ⚠ Calor Gaz ✈ WS
Last arrival time: 22:00
➜ Take A148 (Cromer Road) for 4 miles to Hillington. Continue through village and turn left onto B1153 to Great Bircham. Proceed through Bircham and on a left hand bend fork right onto B1155, follow to main crossroads (Fakenham right, Docking left). Continue straight over, site is situated 200 yards on left.

KINGSBRIDGE Devon 2C4

Camping & Caravanning Club Site

Middle Grounds, Slapton, Kingsbridge TQ7 1QW
☎ 01548-580538
Open March-November ▲ ⌘ ⛟
Size 5.5 acres, 115 touring pitches, 24 with electric hookup, 6 ☗, 9 WCs, 1 CWP
£ car/tent £11.50-£14.60, car/caravan £11.50-£14.60, motorhome £11.50-£14.60, motorbike/tent £11.50-£14.60, children £1.60
☾ MasterCard Visa
⛺ ⛺¼ ✗¼ ● ▯ ☏ ▤ ▦ ☐ ▥ GR ☒ TV ⚠ Calor ♿ ✈ WS
Last arrival time: 23:00
➜ On A379 from Kingsbridge, the site entrance is ¼ mile from A379, beyond the brow of the hill approaching Slapton village.

Karrageen Camping & Caravan Park

Bolberry, Malborough, Kingsbridge TQ7 3EN
☎ 01548-561230 Fax 01548-560192
Open 15 March-15 November ▲ ⌘ ⛟

A small family park offering panoramic rural and sea views - the closest park to the beaches at Hope Cove and only ¾ mile from the National Trust Coastal Path. Level pitches with a view, disabled/family shower room.
Size 7.5 acres, 75 touring pitches, 54 with electric hookup, 75 level pitches, 20 static caravans, 9 ☗, 10 WCs, 1 CWP
£ car/tent £6-£8.50, car/caravan £7-£10, motorhome £6-£8.50, motorbike/tent £6-£7.50, children £0.50
⛺ ● ▯ ☏ ▯ Calor Gaz ♿ ✈
➜ Take A381 from Kingsbridge to Salcombe. Turn sharp right through Malborough, after 0.6 mile turn right signposted Bolberry. After 0.9 mile site is on right. Reception on left at Karrageen House.

LACOCK Wiltshire 4A3

Piccadilly Caravan Site

Folly Lane West, Lacock SN15 2LP
☎ 01249-730260
Open 1 April-31 October ▲ ⌘ ⛟

Located in countryside half a mile from the historic National Trust village of Lacock, the site is an ideal touring centre for Bath and the Cotswolds.
Size 2.5 acres, 40 touring pitches, 34 with electric hookup, 40 level pitches, 4 ☗, 6 WCs, 1 CWP
£ car/tent £7-£8.50, car/caravan £7-£8.50, motorhome £7-£8.50, motorbike/tent £7-£8.50
⛺¼ ✗¼ ▯ ☏ ▯ Calor Gaz ✈
Last arrival time: 22:00
➜ Turn right off A350 Chippenham to Melksham road signposted Gastard (with caravan symbol) into Folly Lane West. Site on left in 300 yards.

Hints & Tips

In winter take your seat cushions home. Not only will they keep dry but a caravan without cushions is a less attractive prospect to thieves.

88

Land's End

| LAND'S END Cornwall | 2A4 |

Cardinney Caravan & Camping Park
Land's End TR19 6HJ
☎ 01736-810880
Open February-November ▲ 🚐 🚗
Size 4.5 acres, 105 touring pitches, 50 with electric hookup, 40 level pitches, 2 static caravans, 6 🚿, 11 WCs, 1 CWP
£ car/tent £4.50-£7.50, car/caravan £4.50-£7.50, motorhome £4.50-£7.50, motorbike/tent £4.50-£7.50, children £0.50-£0.75
Rental 🚐 from £75-£195
cc MasterCard Visa
🐕 ✕ 🍴 🛒 🎮 📺 Calor Gaz 🐾
Last arrival time: 00:00
➜ 5 miles W of Penzance on A30. Towards Land's End, park on right before village of Crows-an-Wra.

| LANGPORT Somerset | 3E2 |

Bowdens Crest Caravan Park
Bowdens, Langport TA10 0DD
☎ 01458-250553 Fax 01458-250553
Open 16 March-30 November ▲ 🚐 🚗

Tranquil site overlooking the Somerset Levels with short breaks available. Vineyard and woodland walks, near cycle and walking routes and fishing. Separate rally field available.
Size 16 acres, 30 touring pitches, 28 with electric hookup, 30 level pitches, 30 static caravans, 4 🚿, 7 WCs, 1 CWP
£ car/tent £7, car/caravan £7, motorhome £7, motorbike/tent £7, children £1
Rental 🚐 £100-£245 per week
cc MasterCard Visa
🐕 🛒 Calor Gaz ♿ 🐾 WS
Last arrival time: 23:00
➜ Off A372 between Langport and Bridgwater.

| LEEDS West Yorkshire | 11D3 |

Moor Lodge Caravan Park
Blackmoor Lane, Bardsey, Leeds LS17 9DZ
☎ 01937-572424
Open all year ▲ 🚐 🚗

Peaceful, immaculate, countryside park.
Size 7.5 acres, 12 touring pitches, 12 with electric hookup, 12 level pitches, 60 static caravans, 4 🚿, 4 WCs, 1 CWP
£ car/tent £7.50, car/caravan £7.50, motorhome £7.50, motorbike/tent £7.50, children £1
🐕¼ ✕¼ 🍴 🛒 Calor Gaz ♿ 🐾 WS
➜ Take A58 from Leeds towards Wetherby. Cross over roundabout on outskirts of Leeds. After one third of a mile when street lights finish, turn left at next crossroad and follow caravan signs.

Roundhay Caravan & Camping Park
Elmete Lane, Leeds LS8 2LQ
☎ 0113-265 9354 Fax 0113-237 0077
Open 1 March-8 November ▲ 🚐 🚗

Set in 700 acres of glorious parkland, including one of the top attractions in England, Tropical World. The site is an ideal touring base for the city of Leeds, Royal Armouries, York, Harrogate and the Yorkshire Dales.
Size 6 acres, 60 touring pitches, 50 with electric hookup, 60 level pitches, 4 🚿, 6 WCs, 1 CWP
£ car/tent £6, car/caravan £9.50, motorhome £9, motorbike/tent £6
🐕 🍴¼ 🛒 ⚡ 🏔 Calor Gaz ♿ 🐾
Last arrival time: 22:00
➜ Signposted from A58.

| LEEK Staffordshire | 7E1 |

Camping & Caravanning Club Site
Blackshaw Grange, Blackshaw Moor, Leek ST13 8TL
☎ 01538-300285
Open January-December ▲ 🚐 🚗
Size 6 acres, 60 touring pitches, 30 with electric hookup, 4 🚿, 6 WCs, 1 CWP

Lewes

£ car/tent £10.40-£13.60, car/caravan £10.40-£13.60, motorhome £10.40-£13.60, motorbike/tent £10.40-£13.60, children £1.50
cc MasterCard Visa
Calor WS
Last arrival time: 23:00
→ Just two miles from Leek on the main A53 Leek to Buxton Road. The site is located 200 yards past the sign for "Blackshaw Moor" on the left hand side of the road.

LEISTON Suffolk   9F4

Cakes & Ale Park
Abbey Lane, Theberton, Leiston IP16 4TE
☎ 01728-831655 Fax 01473-736270
Open 1 April-31 October

A fully serviced site in tranquil parkland with a golf driving range and practice nets, and a large mown recreation area. Nearby is an indoor pool and the area offers superb walking and cycling. Minsmere, Dunwich, Southwold, Aldeburgh and Snape are within easy distance.
Size 45 acres, 50 touring pitches, 50 with electric hookup, 50 level pitches, 150 static caravans, 20, 20 WCs, 2 CWPs
£ car/tent £10-£14, car/caravan £10-£14, motorhome £10-£14, motorbike/tent £10-£14
Rental from £180 weekly.
cc MasterCard Visa
Calor Gaz WS
Last arrival time: 21:00
→ From A12 take B1121 to Saxmundham. At the crossroads in Saxmundham, take B1119 to Leiston. Turn onto minor road 3 miles from Saxmundham and follow signs.

LEOMINSTER Herefordshire   7D3

Shobdon Airfield Touring Site
Leominster HR6 9NR
☎ 01568-708369 Fax 01568-708935
Open February-6 January
Size 5 acres, 35 touring pitches, 4 with electric hookup, 35 level pitches, 12 static caravans, 8, 8 WCs, 1 CWP

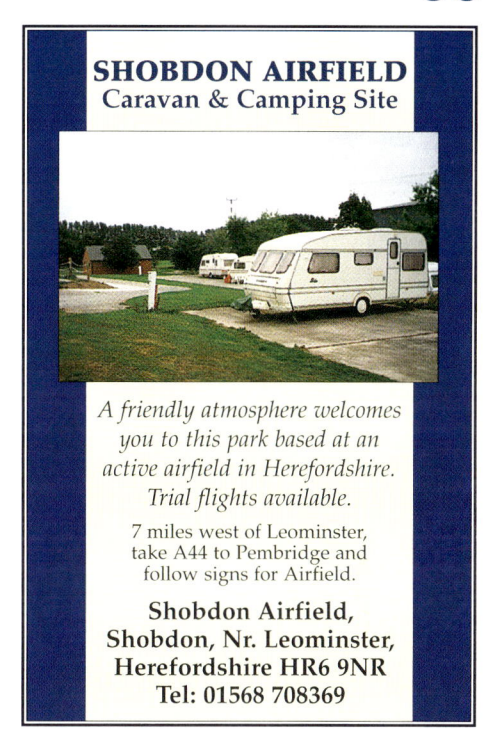

SHOBDON AIRFIELD
Caravan & Camping Site

A friendly atmosphere welcomes you to this park based at an active airfield in Herefordshire. Trial flights available.

7 miles west of Leominster, take A44 to Pembridge and follow signs for Airfield.

**Shobdon Airfield,
Shobdon, Nr. Leominster,
Herefordshire HR6 9NR
Tel: 01568 708369**

£ car/tent £2-£6, car/caravan £3.50-£5, motorhome £3.50-£5, motorbike/tent £2-£6, children £2-£6
cc MasterCard Visa
WS
Last arrival time: 21:00
See advert on this page

LEWES East Sussex   5D4

Bluebell Holiday Park
The Broyle, Shortgate, Ringmer, Lewes BN8 6PJ
☎ 01825-840407
Open 1 April-31 October

Quiet rural park sheltered by trees. No club, swimming pool or playground, just peace and quiet, and an abundance of wild life. Luxury caravans for hire.
Size 2.5 acres, 20 touring pitches, 10 with electric hookup, 20 level pitches, 4 static caravans, 4, 7 WCs, 1 CWP

Bluebell Holiday Park

£ car/tent £7.50, car/caravan £7.50, motorhome £7.50, motorbike/tent £7.50
Rental £90-£250
✕¼ ●¼ Calor Gaz
Last arrival time: 21:00
➜ From A22 Halland roundabout take B2192 to Ringmer. Site is 1½ miles on left behind Bluebell Inn.

LEYBURN North Yorkshire   10C2

Constable Burton Hall Caravan Park
Leyburn DL8 5LJ
☎ 01677-450428   Fax 01677-450622
Open April-October
Size 10 acres, 120 touring pitches, 120 with electric hookup, 120 level pitches, 9, 13 WCs, 3 CWPs
£ car/tent £7.50-£8.50, car/caravan £7.50-£8.50, motorhome £7.50-£8.50, children £0.75
✕¼ ●¼ Calor Gaz
Last arrival time: 22:00
➜ 8 miles W of A1 on A684 between Bedale and Leyburn.

LINGFIELD Surrey   5D3

Long Acres Caravan & Camping Park
Newchapel Road., Lingfield RH7 6LE
☎ 01342-833205   Fax 01342-834307
Open all year
Size 40 acres, 60 touring pitches, 60 with electric hookup, 50 level pitches, 6, 10 WCs, 3 CWPs
£ car/tent £8, car/caravan £8, motorhome £8, motorbike/tent £8, children £1.50
✕¼ ●¼ Calor Gaz WS
Last arrival time: 21:00
➜ From M25 junction 6 take A22 to East Grinstead. At Newchapel roundabout turn left onto B2028 to Lingfield. Site is on right (700 yards).

LONDON   5D2

For sites within the M25 see under LOUGHTON in the North and CHERTSEY in the South.

LONGTOWN Cumbria   13E4

Camelot Caravan Park
Sandysike, Longtown CA6 5SZ
☎ 01228-791248
Open March-October
Size 5 acres, 20 touring pitches, 6 with electric hookup, 20 level pitches, 2, 4 WCs, 1 CWP
£ car/tent £5.70-£6, car/caravan £6.70-£7, motorhome £6.70-£7, motorbike/tent £5.70-£6, children £0.50
Calor Gaz WS

Last arrival time: flexible
➜ Leave M6 at junction 44. Site on right off A7 in 4 miles, 1 mile S of Longtown.

LOOE Cornwall   2B4

Carbeil Caravan & Camping Park
Downderry, Looe
☎ 01503-250636   Fax 01503-250636
Open 31 March-31 October

A family-run site nestling in a picturesque valley. An ideal location for exploring local towns, villages and beaches.
Size 1.25 acres, 22 touring pitches, 6 with electric hookup, 4 static caravans, 4, 7 WCs, 1 CWP
Rental
✕ ● WS
Last arrival time: 21:30
➜ From A387, turn S onto B3247 for Seaton, and continue towards Downderry. Left at St Nicholas Church for site.

Looe Valley Touring Park
Polperro Road, Looe PL12 2JS
☎ 01503-262425   Fax 01503-265411
Open May-end September

Level well drained pitches, set in glorious countryside and close to sandy beaches. Electrical hookups, free swimming pool, entertainment and children's club. New management for 1999.

Looe

Looe Valley Touring Park

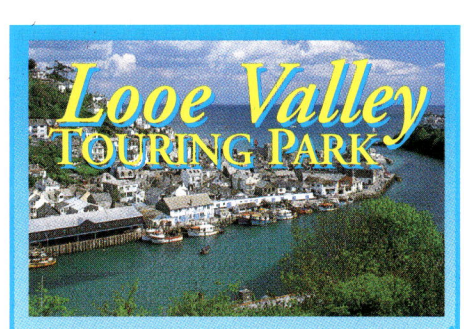

Looe Valley, formerly Treble B, is set in glorious countryside and is ideally situated for touring beautiful South East Cornwall.

- NEW for '99 ~ Eurotents
- FREE heated swimming pool
- Licensed club
- FREE entertainment & children's club
- TV & Games rooms
- Shop, Restaurant, Takeaway & Laundry
- 4 large toilet blocks
- FREE hot water for washing & showers
- Level well drained pitches with electric hook-ups
- Holiday homes & apartments available
- Rallies welcome
- Semi seasonal pitches & winterisation available

Looe Valley Touring Park, Polperro Road, Looe PL13 2JS

01503 262425
FAX: 01503 265411 Quote:RC

Size 22 acres, 557 touring pitches, 265 with electric hookup, 450 level pitches, 30 static caravans, 44, 100 WCs, 4 CWPs
£ car/tent £7-£10.90, car/caravan £7-£10.90, motorhome £7-£10.90, motorbike/tent £7-£10.90
Rental Chalet. £63-£350
CC MasterCard Visa
Calor Gaz WS
Last arrival time: 23:00
➜ 2 miles W of Looe on A387. Observe sign. See advert on this page

Polborder House Caravan & Camping Park
Bucklawren Road, St Martins, Looe PL13 1QR
☏ 01503-240265 Fax 01503-240700
Open April-October
Size 3 acres, 31 touring pitches, 28 with electric hookup, 36 level pitches, 5 static caravans, 9, 16 WCs, 1 CWP
£ car/tent £6-£8.50, car/caravan £6-£8.50, motorhome £6-£8.50, motorbike/tent £4-£5, children £0.75-£1
Rental Chalet. £120-£295
Calor Gaz
Last arrival time: 22:00
➜ 2½ miles E of Looe, turn off B3253 signposted Polborder & Monkey Sanctuary. Site ½ mile on right.

Tencreek Caravan Park
Looe PL13 2JR
☏ 01503-262447 Fax 01503-262447
Open all year

Site offering panoramic views of sea and countryside, perfectly situated for Looe and Polperro. Facilities include heated swimming pool, laundry and clubhouse with entertainment.
Size 16 acres, 250 touring pitches, 200 with electric hookup, 250 level pitches, 62 static caravans, 24, 40 WCs, 2 CWPs
£ car/tent £7.30-£11.75, car/caravan £7.30-£11.75, motorhome £7.30-£11.75, motorbike/tent £7.30-£11.75, children £1.30-£1.85
Rental £90-£340 weekly
CC MasterCard Visa
Calor Gaz WS
Last arrival time: 23:00
➜ From A38 turn right onto A387 for Looe. Travel through Looe town, over bridge and up hill. Approximately 1½ miles from bridge.

Trelay Farmpark
Pelynt, Looe PL13 2JX
☏ 01503-220 900 Fax 01503-220900
Open Easter-end October
Size 5 acres, 55 touring pitches, 23 with electric hookup, 27 level pitches, 20 static caravans, 5, 11 WCs, 1 CWP
£ car/tent £7-£8.50, car/caravan £7-£8.50, motorhome £7-£8.50, motorbike/tent £7-£8.50, children £1-£1.50
Rental £140-£250
Calor
Last arrival time: 23:00
➜ From A38 2 miles W of Liskeard at Dobwalls turn onto A390 for Lostwithiel. Shortly after East Taphouse turn left onto B3359 to Pelynt. Trelay is ½ mile past Pelynt on left. Or from A387 Polperro/Looe road, take A3359 ½ mile before Pelynt on right.

Hints & Tips

Tiredness can kill. If you are planning a long journey make sure you plan some breaks.

ENGLAND

Lostwithiel

LOSTWITHIEL Cornwall — 2B4

Powderham Castle Touring Park
Lanlivery, Lostwithiel PL30 5BU
☎ 01208-872277
Open 1 April-31 October

A quiet, uncommercialised park appealing to the more discerning tourist. Spacious perimeter pitches in enclosed paddocks. Approved and recommended by all revelant touring organisations.
Size 10 acres, 75 touring pitches, 75 with electric hookup, 75 level pitches, 38 static caravans, 8 🚿, 20 WCs, 2 CWPs
£ car/tent £6.50-£9, car/caravan £6.50-£9, motorhome £6.50-£9, motorbike/tent £4-£6, children £0.50-£1.20
Calor Gaz WS
Last arrival time: 22:00
➔ 1½ miles SW of Lostwithiel on A390, turn right at sign to the site. Go up road for 400 yards.

LOUGHTON Essex — 5D2

Debden House Campsite
Debden Green, Loughton IG10 2PA
☎ 0181-508 3008   Fax 0181-508 0284

Set within the beautiful countryside of Epping Forest, but within easy reach of London by road or Underground. Newly refurbished toilet blocks on site.
Size 48.5 acres, 150 touring pitches, 60 with electric hookup, 150 level pitches, 10 🚿, 18 WCs, 2 CWPs
Calor Gaz

DEBDEN HOUSE CENTRE
LONDON'S FOREST CAMPSITE

A 50-acre site of flat and gently sloping meadowland encompassed by the beautiful woodlands of Epping Forest.

Electric Hookups • Spacious Pitches • Shop • Cafe
Laundrette • Showers • Children's Play Area • Telephone
Postbox • New Orienteering Course

LOCALLY: Historic buildings, Swimming, Horseriding, Golf, Bicycle hire and a wide range of Shopping and Dining outlets.

40 mins. from central London by Central line LT
(from Debden or Loughton).
Ideal base for Tourers/Sightseers.

OPEN APRIL 1ST – OCTOBER 31ST

NEWHAM

Further details
DEBDEN GREEN,
LOUGHTON, ESSEX IG10 2PA
Tel: 0181 508 3008   Fax: 0181 508 0284

Last arrival time: 23:30
➔ From M25 junction 26 take A121 to Loughton. At double mini roundabout, turn left onto A1168 Rectory Lane, then take second left into Pyrles Lane.
See advert on this page

LOWESTOFT Suffolk — 9F3

Camping & Caravanning Club Site
Suffolk Wildlife Park, Whites Lane, Kessingland, Lowestoft
☎ 01502-742040
Open March-November
Size 6.5 acres, 90 touring pitches, 53 with electric hookup, 10 🚿, 9 WCs, 1 CWP
£ car/tent £10.40-£13.60, car/caravan £10.40-£13.60, motorhome £10.40-£13.60, motorbike/tent £10.40-£13.60, children £1.50
ℂℂ MasterCard Visa
Calor WS
Last arrival time: 23:00
➔ On A12 from Lowestoft at Kessingland roundabout follow Wildlife Park signs, turn right through park entrance.

Carlton Manor Caravan Site
Chapel Road, Carlton Colville, Lowestoft NR33 8BL
☎ 01502-566511   Fax 01502-573949
Open 1 April-31 October
Size 9.5 acres, 90 touring pitches, 60 with electric hookup, 12 🚿, 10 WCs, 2 CWPs

Lyndhurst

CARLTON MANOR

The touring caravan park is set in 9 acres of beautiful parkland, with childrens play area bouncy castle. The park is open from Easter through to October 31st, licensed for 90 units and has ample electric hook up and wash room facilities.

Facilities at a glance: Easily accessible and level siting. Full use of the hotel facilities. Restaurant. Bar/TV lounge.

Places of interest nearby: Oulton Broad, Gateway to the Broads network. Lowestoft (centre), all major shops in the high street. Beach (2 miles) holds the EC Blue flag award. East Anglian Transport Museum situated next door to our hotel.

Carlton Colville, Lowestoft, Suffolk NR33 8BL
Tel: (01502) 566511 Fax: (01502) 573949

£ car/tent £5.50-£8.25, car/caravan £7-£9.75, motorhome £7.50, motorbike/tent £5.50-£8.25
cc MasterCard Visa
✕ ⛟ 📞 ⊟ ⚠ ⚡ Calor ★ WS
➜ From A12 or A146 follow signs to Transport Museum. Site next door on B1384.
See advert on this page

Whitehouse Farm
Gisleham, Kessingland NR33 8DX
📞 01502-740248 Fax 01502-740248
Open Easter-October ⛺ 🚐 🚍
Size 5 acres, 40 touring pitches, 34 with electric hookup, 40 level pitches, 6 🚿, 6 WCs, 1 CWP
£ car/tent £7-£8, car/caravan £7-£8, motorhome £7-£8
⛟¼ ✕¼ ⛟¼ 📞 ⊟ ⚠ Calor Gaz ♿ ★ WS
Last arrival time: 22:00
➜ In Kessingland (A12), turn W opposite Wildlife Park. Right at second junction, site 220 yards.

LYME REGIS Dorset   3E3

Hook Farm Camping & Caravan Park
Gole Lane, Uplyme, Lyme Regis DT7 3UU
📞 01297-442801 Fax 01297-442801
Open all year ⛺ 🚐 🚍
Size 10 acres, 100 touring pitches, 24 with electric hookup, 8 🚿, 24 WCs, 1 CWP
£ car/tent £7-£9, motorhome £6-£8, children £1-£1.50
Rental ⛺ 🚐 farmhouse B&B available
⛟ ⊟ 📞 ⊟ ⚠ Calor Gaz ♿ ★

Last arrival time: flexible
➜ From A3052 turn right 2 miles W of Lyme Regis, from A35, two miles along B3165 to Uplyme.

Shrubbery Caravan Park
Rousdon, Lyme Regis DT7 3XW
📞 01297-442227
Open March-November ⛺ 🚐 🚍

The park is a quiet, level site covering about ten acres situated between Lyme Regis and Seaton. This part of Devon remains unspoilt by commercialism and has uncrowded beaches.
Size 10.5 acres, 120 touring pitches, 90 with electric hookup, 120 level pitches, 14 🚿, 21 WCs, 1 CWP
£ car/tent £6.25-£7.75, car/caravan £6.25-£7.75, motorhome £5.50-£7, motorbike/tent £5.50-£7, children £0.75
⛟¼ ⊟ 📞 ⊟ ⚠ Calor Gaz ♿ ★ WS
Last arrival time: 22:00
➜ 3 miles W of Lyme Regis on A3052 at village of Rousdon.

LYNDHURST Hampshire   4B4

Forestry Commission Denny Wood
Beaulieu Road, Lyndhurst SO43 7FZ
📞 01703-283771
Open end March-end September 🚐 🚍
Size 15 acres, 170 touring pitches, 100 level pitches, 1 CWP
£ car/caravan £5.50-£6.70, motorhome £5.50-£6.70
cc MasterCard Visa
Last arrival time: 22:00
➜ Take B3056 from Lyndhurst. Site is 2.5 miles on right.

Forestry Commission Matley Wood Campsite
Beaulieu Road, Lyndhurst SO43 7FZ
📞 01703-283771
Open end March-end September 🚐 🚍
Size 15 acres, 70 touring pitches, 70 level pitches, 1 CWP
£ car/caravan £5.50-£6.70, motorhome £5.50-£6.70
cc MasterCard Visa
★
Last arrival time: 22:00
➜ Take B3056 from Lyndhurst. Site is two miles on left.

ENGLAND

94

Lyndhurst

Forestry Commission Ocknell Campsite
Fritham, Lyndhurst SO43 7NH
☎ 01703-283771 Fax 01703-283929
Open end March-end September ▲ ⊕ ⊟
Size 47 acres, 480 touring pitches, 200 level pitches, 19 WCs, 2 CWPs
£ car/tent £6-£8.70, car/caravan £6-£8.70, motorhome £6-£8.70, motorbike/tent £6-£8.70
cc MasterCard Visa
Last arrival time: 22:00
➡ From A31 take B3079 at Cadnam through Brook and Fritham.

LYNTON Devon   2C2

Camping & Caravanning Club Site
Caffyns Cross, Lynton EX35 6JS
☎ 01598-752379
Open March-November ▲ ⊕ ⊟
Size 5.5 acres, 105 touring pitches, 50 with electric hookup, 10, 17 WCs, 1 CWP
£ car/tent £10.40-£13.60, car/caravan £10.40-£13.60, motorhome £10.40-£13.60, motorbike/tent £10.40-£13.60, children £1.50
cc MasterCard Visa
WS
Last arrival time: 23:00
➡ Turn N off A39, signposted Caffyns, then turn right.

Channel View Caravan Park
Manor Farm, Barbrook, Lynton EX35 6LD
☎ 01598-753349
Open March-October ▲ ⊕ ⊟

A warm welcome awaits you at this quiet family run site. Situated on the edge of Exmoor National Park with spectacular views.
Size 9 acres, 70 touring pitches, 40 with electric hookup, 40 level pitches, 29 static caravans, 11, 20 WCs, 1 CWP
£ car/tent £7-£8, car/caravan £7.50-£8.50, motorhome £7-£8, motorbike/tent £7-£7.50, children £0.50-£1
Rental ⊕ £30 per night
cc MasterCard Visa
Last arrival time: 22:00
➡ On main A39, ½ mile from Barbrook village.

LYTHAM ST ANNES Lancashire   10B4

Bank Lane Caravan Park
Warton, Preston
☎ 01772-633513
Open March-October ▲ ⊕ ⊟

Bank Lane Caravan Park has been architecturally designed, popular and highly praised by visitors. With modern facilities all holiday homes are situated in spacious cul-de-sacs. Tourers very welcome.
Size 15 acres, 50 touring pitches, 50 with electric hookup, 40 level pitches, 160 static caravans, 5, 8 WCs, 2 CWPs
£ car/tent £7-£8, car/caravan £7, motorhome £7, motorbike/tent £7, children £7
Calor & ⊁ WS
Last arrival time: 22:00
➡ M6 (jn 31) to Blackpool. Join A584 Freckleton/Lytham, past BAE. Turn left at art gallery/ladies hairdressers. Follow the lane to site.

Eastham Hall Caravan Park
Saltcotes Road, Lytham St Annes FY8 4LS
☎ 01253-737907
Open 1 March-31 October ⊕ ⊟
Size 25 acres, 140 touring pitches, 72 with electric hookup, 140 level pitches, 250 static caravans, 10, 52 WCs, 10 CWPs
£ car/caravan £10-£11.50, motorhome £10-£11.50, children £0.75-£1
Calor Gaz & ⊁ WS
Last arrival time: 20:00
➡ Take A584 from Preston, turn right onto B5259 and site is ¾ mile on the right.

MABLETHORPE Lincolnshire   11F4

Camping & Caravanning Club Site
Highfield, Church Lane, Mablethorpe LN12 2NU
☎ 01507-472374
Open March-September ▲ ⊕ ⊟
Size 6 acres, 105 touring pitches, 60 with electric hookup, 4, 11 WCs,
£ car/tent £9.60-£12.10, car/caravan £9.60-£12.10, motorhome £9.60-£12.10, motorbike/tent £9.60-£12.10, children £1.50
cc MasterCard Visa

Maidenhead

⚡¼ ✕¼ 🚐 🚐¼ 🚿 📞 ▶ 💧 GR 🍳 TV ⛽ Calor ♿ 🐕 WS
Last arrival time: 23:00
➡ On outskirts of Mablethorpe, on A1104, just after the "Welcome to Mablethorpe" sign, petrol station on right, turn into Church Lane and drive 800 yards to end of lane. The site is on right.

Golden Sands Holiday Park
Quebec Road, Mablethorpe LN12 1QJ
📞 01507-477871
Open Easter-October 🚶 🚐 🚌
Size 23 acres, 320 touring pitches, 189 with electric hookup, 320 level pitches, 1,300 static caravans, 3 CWPs
Rental 🚐
ℂℂ MasterCard Visa
⚡ ✕ 🚐 🚿 📞 ▶ 🍳 ⛽ ⚔ Calor Gaz 🐕
➡ From Mablethorpe town centre follow seafront road to N end for Golden Sands. About 1 mile.

Kirkstead Holiday Park
North Road, Trusthorpe, Mablethorpe LN12 2QD
📞 01507-441483
Open March-December 🚶 🚐 🚌
Size 6 acres, 60 touring pitches, 50 with electric hookup, 60 level pitches, 60 static caravans, 6 🚿, 10 WCs, 1 CWP
£ car/tent £6, car/caravan £6.50-£10, motorhome £6.50-£10, motorbike/tent £6
Rental 🚐 £80-£200
⚡ ⚡¼ ✕ ✕¼ 🚐 🚐¼ 🚿 📞 ▶ 🍳 GR TV ⚔ Calor ♿ 🐕 WS
Last arrival time: 00:00
➡ On A52 coast road between Mablethorpe and Sutton-on-Sea. Turn off Trusthorpe Island for signs to Kirkstead Holiday Park.

Trusthorpe Springs Leisure Park
Trusthorpe Hall, Mile Lane, Trusthorpe, Mablethorpe LN12 2QQ
📞 01507-441333 Fax 01507-441333
Open 1 March-30 November 🚐 🚌
Size 4 acres, 22 touring pitches, 22 with electric hookup, 22 level pitches, 109 static caravans, 8 🚿, 30 WCs, 5 CWPs
£ car/caravan £6-£7.50
Rental 🚶 🚐 £25 daily, £185 weekly.
℃ℂ MasterCard Visa
⚡ ✕ 🚐 🚿 📞 ▶ ⛽ ⚔ Calor ♿ 🐕
Last arrival time: 17:00
➡ Enter Mablethorpe on A1104, right at Cross Inn public house into Mile Lane. Site on corner, 1 mile from Cross Inn.
See advert on this page

MAIDENHEAD Berkshire   4C2

Hurley Caravan & Camping Park
Hurley Farm, Hurley, Maidenhead SL6 5NE
📞 01628-823501 Fax 01628-825533
Open March-October 🚶 🚐 🚌

Hurley Farm is situated on the south bank of the River Thames. An ideal touring centre for London, Windsor (Legoland), Oxford and the Thames Valley.
Size 400 acres, 200 touring pitches, 146 with electric hookup, 200 level pitches, 450 static caravans, 27 🚿, 36 WCs, 4 CWPs
£ car/tent £5.50-£11, car/caravan £6.50-£12, motorhome £6.50-£12, children £1
Rental 🚐 4-6 berth caravans - £140-£280 per week
℃ℂ MasterCard Visa
⚡ ⚡¼ ✕¼ 🚐 📞 ▶ 🍳 Calor Gaz ♿ 🐕
Last arrival time: 22:00
➡ From M4 (jn 8/9) take A404. At the 3rd exit at A4130 signposted Hurley. After 2 miles follow park signs to Shepherd's House, 1m W of Hurley village.

TRUSTHORPE
Springs

Being less than a mile from the coast, the Park offers seaside location but in a woodland setting in the grounds of Trusthorpe Hall, a fine Georgian House built in 1830.
The park has it's own licensed club – The Cartwheel – which throughout the season has much live entertainment for all ages. Children too, are important and facilities are provided for their needs.
The heated swimming pool located in the centre of the park, always catches the sun and provides an ideal focal point during the day for those who just want to relax.

**Trusthorpe Hall, Mile Lane, Trusthorpe,
Mablethorpe, Lincolnshire LN12 2QQ
Tel: (01507) 441384**

ENGLAND

95

Maidstone

MAIDSTONE Kent 5E3

Pine Lodge Touring Park
Ashford Road, Hollingbourne, Maidstone ME17 1XH
01622-730018 Fax 01622-734498
Open all year

Ideally placed for touring Kent (Leeds Castle is only a mile away) and within easy reach of the Channel ports and the Channel Tunnel. New facilities block. Open all year. Sorry no dogs.
Size 7 acres, 100 touring pitches, 80 with electric hookup, 100 level pitches, 8, 11 WCs, 1 CWP
£ car/tent £9-£10, car/caravan £9-£10, motorhome £9-£10, motorbike/tent £7, children £0.50
MasterCard Visa
Calor Gaz WS
Last arrival time: 22:00
→ From junction 8 on A20 roundabout turn off towards Bearsted and Maidstone. Pine Lodge is on left after 1 mile.

RELAX at this scenic riverside park

CALL FREE 0800 146 505 FOR A BROCHURE

Set in 22 acres, this scenic riverside park is the ideal location for that relaxing break away.

A clean site with modern facilities, its own boating lake, two children's play areas, modern toilet and shower facilities, cycling and fishing nearby and over 180 pitches.

SHERWOOD FOREST CARAVAN PARK

Sherwood Forest Caravan Park, nr Edwinstowe, Mansfield, Nottinghamshire, NG1 9HW. Fax: 01623 824 637

MALMESBURY Wiltshire 4A2

Burton Hill Caravan & Camping Park
Burton Hill, Malmesbury SN16 0EH
01666-826880 Fax 01666-822585
Open 1 April-30 November
Size 2 acres, 30 touring pitches, 18 with electric hookup, 30 level pitches, 2, 4 WCs, 1 CWP
£ car/tent £7, car/caravan £7, motorhome £7, motorbike/tent £7, children £0.50
Calor Gaz WS
Last arrival time: 00:00
→ 200 yards S of roundabout at junction of A429, B4014 and B4042, turn W off A429 opposite Malmesbury Hospital (Arches Lane) and follow signs.

MALVERN Worcestershire 7E4

Camping & Caravanning Club Site
Blackmore Camp Site No. 2, Hanley Swan WR8 0EE
01684-310280
Open March-November
Size 12 acres, 200 touring pitches, 102 with electric hookup, 12, 14 WCs, 2 CWPs
£ car/tent £10.40-£13.60, car/caravan £10.40-£13.60, motorhome £10.40-£13.60, motorbike/tent £10.40-£13.60, children £1.50
MasterCard Visa
Calor WS
Last arrival time: 23:00
→ A38 to Upton on Severn. Turn N over river bridge. Take second left, then first left signed Hanley Swan. The site is on right after 1 mile.

MANSFIELD Nottinghamshire 8B2

Sherwood Forest Caravan Park
Cavendish Lodge, Old Clipstone, Mansfield NG21 9HW
0800-146505 Fax 01623-823132
Open March-October

Quiet country park in the heart of Robin Hood country. Some pitches overlook lake and river. Rural atmosphere with wildlife around. Excellent area for walking and cycling.

Market Rasen

Size 22 acres, 170 touring pitches, 137 with electric hookup, 21 🚿, 25 WCs, 5 CWPs
£ car/tent £7.20–£14.45, car/caravan £7.20–£14.45, motorhome £7.20–£14.45, motorbike/tent £7.20–£14.45
℃ MasterCard Visa
🏪 ✕¼ 🚰¼ 🔌 🔋 GR 📶 TV ⛽ Calor Gaz ♿ 🐕
➡ Best approach is via Ollerton-Mansfield road A6075; turn S towards Old Clipstone opposite turning to Warsop and ½ mile to park. From M1 take exit 27 from S and 30 from N.
See advert on opposite page

MANSTON Kent   5F2

Pine Meadow Caravan Park
Spratling Court Farm, Manston CT12 5AN
☎ 01843-587770 Fax 01843-851177
Open April-end September ⛺ 🚐 🚙
Size 3 acres, 40 touring pitches, 40 with electric hookup, 40 level pitches, 4 🚿, 4 WCs, 1 CWP
£ car/tent £8–£11.20, car/caravan £8–£11.20, motorhome £8–£11.20
🏪¼ ✕¼ 🚰¼ 🔌 P ⛽ Calor
Last arrival time: 22:00
➡ From A256 junction take B2050 W towards Manston village, in 300 yards turn right, signposted Greensole Lane/Pine Meadow.

MARDEN Kent   5E3

Tanner Farm Caravan & Camping Park
Goudhurst Road, Marden TN12 9ND
☎ 01622-832399 Fax 01622-832472
Open all year ⛺ 🚐 🚙

Secluded Park in centre of 150 acre farm. Immaculate facilities. Two centrally-heated toilet/shower units with privacy cubicles. Ideal touring centre. Shire horses kept.
Size 15 acres, 100 touring pitches, 100 with electric hookup, 95 level pitches, 13 🚿, 16 WCs, 4 CWPs
£ car/tent £7.50–£11, car/caravan £6.20–£11, motorhome £6.20–£11, motorbike/tent £7.50–£11, children £1.10–£1.20
℃ MasterCard Visa
🏪 🔋 🔌 🔋 📶 ⛽ Calor Gaz ♿ 🐕 WS
Last arrival time: 20:00
➡ From A229 or A262 onto B2079 midway between villages of Marden and Goudhurst.

MARGATE Kent   5F2

Frost Farm Caravan Site
St Nicholas-at-Wade, Birchington, Margate
☎ 01843-847219
Open March-October 🚐 🚙
Size 3 acres, 12 touring pitches, 8 with electric hookup, 6 level pitches, 48 static caravans, 2 🚿, 8 WCs, 1 CWP
£ car/caravan £6–£8, motorhome £6–£8
🏪¼ ✕¼ 🚰¼ 🔌 ⛽ Calor 🐕 WS
Last arrival time: 22:00
➡ Site on A299, to St Nicholas roundabout, return on London side ¼ mile.

St Nicholas Camping Site
Court Road, St Nicholas-at-Wade, Birchington, Margate
☎ 01843-847245
Open 1 March-31 October ⛺ 🚐 🚙
Size 3 acres, 75 touring pitches, 16 with electric hookup, 75 level pitches, 4 🚿, 8 WCs, 1 CWP
£ car/tent £7–£8.50, car/caravan £6.50–£8.50, motorhome £7–£8, motorbike/tent £7–£8
🏪 🏪¼ ✕¼ 🚰¼ 🔋 ⛽ Calor Gaz ♿ 🐕
➡ Signposted off A299 and off A28 near Birchington.

MARKET RASEN Lincolnshire   8C1

Market Rasen Racecourse
Legsby Road, Market Rasen LN8 3EA
☎ 01673-842307 Fax 01673-844532
Open 9 April-5 October ⛺ 🚐 🚙

Rural site, with phone, TV room, playground, games area, reduced admission to racing, 9 hole pay and play golf course. Shop and restaurant one mile. Swimming pool 15 miles.
Size 2 acres, 55 touring pitches, 35 with electric hookup, 55 level pitches, 6 🚿, 6 WCs, 1 CWP
£ car/tent £5.50–£6.70, car/caravan £5–£6.20, motorhome £5–£6.20, motorbike/tent £5.50–£6.70, children £1–£1.10
℃ MasterCard Visa
🏪 🔋 🔌 P GR ⛽ Calor Gaz 🐕
Last arrival time: 22:00
➡ S off A631 on E outskirts of Market Rasen. Site is on left after ¾ mile.

ENGLAND

98

Market Rasen

Walesby Woodlands
Walesby, Market Rasen LN8 3UN
01673-843285
Open 1 March-1 November
Size 2.5 acres, 64 touring pitches, 60 with electric hookup, 64 level pitches, 4, 12 WCs, 2 CWPs
£ car/tent £7.50, car/caravan £7.50, motorhome £7.50, motorbike/tent £7.50, children £1-£1.25
Calor Gaz WS
Last arrival time: 21:30
➜ In Market Rasen, adjacent to the railway bridge, take the B1203 to Tealby. After ¾ mile turn left onto an unclassified road to Walesby. After ¼ mile the site is signposted on left.

| MARLBOROUGH Wiltshire | 4A2 |

Forestry Commission Postern Hill C & C Site
Postern Hill, Marlborough SN8 4ND
01672-515195
Open mid March-end October
Size 28 acres, 170 touring pitches, 78 with electric hookup, 100 level pitches, 8 WCs, 1 CWP
£ car/tent £6-£7.50, car/caravan £6-£7.50, motorhome £6-£7.50, motorbike/tent £6-£7.50
MasterCard Visa
Last arrival time: 22:00
➜ 1 mile S of Marlborough on A346 at the N end of Savernake Forest.

| MARTOCK Somerset | 3E2 |

Southfork Caravan Park
Parrett Works, Martock TA12 6AE
01935-825661 Fax 01935-825122
Open all year

Small, peaceful, family-run park in open countryside near River Parrett. Level, clean, immaculately maintained with modern heated toilet block and free hot showers. Numerous places of interest nearby for all age groups. Caravan servicing, repairs, parts and accessories.
Size 2 acres, 30 touring pitches, 20 with electric hookup, 30 level pitches, 3 static caravans, 4, 5 WCs, 1 CWP
£ car/tent £6-£9, car/caravan £6-£9, motorhome £6-£9, motorbike/tent £6-£9, children £1
Rental £100-£220

MasterCard Visa
Calor Gaz
Last arrival time: 22:00
➜ From A303 E of Ilminster at South Petherton roundabout, take first exit towards South Petherton and follow camping signs.

| MASHAM North Yorkshire | 11D2 |

Fearby Caravan Site
Black Swan Hotel, Fearby, Masham HG4 4NF
01765-689477 Fax 01765-689477
Open 1 March-31 October

The site overlooks the Burn Valley and has been designated as an area of outstanding natural beauty by the Countryside Commission.
Size 3 acres, 50 touring pitches, 50 with electric hookup, 50 level pitches, 3 static caravans, 4, 9 WCs, 1 CWP
£ car/tent £7-£9, car/caravan £8-£9, motorhome £8-£9, motorbike/tent £7-£8
Rental Chalet. £95-£275
Visa
Calor Gaz WS
Last arrival time: 22:00
➜ Turn left off A6108 ¼ mile NW of Masham. Site is 2 miles, at rear of Black Swan.

| MATLOCK Derbyshire | 8A2 |

Darwin Forest Country Park
Two Dales, Matlock DE4 5LN
01629-732428 Fax 01629-735015
Open March-December

Mevagissey

A luxurious family park set in 44 acres of magnificent woodland, featuring every comfort in a spacious and peaceful environment. Pine lodges for hire.
Size 44 acres, 48 touring pitches, 48 with electric hookup, 48 level pitches, 16 ⚲, 21 WCs, 1 CWP
£ car/caravan £10-£12, motorhome £10-£12
Rental Lodges. £190
CC MasterCard Visa
Last arrival time: 21:00
➜ M1, junction 29 to Chesterfield - A632 towards Matlock, turn right on to B5057 towards Two Dales. Park is on right, 2 miles before village.

MERSEA ISLAND Essex   5E1

Waldegraves Holiday Park
West Mersea, Mersea Island CO5 8SE
☎ 01206-382898 Fax 01206-385359
Open March-November
Size 25 acres, 120 touring pitches, 120 with electric hookup, 120 level pitches, 205 static caravans, 20 ⚲, 20 WCs, 4 CWPs
£ car/tent £8-£13, car/caravan £8-£13, motorhome £8-£13, motorbike/tent £8-£13
Rental £150-320
CC MasterCard Visa
Calor Gaz WS
Last arrival time: 22:00
➜ B1025 from Colchester to Mersea. Follow brown tourist signs to East Mersea and on to Waldegraves.

MEVAGISSEY Cornwall   2B4

Penhaven Touring Park
Pentewan PL26 6DL
☎ 01726-843687 Fax 01726-843
Open Easter-31 October
Size 13 acres, 105 touring pitches, 78 with electric hookup, 105 level pitches, 16 ⚲, 20 WCs, 2 CWPs
£ car/tent £8-£13, car/caravan £8-£17, motorhome £8-£17, motorbike/tent £8-£13, children £1.40
CC MasterCard Visa
Calor Gaz WS
Last arrival time: 21:00
➜ S of St Austell, on B3273 turning on left 1 mile after village of London Apprentice.

Sea View International
Boswinger, Gorran, St Austell PL26 6LL
☎ 01726-843425 Fax 01726-843358
Open April-October

A peaceful, landscaped, level park close to beautiful beaches. Acres of recreational space with badminton, tennis court, volleyball and putting green.
Size 16 acres, 165 touring pitches, 150 with electric hookup, 165 level pitches, 38 static caravans, 15 ⚲, 30 WCs, 2 CWPs
£ car/tent £7.50-£16.50, car/caravan £7.50-£16.50, motorhome £7.50-£16.50, children £2-£2.50
Rental Chalet. £100-£499
CC MasterCard Visa
Calor Gaz
Last arrival time: 22:00
➜ From St Austell take B3273 signed Mevagissey. Prior to village follow brown tourism signs and turn right signed Gorran. After 6 miles follow directional signs on right.

Tregarton Park
Gorran, St Austell PL26 6NF
☎ 01726-843666 Fax 01726-844481
Open 1 April-30 September

A friendly, family run park offering touring and camping facilities of the highest standard. 12 acres of sheltered grassland without the holiday camp atmosphere. Reserved for families and couples only.
Size 12 acres, 150 touring pitches, 120 with electric hookup, 80 level pitches, 10 ⚲, 15 WCs, 2 CWPs
£ car/tent £6-£12.90, car/caravan £6-£12.90, motorhome £6-£12.90, motorbike/tent £6-£12.90, children £1-£1.50
CC MasterCard Visa
Calor Gaz
Last arrival time: 21:00
➜ At the top of Pentewen Hill, turn right to Gorran, then follow brown tourist signs.

100

Milford-on-Sea

MILFORD-ON-SEA Hampshire   4B4

Lytton Lawn Camping & Caravan Park
Lymore Lane, Milford-on-Sea, Lymington SO41 0TX
📞 01590-648331   Fax 01590-645610
Open 1 March-5 January

Shorefield's touring park at Lytton Lawn offers peace, quiet and superb facilities, just 800 yards from the beach and 3 miles from the New Forest.
Size 5 acres, 126 touring pitches, 126 with electric hookup, 68 level pitches, 14, 28 WCs, 2 CWPs
£ car/tent £9.45-£23.10, car/caravan £9.45-£23.10, motorhome £9.45-£23.10, motorbike/tent £9.45-£23.10
MasterCard Visa
Calor Gaz
Last arrival time: 22:00
➜ From Lymington take A337 to Everton, then left onto B3058 towards Milford-on-Sea. Lytton Lawn is ¼ mile on left.
See advert on page 125

MINEHEAD Somerset   3D2

Blue Anchor Bay Caravan Park
Minehead TA24 6JT
📞 01643-821360   Fax 01643-821572
Open March-October

Peaceful beach side location bordered by the West Somerset Railway. Ideal for exploring Exmoor and the beautiful Somerset coast.
Size 29 acres, 103 touring pitches, 103 with electric hookup, 103 level pitches, 300 static caravans, 8, 15 WCs, 1 CWP
£ car/caravan £6-£14.50, motorhome £6-£14.50
Rental

MasterCard Visa
Calor Gaz
Last arrival time: 23:00
➜ From junction 25 on M5, take A358 signed Minehead. After about 12 miles, turn left onto A39 at Williton. After about four miles, turn right onto B3191 at Carhampton. Park is 1½ miles on right.

Camping & Caravanning Club Site
Hill Road, North Hill, Minehead TA24 5SF
📞 01643-704738
Open March-September
Size 3.75 acres, 60 touring pitches, 12 with electric hookup, 6, 8 WCs, 1 CWP
£ car/tent £7.30-£8.95, car/caravan £7.30-£8.95, motorhome £7.30-£8.95, motorbike/tent £7.30-£8.95, children £1.50
MasterCard Visa
Calor   WS
Last arrival time: 23:00
➜ From A39 head towards town centre, in main street turn opposite W.H. Smith to Blenheim Road and turn left in 50 yards (by pub with red & white mushroom) into Martlet Road (camp site sign), uphill, left round hairpin at Memorial, right at cottages, past the church on the right, continue up to site on right.

MODBURY Devon   2C4

Camping & Caravanning Club Site
California Cross, Ivybridge, Modbury PL21 0SG
📞 01548-821297
Open March-November
Size 3.66 acres, 80 touring pitches, 40 with electric hookup, 6, 9 WCs, 1 CWP
£ car/tent £10.40-£13.60, car/caravan £10.40-£13.60, motorhome £10.40-£13.60, motorbike/tent £10.40-£13.60, children £1.50
MasterCard Visa
Calor   WS
Last arrival time: 23:00
➜ From A38, take A3121 and continue to the crossroads. Straight across onto B3196 (Loddiswell signpost) to California Cross hamlet. Turn left after California Cross hamlet sign and before the petrol station. The site is on right.

Moor View Touring Park
California Cross, Nr Modbury PL21 0SG
📞 01548-821485   Fax 01548-821485
Open 1 May-end September

Morecambe

Quiet country park, superb moorland views, sheltered spacious level pitches, modern and scrupulously clean toilets and showers with free hot water. Shop and take-away. Dogs welcome.
Size 5.5 acres, 68 touring pitches, 68 with electric hookup, 68 level pitches, 6 🚿, 9 WCs, 1 CWP
£ car/tent £6.50-£9.50, car/caravan £6.50-£9.50, motorhome £6.50-£9.50, motorbike/tent £6.50-£9.50, children £1.50
cc MasterCard Visa
🛒 ✗¼ 🛁 ⌂ 🚻 GR 🔌 TV ⚠ Gaz 🐕
Last arrival time: 22:00
➡ From A38, 25 miles W of Exeter, leave at Wrangaton Cross (A3121). After 3 miles after Loddiswell Road leave BP garage on left and follow Modbury (B3207) road. Park is ½ mile on left.

Pennymoor Camping & Caravan Park
Modbury PL21 0SB
📞 01548-830269
Open 15 March-15 November 🏕 🚐 🚙

Immaculate, peaceful site with panoramic views. Close to many beaches, towns and numerous attractions. Childrens equipped play area, shop, electric hook-up, superb toilet/showers block. Luxury caravans for hire.
Size 12 acres, 154 touring pitches, 50 with electric hookup, 120 level pitches, 70 static caravans, 15 🚿, 28 WCs, 2 CWPs
£ car/tent £5.50-£9, car/caravan £5.50-£9, motorhome £4.50-£8, motorbike/tent £5
Rental 🚐 from £80-£310
🛒 ⌂ 🚻 🔌 ⚠ Calor Gaz ♿ 🐕
Last arrival time: 22:00
➡ From Exeter, leave A38 at Wrangaton Cross, left then straight ahead at next crossroads. Continue for 4 miles. Pass garage on your left, then second left and site is 1 mile.

MORECAMBE Lancashire	10B3

Melbreak Caravan Park
Carr Lane, Middleton, Morecambe LA3 3LH
📞 01524-852430
Open 1 March-30 October 🏕 🚐 🚙

Small family site with modern fully-tiled toilet blocks situated four miles from Morecambe and six miles from Lancaster, within reach of the Lake District and Yorkshire Dales.
Size 2 acres, 30 touring pitches, 30 with electric hookup, 30 level pitches, 10 static caravans, 4 🚿, 7 WCs, 1 CWP
£ car/tent £6-£6.50, car/caravan £6.50-£7, motorhome £6.75-£7, motorbike/tent £5.75-£6
🛒 ⌂ 🚻 Calor Gaz 🐕
Last arrival time: 21:00
➡ Take A683 S from Lancaster. At second large roundabout turn left to Middleton. Follow signs for site.

Riverside Caravan Park
Oxcliffe Hill Farm, Heaton-with-Oxcliffe, Morecambe LA3 3ER
📞 01524-844193 Fax 01524-65522
Open March-October 🏕 🚐 🚙

Quiet site, but only 5-10 minutes from centre of Morecambe or Lancaster. Old world pub next to site entrance. Restaurant 30 yards. Swimming pool 2 miles. No motorcycles.
Size 2.5 acres, 50 touring pitches, 50 with electric hookup, 50 level pitches, 4 🚿, 8 WCs, 1 CWP
£ car/tent £6-£8, car/caravan £6-£8, motorhome £6-£8
🛒¼ ✗¼ 🛁 🚻 ⚠ Calor ♿ 🐕 WS
Last arrival time: 22:00
➡ Leave M6 junction 34, follow signs for Morecambe. Cross river and follow signs for Overton and Middleton. Site gate next to Golden Ball Inn, where river and road run next to each other.

ENGLAND

101

Venture Caravan Park
Langridge Way, Westgate, Morecambe LA4 4TQ
☎ 01524-412986 Fax 01524-855884
Open all year ⓘ 🚐 🚍

18 acre site with level grass pitches. Quiet, but only three quarters of a mile to all town amenities.
Size 18 acres, 100 touring pitches, 70 with electric hookup, 100 level pitches, 200 static caravans, 20 ⓘ, 20 WCs, 2 CWPs
£ car/tent £9-£11, car/caravan £7-£13, motorhome £7-£13, motorbike/tent £9-£11
Rental 🚐 £100-£260
🚿 ✕ 🍴 🛒 🔌 🚽 🎲 📺 🧺 ⚡ Calor Gaz ♿ 🐕 WS
Last arrival time: 23:00
➜ M6 junction 34 to Lancaster, then A589 to Morecambe. At third roundabout by Shrimp Public House, take left along Westgate, ½ mile right at school into Langridge Way. Straight on ahead for site.

MORPETH Northumberland	13F3

Percy Wood Caravan Park
Swanland, Morpeth NE65 9JW
☎ 01670-787649 Fax 01670-787034
Open 1 March-31 January ⓘ 🚐 🚍

Secluded woodland site with plenty of wildlife, adjacent to forest walks.
Size 67 acres, 60 touring pitches, 60 with electric hookup, 60 level pitches, 60 static caravans, 6 ⓘ, 10 WCs, 2 CWPs
£ car/tent £8, car/caravan £9.50, motorhome £9.50, motorbike/tent £8, children £1
Rental 🚐 £85-£290
℃ MasterCard Visa
🚿 🚿¼ ✕¼ 🍴¼ 🛒 🔌 🚽 🎲 📺 🧺 ⚡ Calor Gaz 🐕
Last arrival time: 22:00
➜ 2 miles off A1 to Swarland, 6 miles S of Alnwick.

MUNDESLEY-ON-SEA Norfolk	9F2

Sandy Gulls Clifftop Touring Park
Cromer Road, Mundesley-on-Sea NR11 8DF
☎ 01263-720513
Open March-November ⓘ 🚐 🚍

Set on a clifftop with panoramic sea views, half a mile from the village. Only a ten minute drive to the Broads National Park and centrally situated for all attractions.
Size 20 acres, 40 touring pitches, 40 with electric hookup, 20 level pitches, 100 static caravans, 10 ⓘ, 20 WCs, 2 CWPs
£ car/tent £8-£13, car/caravan £8-£13, motorhome £8-£13
Rental 🚐 Chalet. £160-£220
🚿¼ ✕¼ 🍴¼ 🛒 🔌 🚽 Calor ♿ 🐕
Last arrival time: 22:00
➜ 5 miles S of Cromer on the coast road.

Woodland Caravan Park
Trimingham, Mundesley NR11 8AL
☎ 01263-579208 Fax 01263-833071
Open March-October 🚐 🚍
Size 43 acres, 150 touring pitches, 80 with electric hookup, 100 level pitches, 150 static caravans, 14 ⓘ, 30 WCs, 2 CWPs
£ car/caravan £6.70-£10.85, motorhome £6.70-£10.85
℃ MasterCard Visa
🚿 ✕ 🍴 🛒 🔌 🚽 🎲 📺 🧺 ⚡ Calor ♿ 🐕 WS
➜ On coast road between Cromer and Mundesley.

NEW MILTON Hampshire	4A4

Bashley Park
Sway Road, New Milton BH25 5QR
☎ 01425-612340 Fax 01425-612602
Open 1 March-31 October 🚐 🚍

Newhaven

Set in a wooded country estate close to Bournemouth, the New Forest and Solent Beaches, this family park has a vast range of sporting and entertainment facilities.
Size 100 acres, 420 touring pitches, 420 with electric hookup, 350 level pitches, 380 static caravans, 37 🚿, 72 WCs, 4 CWPs
£ car/caravan £10.50-£26.50, motorhome £10.50-£26.50
Rental
MasterCard Visa
Calor
Last arrival time: 21:00
➜ Take A35 Lyndhurst to Bournemouth for 10 miles. Take B3055 signed Swayford for 2½ miles, then straight over at crossroads. Park is ¼ mile on left.

Forestry Commission Setthorns Campsite

Wootton, New Milton BH25 5UA
☎ 01703-283771 Fax 01703-283929

Size 15 acres, 320 touring pitches, 120 with electric hookup, 100 level pitches, 2 CWPs
£ car/caravan £5.20-£8, motorhome £5.20-£8
MasterCard Visa

Last arrival time: 22:00
➜ Signposted from B3058 New Milton to Brockenhurst road.

NEW ROMNEY Kent	5E3

Marlie Farm Holiday Village

Dymchurch Road, New Romney TN28 8UE
☎ 01797-363060
Open March-January

Friendly, modern park with good facilities. Indoor leisure complex with pool, sauna & bubble spa. Clubhouse, children's play area & amusements. Popular touring base for south coast.
Size 120 acres, 350 touring pitches, 100 with electric hookup, 350 level pitches, 222 static caravans, 14 🚿, 52 WCs, 1 CWP
£ car/tent £8-£11, car/caravan £8-£11, motorhome £8-£11, motorbike/tent £8-£11, children £2-£2.90
Rental Various rental prices
Calor
➜ Take A259 main coast road, ¼ mile E of New Romney, 16 miles W of Folkestone

NEWBY BRIDGE Cumbria	10B2

Newby Bridge Caravan Park

Canny Hill, Newby Bridge LA12 8NF
☎ 015395-31030 Fax 015395-30105
Open March-October
Size 25 acres, 20 touring pitches, 20 with electric hookup, 20 level pitches, 69 static caravans, 4 🚿, 8 WCs, 1 CWP
£ car/caravan £9-£12.50, motorhome £9-£12.50
Rental Chalet. £75-£385
¼ ¼ ¼ Calor WS
Last arrival time: 20:00
➜ Just before entering Newby Bridge from motorway turn left at Canny Hill signpost. Park entrance is 200 yards on right.

Oak Head Caravan Park

Ayside, Newby Bridge LA11 6JA
☎ 01539-531475
Open March-October
Size 3.5 acres, 60 touring pitches, 30 with electric hookup, 50 level pitches, 71 static caravans, 8 🚿, 33 WCs, 1 CWP
£ car/tent £5-£7, car/caravan £7-£8, motorhome £5-£7, motorbike/tent £5
Rental
Calor Gaz WS
Last arrival time: flexible
➜ M6 junction 36 onto A590. Follow signs for Newby Bridge for 14 miles. Caravan sign is on left of A590. Site is 1½ miles S of Newby Bridge.

NEWHAVEN Derbyshire	8A2

Newhaven Caravan & Camping Park

Newhaven SK17 0DT
☎ 01298-84300
Open 1 March-31 October

Delightful site in the heart of the Peak District with excellent facilities and free hot water. Alton Towers, Chatsworth House, Haddon Hall, Harwick Hall, all within easy reach.

103

ENGLAND

Newhaven

← Newhaven Caravan & Camping Park

Size 30 acres, 125 touring pitches, 73 with electric hookup, 80 level pitches, 70 static caravans, 8 🚿, 18 WCs, 2 CWPs
£ car/tent £7-£8, car/caravan £7-£8, motorhome £7-£8, motorbike/tent £7-£8
⛺ ✕¼ 🔲 🔋 GR ⚠ Calor Gaz 🐕 WS
➜ Halfway between Ashbourne and Buxton on A515 at junction with A5012.

NEWMARKET Suffolk 9D4

Camping & Caravanning Club Site
Rowley Mile Racecourse, Newmarket CB8 8JL
☎ 01638-663235
Open March-September ⛺ 🚐 🚙
Size 10 acres, 90 touring pitches, 36 with electric hookup, 6 🚿, 14 WCs, 1 CWP
£ car/tent £9.60-£12.10, car/caravan £9.60-£12.10, motorhome £9.60-£12.10, motorbike/tent £9.60-£12.10, children £1.50
㏄ MasterCard Visa
⛺ ⛺¼ ✕¼ 🔲 🍺¼ 🔲 🔋 P J GR Q TV ⚠ Calor ♿ 🐕 WS
Last arrival time: 23:00
➜ From the A1304 follow signs to the racecourse. Drive down the Rowley Mile which is signposted to the site, keeping the grandstand on your left.

NEWQUAY Cornwall 2A3

Camping & Caravanning Club Site
Tregurrian, Watergate Bay, Newquay TR8 4AE
☎ 01637-860448
Open March-September ⛺ 🚐 🚙
Size 4.5 acres, 90 touring pitches, 42 with electric hookup, 5 🚿, 10 WCs, 2 CWPs
£ car/tent £8.40-£9.40, car/caravan £8.40-£9.40, motorhome £8.40-£9.40, motorbike/tent £8.40-£9.40, children £1.10
㏄ MasterCard Visa
⛺ ⛺¼ ✕¼ 🍺 🍺¼ 🔲 🔋 P J GR Q TV ⚠ Calor ♿ 🐕 WS
Last arrival time: 23:00
➜ Leave A30 after prominent railway bridge by turning right signposted Newquay Airport, at roundabout on A39 join A3059 for Newquay, 1½ miles on after passing a service station on right turn right signposted Newquay Airport, continue on road past airport, at junction turn left for Tregurrian, follow Watergate Bay camp signs to site.

Hendra Holiday Park
Newquay TR8 4NY
☎ 01637-875778 Fax 01637-879017
Open April-October ⛺ 🚐 🚙
Size 49 acres, 600 touring pitches, 250 with electric hookup, 600 level pitches, 187 static caravans, 3 CWPs

NEWQUAY CORNWALL

Excellent Camping & Touring Facilities - Luxury Static Caravans

Free Entertainment • Cabaret • Children's Pirate Den
Licensed Bars • Marios Bar • Fish and Chip Shop
Sauna • Supermarket • Food Bar • Amusements
Games Fields • Train Rides • Pitch n Putt • Heated
Swimming Pools and Waterslide • Adventure Playparks

To ensure everyones enjoyment, Hendra Holiday Park caters exclusively for families and couples only!

Brochure Hotline 0500 242523

Hendra Holiday Park, Newquay, Cornwall TR8 4NY
Tel: 01637 875778
e.mail: hendra.uk@dial.pipex.com
http://www.hendra-holidays.com

Hendra HOLIDAY PARK

Newquay

£ car/tent £7.60-£11.30, car/caravan £7.60-£11.30, motorhome £7.60-£11.30, motorbike/tent £7.60-£11.30, children £3.40
Rental from £115-£615
cc MasterCard Visa
WS
➜ A30 to Indian Queens, A392 to Newquay. Hendra is 1½ miles before Newquay town centre.
See advert on opposite page

Monkey Tree Holiday Park
Rejerrah, Newquay TR8 5QL
01872-572032 fax 01872-071298
Open Easter-October
Size 18 acres, 245 touring pitches, 84 with electric hookup, 245 level pitches, 20 static caravans, 18, 34 WCs, 1 CWP
£ car/tent £6.50-£12, car/caravan £6.50-£12, motorhome £6.50-£12, motorbike/tent £6.50-£12, children £1.50-£3
Rental Statics £150-£495, Eurotents £195-250
Calor Gaz WS
Last arrival time: 20:00
➜ A3075 from Newquay to Perranporth. After 4 miles turn left, signposted Zelah. Site is 800 yards.
See advert on this page

Newquay Holiday Parks

FOR FREE BROCHURE PHONE NOW 01637 871111 ext 30

Two superb Holiday Parks to choose from:
NEWQUAY HOLIDAY PARK & HOLYWELL BAY HOLIDAY PARK

Great family value and so much to enjoy!
★ FREE Heated swimming pools with giant water slides ★ FREE Children's playgrounds
★ FREE Nightly entertainment for all the family
★ FREE Children's clubs
★ Pool/Snooker rooms
★ Amusement arcades
★ Crazy Golf

Excellent Facilities
★ Electric Hook-ups
★ Free showers ★ Self-service shop
★ Take-away food ★ Launderette

NEWQUAY HOLIDAY PARKS 30, NEWQUAY, CORNWALL TR8 4HS
http://www.newquay-holiday-parks.co.uk

AA EXCELLENT ROSE AWARD

NEWQUAY
A family holiday & camping park......

AA

★ Situated in rural surrounds & close to beaches
★ Welcoming All Tourers – Pitches from £3.50 per day
★ Also Euro Tents from £100 per week – Luxury Static Caravans from £150 per week
★ Overnight & short stays available

Tel: 01872 572032 to book now or request brochure

The Monkey Tree
Holiday & Camping Park

Tel: 01872 572032 Fax: 01872 571298
Website: www.chycor.co.uk/monkey-tree
E-Mail: walker.group@virgin.net

Lounge Bar Restaurant Take-Away • Ample Toilet & Washing Facilities
Heated Swimming Pool & Sauna • Shop • Games Room & Outdoor Play Area
Free Entertainment & Attractions • Electric Hook-Ups & Winter Storage

TREKENNING TOURIST PARK

An exclusive family run park set in beautiful quiet quiet countryside but only minutes away from sandy beaches.

Facilities include:
Swimming Pools, Bar, Restaurant, TV and Games Room, Play Area, Family Bathrooms/Showers, Shop and Laundry.

Contact John Dave or Tracey.
NEWQUAY, CORNWALL TR8 4JF
Tel: 01637 880462 Fax: 01637 880500
Email: trekenning@aol.com
www.crescom.co.uk/trekenning/

Newquay Holiday Park
Newquay TR8 4HS
01637-871111 Fax 01637-850818
Open 17 May-19 September
Size 23 acres, 357 touring pitches, 156 with electric hookup, 10 level pitches, 140 static caravans, 24, 30 WCs, 4 CWPs
£ car/tent £7.25-£12.35, car/caravan £7.25-£12.35, motorhome £7.25-£12.35, motorbike/tent £7.25-£12.35, children £3.60
Rental £102-£543
MasterCard Visa
Calor Gaz
Last arrival time: 22:00
→ 2 miles from Newquay on A3059 toward St Columb, signposted.
See advert on previous page

Riverside Holiday Park
Newquay TR8 4PE
01637-873617 Fax 01637-873617
Open Easter-December

Riverside family park only 2 miles from Newquay. Luxury lodges and caravans for hire. Tourers/tents are welcome. Electrical hook-ups available. Domed heated pool, lounge bar and river fishing. Families and couples only.
Size 14 acres, 150 touring pitches, 45 with electric hookup, 150 level pitches, 32 static caravans, 13, 10 WCs, 1 CWP
£ car/tent £5.20-£9, car/caravan £5.20-£9, motorhome £4.60-£8, motorbike/tent £4.90-£8.50, children £1.20-£2.10
Rental Lodges. £90-£500
MasterCard Visa
Calor Gaz WS
Last arrival time: 22:00
→ Take M5 to Exeter, then A30, then A392 to Newquay. At Quintrell Downs go straight across at roundabout, then take second turning on left signposted 'Gwills'. Go past Lane Theatre, turn right at crossroads and site is 400 yards on right.

Trekenning Tourist Park
Newquay TR8 4JF
01637-880462 Fax 01637-880500
Open April-September
Size 6.5 acres, 75 touring pitches, 68 with electric hookup, 9, 11 WCs, 1 CWP
£ car/tent £7.50-£10.80, car/caravan £7.50-£10.80, motorhome £7.50-£10.80, motorbike/tent £7.50-£10.80, children £2.55-£3.90
MasterCard Visa
Calor Gaz WS
→ Adjacent to A39 by St Columb Major roundabout.
See advert on this page

Treloy Tourist Park
Newquay TR8 4JN
01637-872063 Fax 01637-872063
Open April-end September

A family-run park with heated pool, licensed club/family room and entertainment. Shop, cafe/takeaway. Electric hook-ups. Golf course, concessionary green fees. Coarse fishing nearby.
Size 11.5 acres, 141 touring pitches, 100 with electric hookup, 100 level pitches, 15, 24 WCs, 1 CWP
£ car/tent £5-£10, car/caravan £5-£10, children £1.50-£2.90
MasterCard Visa
Calor Gaz
Last arrival time: 23:00
→ Just off A3059 (main St Columb Major to Newquay road). 5 minutes to Newquay.

Newquay

Trenance Caravan Park
Edgcumbe Avenue, Newquay TR7 2JY
01637-873447 Fax 01637-852677
Open 1 April-31 October
Size 12 acres, 50 touring pitches, 36 with electric hookup, 16 level pitches, 134 static caravans, 22, 3 CWPs
£ car/tent £6-£10, car/caravan £6-£10, motorhome £6-£10, motorbike/tent £6-£10, children £1.50-£2.50
Rental Chalet. £80-£340
MasterCard Visa
Calor Gaz
Last arrival time: 21:00
→ On the main A3075 Newquay/Truro road. 1 mile from Newquay town centre.
See advert on this page

Trethiggey Touring Park
Quintrell Downs, Newquay TR8 4LG
01637-877672
Open 1 March-1 January
Size 15 acres, 155 touring pitches, 100 with electric hookup, 155 level pitches, 2 static caravans, 8, 21 WCs, 1 CWP
£ car/tent £6-£8.90, car/caravan £6-£8.90, motorhome £5-£7.90, motorbike/tent £5-£7.90, children £1-£2.10
Rental £80-£360
MasterCard Visa
Calor Gaz WS
Last arrival time: 22:30
→ From A30 at Indian Queens take A392 Newquay road. Follow this road for 5 miles to Quintrell Downs roundabout. The site is signposted left on A3058 ½ mile.

Trevornick Holiday Park
Holywell Bay, Newquay TR8 5PW
01637-830531 Fax 01637-831000
Open May-September

Just ½ mile from beach, stunning sea views from immaculately maintained 5 tick park.
Daytime/evening entertainment programme. Fully equipped tents to sleep 6, to rent.
Size 30 acres, 450 touring pitches, 280 with electric hookup, 200 level pitches, 40, 70 WCs, 8 CWPs
£ car/tent £6.50-£11.40, car/caravan £6.50-£11.40, motorhome £6.50-£11.40, motorbike/tent £6.50-£11.40, children £3.50
Rental Eurotents, fully equipped £89-£296 weekly.
MasterCard Visa

TRENANCE CHALET AND CARAVAN PARK

CHALETS & CARAVANS FOR HIRE
TOURING PITCHES & HOOK UPS
MINI-MARKET & OFF LICENCE
TAKE-AWAY & RESTAURANT
LAUNDERETTE & GAMES ROOM
MODERN SHOWER BLOCK
ADJACENT 26 ACRE LEISURE PARK
NEAREST PARK TO
TOWN CENTRE & BEACHES
FAMILIES & COUPLES ONLY

Member B.H.H.P.A.
Graded 4 Ticks Tourist Board

FREE PHONE BROCHURE LINE
0500-131243

EDGCUMBE AVENUE, NEWQUAY
Telephone: 01637 873447

Calor Gaz

→ Take A3075 Newquay to Perranporth road. Turn left for Cubert/Holywell. Go through Cubert and site is ½ mile on right.

Watergate Bay Holiday Park
Tregurrian, Watergate Bay, Newquay TR8 4AD
01637-860387 Fax 01637-860387
Open 1 March-30 November

For a relaxing holiday in beautiful countryside by the sea. Heated pool, licensed club, cafeteria, electronics, laundrette, adventure playground and evening entertainment.
Size 30 acres, 171 touring pitches, 100 with electric hookup, 171 level pitches, 32, 43 WCs, 7 CWPs
£ car/tent £7-£11, car/caravan £7-£11, motorhome £7-£11, motorbike/tent £7-£11
MasterCard Visa
Calor Gaz WS
→ 4 miles N of Newquay on B3276 coast road to Newquay.

ENGLAND

Newquay

White Acres Country Park
White Cross, Newquay TR8 4LW
☎ 01726-860220 Fax 01726-860877
Open Easter-end November
Size 55 acres, 240 touring pitches, 60 with electric hookup, 240 level pitches, 110 static caravans, 4 🚿, 4 WCs,
£ car/tent £6.50-£10, car/caravan £6.50-£10, motorhome £6.50-£10, motorbike/tent £6.50-£10, children £3.20
Rental £170-£695
ℂℂ MasterCard Visa
Last arrival time: 00:00
➡ From A30, take A392 for 1 mile, site on right.

NEWTON ABBOT Devon   3D3

Dornafield Caravan Park
Two Mile Oak, Newton Abbot TQ12 6DD
☎ 01803-812732 Fax 01803-812032
Open 20 March-31 October

Beautiful 14th century farmhouse located in peaceful Devon countryside. Superb facilities for the discerning caravanner with 135 pitches (including 64 full service). Tennis, games room, children's adventure areas and shop. Our brochure is only a phone call away
Size 30 acres, 135 touring pitches, 135 with electric hookup, 135 level pitches, 21 🚿, 34 WCs, 32 CWPs
£ car/tent £8-£12.50, car/caravan £8-£12.50, motorhome £8-£12.50, motorbike/tent £8-£12.50, children £1.10-£1.25
ℂℂ Visa
Last arrival time: 22:00
➡ Take A381, Newton Abbot to Totnes road. From Newton Abbot after 2½ miles turn right at 'Two Mile Oak Inn'. After 5 miles take first turning on left and site is 200 yards on right.

Hints & Tips
Make sure your mirrors are adjusted correctly before moving off.

Lemonford Caravan Park
Bickington, Newton Abbot TQ12 6JR
☎ 01626-821242
Open March-October

One of the prettiest parks in South Devon, landscaped with hedges and trees, with easy access to Torbay, Dartmoor and many major attractions.
Size 7.5 acres, 90 touring pitches, 62 with electric hookup, 90 level pitches, 18 static caravans, 6 🚿, 12 WCs, 3 CWPs
£ car/tent £5-£9, car/caravan £5-£9, motorhome £5-£9, motorbike/tent £8, children £1.10
Calor Gaz WS
Last arrival time: 22:00
➡ From Exeter take A38 towards Plymouth to B382. At roundabout, take third exit to Bickington. From Plymouth take A383 turn off to Bickington.

Ross Park
Park Hill Farm, Ipplepen, Newton Abbot TQ12 5TT
☎ 01803-812983 Fax 01803-812983
Open all year

Welcoming, tranquil, rural park with private pitches and splendid views of Dartmoor. Centrally heated showers and toilets. 16 amp hookup. Magnificent floral displays. Heated tropical conservatory. Restaurant.
Size 26 acres, 110 touring pitches, 110 with electric hookup, 110 level pitches, 11 🚿, 19 WCs, 1 CWP
£ car/tent £6.80-£10.20, car/caravan £6.80-£10.20, motorhome £6.80-£10.20, children £1.75
Calor Gaz WS
Last arrival time: 21:00
➡ 3 miles from Newton Abbot, 6 miles from Totnes on A381. At Park Hill crossroads and Jet filling station, take road sign to Woodlands and brown tourist road sign Ross Park.

Norwich

NORTHALLERTON North Yorkshire 11D2

Cote Ghyll Caravan Park
Osmotherley, Northallerton OL6 3AH
☎ 01609-883425
Open April-October
Size 7 acres, 57 touring pitches, 57 with electric hookup, 27 level pitches, 17 static caravans, 10, 17 WCs, 2 CWPs
£ car/tent £5.75-£6.50, car/caravan £6.50, motorhome £6, motorbike/tent £6, children £0.50
Calor Gaz
Last arrival time: 22:00
➡ Take A19 to A684. Follow signpost for Osmotherley to village centre. Turn left up hill. Site is ½ mile on right.

NORTHAMPTON Northamptonshire 8B4

Billing Aquadrome
Crow Lane, Great Billing, Northampton NN3 9DA
☎ 01604-408181 Fax 01604-784412
Open March-November

235 acres of level parkland for seasonal holiday homes or touring units. Funfair, bars, restaurants, national events throughout the year, jet skis, go-karts and much more.
Size 237 acres, 755 touring pitches, 400 with electric hookup, 755 level pitches, 800 static caravans, 66, 217 WCs, 14 CWPs
£ car/tent £10-£12, car/caravan £10-£12, motorhome £10-£12, motorbike/tent £10-£12
Rental from £140 weekly.
ℂℂ MasterCard Visa
Calor Gaz WS
Last arrival time: 24 hours
➡ Junction 15 M1, 10 miles away, follow signpost.

NORWICH Norfolk 9F3

Camping & Caravanning Club Site
Martineau Lane, Lakenham, Norwich NR1 2HX
☎ 01603-620060
Open March-November
Size 2.5 acres, 50 touring pitches, 16 with electric hookup, 4, 6 WCs, 1 CWP

£ car/tent £11.40-£13.60, car/caravan £10.40-£13.60, motorhome £10.40-£13.60, motorbike/tent £10.40-£13.60, children £1.60
ℂℂ MasterCard Visa
Calor WS
Last arrival time: 23:00
➡ From A47 join A146 towards city centre, at traffic lights turn left to next set of traffic lights, under low bridge to Cock public house, turn left. The site is on right in 150 yards.

Dower House Touring Park
East Harling, Norwich NR16 2SE
☎ 01953-717314 Fax 01953-717843
Open 15 March-31 October

This family run touring park deep in the heart of the Thetford Forest provides the ideal break. Set in rural tranquillity with excellent facilities, including a pub and outdoor pool.
Size 20 acres, 80 with electric hookup, 160 level pitches, 11, 20 WCs, 3 CWPs
£ car/tent £6.95-£9.45, car/caravan £6.95-£9.45, motorhome £6.95-£9.45, motorbike/tent £6.95-£9.45, children £0.40-£0.90
ℂℂ MasterCard Visa
Calor Gaz WS
Last arrival time: 21:00
➡ From Thetford, take A1066 E for 5 miles, fork left at camping sign onto East Harling road. Site is on left after 2 miles.

Haveringland Hall Caravan Park
Cawston, Norwich NR10 4PN
☎ 01603-871302
Open March-October
Size 35 acres, 40 touring pitches, 22 with electric hookup, 20 level pitches, 55 static caravans, 10, 18 WCs, 1 CWP
£ car/tent £6.50-£8.50, car/caravan £7.50-£8.50, motorhome £7.50-£8.50, motorbike/tent £6.50-£8.50, children £1
Rental
Calor Gaz WS
Last arrival time: 22:00
➡ From Norwich N on A140 for 3¾ miles, fork left on B1149 for 2¾ miles. 3 miles past turn left into unclassified road, after 1¼ miles turn right and continue to site on right in ½ mile.

ENGLAND

Norwich

THORNTON'S HOLT
CAMPING PARK

'The Indoor Swimming Pool and Patio'

Situated where the peace of the countryside meets the culture and life of the City of Nottingham, this sheltered Park offers the following attractions:

- ☆ 90 pitches, most with electric H.U.
- ☆ Good central amenities
- ☆ Outdoor play area & games barn
- ☆ Indoor heated swimming pool
- ☆ Shop & information centre
- ☆ Pub & restaurant within 150 metres
- ☆ Regular & frequent bus service to Nottingham.

STRAGGLETHORPE, RADCLIFFE-ON-TRENT, NOTTINGHAM NG12 2JZ
Tel: 0115 9332125 Fax: 0115 9333318

Swans Harbour Caravan Park
Barford Road, Marlingford, Norwich NR9 4BE
☏ 01603-759658
Open all year

Situated just outside the historic city of Norwich, this site is perfectly placed for touring Norfolk and the Broads.
Size 4 acres, 25 touring pitches, 25 with electric hookup, 25 level pitches, 2, 6 WCs, 1 CWP
£ car/tent £5, car/caravan £5, motorhome £5, motorbike/tent £5, children £0.30

➔ Take B1108 Norwich-Watton. 2½ miles past Norwich southern bypass, turn right at crossroads to Marlingford. Follow tourist signs to site.

Don't forget to mention the guide
When booking, please remember to tell the site that you chose it from RAC Camping & Caravanning 1999

NOTTINGHAM Nottinghamshire   8B2

Thornton's Holt Camping Park
Stragglethorpe, Radcliffe-on-Trent, Nottingham NG12 2JZ
☏ 0115-933 2125   Fax 0115-933 3318
Open all year
Size 14 acres, 90 touring pitches, 71 with electric hookup, 90 level pitches, 9, 12 WCs, 1 CWP
£ car/tent £7-£8, car/caravan £7-£8, motorhome £7-£8, motorbike/tent £7-£8, children £0.50-£0.75
Calor Gaz WS
Last arrival time: 21:00

➔ From A52, 3 miles E of Nottingham, turn S at traffic lights towards Cropwell Bishop. Park is ½ mile on left. From A46, 5 miles SE of Nottingham turn N signposted Stragglethorpe. Park is 2½ miles on right.
See advert on this page

OKEHAMPTON Devon   2C3

Bridestow Caravan Park
Bridestowe, Okehampton EX20 4ER
☏ 01837-861261
Open March-end December
Size 5.5 acres, 13 touring pitches, 13 with electric hookup, 13 level pitches, 36 static caravans, 4, 9 WCs, 1 CWP
£ car/tent £6.50, car/caravan £6.50, motorhome £6.50, motorbike/tent £4, children £0.50
Rental from £85-£220
Calor Gaz WS
Last arrival time: 22:30

➔ Turn off A30 at Sourton Cross junction, follow signs to Bridestowe Village. In the village follow signs to the park.

Camping & Caravanning Club Site
Lydford, Nr Okehampton EX20 4BE
☏ 01822-820275
Open March-November
Size 4 acres, 70 touring pitches, 30 with electric hookup, 8, 18 WCs, 1 CWP
£ car/tent £10.40-£13.60, car/caravan £10.40-£13.60, motorhome £10.40-£13.60, motorbike/tent £10.40-£13.60, children £1.50
MasterCard Visa
Calor
Last arrival time: 23:00

➔ From A30 take A386, signposted Tavistock, take A386 until you come to a filling station on your right. Turn right, signposted Lydford, at this junction, go into Lydford, at the War Memorial turn right, the campsite sign is 200 yards. At the fork road take the right fork, the site is 100 yards on the left.

Owermoigne

Dartmoor View Holiday Park
Whiddon Down, Okehampton EX20 2QL
☎ 01647-231545 Fax 01647-231654
Open March-November ⚠ 🚐 🚍

A quiet, friendly and superbly maintained family holiday park within easy reach of the A30 and the perfect base for touring glorious Devon and Cornwall. Letterboxing centre with licensed bar, heated outdoor pool and take-away.
Size 5.5 acres, 75 touring pitches, 40 with electric hookup, 31 static caravans, 4 🚿, 8 WCs, 1 CWP
£ car/tent £6.50-£9, car/caravan £6.50-£9, motorhome £6.50-£9, motorbike/tent £6.50-£9, children £1.35
Rental 🚐 Chalet. £115-£303
CC MasterCard Visa
🛁 ✗¼ 🍴 🛒 🎮 📺 ♿ ⛽ Calor Gaz 🐕 WS
Last arrival time: 22:00
➜ A30 from Exeter to Merry Meet roundabout (17 miles), turn left. Park ½ mile from roundabout on right

Olditch Farm Caravan & Camping Park
Sticklepath, Okehampton EX20 2NT
☎ 01837-840734 Fax 01837-840877
Open 14 March-14 November ⚠ 🚐 🚍

A small family run site, within the Dartmoor National Park - direct walking access to the moor, small play area for children, dogs welcome. Approximately one hour from the coast.
Size 5 acres, 35 touring pitches, 15 with electric hookup, 12 level pitches, 20 static caravans, 4 🚿, 12 WCs, 1 CWP
£ car/tent £5.50-£6.50, car/caravan £5.50-£6.50, motorhome £5.50-£6.50, motorbike/tent £6.50
Rental 🚐 £95-£240
🛁¼ ✗ ✗¼ 🛒 🎮 📺 ♿ ⛽ Calor Gaz 🐕 WS
Last arrival time: 22:00
➜ 3 miles E of Okehampton turn off A30 at Merry Meet roundabout. Site is 3 miles down Old Road.

Yertiz Caravan and Camping Park
Exeter Road, Okehampton EX20 1QF
☎ 01837-52281
Open all year ⚠ 🚐 🚍
Size 3.5 acres, 30 touring pitches, 22 with electric hookup, 8 level pitches, 4 static caravans, 3 🚿, 5 WCs, 1 CWP
£ car/tent £4.50-£7, car/caravan £5-£7, motorhome £5-£7, motorbike/tent £4.50-£5.50, children £0.50
Rental 🚐 £90-£220
🛁¼ ✗¼ 🍴¼ 🛒 ⛽ Calor Gaz ♿ 🐕
Last arrival time: 23:30
➜ From Exeter on the A30 take the B3260 signposted Okehampton. Site on left 50 yards past Moorcroft Inn.

OSWESTRY Shropshire   7D2

Royal Hill Inn
Edgerley, Kinnerley, Oswestry SY10 8ES
☎ 01743-741242
Open April-October ⚠ 🚐 🚍
Size 2.5 acres, 25 touring pitches, 4 static caravans, 2 🚿, 2 WCs, 1 CWP
£ car/tent £4.50, car/caravan £4.50, motorhome £4.50, motorbike/tent £4.50
Rental 🚐 £80-£100
🛒 🎮 ⛽ Calor ♿ 🐕
Last arrival time: 22:00
➜ From A5 (Shrewsbury), left at Melverley sign, left out of Pentre at post office. Site 1 mile from Pentre next to Severn River.

OWERMOIGNE Dorset   3F3

Sandyholme Holiday Park
Moreton Road, Owermoigne DT2 8HZ
☎ 01305-852677 Fax 01305-854677
Open Easter-31 October ⚠ 🚐 🚍

Quiet family run site situated in Hardy countryside near the picturesque village of Owermoigne with all amenities. Central for Weymouth, Dorchester and Lulworth Cove.
Size 6 acres, 65 touring pitches, 58 with electric hookup, 65 level pitches, 35 static caravans, 8 🚿, 20 WCs, 1 CWP
£ car/tent £5.50-£10.50, car/caravan £5.50-£10.50, motorhome £5.50-£10.50, motorbike/tent £5-£10
Rental 🚐 £115-£310

ENGLAND

Owermoigne

← **Sandyholme Holiday Park**

《 MasterCard Visa
Calor Gaz WS
Last arrival time: 22:00

→ Turn off A352 Dorchester/Wareham road through village of Owermoigne for 1 mile.

OXFORD Oxfordshire 4B2

Cassington Mill Caravan Park
Eynsham Road, Cassington, Oxford OX8 1DB
☎ 01865-881081 Fax 01865-884167
Open 1 April-31 October

A quiet, grassy site, with the River Evenlode running through the park. Restaurant one mile. Swimming pool seven miles.
Size 4 acres, 83 touring pitches, 70 with electric hookup, 83 level pitches, 35 static caravans, 4, 30 WCs, 2 CWPs
£ car/tent £8-£9.50, car/caravan £8-£9.50, motorhome £8-£9.50, motorbike/tent £6-£6.50, children £2
《 MasterCard Visa
Calor Gaz WS
Last arrival time: 21:00

→ A40 W of Oxford, second left, signposted.

Diamond Farm Caravan & Camping Park
Bletchingdon, Oxford OX5 3DR
☎ 01869-350909 Fax 01869-350918
Open all year

A small family run site set in the heart of the countryside. Offering first class facilities. Only 3 miles from junction 9 of the M40.
Size 3 acres, 37 touring pitches, 26 with electric hookup, 37 level pitches, 4, 8 WCs, 1 CWP
£ car/tent £7-£10, car/caravan £7-£10, motorhome £7-£10, motorbike/tent £7-£10, children £1.50
Calor Gaz
Last arrival time: 22:00

→ From M40 junction 9 follow A34 for about 3 miles towards Oxford. Take second exit off A34 and follow signs for Bletchingdon.

Oxford Camping International
426 Abingdon Road, Oxford OX1 4XN
☎ 01865-246551 Fax 01865-240145
Open all year

Situated on the edge of Oxford, just over one mile from the historic centre and ½ mile from the River Thames, with good access to the M4/M40.
Size 5 acres, 129 touring pitches, 90 with electric hookup, 129 level pitches, 10, 21 WCs, 1 CWP
£ car/tent £8.95, car/caravan £8.95, motorhome £8.95, motorbike/tent £7.80
《 MasterCard Visa
¼ ×¼ ¼ Calor Gaz
Last arrival time: 22:00

→ On S side of Oxford, take A4144 to city centre from ring road, ¼ mile on left. Rear of Touchwoods Outdoor Life Centre.

PADSTOW Cornwall 2B3

Carnevas Holiday Park
St. Merryn, Padstow PL28 8PN
☎ 01841-520230 Fax 01841-520230
Open April-October

Size 12 acres, 195 touring pitches, 50 with electric hookup, 75 level pitches, 9 static caravans, 18, 21 WCs, 1 CWP
£ car/tent £5.50-£9, car/caravan £5.50-£9, motorhome £5.50-£9, motorbike/tent £5.50-£9, children £0.80
Rental Chalet. £100-£395
Calor Gaz

→ From village of St Merryn take B3276 towards Porthcothan Bay, turn right off Tredrea Inn and park is ¼ mile on right.

Dennis Cove Camping
Padstow PL28 8DR
☎ 01841-532349
Open Easter-30 September
Size 5 acres, 62 touring pitches, 22 level pitches, 7, 18 WCs, 1 CWP

Paignton

£ car/tent £7.80-£11, car/caravan £7.80-£11, motorhome £7.80-£11, motorbike/tent £7.80-£11, children £1.10-£1.60

¼ ✗ ✗¼ ● ●¼ ⊡ 🔲 ⟶ ⚠ ⊕ Calor Gaz ☂

Last arrival time: 23:00

➡ From A389 turn right at town sign, then second right into Dennis Lane. Camp site is at the end of lane.

Maribou Holidays

St Merryn, Padstow PL28 8QA
📞 01841-520520 Fax 01841-521154
Open Easter-October 🅰 ⛺ 🚐

Size 26 acres, 100 touring pitches, 20 with electric hookup, 80 level pitches, 100 static caravans, 6 🚿, 20 WCs, 1 CWP

£ car/tent £4.50-£8, car/caravan £4.50-£8, motorhome £4.50-£8, motorbike/tent £8

Rental ⛺ Chalet. £95-£325

¼ ● ⊡ 🔲 GR ⚠ ⊕ Calor ☂

Last arrival time: 21:00

➡ From Wadebridge SW on A39 to first roundabout. Right onto B3274. Second left to St Merryn, over crossroads to site in 1 mile.

Music Water Touring Site

Rumford, Padstow PL27 7SJ
📞 01841-540257 Fax 01841-540257
Open April-October 🅰 ⛺ 🚐

Size 8 acres, 140 touring pitches, 60 with electric hookup, 130 level pitches, 7 static caravans, 8 🚿, 18 WCs, 2 CWPs

£ car/tent £4-£7, car/caravan £4-£7, motorhome £4-£7, motorbike/tent £4-£7, children £1

Rental ⛺

¼ ✗ ● ⊡ 🔲 ⟶ GR ⚠ ⊕ Calor Gaz ☂ WS

➡ From junction of A39 and B3274 (N of St Columb Major), N on B3274 signed Padstow for 2 miles, turn left to site on right in just over ¼ mile.

Trevean Farm Caravan & Camping Site

St Merryn, Padstow PL28 8PR
📞 01841-520772
Open 1 April-31 October 🅰 ⛺ 🚐

Size 2 acres, 36 touring pitches, 12 with electric hookup, 36 level pitches, 3 static caravans, 4 🚿, 7 WCs, 1 CWP

£ car/tent £5.50, car/caravan £5.50, motorhome £5.50, motorbike/tent £4, children £0.50

Rental ⛺ £100-£260

¼ ⊡ 🔲 ⚠ Calor Gaz ☂ WS

Last arrival time: 22:00

➡ From St Merryn village take B3276 Newquay road for 1 mile. Turn left for Rumford. Site is ¼ mile right.

PAIGNTON Devon	3D3

Beverley Park Holiday Centre

Goodrington Road, Paignton TQ4 7JE
📞 01803-843887 Fax 01803-845427
Open Easter-November 🅰 ⛺ 🚐

Superb holiday park overlooking Torbay, offering the very best in touring park facilities. The perfect centre for exploring Devon.

Size 21 acres, 194 touring pitches, 190 with electric hookup, 40 level pitches, 198 static caravans, 24 🚿, 48 WCs, 3 CWPs

£ car/tent £7.50-£13.50, car/caravan £9-£15, motorhome £9-£15, motorbike/tent £7.50-£13.50, children £1.80

Rental ⛺ £88-£515

㏄ MasterCard Visa

¼ ✗ ● ⊡ 🔲 ⟶ 🎣 🎳 GR ⚠ ⊕ Calor Gaz ♿

Last arrival time: 22:00

➡ 2 miles S of Paignton on A380, then take A3022 and turn left into Goodrington Road.

Grange Court Holiday Centre

Grange Road, Goodrington, Paignton TQ4 7JP
📞 01803-558010 Fax 01803-663336
Open 15 February-15 January 🅰 ⛺ 🚐

Superb family park with extensive entertainment and leisure facilities including a new indoor pool complex and licensed club. Panoramic view across Torbay.

Size 65 acres, 157 touring pitches, 157 with electric hookup, 90 level pitches, 530 static caravans, 33 🚿, 35 WCs, 3 CWPs

£ car/tent £8.50-£21, car/caravan £8.50-£21, motorhome £8.50-£21

Rental ⛺

㏄ MasterCard Visa

¼ ✗ ● ⊡ 🔲 ⟶ 🎳 GR ⚠ ⊕ Calor Gaz

Last arrival time: 22:00

➡ From junction of A380 (Paignton ring road) and A385, travel S on A380 for 1 mile. Turn left into Goodrington Road. After ¾ mile turn left into Grange Road. The park is signposted.

Paignton

LOWER YALBERTON Holiday Park

- Touring Caravans • Tents
- Holiday Vans • Bar
- Heated Pool • Snack Bar
- Launderette • Family Room
- Entertainment

LONG ROAD, PAIGNTON, DEVON TQ4 7PQ
Tel: 01803 558127

Higher Well Farm Holiday Park
Stoke Gabriel, Paignton TQ9 6RN
01803-782289
Open Easter-October
Size 12 acres, 30 touring pitches, 30 with electric hookup, 28 level pitches, 18 static caravans, 12, 22 WCs, 1 CWP
£ car/tent £6.30, car/caravan £6.30, motorhome £6.30, children £1
Rental £125-£340 weekly. £18 nightly.
Calor Gaz
Last arrival time: 22:00
→ Take A385 from Paignton to Totnes and turn left at Parker Arms pub. Head straight on for 1½ miles and turn left.

Holly Gruit Camp
Brixham Road, Paignton TQ4 7BA
01803-550763
Open end May-end September
Size 3 acres, 70 touring pitches, 70 level pitches, 4, 11 WCs,
£ car/tent £8-£9, motorbike/tent £8-£9
Calor Gaz
Last arrival time: 23:00
→ From junction of A3022 and A385 (1 mile W of Paignton), travel S on A3022 for ¾ mile. Site signposted.

Lower Yalberton Holiday Park
Long Road, Lower Yalberton, Paignton TQ4 7PQ
01803-558127 Fax 01803-558127
Open May-September
Size 25 acres, 550 touring pitches, 90 with electric hookup, 8 static caravans, 22, 3 CWPs
£ car/tent £7-£9, car/caravan £8-£11, motorhome £8-£9.50, motorbike/tent £9, children £1-£1.75
Rental £130-£330 weekly.
MasterCard Visa
Calor Gaz
Last arrival time: 20:30
→ 2½ miles from Paignton. 5 miles from Torquay. 3 miles from Brixham. 1 mile S of intersection of A385 and A3022 Paignton ring road. Turn W off the A3022 into Long Road for ¾ mile
See advert on this page

Ramslade Touring Park
Stoke Road, Stoke Gabriel TQ9 6QB
01803-782575 Fax 01803-782828
Open mid March-31 October
Size 8.5 acres, 135 touring pitches, 135 with electric hookup, 135 level pitches, 12, 20 WCs, 4 CWPs
£ car/tent £8.80-£12.30, car/caravan £8.80-£12.30, motorhome £8.80-£12.30, motorbike/tent £8.80-£12.30, children £1.10-£1.20
MasterCard Visa
Calor Gaz WS
Last arrival time: 21:00
→ Turn off A385 Paignton to Totnes road at Parkers Arms, Ramslade is 1½ miles on right, near Stoke Gabriel.

Widend Touring Park
Berry Pomeroy Road, Marldon, Paignton TQ3 1RT
01830-550116
Open Easter-October
Size 22 acres, 184 touring pitches, 133 with electric hookup, 174 level pitches, 17, 28 WCs, 3 CWPs
£ car/tent £5.50-£9.50, car/caravan £5.50-£10, motorhome £5.50-£10, children £1-£1.50
MasterCard Visa
Calor Gaz
Last arrival time: 21:00
→ Follow A380 Torbay ring road. At second roundabout turn towards Marldon. At next roundabout turn second left into Five Lanes - Singmore Hotel on corner. Head towards Berry Pomeroy and Totnes following camping signs. Widend is 1 mile from ring road.

Hints & Tips

Tyres are your only contact with the road. Look after them and you will improve the safety and behaviour of your unit. Never mix cross ply and radials on the same axis.

Penrith

PAR Cornwall 2B4

Par Sands Holiday Park
Par Beach, Par PL24 2AS
☎ 01726-812868 Fax 01726-817899
Open 1 April-31 October

A flat, grassy site alongside a large, safe, sandy beach. Ideal position for touring Cornwall. Modern toilet and shower facilities, electric hook-ups, super pitches and baby's bathroom.
Size 23 acres, 199 touring pitches, 114 with electric hookup, 199 level pitches, 210 static caravans, 20 ☏, 26 WCs, 2 CWPs
£ car/tent £6-£14, car/caravan £6-£14, motorhome £6-£14, motorbike/tent £6-£14, children £1
Rental Holiday homes - £110-£440
CC MasterCard Visa

➜ Signposted ½ mile E of Par on A3082, heading towards Fowey.

PATELEY BRIDGE North Yorkshire 10C3

Studfold Farm
Lofthouse, Harrogate HG3 5SG
☎ 01423-755210
Open April-October
Size 3 acres, 20 touring pitches, 20 with electric hookup, 20 level pitches, 60 static caravans, 8 ☏, 15 WCs, 1 CWP
£ car/tent £6-£9, car/caravan £7-£9, motorhome £6-£9, children £1.50
Rental £120 per week

➜ 7 miles from Pateley Bridge.

Hints & Tips

If you have any information concerning caravan theft contact the confidential freephone Crimestoppers Line on 0800 555111.
You may be entitled to a reward and there is no need to give your name if you don't want to.

LOWTHER CARAVAN PARK

We should like to extend an invitation to all those who have not yet discovered Lowther Caravan Park – a renowned haven of peace and tranquillity, set in 50 acres of natural parkland, home of the rare and fascinating red squirrel.

EAMONT BRIDGE, PENRITH, CUMBRIA CA10 2JB
Tel: (01768) 863631
Fax: (01768) 868126

PENRITH Cumbria 10B1

Lowther Holiday Park
Eamont Bridge, Penrith CA10 2JB
☎ 01768-63631 Fax 01768-868126
Open March-November
Size 50 acres, 221 touring pitches, 175 with electric hookup, 200 level pitches, 403 static caravans, 25 ☏, 30 WCs, 2 CWPs
£ car/tent £6.50-£13.50, car/caravan £6.50-£13.50, motorhome £6.50-£13.50, motorbike/tent £6.50-£13.50
Rental from £150-£310
CC MasterCard Visa

Last arrival time: 22:00
➜ From roundabout (junction of A6, A66 and A686) S of Penrith, travel on A6 for ½ mile, then right along W bank of River Lowther to site.
See advert on this page

Thacka Lea Caravan Site
Penrith CA11 9HX
☎ 01768-863319
Open March-October
Size 1 acre, 25 touring pitches, 24 with electric hookup, 25 level pitches, 2 ☏, 7 WCs, 1 CWP
£ car/caravan £6, motorhome £6

➜ Off A6 N of Penrith.

Penruddock

PENRUDDOCK Cumbria   10B1

Beckses Caravan Site
Penruddock CA11 ORX
☎ 01768-483224   Fax 01768-483006
Open Easter-31 October

A small pleasant site on the fringe of the Lake District National Park, offering modern facilities to pitch tents or caravans. Hire of luxury caravans available.
Size 20 acres, 23 touring pitches, 23 with electric hookup, 15 level pitches, 18 static caravans, 6, 10 WCs, 1 CWP
£ car/tent £5, car/caravan £6.50, motorhome £6.50, motorbike/tent £5
Rental £140 - £200 weekly.
¼ Calor Gaz
Last arrival time: 22:00
➜ From M6 junction 40 take A66 W to Keswick. Take B5288 on the right.

PENZANCE Cornwall   2A4

Camping & Caravanning Club Site
Higher Tregiffian Farm, St Buryan, Penzance TR19 6JB
☎ 01736-871588
Open March-September
Size 4 acres, 75 touring pitches, 38 with electric hookup, 6, 9 WCs, 1 CWP
£ car/tent £10.40-£13.60, car/caravan £10.40-£13.60, motorhome £10.40-£13.60, motorbike/tent £10.40-£13.60, children £1.50
cc MasterCard Visa
¼ X¼ ¼ Calor WS
Last arrival time: 23:00
➜ Follow the A30 towards Lands End. Turn right on to the A3306 St Just/Pendeen Road. The site is 50 yards on the left.

Kenneggy Cove Holiday Park
Higher Kenneggy, Rosudgeon, Penzance TR20 9AU
☎ 01736-763453   Fax 01736-763453
Open 31 March-31 October

In a superb location overlooking Mount's Bay and Lizard Penninsula, this is a quiet family site ideally situated for walking and exploring West Cornwall.
Size 4 acres, 60 touring pitches, 21 with electric hookup, 50 level pitches, 9 static caravans, 6, 12 WCs, 1 CWP
£ car/tent £4.30-£7.50, car/caravan £4.30-£7.50, motorhome £4.30-£7.50, motorbike/tent £4.30-£7.50, children £0.75
Rental £110-£285
Calor Gaz WS
Last arrival time: 23:00
➜ 3 miles E of Marazion on A394 just E of Rosudgeon. Turn S for ½ mile to park.

Tower Park Camping and Caravanning
St Buryan, Penzance TR19 6BZ
☎ 01736-810286
Open March-January
Size 12 acres, 102 touring pitches, 30 with electric hookup, 102 level pitches, 5 static caravans, 10, 12 WCs, 2 CWPs
£ car/tent £5.50-£8.50, car/caravan £5.50-£8.50, motorhome £5.50-£8.50, motorbike/tent £5-£7.50, children £1.50-£2
¼ X¼ Calor Gaz
Last arrival time: 22:00
➜ 3 miles from Penzance on A30 fork left on B3283 to St Buryan. In village take first right and right again. Park is 300 yards on the right on St Just Road.

PERRANPORTH Cornwall   2A4

Blue Seas Holidays
Newquay Road, Goonhavern TR4 9QD
☎ 01872-572176
Open Easter-October

Pickering

Eight static luxury caravans with sea and beach views on a quiet family park, overlooking Perranporth. Only ten minutes walk to golden sands, lake and shops.
Rental £85-£330 weekly
✗¼ ●¼ Calor
➜ In Perranporth on B3285, 800 yards on right from town centre.

Perran Sands Holiday Super Centre
Perranporth TR6A OAQ
☎ 01872-573551 Fax 01872-571158
Open May-October
Size 500 acres, 350 touring pitches, 232 with electric hookup, 350 level pitches, 36, 44 WCs, 3 CWPs
Rental Chalet.
CC MasterCard Visa
¼ ✗ ✗¼ ● ●¼
Calor Gaz
Last arrival time: 22:00
➜ A30 through Cornwall, turn right on to the B3285 towards Perranporth. Perran Sands is on the right.

Perranporth Camping & Touring Park
Budnick Road, Perranporth TR6 0AQ
☎ 01872-572174
Open Easter-end September

The park is situated in a sheltered valley, ½ mile from the town and beach, adjacent to the golf club and 200 yards from riding stables.
Size 7 acres, 160 touring pitches, 24 with electric hookup, 9 static caravans, 10, 19 WCs, 1 CWP
£ car/tent £8-£11, car/caravan £8-£11, motorhome £8-£11, motorbike/tent £8-£11, children £1-£1.50
Rental
CC MasterCard Visa
✗ ● Calor Gaz
Last arrival time: 23:00
➜ ½ mile NE of Perranporth centre.

Hints & Tips

Tyres are your only contact with the road. Look after them and you will improve the safety and behaviour of your unit. Never mix cross ply and radials on the same axis.

PETWORTH West Sussex   4C3

Camping & Caravanning Club Site
Great Bury, Graffham, Petworth GU28 0QJ
☎ 01798-867476
Open March-November
Size 20 acres, 90 touring pitches, 30 with electric hookup, 6, 11 WCs, 2 CWPs
£ car/tent £10.40-£13.60, car/caravan £10.40-£13.60, motorhome £10.40-£13.60, motorbike/tent £10.40-£13.60, children £1.50
CC MasterCard Visa
¼ ✗¼ ●¼ Calor WS
Last arrival time: 23:00
➜ Coming from Petworth (A285) pass Badgers pub on the left and BP garage on the right. Take the next right, sign posted Selham Graffham (with brown camping sign), follow this sign to the site. Coming from Chichester, A285 through Duncton, turn left at Selham Graffham sign.

PEVENSEY BAY East Sussex   5D4

Camping & Caravanning Club Site
Norman's Bay, Pevensey Bay BN24 6PR
☎ 01323-761190
Open March-November
Size 12 acres, 200 touring pitches, 111 with electric hookup, 14, 24 WCs, 2 CWPs
£ car/tent £11.50-£14.60, car/caravan £11.50-£14.60, motorhome £11.50-£14.60, motorbike/tent £11.50-£14.60, children £1.60
CC MasterCard Visa
¼ ✗¼ ●¼ Calor WS
Last arrival time: 23:00
➜ From the roundabout at the junction of A27/A259 follow the A259 signed Eastbourne. After entering Pevensey Bay village, take the first left (coast road) signed Beachlands only. After 1¼ miles, the site is on the left.

PICKERING North Yorkshire   11E2

Forestry Commission Spiers House C & C
Cropton, Pickering YO18 8ES
☎ 01751-417591
Open end March-end September
Size 15 acres, 150 touring pitches, 75 with electric hookup, 100 level pitches, 13, 19 WCs, 1 CWP
£ car/tent £6.50-£7.90, car/caravan £6.50-£7.90, motorhome £6.50-£7.90, motorbike/tent £6.50-£7.90
CC MasterCard Visa
Calor Gaz
Last arrival time: 22:00
➜ I mile N of Cropton on A170 (Rosedale road), turn right at sign.

ENGLAND

Wayside Caravan Park
Wrelton, Pickering YO18 8PG
☎ 01751-472608 Fax 01751-472608
Open Easter-early October ⚑ 🚐 🚏

Quiet, south facing, sheltered park with country views, with modern toilet facilites and cubicled wash basins. Ideal centre for the North York Moors and the coast.
Size 10 acres, 72 touring pitches, 60 with electric hookup, 72 level pitches, 10 ⚐, 21 WCs, 1 CWP
£ car/tent £7.50, car/caravan £8.50, motorhome £7.50
Last arrival time: 23:00
➜ 2½ miles W of Pickering off A170, signposted at Wrelton, off bypass.

PLYMOUTH Devon 2C4

Brixton Caravan & Camping Park
Venn Farm, Brixton, Plymouth PL8 2AX
☎ 01752-880378
Open March-October ⚑ 🚐 🚏
Size 2 acres, 43 touring pitches, 12 with electric hookup, 12 ⚐, 1 CWP
Last arrival time: 23:00
➜ Located on A379 in Brixton, signposted.

POLZEATH Cornwall 2B3

Southwinds Caravan & Camping Site
Polzeath PL27 6QU
☎ 01208-863267 Fax 01208-862080
Open Easter-October ⚑ 🚐 🚏
Size 6 acres, 50 touring pitches, 40 with electric hookup, 50 level pitches, 8 ⚐, 14 WCs, 1 CWP
£ car/tent £6, car/caravan £8, motorhome £6
⚅ MasterCard Visa
Last arrival time: 23:00
➜ 7 miles N of Wadebridge on B3314.
See advert on opposite page

Tristram Camping & Caravan Park
Polzeath PL27 6SR
☎ 01208-862215 Fax 01208-862080
Open Easter-October ⚑ 🚐 🚏
Size 5 acres, 70 touring pitches, 65 with electric hookup, 60 level pitches, 12 ⚐, 18 WCs, 1 CWP
⚅ MasterCard Visa

➜ From Wadebridge, take B3314 to Polzeath
See advert on opposite page

POOLE Dorset 3F3

Beacon Hill Touring Park
Blandford Road North, Poole BH16 6AB
☎ 01202-631631
Open Easter-end September ⚑ 🚐 🚏

A secluded, peaceful site, yet close to the main routes. An ideal touring base for Dorset, Bournemouth and the New Forest, and only three miles from the Poole ferry terminal. Fishing, tennis, bar (entertainment and take-away during the high season).
Size 30 acres, 170 touring pitches, 140 with electric hookup, 150 level pitches, 22 ⚐, 25 WCs, 3 CWPs
£ car/tent £6.60-£15, car/caravan £7.40-£15, motorhome £6.60-£15, motorbike/tent £6.60-£13
Last arrival time: 23:00
➜ ¼ mile N of junction of A35 and A350 towards Blandford. 3 miles N of Poole.

BEACON HILL TOURING PARK

A secluded, peaceful site, yet close to the main routes. An ideal touring base for Dorset, Bournemouth and the New Forest, and only three miles from the Poole ferry terminal. Fishing, tennis, bar (entertainment and take-away during the high season).

**BLANDFORD ROAD NORTH,
POOLE, DORSET BH16 6AB
Tel: 01202 631631**

STUNNING LOCATIONS EXCELLENT FACILITIES

Polzeath Bay, North Cornwall

SouthWinds

Tristram

COLOUR BROCHURE ON REQUEST

Polzeath is probably one of the most spectacular beaches in Cornwall. Visitors keep coming back year after year to enjoy the beauty and safety of its golden sands and clear blue sea. Polzeath is ideal for families with young children as there are numerous rock pools where they can play and swim in safety. Polzeath also boasts one of the best surfing beaches in Cornwall for the professional as well as the beginner. There are numerous other attractions and activities in the immediate location. At nearby Rock there's sailing, water skiing and wind surfing all within the beautiful Camel estuary.

We have two sites at Polzeath as shown on the aerial picture. Tristram is positioned on the gently sloping cliff overlooking the beach with its own direct access to the beach. The site is fenced off so it is private and safe for children. It also has its own shop and cafe / take away on site. South Winds is very different, many families like the location because it is so quiet and peaceful with beautiful sea and panoramic rural views yet only half a mile from the beach. Both sites have modern toilets, showers and laundry facilities.

Tristram and South Winds

For further information please call us on:
01208 863267 (South Winds)
01208 862215 (Tristram)
Fax: 01208 862080

AA | VISA

ULTIMATE CAMPING & CARAVAN HOLIDAY PARKS IN CORNWALL
South Winds, Polzeath, Cornwall PL27 6QU

ENGLAND

Poole

Pear Tree Touring Park
Organford, Poole BH16 6LA
📞 01202-622434　Fax 01202-631985
Open April-October

Size 7.5 acres, 125 touring pitches, 125 with electric hookup, 125 level pitches, 10, 20 WCs, 2 CWPs

£ car/tent £6.50-£9, car/caravan £6.50-£9, motorhome £6.50-£9, motorbike/tent £6.50-£9, children £1.50

cc MasterCard Visa

Calor Gaz WS

Last arrival time: 21:00

➡ Between A351 at Holton Heath and A35 at Lytchett Minster. Take A351 signposted to Wareham. At Holton Heath crossroads, turn right down road beside garage signposted Organford. About ½ mile down road on left is wide entrance to park.

See advert on this page

Pear Tree Touring Park

FINALIST IN THE CALOR CARAVAN PARK AWARDS 1998. MOST IMPROVED PARK CATEGORY.

A quiet, sheltered, family country park with seven and a half acres of touring and camping pitches. Children's Play Area. The park nestles on the edge of Wareham Forest. Ideal for walking and cycling. Centrally situated for Poole, Swanage and Bournemouth. The Purbeck Hills, lovely sandy beaches at Sandbanks and Studland Bay, and Poole ferry terminal are all within easy reach.

MODERN TOILET BLOCK – SHOP
CALOR & CAMPING GAZ – ELECTRIC HOOK-UPS
SUMMER & WINTER STORAGE AVAILABLE

ORGANFORD, POOLE, DORSET BH16 6LA
Tel: (01202) 622434

Rockley Park
Napier Road, Hamworthy, Poole BH15 4LZ
📞 01202-679393　Fax 01202-683159
Open March-October

A family holiday park in a lovely location overlooking Poole Harbour. Indoor/outdoor heated pools, kids clubs, sailing and scuba diving included in the wide range of leisure facilities. Cafe/snack bar and bars, excellent cabaret entertainment. A 'British Holidays Park'.

Size 87 acres, 73 touring pitches, 8 with electric hookup, 1,077 static caravans, 20, 1 CWP

£ car/tent £9-£20, car/caravan £9-£20, motorhome £13-£20, motorbike/tent £14, children £2

Rental from £157

cc MasterCard Visa

Calor

Last arrival time: 00:00

➡ Leave M27 for Poole and follow signs for Poole town centre. Once in town centre, Rockley Park is signposted.

Organford Manor Caravans & Holidays
Poole BH16 6ES
📞 01202-622202　Fax 01202-623278
Open 15 March-31 October

Quiet secluded site in wooded grounds of the manor house. Touring field is level, sheltered and well-drained with good amenities.

Size 3 acres, 75 touring pitches, 34 with electric hookup, 75 level pitches, 45 static caravans, 6, 8 WCs, 1 CWP

£ car/tent £7.50-£9, car/caravan £7.50-£9, motorhome £6-£7.50, motorbike/tent £6-£7.50

Calor Gaz WS

➡ Take first turning off A35, Poole to Dorchester road after the junction with A315 to Wareham, W of Lychett Minster, from there it is signposted.

Hints & Tips
Make sure your mirrors are adjusted correctly before moving off.

Porlock

121

Sandford Holiday Park
Holton Heath, Poole BH16 6JZ
☎ 01202-631600 Fax 01202-625678
Open Easter-end October ▲ 🚐 🚛

Large, well-organised, family site. Extensive amenities include swimming pool, clubhouse, 3 bars, ballroom, 2 restaurants, TV lounge, family room, children's swimming pool (with 'beach'), tennis courts, crazy golf, shortmat bowls and barbecues.
Size 64 acres, 505 touring pitches, 460 with electric hookup, 505 level pitches, 277 static caravans, 27 ☔, 60 WCs, 2 CWPs
£ car/tent £7.90-£13.40, car/caravan £7.90-£13.40, motorhome £7.90-£13.40, motorbike/tent £7.90-£12.40, children £1.50-£2.50
Rental 🚐 Chalet. £99-£799
CC MasterCard Visa
🛒 ✗ 🍴 📺 📞 📋 ⏵ 📠 🅿 GR 🔧 📺 ⚡ ⛽ Calor ♿ WS
Last arrival time: 00:00
➡ 2½ miles NE of Wareham on A351 turn into Organford Road at Holton Heath crossroads. Site is 50 yards on left.
See advert on this page

South Lytchett Manor Caravan Park
Lytchett Minster, Poole BH16 6JB
☎ 01202-622577
Open 1 April-3 October ▲ 🚐 🚛

Popular rural site situated in lovely parkland surroundings. Ideal base for beautiful beaches, sailing, windsurfing and touring the Purbeck area.
Size 11 acres, 150 touring pitches, 68 with electric hookup, 150 level pitches, 21 ☔, 26 WCs, 1 CWP
£ car/tent £7.40-£9, car/caravan £7.40-£9, motorhome £7.40-£9, motorbike/tent £7.40-£9, children £1.10-£1.45
CC MasterCard Visa
🛒 ✗¼ 🍴¼ 📺 📞 📋 📺 ⚡ Calor Gaz ♿ 🐕 WS
Last arrival time: 22:00
➡ From junction of A35 and A350, travel S on A350 to Upton. Turn right onto B3067 for 1 mile and site is on right.

PORLOCK Somerset   3D2

Burrowhayes Farm Camping & Caravan Site
West Luccombe, Porlock TA24 8HT
☎ 01643-862463
Open 15 March-31 October ▲ 🚐 🚛

Ideally situated for walkers and riders in the glorious Horner Valley, part of the National Trust's Holnicote Estate and Exmoor National Park. The site is surrounded by moors and woods with a stream running alongside. Riding stables operate from the farm.
Size 8 acres, 54 touring pitches, 40 with electric hookup, 40 level pitches, 19 static caravans, 8 ☔, 17 WCs, 2 CWPs

➡

ENGLAND

Beautiful Spaces in Breathtaking Places
Sandford Holiday Park in Dorset...

Set in sixty acres of beautiful woodland. Within easy reach of Bournemouth, Poole & Weymouth & superb sandy beaches. Free heated indoor & outdoor pools. Free nightly entertainment & childrens' clubs. Restaurant, supermarket & launderette. Super hook-ups with TV, electricity and water. New for 1999 - Eurotents.
Sandford Holiday Park - the perfect choice for touring Dorset

WESTSTAR Holiday Parks
For our Latest Brochure & Friendly Service
Call (01202) 631 600 Quote: RC

← Sandyholme Holiday Park

£ car/tent £5.50-£7.50, car/caravan £5.50-£7.50, motorhome £5.50-£7.50, motorbike/tent £5.50-£7.50, children £1
Rental £85-£240
Calor Gaz
➡ Take M5 to Bridgwater, A39 to Minehead, then towards Porlock. 5 miles W of Minehead, take left toward West Luccombe. Site in ¼ mile on right.

PORTHTOWN Cornwall	2A4

Rosehill Touring Park
Porthtowan TR4 8AR
☎ 01209-890802
Open April-October

A quiet, sheltered site just four minutes from the beach. Set on 3 acres with 40 level pitches, hot showers, WC's and a shop.
Size 3 acres, 40 touring pitches, 20 with electric hookup, 40 level pitches, 4, 7 WCs, 2 CWPs
£ car/tent £7-£10, car/caravan £7-£10, motorhome £7-£10, motorbike/tent £7-£10, children £1.50
Calor Gaz
Last arrival time: 21:30
➡ From A30 take St. Agnes road at Chiverton roundabout. Follow Porthtowan signs down the hill into Porthtowan. Park is situated on the left about 100 yards past Beach Road which is on the right.

PORTSMOUTH & SOUTHSEA Hampshire	4B4

Southsea Leisure Park
Melville Road, Southsea PO4 9TB
☎ 01705-735170 Fax 01705-821302
Open all year
Size 12 acres, 188 touring pitches, 188 with electric hookup, 188 level pitches, 45 static caravans, 16, 24 WCs, 4 CWPs
£ car/tent £7-£9, car/caravan £9-£15, motorbike/tent £8.50-£9
Rental
₢ MasterCard Visa
Calor Gaz WS
Last arrival time: 00:00
➡ From M27 take A2030 S for 3 miles, then turn left onto A288, following caravan signs, turn left into Bransbury Road. Site on left, signed.
See advert on this page

Porlock

READING Berkshire	4B2

Loddon Court Farm
Beech Hill Road, Spencers Wood, Reading RG7 1HT
☎ 01189-883153
Open all year
Size 4 acres, 30 touring pitches, 30 level pitches, 4, 8 WCs, 1 CWP
£ car/tent £6, car/caravan £6, motorhome £6, motorbike/tent £6, children £1
Calor WS
Last arrival time: 21:00
➡ Signposted from M4 junction 11 and from Riseley roundabout to A33. Both routes via Spencers Wood village and Beech Hill Road.

Wellington Country Park
Risebey, Reading R67 1SP
☎ 0118-932 6444 Fax 0118-932 6445
Open March-November
Size 350 acres, 58 touring pitches, 45 with electric hookup, 6, 16 WCs,
£ car/tent £7-£12.50, car/caravan £7-£12.50, motorhome £7-£12.50, motorbike/tent £7-£12.50
₢ MasterCard Visa
Last arrival time: 17:30
➡ Between Reading and Basingstoke off B3349.

Southsea Leisure Park

You couldn't get closer to the beach. A fully equipped 12 acre site right by the Solent. Touring and luxury holiday caravans. Heated outdoor pool, restaurant and 2 bars, park, shop, all modern facilities. An ideal stopover for the cross channel ferries (only 10 minutes' drive).
Special off-season rates.
Discounts for OAP's and CC members.

Southsea Leisure Park, Quote RAC C&C 98
Melville Road, Southsea, Hampshire PO4 9TB
Tel: 01705 735070 Fax: 01705 821302

Ringwood

123

RICHMOND North Yorkshire   10C2

Brompton-on-Swale Caravan Park
Brompton-on-Swale, Richmond DL10 7EZ
☎ 01748-824629   Fax 01748-824629
Open 21 March-31 October
Size 10 acres, 150 touring pitches, 145 with electric hookup, 150 level pitches, 22 static caravans, 15, 23 WCs, 2 CWPs
£ car/tent £7.25-£12.05, car/caravan £7.25-£11.05, motorhome £7.25-£11.05, children £0.95-£1.75
Rental Chalet. £145-£225
Calor Gaz
Last arrival time: 22:00
→ Exit A1 at Catterick onto A6136. Follow B6271 through Brompton-on-Swale towards Richmond. Park on left, 1½ SE of Richmond.

Swaleview Caravan Park
Reeth Road, Richmond DL10 4SF
☎ 01748-823106
Open March-October
Situated beside River Swale in a wooded valley in Yorkshire Dales National Park.
Size 12 acres, 25 touring pitches, 25 with electric hookup, 50 level pitches, 100 static caravans, 10, 20 WCs, 1 CWP
£ car/tent £6.10-£7.10, car/caravan £7.10-£7.30, motorhome £6.80-£7.10, motorbike/tent £7.10, children £0.50-£1
Rental £120-£195
Calor Gaz
Last arrival time: 21:00
→ 3 miles W of Richmond on A6108. 7 miles from A1/A1M at Scotch Corner.

RINGWOOD Hampshire   4A4

Oakdene Forest Park
Ringwood BH24 2RZ
☎ 01590-648331   Fax 01590-645610
Open 1 March-5 January

Oakdene is perfect for a family touring holiday, just 9 miles from Bournemouth on the edge of the Avon Forest. Superb facilities plus riding stables.

Size 55 acres, 200 touring pitches, 191 with electric hookup, 200 level pitches, 207 static caravans, 31, 54 WCs, 3 CWPs
£ car/tent £4.98-£19.95, car/caravan £4.98-£19.95, motorhome £4.98-£19.95, motorbike/tent £4.98-£19.95
Rental £110-£490 per week
℃ MasterCard Visa
Calor Gaz
Last arrival time: 22:00
→ M27 W, A31 through Ringwood heading W. Park is on left in 3 miles.
See advert on next page.

Oakhill Farm Caravan Park
St. Leonards, Ringwood BH24 2SB
☎ 01202-876968
Open 1 April-31 October
Size 10 acres, 80 touring pitches, 80 level pitches, 10, 16 WCs, 1 CWP
£ car/tent £6, car/caravan £6, motorhome £6, motorbike/tent £6, children £1
Calor Gaz WS
Last arrival time: 22:00
→ ¾ mile off main A31 at roundabout opposite Boundary Lane, St Leonards. Near hospital.

Red Shoot Camping Park
Linwood, Ringwood BH24 3QT
☎ 01425-473789   Fax 01425-471558
Open March-October

Beautifully situated in the New Forest. Ideal for walking, touring and the nature lover, yet only half an hour from the coast.
Size 4 acres, 105 touring pitches, 45 with electric hookup, 105 level pitches, 6, 18 WCs, 1 CWP
£ car/tent £8.10-£11.10, car/caravan £8.10-£11.10, motorhome £8.10-£11.10, motorbike/tent £8.10-£11.10
Calor Gaz
Last arrival time: 20:30
→ Off A338, 2 miles N of Ringwood, turn right and follow signs to Linwood. Site signed.

ENGLAND

Touring in the Perfect Location

Our Own Riding Stables

Forest Ponies

OAKDENE
FOREST PARK

Oakdene Forest Park will provide you with the perfect location for your touring holiday. There's all-weather fun and excitement for the kids and perfect relaxation for mum and dad. Set in 55 acres on the edge of the beautiful Avon Forest, Oakdene is only 9 miles from Bournemouth's sandy beaches offering the following superb facilities:

- Indoor and outdoor pools
- Our own riding stables
- Children's adventure playground
- Licensed club with entertainment
- Sauna, solarium and mini-gym
- Cafeteria and takeaway
- General store and launderette
- Touring pitches (many with power)
- Rallies welcome

Oakdene, St. Leonards, Ringwood, Hants BH24 2RZ
e-mail: holidays@shorefield.co.uk
http://www.shorefield.co.uk

Oakdene is a member of the Shorefield Group

For a free brochure telephone
01590 648331
Fax 01590 645610
Ref: ORAC
Office open seven days a week

The New Forest

Best of both worlds

Superb Pool

LYTTON Lawn is the perfect location for a relaxing touring holiday. Only 2½ miles from Shorefield Country Park, Lytton Lawn is set in beautiful natural parkland, close to Milford beach and the historic New Forest.

Caravans have individual pitches, with plenty of space for the car, caravan or tent, awning and barbecue.

Facilities include:
- Electricity hook up
- Showers and purpose-built laundrette
- 'Premier pitches' ● Children's area

Plus *FREE* membership of our exclusive Leisure Club, 2½ miles away at Shorefield:
- Indoor/Outdoor pools
- Dance Studio
- Tennis courts
- Top class restaurant
- Sauna, solarium and spa bath
- Special facilities for children
- Nightly entertainment

For a free brochure telephone
01590 648331
Quoting: RAC

Office open seven days a week

SHOREFIELD COUNTRY PARKS

Shorefield Country Parks, Shorefield Road, Milford on Sea, Hampshire SO41 0LH

ENGLAND

Ripon

RIPON North Yorkshire	11D3

River Laver Holiday Park
Studley Road, Ripon HG4 2QR
☎ 01765-690508 Fax 01748-811393
Open 1 March-31 December ▲ 🚐 🚛

A five acre park with 50 touring pitches, situated one mile from the city centre and ideally located for touring the Yorkshire Dales.
Size 5 acres, 50 touring pitches, 50 with electric hookup, 50 level pitches, 50 static caravans, 8 ☗, 10 WCs, 1 CWP
£ car/tent £7-£9, car/caravan £10-£11, motorhome £10-£11, motorbike/tent £7-£9
cc MasterCard Visa
🛁 ✕¼ 🚿¼ 🔲 📞 🔌 Calor Gaz ♿ 🐕 WS
Last arrival time: 21:00
➡ From A1 take A61 or B6265 to Ripon (following signs for Fountains Abbey). Park is situated off B6265, 1 mile from Ripon centre.

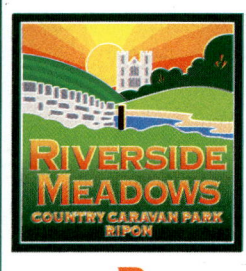

Riverside Meadows Country Caravan Park
Ure Bank Top, Ripon HG4 1JD
☎ 01765-602964 Fax 01765-604045
Open Easter-Oct ▲ 🚐 🚛
Size 26 acres, 175 touring pitches, 60 with electric hookup, 200 static caravans, 12 ☗, 24 WCs, 2 CWPs
£ car/tent £6.50-£10, car/caravan £6.50-£10, motorhome £6.50-£10, children £2
🛁 ✕ 🚿 🔲 📞 🔌 🔳 ⚡ 🔥 Calor 🐕 WS
Last arrival time: Dusk
➡ Leave Ripon N on A61. Cross River Ure and turn W and ahead bear right to site.
See advert on this page

Sleningford Watermill Caravan & Camping
North Stainley, Ripon HG4 3HQ
☎ 01765-635201
Open 1 April-31 October ▲ 🚐 🚛
Size 14 acres, 65 touring pitches, 50 with electric hookup, 55 level pitches, 25 static caravans, 10 ☗, 18 WCs, 6 CWPs
£ car/tent £8-£11, car/caravan £8-£11, motorhome £8-£11, motorbike/tent £8-£11, children £1
Rental Chalet. £150-£185
🛁 🔲 📞 🔌 🔳 ⚡ 🔥 Calor Gaz ♿ 🐕 WS
Last arrival time: 22:00
➡ 5 miles from Ripon on A6108.

ROBERTSBRIDGE East Sussex	5E3

Lordine Court Caravan Park
Ewhurst Green, Staplecross, Robertsbridge TN32 5TS
☎ 01580-830209 Fax 01580-830091
Open Easter-31 October ▲ 🚐 🚛

An inland site with good access to the main coastal resorts. Close to Bodiam Castle and the pretty town of Battle. Shop, licensed bar, pay-phone, children's playground, outdoor pool, restaurant. All year storage.
Size 40 acres, 120 touring pitches, 50 with electric hookup, 60 level pitches, 150 static caravans, 17 ☗, 25 WCs, 1 CWP
£ car/tent £5.50-£15, car/caravan £5.50-£15, motorhome £5.50-£15, motorbike/tent £5.50-£15
Rental 🚐 £100-£285 per week
🛁 ✕ 🚿 🔲 📞 🔌 🔳 ⚡ 🔥 Calor Gaz 🐕 WS
Last arrival time: 22:00
➡ A21 from London, left at Flimwell to Hawkhurst. B2244 at Hawkhurst to Cripps Corner. Left onto B2165 (Northam direction).

Riverside Country
Caravan Park
Dept. E
Ure Bank Top
Ripon HG4 1JD
Telephone:
01765 602964

AA

RELAX IN THE COUNTRY

Peaceful Holidays in the lovely
North Yorkshire Countryside

■ TOURING PITCHES
■ SEASONAL PITCHES
■ LUXURY CARAVANS FOR SALE

■ Walking ■ Fishing
■ Historic Towns & Villages
■ Studley Royal and Harlow Carr

Gardens of International Repute

Rugeley

ROCHDALE Lancashire   10C4

Hollingworth Lake Caravan Park
Rakewood, Littleborough, Rochdale OL15 0AT
☎ 01706-378661
Open all year
Size 7 acres, 45 touring pitches, 35 with electric hookup, 45 level pitches, 8 🚿, 8 WCs, 2 CWPs
£ car/tent £6-£8, car/caravan £6-£8, motorhome £5-£8, motorbike/tent £4-£6
Rental Chalet.
Calor Gaz WS
Last arrival time: 20:00
➜ From M62 junction 21 take B6225 from Hollingworth Lake Country Park, at Fisherman's Inn. Take Rakenwood Road, then second on right.

ROTHBURY Northumberland   13F3

Coquetdale Caravan Park
Whitton, Rothbury NE65 7RU
☎ 01669-620549
Open Easter-31 October
Size 14 acres, 55 touring pitches, 30 with electric hookup, 30 level pitches, 180 static caravans, 10 🚿, 15 WCs, 2 CWPs
£ car/tent £8-£10, car/caravan £8-£12, motorhome £8-£12, motorbike/tent £8-£10
Calor Gaz WS
➜ ½ mile SW of Rothbury on Newton road.

ROYDON Essex   5D2

Roydon Mill Leisure Park
Roydon, Harlow CM19 5EJ
☎ 01279-792777   Fax 01279-792695
Open all year
Size 58 acres, 110 touring pitches, 72 with electric hookup, 110 level pitches, 106 static caravans, 8 🚿, 14 WCs, 2 CWPs
£ car/tent £10-£11, car/caravan £10-£11, motorhome £10-£11, motorbike/tent £10-£11, children £1.80
Rental £160-£300
₡ MasterCard Visa
Calor Gaz WS
Last arrival time: 22:00
➜ From N via A1 or M1/M25/M11. From S take junction 7 off M11 and follow signs to Harlow, then A414 and B181 to Roydon. At end of High Street, just before level crossing.

RUAN MINOR Cornwall   2A4

Gwendreath Farm Caravan Park
Kennack Sands, Ruan Minor, Helston TR12 7LZ
☎ 01326-290666
Open Easter-October

Size 7 acres, 10 touring pitches, 10 with electric hookup, 16 level pitches, 30 static caravans, 4 🚿, 8 WCs, 1 CWP
£ car/tent £5.30-£6.50, car/caravan £5.30-£6.50, motorhome £5.30-£6.50, motorbike/tent £5.30-£6.50, children £1.10-£1.40
Rental £79-£329
₡ MasterCard Visa
Calor Gaz
➜ From Helston take A3083, then left on to B3293 signposted St Keverne. Continue 4 miles to Goonhilly Earth station and take next right then next left. At end of lane turn right over cattle grid and drive through Seaview and stop at second shop.

RUGELEY Staffordshire   7F2

Camping & Caravanning Club Site
Old Youth Hostel, Wandon, Rugeley WS15 1QW
☎ 01889-582166
Open March-November
Size 5 acres, 59 touring pitches, 35 with electric hookup, 6 🚿, 6 WCs, 1 CWP
£ car/tent £10.40-£13.60, car/caravan £10.40-£13.60, motorhome £10.40-£13.60, motorbike/tent £10.40-£13.60, children £1.50
₡ MasterCard Visa
Gaz WS
Last arrival time: 23:00
➜ On A460 to Hednesford turn right at signpost Rawnsley, Hazelslade, then first left, site is ½ mile past golf club.

Silvertrees Caravan Park
Stafford Brook Road, Rugeley WS15 2TX
☎ 01889-582185   Fax 01889-582185
Open 1 April-31 October

Set in the heart of Cannock Chase, Silvertrees is an idyllically peaceful park, set in 30 acres of natural woodlands, graded '4 ticks' and Rose Awarded by the ETB.
Size 30 acres, 50 touring pitches, 50 with electric hookup, 50 level pitches, 50 static caravans, 4 🚿, 9 WCs, 1 CWP
£ car/caravan £8-£10, motorhome £8-£10
Rental £149-£350 (short breaks from £77)
₡ MasterCard Visa
Calor
➜ 2 miles W of Rugeley off A51 on unclassified road signposted Penkridge. Turn right at bottom of hill by white fence. Entrance 100 yards on left.

ENGLAND

St Agnes

ST AGNES Cornwall   2A4

Beacon Cottage Farm
Beacon Drive, St Agnes TR5 0NU
☎ 01872-552347
Open May-October

Small secluded park on a working family farm set in six landscaped paddocks covering two acres. Ten minutes walk to the sandy beach. Beautiful scenery, lovely walks. Quiet and uncommercialised.
Size 4 acres, 50 touring pitches, 27 with electric hookup, 45 level pitches, 4 ⚿, 9 WCs, 1 CWP
£ car/tent £5-£11, car/caravan £5-£11, motorhome £5-£11, motorbike/tent £5-£11, children £1.50-£2.50
Calor Gaz WS
Last arrival time: 20:00
➡ Leave A30 at Chiverton roundabout and take B3277 to St Agnes. On reaching village, turn left, signposted The Beacon and follow signs to park.

Trevarth Holiday Park
Blackwater, St Agnes TR4 8HR
☎ 01872-560266 Fax 01872-560266
Open Easter-mid October

Small family run park in rural area, conveniently situated for the north and south coast resorts.
Size 4.5 acres, 30 touring pitches, 27 with electric hookup, 30 level pitches, 20 static caravans, 3 ⚿, 4 WCs, 1 CWP
£ car/tent £5, car/caravan £5, motorhome £5, motorbike/tent £5, children £1
Rental £90
€€ MasterCard Visa
Calor Gaz WS
Last arrival time: 22:00
➡ 300 yards down Blackwater road, from Chiverton roundabout which is on A30, 4½ miles N of Redruth.

ST AUSTELL Cornwall   2B4

Croft Farm Touring Park
Luxulyan, Bodmin PL30 5EQ
☎ 01726-85028 Fax 01726-850498
Open April-October

Sheltered, secluded and only 3 miles from St Austell Bay, Croft offers a comfortable base for your stay. Silver David Bellamy Conservation Award winners. 3.5 acre dogwalk.
Size 6 acres, 46 touring pitches, 44 with electric hookup, 44 level pitches, 6 static caravans, 8 ⚿, 12 WCs, 2 CWPs
£ car/tent £7.50-£10, car/caravan £7.50-£10, motorhome £7.50-£10, motorbike/tent £7.50-£10, children £1
Rental £80-£230, cottages £172-£415
€€ MasterCard Visa
Calor Gaz
➡ From A30 Bodmin turn left at A391 to St Austell. Continue to Bugle, turn left at crossroad (traffic lights) onto B3374 to Penwithick. Continue to Penwithick, turn left to Trethurgy/Luxulyan. At T-junction turn left. Park is on left hand side in ½ mile.

Trencreek Farm Holiday Park
Hewaswater, St Austell PL26 7JG
☎ 01726-882540 Fax 01726-882540
Open April-October
Size 56 acres, 196 touring pitches, 100 with electric hookup, 30 level pitches, 32 static caravans, 14 ⚿, 25 WCs, 3 CWPs
£ car/tent £5-£11
Rental Chalet.
€€ MasterCard Visa
Calor Gaz
Last arrival time: 24 hours
➡ Off B3287 1 mile from junction with A390 to St Mawes and Tregony.

Trevor Farm Camping & Caravan Site
Gorran, St Austell PL26 6LW
☎ 01726-842387 Fax 01726-842387
Open 1 April-end October

St Ives

Level meadow site on working farm. 50 pitches, including 28 electric hook-ups. 1 mile to coastal walks and beach.
Size 4 acres, 50 touring pitches, 28 with electric hookup, 50 level pitches, 4 🚿, 12 WCs, 1 CWP
£ car/tent £6.50-£12, car/caravan £6.50-£12, motorhome £6.50-£12, motorbike/tent £6.50-£12

Last arrival time: 20:00
➜ From St Austell S on B3273, 3¼ miles past Pentewan, turn right signed Gorran. After 4½ miles bear right. After ¼ mile turn right to site.

Trewhiddle Holiday Estate
Trewhiddle, Pentewan Road, St Austell PL26 7AD
📞 01726-67011 **Fax** 01726-67010

A country park in the peaceful Pentewan Valley, with the sea nearby. 16 acre family site ideally situated for exploring Cornwall. Excellent facilities for family holidays.
Size 16 acres, 105 touring pitches, 50 with electric hookup, 50 static caravans, 9 🚿, 16 WCs, 1 CWP
£ car/tent £6-£10, car/caravan £6-£10, motorhome £6-£10, motorbike/tent £6-£10, children £1
Rental Chalet. £130-£360
㏄ MasterCard Visa

Last arrival time: 22:00
➜ From St Austell take B3273 to Mevagissey. Site entrance is ¾ mile on right from roundabout.

ST IVES Cornwall   2A4

Ayr Holiday Park
Higher Ayr, St Ives TR26 1EJ
📞 01736-795855 **Fax** 01736-798797
Open 1 April-31 October

The only holiday park in St Ives itself, with easy access to the beaches, town centre and coastal footpath. Beautiful views over St Ives Bay.
Size 4 acres, 40 touring pitches, 35 with electric hookup, 20 level pitches, 43 static caravans, 10 🚿, 11 WCs, 1 CWP
£ car/tent £8.25-£14.50, car/caravan £9.25-£14.50, motorhome £8.50-£13.50, motorbike/tent £14.50, children £1-£1.75
Rental Chalet. £140-£550
㏄ MasterCard Visa

Last arrival time: 20:00
➜ From the A30 follow the holiday route to St Ives joining B3311 and B3306. ½ mile from St Ives turn left at mini roundabout following signs to Ayr and Porthmeor Beach.
See advert on this page

ENGLAND

Ayr Holiday Park

The only holiday park in St Ives itself, less than ½ mile from the harbour, town centre and beaches.

Beautiful views over St Ives Bay. Holiday caravans and chalets, also touring van and tent pitches. Electric hook-ups, free showers, modern clean amenities.

Signposted from B3306, ½ mile west of town centre.

For brochure write to:
**RC Baragwanath,
Ayr Holiday Park, Ayr, St Ives,
Cornwall TR26 1EJ
Tel: (01736) 795855**

St Ives

Camping International

Highly popular family touring park for the more discerning camper/caravanner. Clean park with a friendly atmosphere. Lots of facilities. Marked, level pitches. Statistically the best sunshine record in UK.

RATED AS ONE OF THE TOP 100 PARKS IN UK BY AA, PRACTICAL CARAVAN AND CARAVAN PLUS.

229 Ringwood Road, St. Leonards, Ringwood, Hants. BH24 2SD. Tel: (01202) 872817 Fax: 861292

Polmanter Tourist Park
Halstown, St Ives TR26 3LX
01736-795640 Fax 01736-795640
Open Easter-31 October

Award winning park, with excellent facilities including a heated swimming pool, located within easy walking distance of St Ives and its glorious beaches, just one mile away.
Size 13 acres, 240 touring pitches, 188 with electric hookup, 230 level pitches, 34, 40 WCs, 4 CWPs
£ car/tent £14, car/caravan £14, motorhome £14, motorbike/tent £14, children £1.75-£2.50
MasterCard Visa
Calor Gaz
Last arrival time: 21:00
➔ Off A30 to St Ives (A3074). First left at mini-roundabout. Take holiday route (HR) to St Ives (Halstown). Right at Halstown Inn, then first left.

Trevalgan Family Camping Park
St Ives TR26 3BJ
01736-796433 Fax 01736-796433
Open 1 May-30 September

Size 5 acres, 120 touring pitches, 22 with electric hookup, 120 level pitches, 10, 15 WCs, 1 CWP
£ car/tent £7-£10.50, car/caravan £7-£10.50, motorhome £7-£10.50, motorbike/tent £7-£10.50, children £2-£4.50
MasterCard Visa
Calor Gaz WS
Last arrival time: 23:30
➔ Take A30 to B3306 and follow signs for park.

ST LEONARDS Hampshire 4A4

Camping International
229 Ringwood Road, St Leonards BH24 2SD
01202-872817 Fax 01202-861292
Open 1 March-October

A clean, friendly, family park with level, marked pitches surrounded by trees and lots of facilities. Ideal for the New Forest, Bournemouth and the coast.
Size 9 acres, 205 touring pitches, 165 with electric hookup, 205 level pitches, 16, 22 WCs, 2 CWPs
£ car/tent £7.70-£11.30, car/caravan £7.70-£11.30, motorhome £7.70-£11.30, motorbike/tent £7.70-£11.30, children £1.50-£1.70
MasterCard Visa
Calor Gaz WS
Last arrival time: 22:00
➔ On main A31 2½ miles W of Ringwood. Entrance in Boundary Lane.
See advert on this page

ST MAWES Cornwall 2B4

Trethem Mill Touring Park
St Just-in-Roseland, St Mawes TR2 5JF
01872-580504 Fax 01872-580968
Open 1 April-18 October

Discover the beautiful Roseland, staying on our exclusive, peaceful park, offering immaculate facilties

Salcombe

in tranquil countryside setting. Ideal for beaches, walking, watersports, gardens and touring Cornwall.
Size 11 acres, 84 touring pitches, 50 with electric hookup, 40 level pitches, 8 🚿, 16 WCs, 1 CWP
£ car/tent £6.50-£10.50, car/caravan £6.50-£10.50, motorhome £6.50-£10.50, motorbike/tent £6.50-£10.50, children £1.50-£2
℆ MasterCard Visa
🛒 🎮 📶 🅿 🎬 △ Calor Gaz ♿ 🐕
Last arrival time: 21:00
➔ From Tregony follow A3078 to St Mawes. 2 miles after passing through Trewithian look for sign.

ST NEOTS Cambridgeshire 8C4

Camping & Caravanning Club Site

Rush Meadow, St Neots PE19 2UD
📞 01480-474404
Open March-November 🏕 🚐 🚙
Size 10 acres, 180 touring pitches, 77 with electric hookup, 12 🚿, 18 WCs, 2 CWPs
£ car/tent £11.50-£14.60, car/caravan £11.50-£14.60, motorhome £11.50-£14.60, motorbike/tent £11.50-£14.60, children £1.60
℆ Visa
🛒 🛒¼ ✕¼ 🍴 🍺¼ 🎮 🅿 🎬 📺 Calor ♿ 🐕 WS
Last arrival time: 23:00
➔ From A1 take A428 to Cambridge, second roundabout left to Tesco's, past the sports centre, follow international camping signs to the site.

SALCOMBE Devon 2C4

Alston Farm Caravan Site

Salcombe TQ7 3BJ
📞 01548-561260 **Fax** 01548-561260
Open Easter-end October 🏕 🚐 🚙
Size 12 acres, 150 touring pitches, 50 with electric hookup, 150 level pitches, 40 static caravans, 18 🚿, 35 WCs, 1 CWP
£ car/tent £6-£7, car/caravan £6-£9, motorhome £6-£7, motorbike/tent £6-£7, children £0.50
🛒 🎮 📺 Calor Gaz ♿ 🐕 WS
➔ Signposted on left on A381 Kingsbridge to Salcombe main road.

Bolberry House Farm Camping & Caravan

Bolberry, Malborough, Kingsbridge TQ7 3DY
📞 01548-561251
Open Easter-October 🏕 🚐 🚙
Size 5.5 acres, 70 touring pitches, 36 with electric hookup, 50 level pitches, 10 static caravans, 8 🚿, 12 WCs, 1 CWP
£ car/tent £6-£8, car/caravan £7-£8.50, motorhome £7-£8.50, motorbike/tent £6
Rental 🚐
🛒¼ ✕¼ 🍺¼ 🎮 📺 Calor Gaz 🐕
➔ Take A381 from Kingsbridge towards Salcombe. Turn sharp right, through village of Malborough and follow signs to Bolberry. Park is on right on outskirts of hamlet.

Higher Rew Caravan Park

Malborough, Kingsbridge, Salcombe TQ7 3DW
📞 01548-842681
Open Easter-October 🏕 🚐 🚙

Quiet family park in area of outstanding natural beauty, adjoining National Trust land, only one mile from South Sands and Salcombe Estuary. Cliff walks are nearby.
Size 5 acres, 75 touring pitches, 40 with electric hookup, 75 level pitches, 8 🚿, 10 WCs, 1 CWP
£ car/tent £6-£8, car/caravan £6-£8, motorhome £6-£8, motorbike/tent £6-£8
🎮 🛒 📶 📺 🔍 Calor Gaz 🐕
Last arrival time: 22:00
➔ From A381 at Malborough turn right and follow signs to Soar for 1 mile, then turn left at Rew Cross signpost to Higher Rew.

Sun Park Caravan & Camping Park

Soar Mill Cove, Malborough, Salcombe TQ7 3DS
📞 01548-561378
Open Easter-31 October 🏕 🚐 🚙

Quality caravans and modern camping facilities on peaceful family run site surrounded by National Trust land. Walking distance of sandy cove. Where better to come and unwind.
Size 5 acres, 75 touring pitches, 18 with electric hookup, 75 level pitches, 34 static caravans, 8 🚿, 10 WCs, 1 CWP
£ car/tent £5-£9, car/caravan £5-£9, motorhome £5-£9, motorbike/tent £5-£9
Rental 🚐 £85-£295
🎮 🛒 📶 📺 △ Calor Gaz 🐕
Last arrival time: 21:00
➔ From A38, turn left at Totnes and Kingsbridge sign. Bypass Kingsbridge by following signs to Salcombe. On entering village of Malborough turn sharp right signposted Soar. Pass through village and keep on road following signs to Soar Mill Cove and Sun Park. Site 1½ miles down this road on right.

ENGLAND

Salisbury

SALISBURY Wiltshire　　　　　　　　　3F2

Alderbury Caravan and Camping Park
Old Southampton Road, Whaddon, Salisbury
☎ 01722-710125
Open all year ⅄ 🚐 🚛
Size 1.5 acres, 39 touring pitches, 26 with electric hookup, 39 level pitches, 4 🚿, 6 WCs, 2 CWPs
£ car/tent £7.50, car/caravan £7.50, motorhome £7.50, motorbike/tent £7.50, children £1
⅄¼ ✕¼ 🍴¼ 🔌 🐕 ✈
Last arrival time: 21:00
➜ From Salisbury take A36 Southampton road for 3 miles. Along dual carriageway take slip road marked Alderbury/Whaddon, turn right over flyover then left for site opposite Three Crowns pub.

Camping & Caravanning Club Site
Hudson's Field, Castle Road, Salisbury SP1 3RR
☎ 01722-320713
Open March-November ⅄ 🚐 🚛
Size 4.5 acres, 150 touring pitches, 68 with electric hookup, 12 🚿, 16 WCs, 2 CWPs
£ car/tent £11.50-£14.60, car/caravan £11.50-£14.60, motorhome £11.50-£14.60, motorbike/tent £11.50-£14.60, children £1.60
CC MasterCard Visa
⅄ ⅄¼ ✕¼ 🍴 🍴¼ 🔌 🚻 🅿 💧 🚩 📞 📺 Calor ♿ ✈ WS
Last arrival time: 23:00
➜ 1½ miles from Salisbury and 7 miles from Amesbury on A345 turn into Castle Road. Large open field next to Old Sarum.

Coombe Touring Caravan Park
Race Plain, Netherhampton, Salisbury SP2 8PN
☎ 01722-328451　Fax 01722-328451
Open all year ⅄ 🚐 🚛

Family park with lovely views, centrally heated, modern toilet block, in landscaped park.
Size 3 acres, 50 touring pitches, 48 with electric hookup, 50 level pitches, 6 🚿, 12 WCs, 2 CWPs
£ car/tent £5.50-£8, car/caravan £5.50-£8, motorhome £5.50-£8, motorbike/tent £5.50-£8, children £1-£1.50
⅄ 🔌 🚻 🅿 ♨ Calor Gaz ♿ ✈
Last arrival time: 21:00
➜ A36 Salisbury to Warminster road. Turn onto A3094 at traffic lights. Cross on bend at top of hill. Take third left behind racecourse. Site is on right.

Hillcrest Camp Site
Southampton Road, Whiteparish, Salisbury SP5 2QW
☎ 01794-884471　Fax 01794-884471
Open all year ⅄ 🚐 🚛
Size 2.5 acres, 30 touring pitches, 12 with electric hookup, 15 level pitches, 3 🚿, 5 WCs, 1 CWP
£ car/tent £7.10, car/caravan £7.10, motorhome £7.10, motorbike/tent £7.10, children £1.60
🚩 🔌 🚩 Calor Gaz ✈
Last arrival time: 22:00
➜ The entrance is off A36, Southampton to Salisbury road, 1¼ miles SE of junction with A27. 8 miles from Salisbury, 13 miles from Southampton.

Stonehenge Touring Park
Orcheston, Salisbury SP3 4SH
☎ 01980-620304　Fax 01980-621121
Open all year ⅄ 🚐 🚛
Size 2 acres, 30 touring pitches, 20 with electric hookup, 30 level pitches, 3 static caravans, 4 🚿, 5 WCs, 1 CWP
£ car/tent £6-£9.50, car/caravan £6-£9.50, motorhome £6-£9.50, motorbike/tent £6-£9.50, children £0.75-£1.50
Rental Chalet. From £70 for a short break.
⅄ ✕ 🍴 🚩 🔌 🚩 ♨ ⛽ Calor Gaz ✈
Last arrival time: 21:30
➜ Off A360 Salisbury to Devizes road.

SANDRINGHAM Norfolk　　　　　　　　9D2

Camping & Caravanning Club Site
The Sandringham Estate, Double Lodges, Sandringham PE35 6EA
☎ 01485-542555
Open February-November ⅄ 🚐 🚛
Size 22 acres, 250 touring pitches, 153 with electric hookup, 22 🚿, 28 WCs,
£ car/tent £13.60-£14.60, car/caravan £13.60-£14.60, motorhome £13.60-£14.60, motorbike/tent £13.60-£14.60, children £1.60
CC MasterCard Visa
⅄ ⅄¼ ✕ ✕¼ 🍴¼ 🔌 🚻 🅿 💧 🚩 📞 📺 ♨ Calor ♿ ✈ WS
Last arrival time: 23:00
➜ From A148 (Kings Lynn to Cromer) turn left onto B1440, signposted West Newton. Follow the signs to site. From A149 (Hunstanton to Kings Lynn) turn left at sign indicating tent and caravan, travel ½ mile to crossroads and turn right. Take second turning on left to site.

SANDWICH Kent　　　　　　　　　　　5F3

Sandwich Leisure Park
Woodnesborough Road, Sandwich CT13 0AA
☎ 01227-771777　Fax 01227-273512
Open 1 March-31 October ⅄ 🚐 🚛

Scarborough

133

Well maintained location adjoining open farmland, a few minutes walk from the town centre with a wealth of olde worlde pubs, restaurants and shops. Warm welcome awaits you.
Size 15 acres, 100 touring pitches, 100 with electric hookup, 100 level pitches, 100 static caravans, 8 ⓡ, 16 WCs, 2 CWPs
£ car/tent £6.80-£9.80, car/caravan £6.80-£9.80, motorhome £6.80-£9.80, motorbike/tent £6.80-£9.80
Rental
♿¼ ✕¼ 🔲 📞 ⚠ Calor Gaz 🐕 WS
Last arrival time: 22:00
➡ A257 to Sandwich town centre, then on to Woodnesborough, over level crossing and take immediate right.
See advert on this page

SANDWICH LEISURE PARK

*Well maintained; close to Channel crossings, adjoining open farm land.
Wealth of Olde Worlde pubs, restaurants and shops within five minutes walk.
Warm welcome awaits.
Directions – A257 to Sandwich, left at the Guild Hall into Woodnesborough Road, 300 yards along, over level crossing and turn right.
Open March to October.*

WOODNESBOROUGH ROAD, SANDWICH, KENT CT13 0AA
Tel: 01304-612681 Fax: 01227-273512

SAXMUNDHAM Suffolk   9F4

Whitearch (Touring Caravan) Park
Main Road, Benhall, Saxmundham IP17 1NA
📞 01728-604646 Fax 01728-604646
Open April-October

Set in Suffolk, with all its rural charm, on 14½ acres offering 30 pitches and close to Heritage Conservation land and Snape Concert Hall.
Size 14.5 acres, 30 touring pitches, 30 with electric hookup, 30 level pitches, 4 ⓡ, 6 WCs, 2 CWPs
£ car/tent £8.50, car/caravan £8.50, motorhome £8.50, motorbike/tent £8.50, children £0.50
♿ 📞 🔲 ⚠ Calor Gaz ♿ 🐕
➡ From Ipswich on A12 towards Lowestoft turn off onto B1121 to Saxmundham. Entrance 20 yards on right.

SCARBOROUGH North Yorkshire   11E2

Cayton Village Caravan Park
D14 Mill Lane, Cayton Bay, Scarborough YO11 3NN
📞 01723-583171
Open Easter-1 October

A spacious, level, landscaped park sheltered by trees. Three miles south of Scarborough. Half a mile from beach. Adjoining village church, inns, fish shop and bus service.
Size 11 acres, 200 touring pitches, 170 with electric hookup, 200 level pitches, 18 ⓡ, 34 WCs, 3 CWPs
£ car/tent £5-£8, car/caravan £5-£8, motorhome £5-£8, motorbike/tent £5-£8
♿ ♿¼ ✕¼ 🍴 🍴¼ 🔲 📞 ⚠ Calor Gaz ♿ 🐕
Last arrival time: 20:00
➡ On A165 turn right at Cayton Bay traffic lights onto Mill Lane. The park is ½ mile on right hand side. On A64 take B1261 signposted Filey. At Cayton Village turn second left after Blacksmiths Arms onto Mill Lane. Park is on left in 500 yards.

ENGLAND

Scarborough

Flower of May
HOLIDAY PARK

THE HAPPY FAMILY HOLIDAY PARK
*Exciting Leisure Complex including indoor heated swimming pool, squash courts, fully equipped gym, games room.
Also huge outdoor play area, bars, self service shop, fish & chip shop, café.*
WINNER 1995 BEST NORTHERN CAMPSITE
**FLOWER OF MAY HOLIDAY PARK, DEPT. E,
LEBBERSTON CLIFF, SCARBOROUGH YO11 3NU
Tel: (01723) 584311**

Flower Of May Caravan Park
Lebberston Cliff, Scarborough YO11 3NU
01723-582324
Open Easter-end October

Acclaimed privately owned park, constantly being updated to provide the most comprehensive facilities. Located on the coast between Scarborough and Filey. Fifty caravans for hire (own WCs). No single-sex groups.
Size 20 acres, 300 touring pitches, 270 with electric hookup, 300 level pitches, 184 static caravans, 36 , 36 WCs, 3 CWPs
£ car/tent £7-£11, car/caravan £7-£11, motorhome £7-£11, motorbike/tent £7-£11, children £2
Rental £95-£370
Calor WS
Last arrival time: dusk
➡ 2¼ miles NW of Filey, 5 miles SE of Scarborough on A165. Turn left, then NE to site.
See advert on this page

Jacob's Mount Caravan Park
Stepney Road, Scarborough YO12 5NL
01723-361178 Fax 01723-361178
Open 1 March-31 October

A small family run park with excellent on site facilities, surrounded by mature woodland yet only two miles from Scarborough on the A170. Highly Recommended.
Size 7 acres, 56 touring pitches, 44 with electric hookup, 12 level pitches, 56 static caravans, 4 , 14 WCs, 1 CWP
£ car/tent £6-£9, car/caravan £6-£9, motorhome £6-£9, motorbike/tent £6-£9
Rental £110-£310.
Calor Gaz WS
Last arrival time: 21:00
➡ Approximately 2 miles W of Scarborough on the A170 Scarborough to Thirsk road.

Lebberston Touring Caravan Park
Beckfield, Lebberston, Scarborough YO11 3PF
01723-582254
Open May-September
Size 7.5 acres, 125 touring pitches, 125 with electric hookup, 100 level pitches, 8 , 24 WCs, 2 CWPs
£ car/caravan £6.50, motorhome £6.50
¼ ¼ ¼ Calor Gaz
Last arrival time: 21:00
➡ From A64 or A165, take B1261 to Lebberston. Site signposted.

Merry Lees Caravan Park
Merry Lees, Staxton, Scarborough YO12 4NN
01944-710080 Fax 01944-710470
Open March-October

Scotch Corner

Ideally situated rural park in woodland based around a small lake, habitat of many birds. Central to moorland and coastal attractions; Flamingoland, Millenium, steam railway.
Size 8 acres, 50 touring pitches, 50 with electric hookup, 50 level pitches, 10 static caravans, 6 🚿, 7 WCs, 1 CWP
£ car/tent £5-£9.50, car/caravan £5-£9.50, motorhome £5-£9.50, motorbike/tent £5-£9.50
cc MasterCard Visa
Calor Gaz & 🐕 WS
Last arrival time: 22:00
➡ On the A64, ½ mile past roundabout on left, 6 miles before Scarborough.

Scalby Close Camping Park

Burniston Road, Scarborough YO13 0DA
📞 01723-365908
Open March-October ⛺ 🚐 🚍

Sheltered by mature trees with all pitches on level ground, ideal for touring North York Moors. Three caravans for hire (own WCs). Restaurant half a mile. Swimming pool 1½ miles.
Size 2 acres, 42 touring pitches, 30 with electric hookup, 5 static caravans, 4 🚿, 10 WCs, 1 CWP
£ car/tent £4.25-£8.75, car/caravan £4.25-£8.75, motorhome £4.25-£8.75, motorbike/tent £4.25-£8.75
Rental 🚐 £120-£295
cc MasterCard Visa
🛒 ✕¼ 🍴 🛒 🛢 Calor Gaz 🐕 WS
Last arrival time: 22:00
➡ Site is on A165 2½ miles N of Scarborough.

Scalby Manor Caravan & Camping Site

Burniston Road., Scarborough
📞 01723-366212
Open Easter-end October ⛺ 🚐 🚍
Size 20 acres, 375 touring pitches, 150 with electric hookup, 230 level pitches, 25 🚿, 40 WCs, 2 CWPs
cc MasterCard Visa
🛒 ✕¼ 🍴 🛢 🛒 🏥 Calor Gaz & 🐕
Last arrival time: 19:00
➡ At 2¼ miles N of Scarborough on A165, follow signs for Burniston/Whitley.
See advert on this page

135

SCOTCH CORNER North Yorkshire   11D2

Scotch Corner Caravan Park

Richmond, Scotch Corner DL10 6NS
📞 01748-822530 **fax** 01748-826272
Open April-October ⛺ 🚐 🚍

Landscaped, level, grassed, well-spaced pitches. Booking advisable July/August and bank holiday weekends.
Size 7 acres, 75 touring pitches, 43 with electric hookup, 75 level pitches, 6 🚿, 14 WCs, 1 CWP
£ car/tent £8-£10, car/caravan £8-£10, motorhome £8-£10, motorbike/tent £7-£9, children £1
cc MasterCard Visa
🛒 ✕¼ 🍴¼ 🛢 🛒 🛢 Calor Gaz & 🐕 WS
Last arrival time: 22:30
➡ Leave A1 at Scotch Corner and take A6108 Richmond exit. Proceed 250 yards on dual carriageway, then cross central reservation and return 200 yards to site entrance.

ENGLAND

SCARBOROUGH
Yorkshire's Warmest Welcome

SCALBY MANOR
CARAVAN & CAMPING PARK

This scenic park is set in 20 acres of countryside. A footpath takes you down to the beach and Scarborough's North Bay and with the town centre just three miles away, the setting is just perfect for a relaxing holiday.

Enjoy over 45 miles of superb seaside, set against the backcloth of the North York Moors National Park. Heritage, tradition, festivals… family fun or big time stars… quiet times or 24 hour action. You'll see why there's so much more to the seaside than the sea.

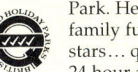

SCARBOROUGH WHITBY FILEY

(For full details of facilities see listing under Scarborough).

FOR DETAILS AND BOOKING FORMS
PLEASE CONTACT:

Scalby Manor Caravan & Camping Park,
Field Lane, Station Road, Scalby,
Scarborough YO13 0DA
Tel: (01723) 366212

VISA Access AA ▶▶▶

Selsey

SELSEY West Sussex	4C4

Warner Farm Touring Park
Warner Lane, Selsey
☎ 01243-604499 Fax 01243-604499
Open 1 March-31 October

Situated in beautiful Sussex, with top family entertainment and two swimming pools. Special offers with great savings in June, July, September and October.
Size 10 acres, 200 touring pitches, 130 with electric hookup, 180 level pitches, 20, 30 WCs, 4 CWPs
£ car/tent £6.50-£17.50, car/caravan £6.50-£20.50, motorhome £6.50-£20.50, motorbike/tent £6.50-£17.50
Rental
cc MasterCard Visa
Calor Gaz
Last arrival time: 22:00

➡ From Chichester A27 take B2145 to Selsey. At Selsey turn right into School Lane and follow signs for park.
See advert on this page

WARNER FARM

Warner Farm Touring Park is the park to aim for.

With first class swimming pools and great entertainment.

Located in sunny Selsey on the south coast with many local places of interest.

Ring now for your free brochure on
(01243) 604499

SETTLE North Yorkshire	10C3

Knight Stainforth Hall Camping & Caravan
Little Stainforth, Settle BD24 ODP
☎ 01729-822200 Fax 01729-823387
Open March-October

Family run camping park catering mainly for families. Situated in the Yorkshire Dales National Park on the west bank of the River Ribble, near waterfall and Pack-horse Bridge.
Size 10 acres, 50 touring pitches, 50 with electric hookup, 80 level pitches, 60 static caravans, 8, 21 WCs, 1 CWP
£ car/tent £8.30, car/caravan £8.30, motorhome £8.30, motorbike/tent £8.30, children £1
cc MasterCard Visa
Calor Gaz
Last arrival time: 21:30

➡ Take A65 Settle to Kendal. Turn off opposite Settle High School on Stackhouse Lane. Site is 2½ miles.

SEVENOAKS Kent	5D3

Camping & Caravanning Club Site
Styants Bottom, Seal, Sevenoaks TN15 0ET
☎ 01732-762728
Open March-November

Size 4 acres, 58 touring pitches, 30 with electric hookup, 4, 7 WCs, 1 CWP
£ car/tent £10.40-£13.60, car/caravan £10.40-£13.60, motorhome £10.40-£13.60, motorbike/tent £10.40-£13.60, children £1.50
cc MasterCard Visa
Calor WS
Last arrival time: 23:00

➡ If travelling along the A25 from Sevenoaks towards Borough Green, turn left just after the Crown Point Inn, which is on the right, down narrow lane to Staynts Bottom. The site is on the left.

SHEFFIELD South Yorkshire	8B1

Greensprings Touring Park
Rockley Abbey, Worsbrough S75 3DS
☎ 01226-288298 Fax 01226-288298
Open 1 April-1 October

Sheringham

Quiet secluded rural setting with pleasant walks. Ideal location for a relaxing break on journeys north and south and as a base for exploring Yorkshire and Derbyshire.
Size 4 acres, 60 touring pitches, 32 with electric hookup, 40 level pitches, 6 ⌂, 9 WCs, 2 CWPs
£ car/tent £6.50, car/caravan £6.50, motorhome £6.50, motorbike/tent £6.50
Calor Gaz
Last arrival time: 21:00
➜ From M1 junction 36, take A61 towards Barnsley. Turn left after ¼ mile onto 'B' road signed Pilley. Follow road for ¾ mile. Site entrance is on left.

SHERIFF HUTTON North Yorkshire 11D3

Camping & Caravanning Club Site
Bracken Hill, Sheriff Hutton YO6 1QG
☎ 01347-878660
Open March-November
Size 10 acres, 88 touring pitches, 41 with electric hookup, 6 ⌂, 9 WCs, 1 CWP
£ car/tent £10.40-£13.60, car/caravan £10.40-£13.60, motorhome £10.40-£13.60, motorbike/tent £10.40-£13.60, children £1.50
⊂⊂ MasterCard Visa
Calor WS
Last arrival time: 22:00
➜ From York, take the signpost Earswick, keep left at the filling station and Ship Inn, the site is second on the right

SHERINGHAM Norfolk 9E2

Beeston Regis Caravan & Camping Park
Cromer Road, West Runton, Sheringham NR27 9NG
☎ 01263-823614 Fax 01263-823614
Open 24 March-31 October
Size 44 acres, 440 touring pitches, 56 with electric hookup, 440 level pitches, 120 static caravans, 16 ⌂, 30 WCs, 2 CWPs
£ car/tent £6-£8, car/caravan £6-£10.90, motorhome £6-£10.90, motorbike/tent £6-£8, children £0.50-£0.70
Rental from £150-£349
⊂⊂ MasterCard Visa
WS
Last arrival time: 21:30

Beeston Regis
CARAVAN PARK

A lovely 44 acre clifftop park situated close to the town of Sheringham in an area of outstanding natural beauty. We welcome touring caravans, motorhomes and tents and have 56 electric hookups, two shower blocks, a small shop and access to a clean, sandy beach.
Phone for brochure.

Cromer Road, Beeston Regis,
West Runton, Norfolk NR27 9NG
Tel: 01263-823614

➜ Take A148 to Sheringham and follow signs. At Sheringham roundabout turn right onto A149 coast road to Cromer, ½ mile on left hand side.
See advert on this page

Woodlands Caravan Park
Holt Road, Sheringham NR26 8TU
☎ 01263-823802
Open March-October

Quiet, secluded park surrounded by woodland and fields in a very pleasant area. No motorcycles. 28 days maximum stay. Open March-October.
Size 21 acres, 286 touring pitches, 216 with electric hookup, 250 level pitches, 133 static caravans, 28 ⌂, 74 WCs, 4 CWPs
£ car/caravan £7.25-£11, motorhome £7.25-£11
Calor Gaz
Last arrival time: 00:00
➜ On N side of A148. 4 miles E of Holt.

SIDMOUTH Devon	3D3

Salcombe Regis Camping & Caravan Park
Salcombe Regis, Sidmouth EX10 0JH
☎ 01395-514303 Fax 01395-514303
Open April-November 🏕 🚐 🚛

Quiet family-run park, situated on the edge of the picturesque village of Salcombe Regis in an area of outstanding natural beauty. Ideal base for exploring east Devon. Colour brochure available on request.
Size 16 acres, 100 touring pitches, 100 with electric hookup, 60 level pitches, 10 static caravans, 14 🚿, 14 WCs, 5 CWPs
£ car/tent £6.25-£9, car/caravan £6.25-£9, motorhome £6.25-£9, motorbike/tent £6.25-£9
Rental 🚐 £110-£350
cc MasterCard Visa
🍴 ¼ ✗¼ 🍺¼ ⓘ 🕪 🗓 ⚠ Calor Gaz ♿ 🐕 WS
Last arrival time: 22:00
➜ Signposted off A3052 Exeter to Lyme Regis coast road, 1 mile E of Sidmouth.

SILLOTH Cumbria	10A1

Solway Holiday Village
Silloth CA5 4QQ
☎ 016973-31236 Fax 016973-32553
Open all year 🏕 🚐 🚛

Discover nearby Lake District and Borders. Quality accomodation and spacious touring area. Indoor pool, bowling alley, deer farm, bars, kiddies club. O.A.P. and Rally discounts.
Size 130 acres, 150 touring pitches, 90 with electric hookup, 150 level pitches, 200 static caravans, 5 🚿, 10 WCs, 1 CWP
£ car/tent £6-£11, car/caravan £6-£11, motorhome £6-£11, motorbike/tent £6-£11
Rental 🚐 Chalet. £90-£520 weekly (family of four)

cc MasterCard Visa
🍴 ✗ 🍺 ⓘ 🕪 🗓 🎬 🍴 🅿 🛁 🐕 GR ⓘ TV ⚠ ⚡ Calor Gaz ♿ 🐕 WS
Last arrival time: 21:00
➜ From S: leave M6 junction 41. From N: leave A74 junction 44 - take B5305 to Silloth, turning right on reaching seafront towards Skinburness. The park is about a mile on right.

Stanwix Park Holiday Centre
Greenrow, Silloth CA5 4HH
☎ 016973-32666 Fax 016973-32555
🏕 🚐 🚛

Large, well-run holiday site, with ballroom, disco, bar, play park and riding school. Ideal location for exploring Lake District, Roman wall, Gretna Green. Tennis court. Boating and golf nearby. 80 caravans and 28 chalets for hire (own WCs).
Size 20 acres, 121 touring pitches, 121 with electric hookup, 121 level pitches, 186 static caravans, 15 🚿, 20 WCs, 121 CWPs
£ car/tent £11-£14.50, car/caravan £11-£14.50, motorhome £11-£14.50, motorbike/tent £11-£14.50
Rental 🚐 Chalet. £155-£400
cc MasterCard Visa
🍴 ✗ 🍺 ⓘ 🕪 🗓 🎬 🍴 🅿 🛁 🐕 GR ⓘ TV ⚠ ⚡ Calor Gaz ♿ 🐕 WS
Last arrival time: 22:00
➜ From M6, S take jn 41, N take jn 44 and follow signs for Wigton and Silloth. Site is 1 mile S of Silloth on B5300.
See advert on opposite page

Hints & Tips

Watch your speed. With a load on your back, acceleration will be slower. You will need more time and space for overtaking. Your combination is longer and wider than your car so you will need to take this into consideration before pulling out. Stopping distances will be longer so allow more space between the car in front as your speed increases.

Skegness

Tanglewood Caravan Park
Causeway Head, Silloth CA5 4PE
016973-31253
Open March-October

Natural, tree-sheltered, friendly park, ideal for touring the Lakes and the Borders. Large modern holiday homes for hire with colour TV.
Size 7 acres, 21 touring pitches, 21 with electric hookup, 21 level pitches, 56 static caravans, 4, 12 WCs, 2 CWPs
£ car/tent £6, car/caravan £6, motorhome £6, motorbike/tent £6, children £1-£2
Rental
Calor
Last arrival time: 23:00
→ On B5302, 4 miles on from Abbeytown on left, or, on B5302, 1 mile from Silloth on right.

SKEGNESS Lincolnshire   9D2

Richmond Holiday Centre
Richmond Drive, Skegness PE25 3TQ
01754-762097 Fax 01754-765631
Open 1 March-30 November

Family owned park, with on-site facilities including a Post Office, arcade, launderette, hair salon, leisure complex and heated indoor pool. Live nightly entertainment subject to season.
Size 46 acres, 175 touring pitches, 107 with electric hookup, 175 level pitches, 550 static caravans, 24, 100 WCs, 3 CWPs
£ car/caravan £8-£14.50, motorhome £8-£14.50
Rental £100-£300
Visa
¼ × ×¼ ¼
Calor Gaz WS
→ Follow signs to bus station. Site is 400 yards beyond coach station on right.

STANWIX PARK HOLIDAY CENTRE
Greenrow, Silloth, Cumbria CA5 4HH
Tel: 016973 32666 Fax 016973 32555
e-mail: stanwix.park@btinternet.com
Produce this Ad at time of Booking and SAVE 10% on Camping Charges
WHEN MAKING AN ENQUIRY PLEASE QUOTE REFERENCE NO. RAC

Situated on the Solway Coast. Ideal base to explore The Lake District, Roman Wall, Gretna Green and the Borders. Superb accommodation, apartments and caravan holiday homes. Tent and touring pitches with hook-up's. Leisure centre with pool, gym, tenpin bowling, amusements, family entertainment. Cabaret and dancing. No gimmicks, just pure value for money.

One of Cumbria's Premier Caravan Parks

We are extremely proud of winning the following awards.
1997 CUMBRIA FOR EXCELLENCE AWARD CARAVAN HOLIDAY PARK OF THE YEAR
presented by
The Cumbria Tourist Board

AA Northern Winner
Best Campsite of the Year 1997/98

Send for a colour brochure

Skipsea

SKIPSEA East Yorkshire　　　　　　　　11F3

Far Grange Park
Windhook, Hornsea Road, Skipsea YO25 8SY
☎ 01262-468293　Fax 01262-468648
Open March-Oct & winter weekends

Full facilities for touring caravans, tents and motorhomes. Luxury rose award holiday homes for hire. Holiday homes for sale. Leisure centre and indoor swimming pool.
Size 60 acres, 170 touring pitches, 170 with electric hookup, 170 level pitches, 327 static caravans, 20 ⚿, 76 WCs, 4 CWPs
£ car/tent £10-£14, car/caravan £10-£14, motorhome £10-£14
Rental £150-£320
CC MasterCard Visa
Calor Gaz

→ Halfway between Skipsea and Hornsea on B1242.

SKIRLINGTON LEISURE PARK

Pleasantly situated between the east coast villages of Skipsea and Atwick. It is a family run business with a reputation for high standards.

6-8 Berth Caravans for Hire • Hook ups
Indoor Heated Swimming Pool • Jacuzzi • Sauna • Solarium
Snooker & Pool • 9 Hole Putting Green • Golf Driving Range
Fishing Lake • Children's Play Areas • Duck Pond • Animal Farm
Sandy Beach Nearby.

The Tow Bar Inn offers restaurant & bar meals, a children's room and live entertainment most evenings.

The park is ideally placed for trips to Bridlington, Scarborough, York, the North Yorkshire Moors and many other local attractions.

LOW SKIRLINGTON, SKIPSEA, DRIFFIELD, E. YORKSHIRE YO25 8SY
Tel: 01262 468213/468466

Skirlington Leisure Park
Low Skirlington, Skipsea YO25 8SY
☎ 01262-468213　Fax 01262-468105
Open 1 March-31 October

Situated on the East Yorkshire coast, a family run business with a reputation for high standards and constant updating of all facilities. Please call for a brochure.
Size 80 acres, 275 touring pitches, 275 with electric hookup, 275 level pitches, 465 static caravans, 45 ⚿, 55 WCs, 5 CWPs
£ car/tent £9-£14, car/caravan £9-£14, motorhome £9-£14, motorbike/tent £9-£14
Rental £90-£275
CC MasterCard Visa
Calor Gaz WS

→ M62 signposted to Beverley, follow signs to Hornsea. Brown signposts direct to site once in Hornsea.
See advert on this page

SLIMBRIDGE Gloucestershire　　　　　　　7E4

Tudor Caravan & Camping
Shepherds Patch, Slimbridge GL2 7BP
☎ 01453-890483
Open all year

Size 7.5 acres, 75 touring pitches, 45 with electric hookup, 75 level pitches, 4 ⚿, 12 WCs, 1 CWP
£ car/tent £7-£7.25, car/caravan £7-£7.50, motorhome £7-£7.50, motorbike/tent £7-£7.25, children £0.50
CC MasterCard
Calor
Last arrival time: 22:00

→ From junction of A4135 and A38, 11 miles SW of Gloucester, take road through Slimbridge towards Wild Fowl Trust for 1½ miles. On left immediately before canal bridge.

SLINGSBY North Yorkshire　　　　　　　11E3

Camping & Caravanning Club Site
Railway Street, Slingsby YO6 7AA
☎ 01653-628335
Open March-November

Size 3 acres, 60 touring pitches, 57 with electric hookup, 8 ⚿, 6 WCs, 1 CWP
£ car/tent £11.50-£14.60, car/caravan £11.50-£14.60, motorhome £11.50-£14.60, motorbike/tent

South Molton

£11.50-£14.60, children £1.60
cc MasterCard Visa
♣ ♣¼ ✕¼ ♨¼ ▫ ♦ ▸ ▫ GR ▫ TV ⚠ Calor ♿ 🐕 WS
Last arrival time: 23:00
➧ From A64 turn left, signposted Castle Howard. Taking no turning off, drive straight through Castle Howard Estate until you come to Malton - Helmsly Road. Straight across into the village of Slingsby, through the village, approximately ¼ mile to camp.

SNAINTON North Yorkshire 11E2

Jasmine Park
Cross Lane, Snainton YO13 9BE
📞 01723-859240 Fax 01723-859240
Open March-January ▲ 🚐 🚌

Sheltered, picturesque park in an excellent area for walking and cycling. Local attractions suit all ages and tastes. Many awards including 'Yorkshire in Bloom" and David Bellamy Conservation award.
Size 5 acres, 70 touring pitches, 70 with electric hookup, 70 level pitches, 4 ☂, 14 WCs, 1 CWP
£ car/tent £6-£8.50, car/caravan £6-£8.50, motorhome £6-£8.50, motorbike/tent £6-£8.50, children £0.75
Rental 🚐 £160-£290 per week
♣ ▫ ♦ ▫ Calor Gaz ♿ 🐕 WS
Last arrival time: 9.30
➧ Turn off A170 in Snainton village opposite junior school, signposted. Midway between Scarborough and Pickering.

SNETTISHAM Norfolk 9D2

Diglea Camping & Caravan Park
Beach Road, Snettisham, King's Lynn PE31 7RA
📞 01485-541367
Open 1 April-31 October ▲ 🚐 🚌

Attractive, level, quiet, family run park in a peaceful rural setting, ½ mile from the beach. Ideally situated for exploring the north Norfolk coast and the historic town of King's Lynn.
Size 15 acres, 200 touring pitches, 40 with electric hookup, 200 level pitches, 150 static caravans, 14 ☂, 30 WCs, 2 CWPs
£ car/tent £5.50-£9, car/caravan £5.50-£9, motorhome £5.50-£9, motorbike/tent £5.50-£9
Rental 🚐 £155-£305
♣¼ ✕¼ ♨¼ ▫ ♦ ▫ ⚠ ⛽ Calor Gaz 🐕 WS
Last arrival time: 22:00
➧ From King's Lynn take A149 King's Lynn/Hunstanton road. After approximately 10½ miles turn left at sign marked Snettisham Beach. Park is 1½ miles on left.

SOUTH BRENT Devon 2C3

Edeswell Farm Country Caravan Park
Rattery, South Brent TQ10 9LN
📞 01364-72177 Fax 01364-72177
Open 1 April-31 October ▲ 🚐 🚌
Size 21 acres, 46 touring pitches, 22 with electric hookup, 40 level pitches, 20 static caravans, 10 ☂, 10 WCs, 1 CWP
£ car/tent £8.50-£10.50, car/caravan £8.50-£10.50, motorhome £8.50-£10.50, motorbike/tent £8.50-£10.50, children £1.25
♣ ▫ ♦ ▫ ▫ ▫ GR ▫ ⚠ ⛽ Calor Gaz 🐕 WS
Last arrival time: 20:30
➧ From A38 to Marley Head junction take A385 to Paignton. Site ½ mile on right.

SOUTH MOLTON Devon 2C2

Black Cock Inn & Camping Park
Molland, South Molton EX36 3NW
📞 01769-550297 Fax 01769-550297
Open all year ▲ 🚐 🚌

A traditional stone-built inn with adjacent camping & caravan park. Situated on the edge of Exmoor in a tranquil and scenic setting within easy reach of the North Devon coastline - ideal for touring or just relaxing in peaceful unspoilt surroundings.
Size 7 acres, 65 touring pitches, 40 with electric hookup, 48 level pitches, 2 static caravans, 8 ☂, 15 WCs, 1 CWP

ENGLAND

141

142

South Molton

← **Black Cock Inn & Camping Park**

£ car/tent £7-£9, car/caravan £8-£10, motorhome £7.50-£8.50, motorbike/tent £7-£9
Rental Chalet. from £25 per day.
MasterCard Visa
Calor WS
Last arrival time: 23:00
→ Signed from A361, 4 miles E of South Molton.

SOUTH SHIELDS Tyne & Wear	11D1

Lizard Lane Caravan & Camping Site
Marsden, South Shields NE34 7AB
0191-454 4982
Open 1 March-26 October
Size 4.25 acres, 45 touring pitches, 20 with electric hookup, 45 level pitches, 70 static caravans, 6, 14 WCs, 1 CWP
£ car/tent £6.70-£7.70, car/caravan £6.70-£7.70, motorhome £6.70-£7.70, motorbike/tent £5.20-£5.90, children £1.50-£1.70
¼ ¼ Calor Gaz WS
→ 2 miles S of South Shields on A183.

Sandhaven Caravan Park
Sea Road, South Shields
0191-454 5594
Open 1 March-end October
Size 7 acres, 49 touring pitches, 49 with electric hookup, 49 level pitches, 51 static caravans, 6, 14 WCs, 1 CWP
£ car/tent £8.80-£9.90, car/caravan £8.80-£9.90, motorhome £8.80-£9.90, motorbike/tent £5.80-£6.40
Rental
¼ ¼ Calor Gaz WS
→ Site ¾ mile E of town centre on coast road.

SOUTHAMPTON Hampshire	4B4

Dibles Park Caravan Site
Dibles Road, Warsash, Southampton SO3 9SA
01489-575232
Open 1 March-30 November
Size 5 acres, 15 touring pitches, 15 with electric hookup, 15 level pitches, 4, 7 WCs, 1 CWP
£ car/tent £5-£6, car/caravan £7, motorhome £7
¼ ¼ Calor WS
→ Junction 8 M27 turn left A27 to Sarisbury Green. Right into Barnes Lane, right into Brook Lane, left at Warsash Village then the third turning on right.

SOUTHMINSTER Essex	5E2

Beacon Hill Leisure Park
St Lawrence Bay, Southminster CM10 7LP
01621-779248 Fax 01621-778106
Open 1 April-31 October

Superb riverside location, with small beach access for all types of water sports, friendly clubhouse. Indoor leisure complex with pool, sauna and bubble spa. Activities for the whole family.
Size 25 acres, 60 touring pitches, 40 with electric hookup, 60 level pitches, 200 static caravans, 10, 24 WCs, 2 CWPs
£ car/tent £10-£11.50, car/caravan £10-£11.50, motorhome £10-£11.50, motorbike/tent £10-£11.50
Rental various rental prices
¼ Calor
→ B1010 to Latchingdon. At mini roundabout take Bradwell Road. At St Lawrence take left turn at sign for St Lawrence Bay. ¼ mile to site.

SOUTHPORT Lancashire	10B4

Leisure Lakes Caravan Park
Mere Brow, Tarleton, Southport PR4 JX
01772-813446 Fax 01772-816250
Open all year

A 90 acre site with two lakes for fishing, windsurfing, canoeing and jet skis. Also mountain bike hire. Pub on site serving meals.
Size 90 acres, 87 touring pitches, 80 with electric hookup, 87 level pitches, 6, 11 WCs, 2 CWPs
£ car/caravan £9.90, motorhome £9.90
MasterCard Visa
¼ ¼ Calor Gaz
Last arrival time: 21:00
→ From Southport, take A565 N for 3½ miles, then turn right onto B5246 to Mere Brow village, site entrance is 500 yards on right.

Stourport-on-Severn

STAMFORD Lincolnshire 8C3

Casterton Caravan Site

Casterton Hill, Casterton, Stamford PE9 4DE
☎ 01780-481481 Fax 01780-55753
Open all year
Size 4 acres, 32 touring pitches, 32 with electric hookup, 32 level pitches, 3 static caravans, 2 ☗, 4 WCs, 2 CWPs
£ car/tent £4.95-£5.95, car/caravan £4.95-£5.95, motorhome £4.95-£5.95, motorbike/tent £4.95-£5.95, children £1.20-£1.30
Rental Chalet £69-£128
Calor Gaz WS
Last arrival time: 00:00
➡ From the A1/A606 junction, follow the Ministry signs for the services, 450 yards.

Tallington Lakes

Barholm Road, Tallington, Stamford PE9 4RT
☎ 01778-347000 Fax 01778-346213
Open all year
Size 200 acres, 100 touring pitches, 60 with electric hookup, 100 level pitches, 230 static caravans, 3 ☗, 5 WCs, 1 CWP
£ car/tent £7.50-£9, car/caravan £8.50-£10, motorhome £8.50-£10, motorbike/tent £7.50
Rental
CC MasterCard Visa
Calor WS
Last arrival time: 20:00
➡ On A16 between Stamford and Market Deeping.

STANDLAKE Oxfordshire 4B2

Hardwick Parks

Downs Road, Off Witney Road, Standlake OX8 7PZ
☎ 01865-300501 Fax 01865-300037
Open 1 April-31 October
Size 180 acres, 250 touring pitches, 86 with electric hookup, 250 level pitches, 117 static caravans, 20 ☗, 18 WCs, 1 CWP
£ car/tent £7.50-£9.50, car/caravan £7.50-£9.50, motorhome £7.50-£9.50, motorbike/tent £5, children £0.50
CC MasterCard Visa
Calor Gaz WS
Last arrival time: 20:00
➡ Signposted from A415, 4½ miles S of Witney. See advert on this page.

STOKE-ON-TRENT Staffordshire 8A2

Trentham Caravan & Camping Park

Trentham, Stoke-on-Trent ST4 8AX
☎ 01782-657519
Open all year

Set in the 1000-acre Tretham Gardens, this park has woodland or more open pitches. The River Trent, lake and gardens are all accessible from the park.
Size 35 acres, 250 touring pitches, 24 ☗, 92 WCs,
➡ From M6 junction 15 onto A500, then take first slip road, signed A34 Stone and Stafford. Site 1 mile on right.

STOURPORT-ON-SEVERN Worcestershire 7E3

Redstone Caravan Park

The Rough, Stourport-on-Severn DY13 0LD
☎ 01299-823872 Fax 01299-828026
Open 1 February-31 December
Size 12 acres, 36 touring pitches, 28 with electric hookup, 36 level pitches, 290 static caravans, 8 ☗, 24 WCs, 2 CWPs
£ car/caravan £8-£11, motorhome £8-£11
Calor Gaz
Last arrival time: 21:00
➡ A451 from Kidderminster, over bridge, second left into The Rough.

CARAVANNING for INDIVIDUALISTS

"A hidden world in which to do as much or as little as you like. 180 acres of lakes, parkland and riverbank just waiting to be discovered"

- Air Conditioned Showerblock
- Fully equipped Shop & Launderette
- Floating Clubhouse/Bar
- Long Term Tourers
- Rally Field
- Water Skiing
- Jet Skiing
- Windsurfing
- Fishing
- Dogs Welcome
- Holiday Homes for Sale

HARDWICK Parks

DOWNS RD, STANDLAKE, OXFORDSHIRE
01865 300501 (General) 01865 300841 (Watersports)

Stratford-upon-Avon

STRATFORD-UPON-AVON Warwickshire	7F3

Dodwell Park
Evesham Road, Stratford-upon-Avon CV37 9ST
☏ 01789-204957 Fax 01926-336476
Open all year

Set in beautiful countryside two miles from Stratford-upon-Avon, this is an ideal site for visiting the Cotswolds and Warwick Castle.
Size 17 acres, 50 touring pitches, 50 with electric hookup, 40 level pitches, 6, 7 WCs, 1 CWP
£ car/tent £8-£9, car/caravan £8-£9, motorhome £8-£9, motorbike/tent £6-£7, children £0.70
CC MasterCard Visa
Calor Gaz
Last arrival time: 21:30

→ From Stratford-upon-Avon take B439 to Bidford for 2 miles. Park lies on left (not racecourse site).

Island Meadow Caravan Park
The Mill House, Aston Cantlow B95 6JP
☏ 01789-488273 Fax 01789-488273
Open 1 March-31 October

Quiet, peaceful, secluded riverside park beside picturesque and historic village. Ideal centre for Shakespeare's country, only six miles from Stratford-upon-Avon. English Tourist Board grading four ticks.
Size 7 acres, 24 touring pitches, 24 with electric hookup, 24 level pitches, 56 static caravans, 4, 11 WCs, 1 CWP
£ car/tent £7.50, car/caravan £9.50, motorhome £9.50, motorbike/tent £7.50, children £0.50
Rental £170 (low season)-£295 (high season)
Calor Gaz
Last arrival time: 21:00

→ From A46 Stratford to Alcester, or from A3400 Stratford to Henley-in-Arden, follow signs for Aston Cantlow village.

SUDBURY Suffolk	9E4

Willowmere Caravan & Camping Park
Bures Road, Sudbury CO10 0NN
☏ 01787-375559
Open Easter-October

Size 3 acres, 40 touring pitches, 24 with electric hookup, 40 level pitches, 8 static caravans, 4, 8 WCs, 1 CWP
£ car/tent £7-£9, car/caravan £9, motorhome £9, motorbike/tent £9
¼ ¼ Calor
Last arrival time: 24 hours

SWANAGE Dorset	3F3

Ulwell Cottage Caravan Park
Swanage
☏ 01929-422823 Fax 01929-421500
Open 1 March-7 January

Friendly "Village Inn", heated indoor pool, shop. One mile from the beach. Ideal for families, walkers, golfers and all watersports. Some "all service" hard standing pitches. Luxury caravans some with heating throughout.
Size 13 acres, 77 touring pitches, 60 with electric hookup, 40 level pitches, 140 static caravans, 24, 22 WCs, 4 CWPs
£ car/tent £10-£18, car/caravan £10-£18, motorhome £10-£18
Rental Chalet. £120-£450
CC MasterCard Visa
Calor Gaz
Last arrival time: 22:00

→ Take A351 to Swanage and on seafront turn left. Follow this road towards Studland for 1½ miles and turn left just before telephone kiosk on left.

Hints & Tips
Tiredness can kill. If you are planning a long journey make sure you plan some breaks.

Taunton

Woody Hydt Campsite
Corfe Castle, Swanage BH20 5HT
☎ 01929-480274
Open March-October ▲ 🚐

Set in the heart of the Purbeck countryside, with Swanage steam railway running past the site. Near to the glorious beaches at Studland.
Size 13 acres, 160 touring pitches, 8 with electric hookup, 8 🚿, 15 WCs.
£ car/tent £7-£10, motorhome £7-£10, motorbike/tent £7-£10, children £1.35
🛒 🔌 🍴 ⛺ Calor Gaz 🐕
➔ A351 between Corfe Castle and Harmanns Cross.

TAMWORTH Staffordshire   7F2

Camping & Caravanning Club Site
Kingsbury Water Park, Bodymoor Heath, Sutton Coldfield B76 0DY
☎ 01827-874101
Open March-November ▲ 🚐
Size 18 acres, 120 touring pitches, 60 with electric hookup, 8 🚿, 12 WCs, 1 CWP
£ car/tent £7.50-£10.75, car/caravan £7.50-£10.75, motorhome £7.50-£10.75, motorbike/tent £7.50-£10.75, children £1.50
CC MasterCard Visa
🛒 🛁¼ ✕¼ 🍽 🍴¼ 📺 🔌 ▶ 📧 🔳 🎮 📺 ⛺ Calor ♿ 🐕 WS
Last arrival time: 23:00
➔ M42 (jn 9) take B4097 Kingsbury road. At roundabout turn left, continue past main entrance to water park, over motorway, take next right, follow lane for ½ mile to site.

Drayton Manor Park
Tamworth B78 3TW
☎ 01827-287979 Fax 01827-288916
Open Easter-end October ▲ 🚐
Size 4 acres, 75 touring pitches, 37 level pitches, 12 🚿, 15 WCs, 2 CWPs
£ car/tent £9-£11, car/caravan £9-£11, motorhome £9-£11
CC MasterCard Visa
🛒 🛁¼ ✕ ✕¼ 🍽 🍴¼ 🔌 ▶ 🏠 Gaz ♿ 🐕
➔ From M42 junction 9 or 10 take A5404 or A446 onto A4091.
See advert on this page

TAUNTON Somerset   3D2

Ashe Farm Camping & Caravan Site
Thornfalcon, Taunton TA3 5NW
☎ 01823-442567 Fax 01823-443372
Open 1 April-31 October ▲ 🚐 🚗

Peaceful, family run site with lovely views of the hills. Central for touring and within easy reach of the coast, hills and Somerset Levels.
Size 7 acres, 30 touring pitches, 30 with electric hookup, 30 level pitches, 3 static caravans, 6 🚿, 10 WCs, 2 CWPs
£ car/tent £6, car/caravan £6-£7.50, motorhome £6-£7.50, motorbike/tent £6, children £1
Rental 🚐 £110-£140 week.
🛒 ✕¼ 🍽¼ 🔌 🍴 📧 🔳 🎮 ⛺ Calor Gaz ♿ 🐕 WS
Last arrival time: 00:00
➔ Leave M5 at junction 25. Take A358 Chard road for 2½ miles. Along dual carriageway, turn right at Nags Head pub. Site ¼ mile on right.

ACRES OF FUN
Enjoy a stay at Drayton Manor on a 4-acre site in one of the country's most popular theme parks.
There are 75 pitches on close mown grass and a full range of facilities (including disabled toilet and shower).
Prices include admission to park and zoo. £9 per night per visit (up to 4 people) Sunday – Thursday. £11 per night Friday and Saturday.

For more information, phone 01827 287979. Off Junction 9, M42 nr Tamworth, Staffs B78 3TW.

Drayton Manor Family Theme Park

ENGLAND

Taunton

Holly Bush Park
Culmhead, Taunton TA3 7EA
01823-421515 Fax 01823-421885
Open all year

A beautiful, quiet, family run site in an area of outstanding natural beauty. Numerous places of interest are within easy reach, including National Trust properties.
Size 2 acres, 40 touring pitches, 26 with electric hookup, 40 level pitches, 6, 9 WCs, 1 CWP
£ car/tent £6-£7.50, car/caravan £6-£7.50, motorhome £6-£7.50, motorbike/tent £6-£7.50, children £1.25
Rental & equipment £10 daily.
Calor Gaz WS
Last arrival time: 22:00
➜ Take Jn25 of M5, follow signs for Taunton, Corfe and the racecourse. 3½ miles after Corfe, turn right at crossroads. After 500 yards, turn right at give way sign. Site is 150 yards on the left past Holman Clavel Pub.

Harford Bridge Park

Set within Dartmoor National Park on the River Tavy. Spacious camping pitches and luxury self-catering caravan holiday homes. Ideal for touring, walking and relaxing.

**PETER TAVY,
TAVISTOCK, DEVON PL19 9LS
Tel: (01822) 810349**

TAVISTOCK Devon 2C3

Harford Bridge Holiday Park
Peter Tavy, Tavistock PL19 9LS
01822-810349 Fax 01822-810028
Open mid March-mid November
Size 16 acres, 120 touring pitches, 40 with electric hookup, 120 level pitches, 16 static caravans, 12, 14 WCs, 1 CWP
£ car/tent £6-£9, car/caravan £6-£9, motorhome £6-£9, motorbike/tent £6-£9, children £1-£1.50
Rental Chalet. £100-£300
CC MasterCard Visa
Calor Gaz
Last arrival time: 21:00
➜ Off A386 Tavistock to Okehampton road. 2 miles N of Tavistock, take the Peter Tavy turn.
See advert on this page

Higher Longford Farm
Moorshop, Tavistock PL19 9JY
01822-613 360 Fax 01822-618 722
Open all year
Size 6 acres, 52 touring pitches, 40 with electric hookup, 52 level pitches, 10, 14 WCs, 2 CWPs
£ car/tent £7.50-£8.50, car/caravan £7.50-£8.50, motorhome £7.50-£8.50, motorbike/tent £5.50-£6.50, children £0.50-£0.75
Rental Chalet. £90-£160
Calor Gaz WS
➜ Take B3357 Tavistock to Princetown. The road is 2½ miles from Tavistock on right before Park Hill.

Langstone Manor Camping & Caravan Park
Moortown, Tavistock PL19 9TZ
01822-613371 Fax 01822-613371
Open 15 March-15 November
Size 5.5 acres, 40 touring pitches, 14 with electric hookup, 40 level pitches, 25 static caravans, 6, 7 WCs, 1 CWP
£ car/tent £6-£8, car/caravan £6-£8, motorhome £6-£8, motorbike/tent £6-£8, children £1
Rental £150-£250, flat £125-£220
Calor Gaz
Last arrival time: 23:00
➜ Take B3357 from Tavistock to Princetown. After 2 miles, turn right at crossroads. Pass over cattle grid and turn left. Follow signs to site ½ mile on right.

TEBAY Cumbria 10B2

Tebay Caravan Park
Tebay CA10 3SB
015396-24511 Fax 015396-24511
Open mid March-31 October
Size 4 acres, 70 touring pitches, 60 with electric hookup, 70 level pitches, 4 static caravans, 6, 10 WCs
£ car/tent £6.50-£8.50, car/caravan £6.50-£8.50, motorhome £6.50-£8.50, motorbike/tent £6.50-£8.50

Tenterden

⚜ ✕ ⛟ 📞 ⚐ Calor ♿ ✈ WS
➜ Leave M6 1 mile N of jn 38 signed Westmorland Services. Access also from southbound services.

TELFORD Shropshire 7E2

Ironbridge
VALLEY OF INVENTION

Ideal for a short break... whatever the weather

Ironbridge is six square miles of pure history and stunning beauty. This picturesque valley in Shropshire is full of unique Museums and Monuments. 5 miles from Junction 4 off the M54.

1998 ATTRACTION OF THE YEAR in the Heart of England

The IRONBRIDGE GORGE MUSEUMS
Ironbridge Telford Shropshire TF8 7AW
Tel 01952 433 522 or 432 166

Camping & Caravanning Club Site
Ring Bank, Haughton, Telford TF6 6BU
📞 01743-709334
Open March-November ⚜ ⚘ ⚙
Size 18 acres, 160 touring pitches, 40 with electric hookup, 2 CWPs
£ car/tent £8.40-£9.40, car/caravan £8.40-£9.40, motorhome £8.40-£9.40, motorbike/tent £8.40-£9.40, children £1.10
cc MasterCard Visa
⚜ ⚜¼ ✕¼ ⛟ ⛟¼ 🛁 📞 ☎ 🛒 ⚐ 🛒 ⚐ 📺 ⚠ Calor ♿ ✈ WS
Last arrival time: 23:00
➜ 2½ miles from Shawbury on A53 turn left signed Haughton and Upton Magna. After 1½ miles site is on right. From A5/A49 take B5062 signposted Newport. Pass Haughmond Abbey on left and take left turn signed Hadnall. In about 1 mile, site is on the left.

Severn Gorge Caravan Park
Bridgnorth Road, Tweedale, Telford TF7 4JB
📞 01952-684789 Fax 01952-684789
Open all year ⚜ ⚘ ⚙

Set amongst woodland. This well organised site provides a perfect base for exploring Ironbridge and the rest of Shropshire. Open all year. Brochures available on request.
Size 16 acres, 110 touring pitches, 66 with electric hookup, 110 level pitches, 6 🚿, 11 WCs, 2 CWPs
£ car/tent £8.50-£10, car/caravan £8.50-£10, motorhome £8.50-£10, children £1
⚜ ⚜¼ ✕¼ ⛟¼ 🛁 📞 ☎ ⚐ ⚠ Calor Gaz ♿ ✈ WS
Last arrival time: 23:00
➜ From M54 junction 4 follow signs for Kidderminster for 1 mile, then take A442 signposted Kidderminster for 3 miles and follow signs for Tweedale. At Cuckoo Oak roundabout take third exit. Site 300 yards on right.

TENTERDEN Kent 5E3

Woodlands Caravan Park
Tenterden Road, Biddenden TN27 8BT
📞 01580-291216 Fax 01580-291216
Open 1 March-31 October ⚜ ⚘ ⚙

In the heart of the beautiful Kent countryside, Woodlands offers a perfect base for visiting all tourist attractions. Located in a picturesque and tranquil location. The Channel Tunnel is only 35 minutes drive. Please call for our brochure.
Size 24 acres, 100 touring pitches, 36 with electric hookup, 100 level pitches, 13 static caravans, 8 🚿, 16 WCs, 1 CWP
£ car/tent £8.50-£10, car/caravan £8.50-£10, motorhome £8.50-£10, motorbike/tent £6.50-£8, children £2-£2.50
⚜ ⚜¼ 🛁 📞 ☎ ⚐ ⚠ ⚐ Calor Gaz ♿ ✈ WS
➜ Situated on A262 3 miles N of Tenterden, 1½ miles S of Biddenden.

Hints & Tips

Tyres are your only contact with the road. Look after them and you will improve the safety and behaviour of your unit. Never mix cross ply and radials on the same axis.

THETFORD Norfolk	9E3

Forestry Commission Thorpe Woodland
Shadwell, Thetford IP24 2RX
☎ 01842-751042
Open end March-end October
Size 60 acres, 138 touring pitches, 34 with electric hookup, 100 level pitches, 1 CWP
£ car/tent £4-£5.20, car/caravan £4-£5.20, motorhome £4-£5.20, motorbike/tent £4-£5.20
cc MasterCard Visa
Last arrival time: 22:00
➡ At 5 miles E of Thetford on A1066, bear left to East Harling. Site entrance ¼ mile on left. Visitors must have their own toilets.

THRAPSTON Northamptonshire	8C3

Mill Marina Caravan Park
Midland Road, Thrapston NN14 4JR
☎ 01832-732850
Open 1 April-31 October
Size 10 acres, 45 touring pitches, 38 with electric hookup, 45 level pitches, 6 static caravans, 4 🏠, 5 WCs, 1 CWP
£ car/tent £7.50-£8.50, car/caravan £9.50-£10.50, motorhome £8.50-£9.50, motorbike/tent £7.50-£8.50
Rental £110-£160
Calor Gaz
Last arrival time: 21:00
➡ Take junction 13 on A14 and/or Thrapston exit from A605. Follow Thrapston and camping signs.

THIRSK North Yorkshire	11D2

York House Caravan Park
Balk, Thirsk YO7 2AQ
☎ 01845-597495 Fax 01845-597495
Open 1 April-31 October
Size 14 acres, 80 touring pitches, 30 with electric hookup, 60 level pitches, 170 static caravans, 10 🏠, 22 WCs, 1 CWP
£ car/tent £5.80-£8, car/caravan £8, motorhome £8
Calor WS
➡ From Thirsk, travel E on A170 for 2 miles, turn S for 1 mile, left to site on left in ½ mile.
See advert on this page

TILSHEAD Wiltshire	4A3

Brades Acre Caravan Site
Tilshead, near Salisbury, SP3 4RX
☎ 01980-620402
Size 1.5 acres, 26 touring pitches, 21 with electric hookup, 26 level pitches, 2 🏠, 4 WCs, 1 CWP
£ car/tent £6-£7, car/caravan £6-£7, motorhome £6-£7, motorbike/tent £6-£7, children £0.75
cc Visa
¼ ¼ ¼ Calor WS
Last arrival time: 21:00
➡ 14 miles from Salisbury on A360 to Devizes.

YORK HOUSE
Caravan Park

At the foot of the Hambleton Hills in the heart of Herriot country York House provides an ideal centre for quiet family holidays or walking enthusiasts. Fourteen acres of land, a trout stream and play area further enhance the site's appeal.

Upgraded toilet facilities including disabled access and new children's play area planned for the 1999 season.

BALK, THIRSK, NORTH YORKSHIRE YO7 2AQ
Tel: 01845-597495

Truro

149

TINTAGEL Cornwall 2B3

Headland
Atlantic Road, Tintagel PL34 0DE
☎ 01840-770239 Fax 01840-770239
Open Easter-31 October

A quiet, family run park in King Arthur's Tintagel. Overlooking cliffs, close to coast path, beaches, shops, pubs etc. Ideal for walking and touring.
Size 5 acres, 60 touring pitches, 18 with electric hookup, 20 level pitches, 30 static caravans, 7 ℞, 11 WCs, 3 CWPs
£ car/tent £6.50-£9, car/caravan £7-£10, motorhome £6-£8, motorbike/tent £6.50-£9, children £0.50-£1
Rental £110-£325
ℂℂ MasterCard Visa
Last arrival time: 21:00
➜ Signposted from B3263 through village to Headland.

TIVERTON Devon 3D2

Minnows Camping & Caravan Park
Sampford Peverell, Tiverton EX16 7EN
☎ 01884-821770
Open March-January

Quiet, landscaped park alongside the Grand Western Canal. Abounding with wild flowers and birdlife. Ideal walking, cycling and fishing with pub nearby. Excellent touring centre.
Size 2 acres, 41 touring pitches, 31 with electric hookup, 41 level pitches, 4 ℞, 6 WCs, 1 CWP
£ car/tent £6-£10, car/caravan £6-£11, motorhome £6-£11, motorbike/tent £6-£10, children £1.10-£1.20
ℂℂ MasterCard Visa
Last arrival time: 20:00
➜ From M5 junction 27 onto A361, exit after 600 yards signed Sampford Peverell, right at roundabout over bridge - site ahead.

TORQUAY Devon 3D3

Widdicombe Farm Caravan Park
Marldon, Torquay TQ3 1ST
☎ 01803-558325 Fax 01803-558325
Open Easter-5 November
Size 30 acres, 200 touring pitches, 170 with electric hookup, 170 level pitches, 3 static caravans, 18 ℞, 20 WCs, 3 CWPs
£ car/tent £6-£10, car/caravan £6-£10, motorhome £6-£10, motorbike/tent £6-£10
Rental £90-£250 weekly.
ℂℂ Visa
Calor Gaz WS
Last arrival time: 21:00
➜ On A380 Torquay to Paignton/Brixham ring road.

TRURO Cornwall 2B4

Camping & Caravanning Club Site
Tretheake Manor, Veryan, Truro TR2 5PP
☎ 01872-501658
Open March-November
Size 17 acres, 150 touring pitches, 77 with electric hookup, 10 ℞, 15 WCs, 1 CWP
£ car/tent £11.50-£14.60, car/caravan £11.50-£14.60, motorhome £11.50-£14.60, motorbike/tent £11.50-£14.60, children £1.60
ℂℂ MasterCard Visa
Calor WS
Last arrival time: 23:00
➜ On A390 from St Austell, leave at A3078 sign on the left, turn left at the filling station and follow the international signs.

Carnon Downs Caravan & Camping Park
Carnon Downs, Truro TR3 6JJ
☎ 01872-862283 Fax 01872-862800
Open 1 April-31 October
Size 14 acres, 150 touring pitches, 100 with electric hookup, 150 level pitches, 11 ℞, 19 WCs, 2 CWPs
£ car/tent £6-£12, car/caravan £7-£12, motorhome £7-£12, motorbike/tent £6-£12, children £1.75
ℂℂ MasterCard Visa
Calor Gaz WS
➜ On A39 2½ miles W of Truro. Left side of Truro to Falmouth road.

Cosawes Caravan Park
Truro, Perranarworthal TR3 7QS
☎ 01872-863724 Fax 01872-870268
Open all year
Size 100 acres, 40 touring pitches, 24 with electric hookup, 100 static caravans, 4 ℞, 6 WCs, 1 CWP
£ car/tent £6-£7, car/caravan £7-£7.50, motorhome £6.50, motorbike/tent £6
Rental £105-£210
Calor WS
➜ 6 miles W of Truro on A39.

ENGLAND

Truro

Ringwell Valley Holiday Park
Bissoe Road, Carnon Downs, Truro TR3 6LQ
☎ 01872-862194 Fax 01872-864343
Open April-October

Situated between Truro and Falmouth. Relax on a small picturesque family park overlooking country views. New luxury caravans. Bar, restaurant and swimming pool. All the facilities without the crowds.
Size 12 acres, 35 touring pitches, 25 with electric hookup, 25 level pitches, 38 static caravans, 7, 17 WCs, 1 CWP
£ car/tent £7-£11.50, car/caravan £7-£11.50, motorhome £6-£10.50, motorbike/tent £7-£11.50
Rental £100-£475
CC MasterCard Visa
Calor Gaz WS
Last arrival time: 21:30
➜ From Truro take A39 Falmouth road to roundabout in 2 miles. Follow signs to Carnon Downs, then turn right into Bissoe Road to site ¾ mile on right.

Summer Valley Touring Park
Shortlanesend, Truro TR4 9DW
☎ 01872-277878
Open 1 April-31 October

An award-winning park, centrally located for Cornwall's beaches, gardens and historic houses. Ideal for visiting in the spring for the gardens, and in the autumn for quieter moments.
Size 3 acres, 60 touring pitches, 26 with electric hookup, 30 level pitches, 6, 9 WCs, 1 CWP
£ car/tent £6.50-£8.50, car/caravan £6.50-£8.50, motorhome £6.50-£8.50, motorbike/tent £6.50-£8.50, children £0.75
CC MasterCard Visa
Calor Gaz
Last arrival time: 21:00
➜ From A30 turn left onto B3284 Truro road and site is 1½ miles. Or take B3284 from Truro and site is 2½ miles.

TUXFORD Nottinghamshire 8B1

Greenacres Touring Park
Lincoln Road, Tuxford NG22 0JN
☎ 01777-870264 Fax 01777-872512
Open 15 March-31 October
Size 4 acres, 69 touring pitches, 60 with electric hookup, 60 level pitches, 19 static caravans, 4, 11 WCs, 1 CWP
£ car/tent £6.75, car/caravan £6.75, motorhome £6.75, motorbike/tent £6.75, children £0.50
Rental £75-£150
Calor Gaz WS
➜ From A1 follow signs. Site is on A6075, 300 yards on left after Fountain pub.

Orchard Park Touring C & C Park
Marnham Road, Tuxford NG22 0PM
☎ 01777-870228
Open March-October

A quiet sheltered level site set in an old orchard, with excellent facilities. Ideal for the Sherwood Forest and Robin Hood country.
Size 8 acres, 65 touring pitches, 65 with electric hookup, 65 level pitches, 5, 7 WCs, 1 CWP
£ car/tent £7, car/caravan £7, motorhome £7, motorbike/tent £7, children £0.50
Calor Gaz WS
Last arrival time: 22:00
➜ Turn off A1 onto A6075 (A57 Lincoln road), turn right after ¾ mile into Marnham Road, site on right after ¾ mile.

ULLSWATER Cumbria 10B2

Cove Caravan & Camping Park
Watermillock, Penrith CA11 0LS
☎ 017684-86549
Open 1 March-31 October
Size 5 acres, 50 touring pitches, 17 with electric hookup, 25 level pitches, 39 static caravans, 4, 8 WCs, 1 CWP
£ car/tent £6.80-£7.20, car/caravan £8.50-£9, motorhome £6.80-£7.20, motorbike/tent £6.80-£7.20
Rental £200-£240

Ullswater

⛺¼ 🏠 📞 🗑 ⚠ Calor Gaz ♿ 🐕
Last arrival time: 21:30
➔ From M6 junction 40 take A66 to Keswick and at next roundabout take A592 to Ullswater. At 'T' junction turn right. At Brackenrigs Inn turn right and park is 1½ miles on left.

Hillcroft Park

Pooley Bridge, Ullswater CA10 2LT
📞 01768-486363 Fax 01768-486010
Open 6 March-14 November ⛺ 🚐 🚙
Size 21 acres, 25 touring pitches, 6 with electric hookup, 6 level pitches, 200 static caravans, 20 🚻, 36 WCs, 3 CWPs
£ car/tent £9-£12, car/caravan £12, motorhome £9-£12, motorbike/tent £9-£11, children £1.50
⛺ ✕¼ 🍴¼ 🏠 📞 🗑 ⚠ Calor Gaz ♿ 🐕
➔ From M6 junction 40 take A66 towards Keswick, then A592 to Ullswater. At the head of the lake turn left, go through Pooley Bridge and bear right at church. Head straight through crossroads to site on left.

Park Foot Caravan & Camping Park

Howtown Road, Pooley Bridge, Ullswater CA10 2NA
📞 01768-486309 Fax 01768-486041
Open 15 March-31 October ⛺ 🚐 🚙

A family park set in the magnificent Lakeland Fells. With access to Lake Ullswater for boat launching and car parking. Children's playground, graded excellent by the Tourist Board.
Size 30 acres, 290 touring pitches, 70 with electric hookup, 200 level pitches, 129 static caravans, 24 🚻, 50 WCs, 2 CWPs
£ car/tent £7.50-£11, car/caravan £12-£15, motorhome £7.50-£11, motorbike/tent £7.50-£11, children £1
Rental Houses/log cabins - £45 night, £180-£480 week.
⛺ ✕ 🍴 🏠 📞 🗑 🏪 🎣 🏊 GR 🎮 📺 ⚠ 🔌 Calor Gaz ♿ 🐕
Last arrival time: 23:00
➔ From M6 junction 40 take A66 Keswick road. Take A592 to Ullswater. At 'T' junction turn left. At Pooley Bridge turn right and right again at crossroads. Site is 1 mile down Howtown Road on left.

Quiet Site

Watermillock, Ullswater CA11 0LS
📞 01768-486337 Fax 01768-486610
Open 1 March-14 November ⛺ 🚐 🚙
Idyllic setting amongst the fells. Large adventure playground and 'probably' the best campsite bar in Britain. Voted Best Site in Britain. AA Northern Campsite of the Year. Top 100 Park. ETB Excellent grading.
Size 6 acres, 60 touring pitches, 47 with electric hookup, 53 level pitches, 23 static caravans, 8 🚻, 15 WCs, 1 CWP
£ car/tent £8-£10, car/caravan £9-£11, motorhome £8-£10, motorbike/tent £7-£9, children £1
Rental ⛺ 🚐
⛺ 🏠 📞 🗑 GR 🎮 ⚠ 🔌 Calor Gaz 🐕 WS
Last arrival time: 21:00
➔ From M6 junction 40 take A66 to Keswick. After ¾ mile turn left onto A592 (signed Ullswater). After 4 miles turn right at T-junction. After 1½ miles turn right at Bracherigg Hotel. Site is on right after 1½ miles.

Ullswater Caravan Camping Site

Watermillock, Ullswater CA11 0LR
📞 01768-486666 Fax 01768-486095
Open 1 March-14 November ⛺ 🚐 🚙

Situated in scenic countryside with its own lake access and ½ mile from Lake Ullswater. Ideal for touring the Lake District.
Size 14 acres, 155 touring pitches, 40 with electric hookup, 40 level pitches, 55 static caravans, 14 🚻, 21 WCs, 2 CWPs
£ car/tent £9, car/caravan £10, motorhome £9, motorbike/tent £8, children £1
Rental 🚐 Chalet. £165-£360
CC MasterCard Visa
⛺ 🍴 🏠 📞 🗑 GR 📺 ⚠ 🔌 Calor Gaz ♿ 🐕
Last arrival time: 21:00
➔ From M6 junction 40 take A592 to Ullswater, turn right at telephone kiosk, signposted Longthwaite and Watermillock church.

Hints & Tips

Tyres are your only contact with the road. Look after them and you will improve the safety and behaviour of your unit. Never mix cross ply and radials on the same axis.

ENGLAND

151

Ullswater

WATERFOOT CARAVAN PARK

Peaceful partially wooded site near to and with views over Ullswater. Children's play area. Licensed bar and shop. Ideal area for walking both around the Lake and on Lakeland fells.

POOLEY BRIDGE CA11 0JF
Telephone: 017684-86302

Waterfoot Caravan Park
Pooley Bridge, Ullswater CA11 0JF
☎ 01768-486302
Open March-October

22 acres with level and sloping pitches. Sheltered quiet country park. Touring vans only. 5 mins walk to lake, good access to Lakeland Fells for walking.
Size 22 acres, 57 touring pitches, 57 with electric hookup, 36 level pitches, 123 static caravans, 6 🚿, 10 WCs, 1 CWP
£ car/caravan £11.50-£13, motorhome £11.50-£13
Calor Gaz
Last arrival time: dusk
➡ From junction 40 of M6 take A66 for 1 mile and then A592 to Ullswater. Park is on right 6 miles from M6.
See advert on this page

UMBERLEIGH Devon 2C2

Camping & Caravanning Club Site
Over Weir, Umberleigh EX37 9DU
☎ 01769-560009
Open March-November
Size 4 acres, 60 touring pitches, 33 with electric hookup, 6 🚿, 9 WCs, 1 CWP
£ car/tent £10.40-£13.60, car/caravan £10.40-£13.60, motorhome £10.40-£13.60, motorbike/tent £10.40-£13.60, children £1.50
cc MasterCard Visa
Calor
WS
Last arrival time: 23:00
➡ On A377 from Barnstaple turn right at Umberleigh sign.

WADEBRIDGE Cornwall 2B3

Gunvenna Touring Caravan & Camping Park
St Minver, Polzeath PL27 6QN
☎ 01208-862405
Open Easter-November

Gunvenna, an attractive site, ideally situated for touring North Cornwall. Beautiful views. Indoor heated pool. From £7.50-£12 per pitch.
Size 10 acres, 200 touring pitches, 24 with electric hookup, 75 level pitches, 6 🚿, 20 WCs, 3 CWPs
Calor
➡ From Wadebridge, travel N on B3314 for 4½ miles to site on right.

Laurels
Whitecross, Wadebridge PL27 7JQ
☎ 01208-813341
Open Easter-October
Size 3 acres, 30 touring pitches, 20 with electric hookup, 30 level pitches, 4 🚿, 8 WCs, 1 CWP
£ car/tent £7, car/caravan £7, motorhome £7, motorbike/tent £7, children £0.50
WS
Last arrival time: 22:00
➡ ½ mile S of Whitecross at A39/A389 junction.

Waltham Abbey

Little Bodieve Holiday Park
Bodieve, Wadebridge PL27 6EG
☎ 01208-812323
Open 1 April-31 October ▲ 🚐 🚚

A Rose Award park. 20 acres of well-mown areas, an ideal touring centre, close to superb beaches. Pets corner, play area, games room, entertainment in the main season, luxury caravans for hire.
Size 22 acres, 195 touring pitches, 60 with electric hookup, 195 level pitches, 76 static caravans, 24 🚿, 20 WCs, 5 CWPs
£ car/tent £6-£9, car/caravan £6-£9, motorhome £6-£9, motorbike/tent £6-£9, children £1.50-£2.20
Rental 🚐 £110-£450
CC MasterCard Visa
🛒 ✗ 🛍 🍴 🎮 🎯 GR 🏊 🏕 Calor Gaz ♿ 🐕 WS
Last arrival time: 20:00
➡ 1 mile N of Wadebridge, just off A39. Take B3314 toward Rock and Port Isaac. Nearest to Camel Trail.

Trewince Holiday Park
St Issey, Wadebridge PL27 7RL
☎ 01280-812830
Open 17 April-31 October ▲ 🚐 🚚

Touring caravans can enjoy the facilities of a 5 Tick Rose Award Park overlooking a wooded valley only 4 miles from picturesque Padstow, the Camel Trail and many sandy beaches.
Size 10 acres, 125 touring pitches, 42 with electric hookup, 22 static caravans, 11 🚿, 12 WCs, 3 CWPs
CC Visa
🛒 🎯 Calor Gaz WS
➡ Take A39 to Wadebridge, then A389 to Padstow. The site is signposted and is on left.

WAKEFIELD West Yorkshire 11D4

Nostell Priory Holiday Park
Nostell, Wakefield WF4 1QD
☎ 01924-863938 Fax 01924-862226

Open April-September ▲ 🚐 🚚
Size 35 acres, 60 touring pitches, 60 with electric hookup, 60 level pitches, 80 static caravans, 8 🚿, 12 WCs, 1 CWP
£ car/tent £8-£9, car/caravan £8-£9, motorhome £8-£9, children £0.50
Rental 🚐 £120-£200
🛒 🍴 🎯 🏊 Calor Gaz 🐕 WS
Last arrival time: 21:00
➡ From A638 Wakefield to Doncaster road turn left at Foulby.

WALLINGFORD Oxfordshire 4B2

Bridge Villa International C & C Site
Crowmarsh Gifford, Wallingford OX10 8HB
☎ 01491-836860 Fax 01491-839103
Open 1 February-31 December ▲ 🚐 🚚
Size 4 acres, 111 touring pitches, 111 with electric hookup
£ car/tent £7, car/caravan £7, motorhome £6, motorbike/tent £5, children £0.50
🛒 🛒¼ ✗¼ 🍴¼ 🎯 🏊 Calor Gaz ♿ 🐕 WS
➡ Site located off A4130.

Riverside Park
Crowmarsh, Wallingford OX10 8EB
☎ 01491-835232 Fax 01865-341035
Open April-September ▲ 🚐 🚚
Size 1 acres, 28 touring pitches, 28 level pitches, 6 🚿, 6 WCs
£ car/tent £7.20-£9.25, car/caravan £7.20-£9.25, motorhome £7.20-£9.25, motorbike/tent £7.20-£9.25, children £0.25
🛒 🛒¼ ✗¼ 🍴 🍴¼ 🎯 🎮 🎯 🏊 ♿
Last arrival time: 22:00
➡ A34 to Didcot, then follow sign to Wallingford. Go over main road bridge and take first left.

WALTHAM ABBEY Essex 5D2

Camping & Caravanning Club Site
Theobalds Park, Bulls Cross Ride, Waltham Abbey EN7 5HS
☎ 01992-620604
Open March-November ▲ 🚐 🚚
Size 14 acres, 150 touring pitches, 30 with electric hookup, 6 🚿, 8 WCs, 1 CWP
£ car/tent £9.60-£12.10, car/caravan £9.60-£12.10, motorhome £9.60-£12.10, motorbike/tent £9.60-£12.10, children £1.50
CC MasterCard Visa
🛒 🛒¼ ✗¼ 🍴 🍴¼ 🎮 🎯 P 🎯 🎮 GR 🏊 Calor ♿ 🐕 WS
Last arrival time: 23:00
➡ Junction 25 on M25, take A10 towards London keeping to right hand lane, turn right at first traffic lights, signposted Crews Hill, turn right at T-junction (opposite Pied Bull), turn right behind dog kennels, site is towards top of lane on right.

ENGLAND

153

154

Wareham

BIRCHWOOD TOURIST PARK

Family-run park, ideally situated for exploring Dorset.
Well Stocked Shop, Off Licence, Take-Away, Free Hot Showers, Children's Paddling Pool, Bike Hire, Pony Riding, Fully-Serviced Pitches

We accept VISA DELTA MasterCard

Birchwood Tourist Park
North Trigon, Wareham, Dorset BH20 7PA
Telephone 01929 554763

WAREHAM Dorset   3F3

Birchwood Tourist Park
Bere Road, Coldharbour, Wareham BH20 7PA
☎ 01929-554763
Open March-October
Size 46 acres, 175 touring pitches, 118 with electric hookup, 175 level pitches, 14, 20 WCs, 2 CWPs
£ car/tent £6.50, car/caravan £6.50, motorhome £6.50, motorbike/tent £6.50, children £0.75
cc MasterCard Visa
Calor Gaz
Last arrival time: 22:00
➡ From A35 E of Bere Regis follow signs to Wareham. Second touring park on left.
See advert on this page

Lookout Holiday Park
Stoborough, Wareham BH20 5AZ
☎ 01929-552546 Fax 01929-552546
Open February-November

A quiet, family park, ideally situated for exploring the Purbecks. Touring pitches available on hardstandings or grass. Fully equipped caravans with colour TV for hire.
Size 15 acres, 150 touring pitches, 107 with electric hookup, 150 level pitches, 90 static caravans, 10, 17 WCs, 2 CWPs
£ car/tent £9-£12, car/caravan £9-£12, motorhome £9-£12, motorbike/tent £9-£12
Rental £95-£355
cc MasterCard Visa
Calor Gaz WS
Last arrival time: 22:00
➡ From centre of Wareham proceed S to Swanage. Cross over River Frome, pass through village of Stoborough. Park on left of main road.

WARRINGTON Cheshire   7E1

Hollybank Caravan Park
Warburton Bridge Road, Rixton, Warrington WA3 6HU
☎ 0161-775 2842
Open all year
Size 9 acres, 75 touring pitches, 60 with electric hookup, 60 level pitches, 7, 10 WCs, 2 CWPs
£ car/tent £9.50-£10.50, car/caravan £10.50-£12, motorhome £10.50-£12, motorbike/tent £8.50-£10, children £1
Calor Gaz WS
Last arrival time: 21:00
➡ 2 miles E of M6 junction 21 on A57 (Irlam). Turn right at lights into Warburton Bridge Road and site is on left.

WASHINGTON West Sussex   4C4

Washington Caravan and Camping Park
London Road, Washington RH20 4AJ
☎ 01903-892869 Fax 01903-893252
Open all year
Size 4.5 acres, 100 touring pitches, 21 with electric hookup, 4, 10 WCs, 1 CWP
£ car/tent £8.50, car/caravan £8, motorhome £8, motorbike/tent £8.50, children £3
cc MasterCard Visa
Calor Gaz
➡ N of Washington on A283. E of roundabout with A24, signposted South Downs Way. Site is below Chanctonbury Ring.

WATCHET Somerset   3D2

Warren Bay Caravan & Camping Park
Watchet TA23 0JR
☎ 01984-631460 Fax 01984-633999
Size 22 acres, 180 touring pitches, 30 with electric hookup, 15 level pitches, 155 static caravans, 12, 27 WCs, 2 CWPs

Weston-super-Mare

£ car/tent £3.50-£4, car/caravan £3.50-£6, motorhome £3.50-£4.50, motorbike/tent £4, children £1
Rental £129-£205
CC MasterCard Visa
Calor Gaz WS
➜ From M5 junction 23 take A39 for 17 miles. Then B3191 at Watchet and follow sign for Blue Anchor.

WELLS Somerset   3E2

Homestead Park

Wookey Hole, Wells BA5 1BW
01749-673022
Open 1 April-31 October
Size 4.5 acres, 50 touring pitches, 6 with electric hookup, 50 level pitches, 2, 14 WCs, 1 CWP
£ car/tent £9, car/caravan £8.80, motorhome £8.20, motorbike/tent £7.30, children £1-£2
Calor Gaz
➜ Leave Wells by A371 towards Cheddar. Turn right for Wookey Hole. Site 1¼ miles on left in village.

Mendip Heights Caravan & Camping Park

Priddy, Wells BA5 3BP
01749-870241 **Fax** 01749-870241
Open 1 March-15 November
Size 4.25 acres, 90 touring pitches, 21 with electric hookup, 40 level pitches, 4, 11 WCs, 1 CWP
£ car/tent £6.40-£7, car/caravan £6.40-£7, motorhome £6.40-£7, motorbike/tent £6.40-£7, children £1.50
Calor Gaz WS
Last arrival time: 22:30
➜ From Wells take A39 towards Bristol for 3 miles. Turn left at Green Ore traffic lights onto B3135 for 5 miles, then turn left at camp site sign.

WEM Shropshire   7D2

Lower Lacon Caravan Park

Wem SY4 5RP
01939-232376 **Fax** 01939-233606
Open all year
Size 48 acres, 270 touring pitches, 120 with electric hookup, 270 level pitches, 50 static caravans, 12, 25 WCs, 3 CWPs
£ car/tent £9.50-£10, car/caravan £9.50-£10, motorhome £9.50-£10, motorbike/tent £9.50-£10, children £1
Rental holiday homes £85-£270
CC MasterCard Visa
Calor Gaz WS
Last arrival time: 24 hours
➜ From A49 take B506 to Wem. Go over level crossing onto B5065 Market Drayton road. Park is 1 mile on left.

WEST WITTERING West Sussex   4C4

Scotts Farm Camping Site

West Wittering PO20 8ED
01243-671720 **Fax** 01243-513669
Open March-October

Spacious family run site set in 30 acres of level grassland. Village and beach within easy walking distance, lovely country walks, play area and modern facilities.
Size 30 acres, 450 touring pitches, 200 with electric hookup, 450 level pitches, 56, 60 WCs, 4 CWPs
£ car/tent £9-£10, car/caravan £9-£10, motorhome £9-£10, motorbike/tent £9-£10
Calor Gaz
Last arrival time: 23:30
➜ A286 from A27 to Chichester. After 4 miles turn left to East Wittering/Bracklesham Bay just past self service station on right. Carry on for 1 mile, turn right past Lively Lady pub. Go past East Wittering village and site on right.

WESTON-SUPER-MARE Somerset   3E1

Airport View Caravan Park

Moor Lane, Worle, Weston-super-Mare BS24 7LA
01934-622168 **Fax** 01934-628245
Open 1 March-31 October
Size 10 acres, 200 touring pitches, 40 static caravans, 10, 15 WCs, 1 CWP
£ car/tent £5-£7.50, car/caravan £5-£7.50, motorhome £5-£7.50, children £0.50
Rental
CC MasterCard Visa
Calor Gaz WS
Last arrival time: 21:00
➜ From A371 turn into Moor Lane. Site 100 yards.

Don't forget to mention the guide
When booking, please remember to tell the site that you chose it from RAC Camping & Caravanning 1999

Weston-super-Mare

TOUR & EXPLORE from "COUNTRY VIEW"

"at the gateway to this lovely corner of the West of England...

...or just relax on our quiet, level, family caravan park adjoining open fields"

- Licensed Clubroom
- Shop, Showers & Launderette
- Heated Pool ◆ Long Term Tourers
- 'Bright Lights' of Weston 3 miles
- Close to National Trust Headland
- 400 yds Beach ◆ 10 mins M5
- Touring Caravans, Tents, Motorhomes (& dogs!) all welcome
- Holiday Homes to Let
- Holiday Homes for Sale

Sand Road, Sand Bay, Weston-super-Mare. Tel 01934 627595

Purn INTERNATIONAL HOLIDAY PARK

Touring, camping, holiday homes, hire, sales. FREE heated swimming pools. Free live entertainment plus dancing, bingo, licensed club and own Anchor Inn Pub.

Open 1 March – 7 November.

Bridgwater Road (A370), Bleadon, Weston-super-Mare BS24 0AN
Tel: 01934-812342

Country View Caravan & Touring Park
Sand Road, Sand Bay, Weston-super-Mare BS22 9UJ
01934-627595
Open March-October
Size 8.5 acres, 120 touring pitches, 82 with electric hookup, 120 level pitches, 65 static caravans, 8, 12 WCs, 1 CWP
£ car/tent £4-£12, car/caravan £6.50-£12, motorhome £6.50-£12, motorbike/tent £4-£12
Rental £90-£295
CC MasterCard Visa
Gaz WS
Last arrival time: 22:00
➡ From M5 (jn 21) follow signs to Weston-super-Mare, and then 100 yards bear left to Kewstoke/Sand Bay. Turn right at Homebase DIY store and go straight over three roundabouts. Turn right into Sand Road and site on right.
See advert on this page

Dulhorn Farm Camping Site
Weston Road, Lympsham, Weston-super-Mare BS24 0JQ
01934-750298 Fax 01934-750913
Open March-October
Size 2 acres, 42 touring pitches, 42 with electric hookup, 42 level pitches, 3 static caravans, 2, 5 WCs, 1 CWP
£ car/tent £7-£8.50, car/caravan £7-£8.50, motorhome £7-£8.50, motorbike/tent £7-£8.50
Rental Chalet. £80-£250
Calor Gaz WS
Last arrival time: 22:00
➡ From A38 take A370 to Weston-super-Mare. Site is 1¼ mile on left.

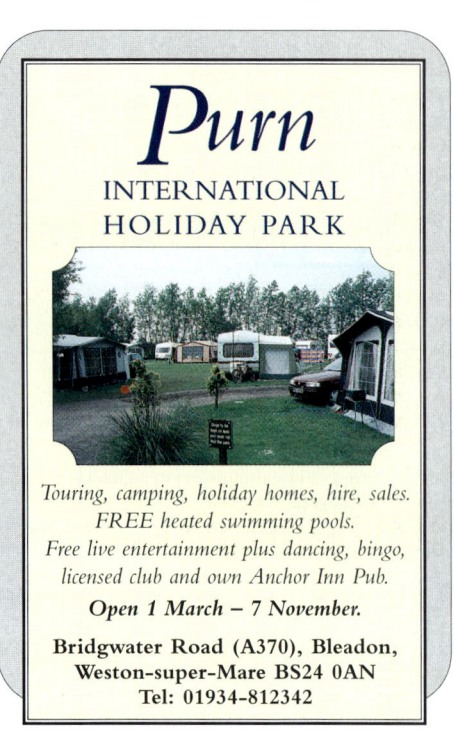

Purn International Holiday Park
Bridgwater Road (A370), Bleadon, Weston-super-Mare BS24 0AN
01934-812342 Fax 01934-812342
Open 1 March-7 November
Size 11 acres, 60 touring pitches, 40 with electric hookup, 60 level pitches, 110 static caravans, 6, 12 WCs, 2 CWPs
£ car/tent £5.50-£9.50, car/caravan £6.50-£9.50, motorhome £6-£9, motorbike/tent £5-£8
Rental £115-£285
Calor Gaz WS
Last arrival time: 00:00
➡ From M5 jn 21 take signs for Weston & Hospital. Turn left at hospital roundabout onto A370. Site 1 mile on right after Anchor Inn pub.
See advert on this page

West End Farm Caravan Park
Locking, Weston-super-Mare BS24 8RH
01934-822529
Open all year
Size 10 acres, 80 touring pitches, 80 with electric hookup, 20 static caravans, 4, 15 WCs, 1 CWP
£ car/tent £7-£10, car/caravan £7-£10, motorhome £7-£10, children £1.50
CC MasterCard Visa
Calor Gaz WS
Last arrival time: 22:00
➡ Leave M5 (jn 21) onto A370. Follow signs to International Helicopter Museum and take next turning on right after museum. Follow signs to site.

Weymouth

WEYMOUTH Dorset   3E3

Bagwell Farm Touring Park
Chickerell, Weymouth DT3 4EA
☎ 01305-782575
Open all year ▲ ⊕ ⊞
Size 14 acres, 320 touring pitches, 174 with electric hookup, 320 level pitches, 12 ⓡ, 38 WCs, 1 CWP
£ car/tent £4-£10, car/caravan £5.50-£10.50, motorhome £5.50-£10.58, motorbike/tent £4-£8.50
㏄ MasterCard Visa
⛱ ✕¼ 🍴 🛒 ☎ 🚿 GR ⚠ Calor Gaz ♿ 🐕 WS
Last arrival time: 21:00
➜ 4 miles W of Weymouth on B3157, 500 yards past Victoria Inn.

East Fleet Farm Touring Park
Chickerell, Weymouth DT3 4DW
☎ 01305-785768
Open 15 March-15 January ▲ ⊕ ⊞

Peaceful and spacious park on the shores of the Fleet overlooking Chesil Bank and the sea. In an area of outstanding natural beauty.
Size 20 acres, 150 touring pitches, 80 with electric hookup, 150 level pitches, 17 ⓡ, 42 WCs, 2 CWPs
£ car/tent £4.50-£9.50, car/caravan £4.50-£9.50, motorhome £4.50-£9.50, motorbike/tent £4.50-£9.50, children £0.25-£0.50
㏄ MasterCard Visa
⛱ ⛱¼ 🍴 🛒 ☎ 🚿 GR ⚠ Calor Gaz ♿ 🐕
➜ Off B3157, left at Chickerell TA camp.

Littlesea Holiday Park
Lynch Lane, Weymouth DT4 9DT
☎ 01305-774414   Fax 01305-760038
Open April-October ▲ ⊕ ⊞
Size 11 acres, 215 touring pitches, 145 with electric hookup, 150 level pitches, 38 ⓡ, 40 WCs, 2 CWPs
Rental ⊕
㏄ MasterCard Visa
⛱ ✕ 🍴 🛒 ☎ 🚿 ⚠ Calor Gaz ♿ 🐕
Last arrival time: 23:00
➜ Leave Dorchester on A354 for Weymouth. Take the third exit at first and second roundabouts. At the third roundabout turn left. Follow the road to the lights, go straight across the lights, right in to Lanehouse Rocks Road, then left in to Lynch Lane.

Osmington Mills
Weymouth DT3 6HB
☎ 01305-832311   Fax 01305-835251
▲ ⊕ ⊞

A family run holiday park where you can enjoy a friendly, relaxed atmosphere in the Dorset coastal countryside, or at nearby Weymouth, with all the facilities of a popular holiday resort.
Size 13 acres, 25 touring pitches, 16 with electric hookup, 25 level pitches, 62 static caravans, 18 ⓡ, 36 WCs, 1 CWP
£ car/tent £6-£15, car/caravan £6-£12, motorhome £6-£15
Rental ⊕ Chalet.
㏄ MasterCard Visa
⛱ ⛱¼ ✕ ✕¼ 🍴 🍴¼ ☎ 🚿 GR ⚠ Calor Gaz 🐕 WS
➜ 5 miles E of Weymouth, off A353 Weymouth to Wareham road, turn S at Osmington to Osmington Mills.
See advert on this page

OSMINGTON MILLS

A family run holiday park where you can enjoy a friendly relaxed atmosphere in the Dorset coastal countryside or at nearby Weymouth with all the facilities of a popular holiday resort.

**OSMINGTON MILLS,
WEYMOUTH,
DORSET DT3 6HB**
Tel: 01305 832311
Fax: 01305 835251

ENGLAND

Weymouth

Pebble Bank Caravan Park
Camp Road, Wyke Regis, Weymouth DT4 9HF
☎ 01305-774844 Fax 01305-774844
Open 1 April-early October

Quiet family park in a picturesque situation close to Weymouth centre, with superb views.
Size 8 acres, 45 touring pitches, 40 with electric hookup, 40 level pitches, 95 static caravans, 5 🚿, 10 WCs, 1 CWP
£ car/tent £5-£10, car/caravan £6-£12, motorhome £5-£10, motorbike/tent £5-£9, children £1
Rental £125-£325
¼ ¼ ¼ Calor Gaz
Last arrival time: 22:00

➜ From harbour roundabout at Weymouth continue up hill to mini roundabout opposite Rodwell pub. Turn right onto Wyke Road. Camp Road is 1 mile further on at apex of sharp right hand bend at bottom of hill.

Sea Barn Farm
Fleet, Weymouth DT3 4ED
☎ 01305-782218 Fax 01305-775396
Open March-October

Part of a 140 acre farm bordering the Fleet Nature Reserve. A delightful scenic walk links to the coastal path. A quiet site for the discerning camper.
Size 12 acres, 250 touring pitches, 16 with electric hookup, 250 level pitches, 15 🚿, 27 WCs, 1 CWP
£ motorhome £6.50-£9.50, motorbike/tent £6.50-£9.50, children £1-£1.50
Rental Chalet. £180 - £390
Calor Gaz
Last arrival time: 21:30

➜ Take B3157 from Weymouth towards Bridport. After 3 miles turn left at mini roundabout to Fleet. Site 1 mile on left.

West Fleet Holiday Farm
Fleet, Weymouth DT3 4EF
☎ 01305-782218 Fax 01305-775396
Open Easter-31 October

Scenic sea and countryside views near the Fleet Nature Reserve. Closely mown grass, tree shelter and tarmac roads on site.
Size 20 acres, 250 touring pitches, 30 with electric hookup, 18 🚿, 28 WCs, 2 CWPs
£ car/tent £7-£11, motorhome £7-£11, motorbike/tent £7-£11, children £1.50
Rental £120-£260, Chalet £180-£390.
Calor Gaz
Last arrival time: 21:30

➜ On coast W of Weymouth. Turn off the B3157 Weymouth to Bridport road at Chickerell mini-roundabout to Fleet. Park is 1 mile on right.
See advert on this page

West Fleet
HOLIDAY FARM

A warm welcome awaits you at this family run camping park. Beautiful location with panoramic views over Dorset coastline and countryside. Sheltered, level grass park. Close to Weymouth.

★ Licensed Club – Bar Meals or Takeaway – Children's Room. Separate games area.
★ Heated Swimming Pool – tree sheltered.
★ Electric hook-up.
★ Luxury Bungalow, 3 bedrooms, in lawned garden. Sea views.
★ 4/6 berth Caravan.

**MR. W. O. COOMBE,
SEA BARN FARM, FLEET,
WEYMOUTH DT3 4ED**
Tel: 01305 782218 Fax: 01305 775396

Wimborne Minster

159

WHITBY North Yorkshire 11E2

Hollins Farm
Glaisdale, Whitby YO21 2PZ
☎ 01947-897516
Open Easter ▲
Size 1 acre, 2 ☻, 3 WCs
£ car/tent £4, motorbike/tent £4, children £1
➔ From A171 take road to Glaisdale for 4 miles. In Glaisdale, opposite phone box, road leads up round church. Come up that road for 1½ miles, to site on left, 100 yards down a tarmac drive.

Middlewood Farm Holiday Park
Fylingthorpe, Robin Hood's Bay, Whitby YO22 4UF
☎ 01947-880414 **Fax** 01947-880414
Open Easter-31 October ▲
Size 6 acres, 20 touring pitches, 20 with electric hookup, 120 level pitches, 30 static caravans, 8 ☻, 18 WCs, 1 CWP
£ car/tent £6.50-£8.50, car/caravan £6.50-£8.50, motorhome £6.50-£7.50, motorbike/tent £6.50-£7.50, children £0.50
Rental £110-£395
Calor Gaz
Last arrival time: 23:00
➔ 2½ miles S of Whitby on A171 turn E on B1447. After 1½ miles turn right to Fylingthorpe. At village crossroads continue straight ahead to park on Middlewood Lane.

Northcliffe Holiday Park
High Hawsker, Whitby YO22 4LL
☎ 01947-880477 **Fax** 01947-880972
Open 15 March-31 October ▲

A secluded family park situated on the beautiful, unspoilt Heritage Coast, between Whitby and Robin Hood's Bay, with panoramic sea views.
Size 26 acres, 30 touring pitches, 30 with electric hookup, 16 level pitches, 161 static caravans, 6 ☻, 10 WCs, 1 CWP
£ car/tent £6-£10.50, car/caravan £6-£10.50, motorhome £6-£10.50, motorbike/tent £6-£8
Rental From £135-£350 weekly
CC MasterCard Visa
Calor Gaz
Last arrival time: 21:00
➔ 3 miles S of Whitby on the A171 turn left onto B1447 (High Hawsker-Robin Hoods Bay). Through village and at top of hill turn left into a private lane for ½ mile.

York House Caravan Park
High Hawsker, Whitby YO22 4LW
☎ 01947-880354
Open 21 March-31 October ▲
Size 4 acres, 59 touring pitches, 59 with electric hookup, 20 level pitches, 41 static caravans, 8 ☻, 13 WCs, 1 CWP
£ car/tent £6.50-£7.50, car/caravan £6.50-£7.50, motorhome £6.50-£7.50, motorbike/tent £5-£7.50, children £0.50
Calor Gaz WS
Last arrival time: 22:00
➔ 3 miles S of Whitby on A171.

WIMBORNE MINSTER Dorset 3F3

Camping & Caravanning Club Site
Sutton Hill, Woodlands, Wimborne Minster BH21 6LF
☎ 01202-822763
Open March-November ▲
Size 12.75 acres, 150 touring pitches, 94 with electric hookup, 12 ☻, 16 WCs, 1 CWP
£ car/tent £11.50-£14.60, car/caravan £11.50-£14.60, motorhome £11.50-£14.60, motorbike/tent £11.50-£14.60, children £1.60
CC MasterCard Visa
Calor WS
Last arrival time: 23:00
➔ Turn left on A354 13 miles from Salisbury onto B3081, the site is 1½ miles W of Verwood

Merley Court Touring Park
Merley, Wimborne Minster BH21 3AA
☎ 01202-881488 **Fax** 01202-881484
Open 1 March-7 January ▲

The first ever English Tourist Board 'Caravan Park of the Year'. Also, Practical Caravan magazine 'Best Family Park' 1993 and 1997. Ideally placed for Bournemouth, Poole and the New Forest.
Size 20 acres, 160 touring pitches, 160 with electric hookup, 160 level pitches, 19 ☻, 37 WCs, 3 CWPs
£ car/tent £6.50-£12, car/caravan £6.50-£12, motorhome £6.50-£12, motorbike/tent £6.50-£12, children £2
CC MasterCard Visa
Calor Gaz
Last arrival time: 22:00
➔ Clearly signposted off A31 Wimborne bypass and A349 Poole junction.

ENGLAND

Wimborne Minster

Springfield Touring Park
Candy's Lane, Corfe Mullen, Wimborne Minster BH21 3EF
☏ 01202-881719
Open Easter-October

Highly commended in Practical Caravan 1996 - 100 Best U.K. Parks. Set in Dorset overlooking the Stour Valley and close to Poole, Bournemouth, the New Forest. Modern facilities, free showers, awnings.
Size 3.5 acres, 45 touring pitches, 45 with electric hookup, 35 level pitches, 6 ☂, 8 WCs, 1 CWP
£ car/tent £6-£8, car/caravan £7-£8, motorhome £7-£8, motorbike/tent £6, children £1.25
Calor Gaz
Last arrival time: 22:00
➜ Turn left off A31 (Ringwood to Dorchester) at roundabout at western end of Wimborne by-pass into road signposted Corfe Mullen. S ¼ mile to Candy's Lane on right, park entrance 300 yards past farm.

Wilksworth Farm Caravan Park
Cranborne Road, Wimborne Minster BH21 4HW
☏ 01202-885467
Open 1 March-30 October

Country park with excellent facilities in a peaceful setting. Tennis courts, games room, heated swimming pool and children's play area are on site. New coffee shop/takeaway.
Size 12 acres, 85 touring pitches, 70 with electric hookup, 75 level pitches, 77 static caravans, 10 ☂, 19 WCs, 1 CWP
£ car/tent £6-£11.50, car/caravan £6-£11.50, motorhome £6-£11.50, motorbike/tent £6, children £1
Rental
Calor Gaz WS
Last arrival time: 21:30
➜ From A31 to Wimborne town centre, then B3078 N to Cranborne. Park is on left.

Woolsbridge Manor Farm Caravan Park
Three Legged Cross, Wimborne Minster BH21 6RA
☏ 01202-826369 fax 01202-813172
Open Easter-October

7 acres of level semi-sheltered spacious pitches set in a quiet working farm location, ideal for families. Walk through fields to Moors Valley Country Park. New Forest only 3½ miles. Graded 4 ticks.
Size 7 acres, 60 touring pitches, 37 with electric hookup, 60 level pitches, 6 ☂, 12 WCs, 2 CWPs
£ car/tent £6-£9, car/caravan £6-£9, motorhome £6-£9, motorbike/tent £6-£9, children £1
Calor Gaz
Last arrival time: 22:00

WINCANTON Somerset   3F2

Wincanton Racecourse
Wincanton BA9 8BJ
☏ 01963-34276
Open end April-end September

A peaceful rural site, 1 mile from Wincanton. Surrounded by numerous places to visit, i.e. the beautiful Stourhead Gardens. Golf course, pay and play.
Size 2 acres, 50 touring pitches, 24 with electric hookup, 50 level pitches, 4 ☂, 7 WCs, 1 CWP
£ car/tent £7.70-£9.50, car/caravan £10.20-£11.50, motorhome £10.20-£11.50, motorbike/tent £6.70-£8.50, children £1.10
cc MasterCard Visa
Calor
Last arrival time: 20:00
➜ From A303 follow signs to Racecourse, 3 miles on B3081.

Windermere

Fallbarrow Park

Beautiful lakeside park with 'state of the art' multi hook-up touring pitches. High standards of park facilities include boat launching and friendly 'Boathouse' pub with delightful beer garden, bar meals and family room.

NATIONAL WINNER
'CAMPSITE OF THE YEAR' 1996/97

RAYRIGG ROAD, WINDERMERE, CUMBRIA LA23 3DL
Tel: (015394) 44428 Fax: (015394) 88736

WINCHESTER Hampshire   4B3

Balldown Camping & Caravan Park
Stockbridge Road, Sparsholt, Winchester SO21 2NA
☎ 01962-776619
Open 1 March-31 October
Size 1.25 acres, 16 touring pitches, 16 with electric hookup, 16 level pitches, 2, 5 WCs, 1 CWP
£ car/tent £6-£8, car/caravan £6-£8, motorhome £6-£8, motorbike/tent £6-£8, children £0.50
Last arrival time: 23:00
➜ 3m N of Winchester on the B3049 to Stockbridge and Salisbury.

WINDERMERE Cumbria   10B2

Fallbarrow Park
Rayrigg Road, Bowness, Windermere LA23 3DL
☎ 015394-44428
Open 15 March-31 October

Beautiful lakeside park with state of the art touring pitches. Just 300 yards from the lakeland village of Bowness. National winner of 'campsite of the year', graded excellent.
Size 32 acres, 83 touring pitches, 83 with electric hookup, 83 level pitches, 248 static caravans, 9, 14 WCs, 2 CWPs
£ car/caravan £11.40-£18.25, motorhome £11.40-£18.25
Rental £125-£515.
₢ MasterCard Visa
Calor
Last arrival time: 23:00
➜ On A591, ½ mile N of Windermere, take A592, signposted Bowness, Barrow. The park is 1½ miles on right.
See advert on this page

Hints & Tips

If you have any information concerning caravan theft contact the confidential freephone Crimestoppers Line on 0800 555111.
You may be entitled to a reward and there is no need to give your name if you don't want to.

Limefitt Park

Spectacular Lakeland valley location. Ten minutes drive Lake Windermere. Tourers and family campers welcome. Friendly Lakeland pub with bar meals. 'Do-it-yourself' Camper's kitchen, Spar shop plus full range of award winning facilities. A truly first class park in breathtaking surroundings.

PATTERDALE ROAD, WINDERMERE, CUMBRIA LA23 1PA
Tel: (015394) 32300 Fax: (015394) 32848

ENGLAND

Windermere

Limefitt Park
Patterdale Road, Windermere LA23 1PA
☎ 015394-32300
Open March-October

Spectacular Lakeland valley location. Ten minutes drive from Lake Windermere. Tourers and family campers welcome. Friendly Lakeland pub with bar meals, plus full range of award winning facilities.
Size 132 acres, 165 touring pitches, 110 with electric hookup, 110 level pitches, 45 static caravans, 16, 24 WCs, 2 CWPs
£ car/tent £9-£12.50, car/caravan £9.50-£13, motorhome £9.50-£13, children £1-£1.25
Rental £160-£390
CC MasterCard Visa
Calor Gaz
Last arrival time: 22:30
➡ At junction on A591 ½ mile N of Windermere, take the A592 to Ullswater and the park is 2½ miles on right.
See advert on previous page

Park Cliffe Camping & Caravan Estate
Birks Road, Tower Wood, Windermere LA23 3PG
☎ 015395-31344 Fax 015395-31971
Open March-November

Flat and gently sloping, grass and hardstanding, rural site with magnificent views over surrounding countryside. Highest tent pitches have commanding views over Lake Windermere and Langdale.
Size 25 acres, 70 touring pitches, 63 with electric hookup, 70 level pitches, 50 static caravans, 10, 19 WCs, 1 CWP
£ car/tent £9.60-£12, car/caravan £11.50-£12, motorhome £11.50-£12, motorbike/tent £9.60-£12, children £1-£1.50
Rental

CC MasterCard Visa
Calor Gaz
Last arrival time: 22:00
➡ M6 junction 36 take A590 to Newby Bridge. Turn right onto A592, go 4 miles and turn right into Birks Road. The park is third of a mile on right.

White Cross Bay Caravan Park
Ambleside Road, Windermere LA23 1LF
☎ 015394-43937 Fax 015394-88704
Open March-14 November
Size 72 acres, 125 touring pitches, 25 with electric hookup, 125 level pitches, 250 static caravans, 45, 80 WCs, 2 CWPs
£ car/caravan £10.50-£16.50, motorhome £10.50-£16.50
Rental Chalet. £150-£660
CC MasterCard Visa
Calor Gaz WS
Last arrival time: 23:00
➡ 2 miles N of Windermere and 3 miles S of Ambleside. Site on W of A591.

WINSFORD Somerset   3D2

Halse Farm
Winsford, Near Minehead TA24 7JL
☎ 01643-851259 Fax 01643-851592
Open mid March-October

Exmoor National Park, small, peaceful, glorious views. Quality heated toilet block. Launderette, pay phone. Disabled facilities. 1 mile from thatched pub, shop.
Size 3 acres, 44 touring pitches, 21 with electric hookup, 44 level pitches, 4, 8 WCs, 1 CWP
£ car/tent £5.50-£7.50, car/caravan £5.50-£7.50, motorhome £5.50-£7.50, motorbike/tent £5.50-£7.50, children £0.50-£1.25
Calor Gaz
Last arrival time: 23:00
➡ Turn off A396 for Winsford. In village turn left in front of Royal Oak, then follow lane for 1 mile. Entrance is immediately on left after cattle grid.

Hints & Tips

Make sure your mirrors are adjusted correctly before moving off.

Woodbridge

WISBOROUGH GREEN West Sussex 4C3

Bat and Ball
New Pound, Wisborough Green RH14 0EH
☎ 01403-700313
Open all year
Size 3 acres, 26 touring pitches, 26 level pitches, 2 WCs, 4 WCs, 1 CWP
£ car/tent £4.50, car/caravan £4.50, motorhome £4.50, motorbike/tent £4.50
➡ Off A272 on B2133 from S to N.

WITTON-LE-WEAR Co. Durham 13F4

Witton Castle Caravan Site
Bishop Auckland, Witton-le-Wear DL14 0DE
☎ 01388-488230 Fax 01388-488008
Open 1 March-31 October
Size 150 acres, 186 touring pitches, 50 with electric hookup, 100 level pitches, 298 static caravans, 9 WCs, 50 WCs, 1 CWP
£ car/tent £7.50-£14.40, car/caravan £7.50-£14.40, motorhome £7.50-£14.40, motorbike/tent £7.50-£14.40, children £0.50
Calor Gaz WS
➡ Signposted on E side of A68 between Toft Hill and Witton-le-Wear. 4 miles W of Bishop Auckland.

WOKINGHAM Berkshire 4C2

California Chalet & Touring Park
Nine Mile Ride, Finchampstead, Wokingham RG40 4HU
☎ 0118-973 3928 Fax 0118-932 8720
Open 1 March-30 October
Size 5.5 acres, 30 touring pitches, 24 with electric hookup, 30 level pitches, 7 WCs, 6 WCs, 1 CWP
£ car/tent £10, car/caravan £10.50-£12, motorhome £10.50-£12, motorbike/tent £10, children £0.50
Rental Chalet.
Last arrival time: 22:00
➡ From M3 junction 3 onto A322 towards Bracknell, turn left onto B3430 towards Finchampstead. Site is on right in 6 miles.

WOODBRIDGE Suffolk 9F4

Forest Camping
Tangham Campsite, Butley, Woodbridge IP12 3NF
☎ 01394-450707
Open 1 April-10 January
Size 7 acres, 90 touring pitches, 66 with electric hookup, 90 level pitches, 6 WCs, 12 WCs, 3 CWPs
£ car/tent £7-£9, car/caravan £7-£9, motorhome £7-£9, motorbike/tent £7-£9, children £1-£2
CC MasterCard Visa
Calor Gaz

Last arrival time: 21:00
➡ Take A1152 off A12 at Woodbridge and then left on B1084 to Orford. After 4 miles turn right into forest.

Moon & Sixpence
Newbourn Road, Waldringfield, Woodbridge IP12 4PP
☎ 01473-736650 Fax 01473-736270
Open 1 April-31 October

Tranquil picturesque location with excellent facilities. Sandy beach, lake, fishing in September and October. Neighbouring golf course, nearby rollerskating, ten pin bowling, indoor bowls, cinemas, water sports.
Size 85 acres, 65 touring pitches, 65 with electric hookup, 65 level pitches, 175 static caravans, 12 WCs, 24 WCs, 1 CWP
£ car/tent £16, car/caravan £16, motorhome £16, motorbike/tent £16
CC MasterCard Visa
Calor Gaz
Last arrival time: 21:00
➡ Turn E off A12 Ipswich Eastern by-pass onto minor road signposted Newbourn and follow signs.

St Margaret's House Caravan Site
Shottisham, Woodbridge IP12 3HD
☎ 01394-411247
Open 1 April-31 October
Size 2.5 acres, 30 touring pitches, 16 with electric hookup, 30 level pitches, 2 WCs, 4 WCs, 1 CWP
£ car/tent £5, car/caravan £5-£6.50, motorhome £5-£6.50, motorbike/tent £5, children £0.25
Calor Gaz
Last arrival time: 22:00
➡ Turn right off A12 onto A1152 signposted Bawdsey/Orford. After 1½ miles fork right onto B1083 signposted Bawdsey. 4 miles to T junction, turn left into Shottisham, the site is on left, 100 yards past Sorrel Horse pub.

Hints & Tips

When braking it will take you an average of 20% more distance to stop. Always avoid violent braking.

Woodhall Spa

WOODHALL SPA Lincolnshire 8C2

Bainland Country Park
Horncastle Road, Woodhall Spa LN10 6UX
☎ 01526-352903 Fax 01526-353730
Open all year

Situated on the edge of the Wolds, surrounded by woodland, ideally central for touring the undiscovered county of Lincolnshire.
Size 50 acres, 150 touring pitches, 150 with electric hookup, 150 level pitches, 10 static caravans, 13, 16 WCs, 53 CWPs
£ car/tent £8.50-£25, car/caravan £8.50-£25, motorhome £8.50-£25, motorbike/tent £8.50-£25
Rental Chalet. £165-£600
CC MasterCard Visa
Calor Gaz WS
Last arrival time: 21:00
➜ Situated on B1191, 6 miles from Horncastle, on left just past WCF petrol station. 1½ miles from Woodhall Spa.

Camping & Caravanning Club Site
Wellsyke Lane, Kirkby-on-Bain, Woodhall Spa LN10 6YU
☎ 01526-352911
Open March-November
Size 6 acres, 110 touring pitches, 66 with electric hookup, 6, 9 WCs, 1 CWP
£ car/tent £11.50-£14.60, car/caravan £11.50-£14.60, motorhome £11.50-£14.60, motorbike/tent £11.50-£14.60, children £1.60
CC MasterCard Visa
Calor WS
Last arrival time: 23:00
➜ From Sleaford or Horncastle take A153 to Haltham. At the garage turn onto the side road, over the bridge, turn left towards Kirkby-on-Bain, at first right (Kirkby Lane) opposite Ebrington Arms, about 1 mile, find the Camping and Caravanning Club signs.

WOOL Dorset 3F3

Whitemead Caravan Park
East Burton Road, Wool BH20 6HG
☎ 01929-462241 Fax 01929-426641
Open March-October
Size 5 acres, 95 touring pitches, 54 with electric hookup, 95 level pitches, 6, 13 WCs, 1 CWP
£ car/tent £5.50-£9.50, car/caravan £5.50-£9.50, motorhome £5.50-£9.50, motorbike/tent £5.50-£9.50, children £0.75
Calor Gaz WS
Last arrival time: 22:00
➜ Off A352 Wareham to Weymouth & Dorchester road (East Burton Road).

WOOLACOMBE Devon 2C2

Twitchen Park
Mortehoe, Woolacombe EX34 7ES
☎ 01271-870476 Fax 01271-870498
Open Easter-end October

Popular family park, close to Woolacombe's glorious sandy beach and coastal walks. A licensed club is on site, with seasonal entertainment, free swimming lessons and more.
Size 45 acres, 51 touring pitches, 51 with electric hookup, 295 static caravans, 24, 46 WCs, 2 CWPs
£ car/tent £6-£18, car/caravan £7.50-£21, motorhome £7.50-£21
Rental
CC MasterCard Visa
Calor Gaz
Last arrival time: 21:00
➜ From A361 10 miles N of Barnstaple take B3343 left for 1¾ miles to Woolacombe. Take right turn signed Mortehoe. Park entrance is 1½ miles on left.

WORCESTER Worcestershire 7E3

Mill House Caravan & Camping Site
Hawford, Worcester WR3 7SE
☎ 01905-451283 Fax 01905-754143
Open April-October
Size 8 acres, 150 touring pitches, 20 with electric hookup, 150 level pitches, 15 static caravans, 4, 9 WCs, 3 CWPs
£ car/tent £5.50, car/caravan £5.50, motorhome £5.50, motorbike/tent £5.50
Calor Gaz
➜ Site is 3 miles N of Worcester, on E of A449.

WORKSOP Nottinghamshire 8B1

Camping & Caravanning Club Site
The Walled Garden, Clumber Park, Worksop S80 3BD
☎ 01909-482303

Yeovil

Open March-November 🏕 🚐 🚗
Size 2.5 acres, 55 touring pitches, 16 with electric hookup, 4 🚿, 6 WCs, 1 CWP
£ car/tent £9.60-£12.10, car/caravan £9.60-£12.10, motorhome £9.60-£12.10, motorbike/tent £9.60-£12.10, children £1.50
℃ MasterCard Visa
Last arrival time: 23:00
➜ From A1 turn onto A614 Southbound. Take the first entrance into Clumber Park (approximately ¼ mile from A1) and follow signs.

YARMOUTH, GREAT Norfolk 9F3

Grange Touring Park

Ormesby St Margaret, Great Yarmouth NR29 3QG
☎ 01493-730306 Fax 01493-730188
Open Easter-mid October 🏕 🚐 🚗
Size 3.5 acres, 70 touring pitches, 60 with electric hookup, 70 level pitches, 10 🚿, 15 WCs, 1 CWP
£ car/tent £6-£10, car/caravan £6-£10, motorhome £6-£10, motorbike/tent £6-£10
℃ Visa
Last arrival time: 21:00
➜ At junction of A149 and B1159, 3 miles N of Caister.

Liffens Holiday Park

Burgh Castle, Great Yarmouth NR31 9QB
☎ 01493-780357 Fax 01493-782383
Open 1 April-30 October 🏕 🚐 🚗

A friendly family holiday park, set in lovely Broadland countryside but only ten minutes from Great Yarmouth.
Size 22 acres, 150 touring pitches, 100 with electric hookup, 150 level pitches, 130 static caravans, 16 🚿, 28 WCs, 1 CWP
£ car/tent £8-£12, car/caravan £8-£12, motorhome £8-£12
Rental Chalet. £80-£375, 6 berth luxury caravans.
℃ MasterCard Visa
Last arrival time: 23:00
➜ From Great Yarmouth take A12 over bridge and after two roundabouts watch for left turn to Burgh Castle. Follow two miles to T junction, turn right and follow signs to Liffens.

Long Beach Estate

Hemsby, Great Yarmouth NR29 4JD
☎ 01493-730023 Fax 01493-730188
Open 22 March-21 October 🏕 🚐 🚗
Size 30 acres, 30 touring pitches, 30 with electric hookup, 130 level pitches, 120 static caravans, 10 🚿, 25 WCs, 2 CWPs
£ car/tent £5-£11, car/caravan £7-£11, motorhome £7-£11, motorbike/tent £5-£7
Rental Chalet.
Last arrival time: 23:00
➜ From B1159 at Hemsby, turn right on Beach Road, then second left (signposted Long Beach).

Wild Duck Caravan Park

Howards Common, Belton, Great Yarmouth NR31 9NE
☎ 01493-780268 Fax 01493-782308
Open March-November 🏕 🚐 🚗
Size 60 acres, 150 touring pitches, 115 with electric hookup, 150 level pitches, 266 static caravans, 20 🚿, 20 WCs,
Rental Chalet.
℃ MasterCard Visa
Last arrival time: 23:00
➜ From Norwich, A47 to Great Yarmouth, follow the Becles Road A143 until dual carriageway, turn right to Belton, right onto Bracon Road, then left onto Station Road, turn right before telephone box, Wild Duck is at top of lane.

Willowcroft Camping & Caravan Park

Staithe Road, Repps-with-Bastwick, Great Yarmouth NR29 5JU
☎ 01692-670380 Fax 01692-670380
Open all year 🏕 🚐 🚗
Size 2 acres, 40 touring pitches, 20 with electric hookup, 40 level pitches, 6 🚿, 9 WCs, 1 CWP
£ car/tent £7.50-£8.50, car/caravan £7.50-£8.50, motorhome £7.50-£8.50, motorbike/tent £7-£8, children £1
Last arrival time: 22:00
➜ In Repps-with-Bastwick (A149) take Church Road. In ½ mile turn into Staithe Road. Site ½ mile on right.

YEOVIL Somerset 3E2

Long Hazel Int. Caravan and Camping Park

High Street, Sparkford, Yeovil BA22 7JH
☎ 01963-440002 Fax 01963-440002
Open March-December 🏕 🚐 🚗
Size 3.5 acres, 76 touring pitches, 50 with electric hookup, 76 level pitches, 3 static caravans, 5 🚿, 8 WCs, 1 CWP
£ car/tent £8-£10, car/caravan £8-£10, motorhome £8-£10, motorbike/tent £8-£10, children £1-£2
Rental £150-£250 per week

ENGLAND

165

← Long Hazel Int. Caravan and Camping Park

Last arrival time: 00:00
→ On A359 off Hazelgrove roundabout, at the junction of A359 and A303. Yeovil 8 miles, Wincanton 7 miles.

YORK North Yorkshire   11D3

Castle Howard Caravan Site
Coneysthorpe, Castle Howard YO6 7DD
☎ 01653-648366 Fax 01653-648529
Open 1 March-31 October
Size 12 acres, 70 touring pitches, 34 with electric hookup, 70 level pitches, 120 static caravans, 6, 15 WCs, 2 CWPs
£ car/tent £7.20, car/caravan £7.20, motorhome £7.20, motorbike/tent £7.20
Calor
Last arrival time: 21:00
→ 15 miles NE of York off A64 (on York-Scarborough road).

Mount Pleasant Holiday Park
Acaster Malbis, York YO23 2UA
☎ 01904-707078 Fax 01904-700888
Open 1 March-30 November

A countryside park yet only five miles from the city centre. Tourers and family tents welcome. An ideal base to tour North Yorkshire and the historical city of York. Full colour brochure available.
Size 18 acres, 60 touring pitches, 40 with electric hookup, 60 level pitches, 165 static caravans, 12, 45 WCs, 2 CWPs
£ car/tent £6, car/caravan £6-£8, motorhome £6-£8, motorbike/tent £6
Rental from £30 per night
« MasterCard Visa
Calor Gaz
Last arrival time: 22:00
→ Turn off A64, follow signs to Bishopthorpe, then for Acaster Airfield (disused). Follow signs for site.

Naburn Lock Caravan Site
Naburn, York YO19 4RU
☎ 01904-728697 Fax 01904-728697
Open March-6 November

Small rural site, with nearby facilities for fishing and horse riding. Restaurant ½ mile, swimming pool four miles.
Size 8 acres, 100 touring pitches, 84 with electric hookup, 100 level pitches, 8, 12 WCs, 2 CWPs
£ car/tent £8-£9.50, car/caravan £9.50, motorhome £9.50, motorbike/tent £8, children £1.25
« MasterCard Visa
Calor Gaz
Last arrival time: 21:00
→ 4 miles S of York. From A19 turn onto B1222. Site is 2½ miles on left.

Poplar Farm Caravan Park
Acaster Malbis, York YO23 2UH
☎ 01904-706548
Open April-October
Size 8 acres, 50 touring pitches, 45 with electric hookup, 50 level pitches, 80 static caravans, 10, 20 WCs, 1 CWP
Rental
Calor Gaz WS
→ S off A64 at Copmanthorpe. Site 2¼ miles.
See advert on this page

POPLAR FARM CARAVAN PARK

Poplar Farm is a family park in the very heart of Yorkshire.

✦ 4 miles from city centre
✦ Riverside location ✦ private fishing
✦ toilets ✦ showers ✦ electric hook-up
✦ touring caravans, motorhomes and tents welcome.

Local bus and river bus operate daily from the park to York.

Ship Inn public house and restaurants offer takeaway, bar snacks and full restaurant facilities everyday.

**ACASTER MALBIS,
YORK YO2 1UH
TEL: 01904 706548**

Scotland

Aberdeen

ABERDEEN Aberdeenshire	15F4

Lower Deeside Caravan Park
Maryculter, Aberdeen AB1 5FX
☎ 01224-733860 Fax 01224-732490
Open all year ⴕ 🚐 🚛

An attractive country site only five miles from Aberdeen. Ideal for touring the Royal Deeside. Shop, games/TV room, laundry and children play area. Luxury caravans and pine lodges for hire.
Size 14 acres, 40 touring pitches, 40 with electric hookup, 40 level pitches, 35 static caravans, 6 🚿, 12 WCs, 1 CWP
£ car/tent £5-£7, car/caravan £7-£9, motorhome £7-£9, motorbike/tent £5-£7
Rental 🚐 Lodges.
₵₵ MasterCard Visa
🛁 ✗¼ 🔲 📞 📷 GR 📞 TV Calor Gaz ♿ 🐕
Last arrival time: 00:00
➡ From Aberdeen take B9077 (SW) for 5 miles from Bridge of Dee roundabout. Adjacent to Old Mill Inn.

ABERFELDY Perthshire	13D1

Aberfeldy Caravan Park
Dunkeld Road, Aberfeldy PH15 2AQ
☎ 01738-639911 Fax 01738-441690
Open late March-late October ⴕ 🚐 🚛

A flat riverside park in spectacular scenery, renowned for its highland hospitality. Senior citizens midweek off-peak reductions.
Size 5.5 acres, 92 touring pitches, 92 with electric hookup, 92 level pitches, 40 static caravans, 18 🚿, 36 WCs, 1 CWP
£ car/tent £7.60, car/caravan £7.80-£8.90, motorhome £7-£8.90, motorbike/tent £6, children £1

₵₵ MasterCard Visa
🛁 ✗¼ ⚱¼ ♿ 🔲 🐕 WS
Last arrival time: 19:00
➡ 9 miles W of A9 (Ballinluig junction) on A827 to Killin.

ABERFOYLE Stirlingshire	12C1

Forestry Commission Cobeland C & C Site
Garthoke, Aberfoyle FK8 3UX
☎ 01877-382392
Open end March-end October ⴕ 🚐 🚛
Size 11 acres, 135 touring pitches, 56 with electric hookup, 80 level pitches, 5 🚿, 19 WCs, 2 CWPs
£ car/tent £7.50-£8.40, car/caravan £7.50-£8.40, motorhome £7.50-£8.40, motorbike/tent £7.50-£8.40, children £1-£1.75
₵₵ MasterCard Visa
🛁 ✗¼ ⚱ 🔲 📞 🔲 Calor Gaz ♿ 🐕 WS
Last arrival time: 22:00
➡ On an unclassified road, 2 miles S of Aberfoyle on A81.

Trossachs Holiday Park
Gartmore, Aberfoyle FK8 3SA
☎ 01877-382614 Fax 01877-382732
Open 1 March-31 October ⴕ 🚐 🚛

A small exclusive enviromental caravan park, 1997 winner - Best park in Scotland. 45 landscaped touring pitches, tents welcome, Thistle award caravans and mountain bikes for hire.
Size 40 acres, 45 touring pitches, 45 with electric hookup, 45 level pitches, 60 static caravans, 4 🚿, 9 WCs, 1 CWP
£ car/tent £9-£11, car/caravan £9-£11, motorhome £9-£11, motorbike/tent £9-£11
Rental 🚐 Chalet. £149-£449
₵₵ MasterCard Visa
🛁 ✗¼ ⚱¼ 🔲 📞 🔲 📷 GR 📞 Calor Gaz 🐕 WS
Last arrival time: 21:00
➡ On E side of A81, 3 miles S of Aberfoyle.

ANNAN Dumfriesshire	13D4

Queensberry Bay Caravan Park
Powfoot, Annan DG12 5PU
☎ 01461-700205
Open April-October ⴕ 🚐 🚛

Arrochar

169

Size 11 acres, 60 touring pitches, 60 with electric hookup, 60 level pitches, 70 static caravans, 8 🚿, 13 WCs, 1 CWP
£ car/tent £8, car/caravan £8, motorhome £8, motorbike/tent £8
Calor Gaz
Last arrival time: 21:00
➦ W of Annan on B724, turn S to Powfoot.

APPLECROSS Ross-shire   14B3

Applecross Camp Site
via Loch Carron, Wester Ross, Applecross IV54 8ND
☎ 01520-744268 Fax 01520-744268
Open Easter-October
Size 6 acres, 60 touring pitches, 10 with electric hookup, 60 level pitches, 3 static caravans, 8 🚿, 12 WCs, 1 CWP
£ car/tent £8, car/caravan £8, motorhome £8, motorbike/tent £8
Rental
C MasterCard Visa
Calor Gaz
Last arrival time: 22:00
➦ From A896 turn left after Kishorn to Applecross - 11 miles. Caravans continue on A896 towards Shielding. After 7½ miles turn left to Applecross - 24 miles.
See advert on this page

ARISAIG Inverness-shire   14B4

Gorten Sands Caravan Site
Gorten Farm, Arisaig PH39 4NS
☎ 01687-450283
Open Easter-30 September

A peaceful, family run hill and coastal farm site in a historic scenic area with safe sandy beaches. The unspoilt location offers views to Skye and the isles.
Size 6 acres, 42 touring pitches, 20 with electric hookup, 42 level pitches, 3 static caravans, 6 🚿, 10 WCs, 1 CWP
£ car/tent £7-£9, car/caravan £7-£8.50, motorhome £7-£8, motorbike/tent £7, children £0.75
Rental £200-£300
¼ ¼ Calor Gaz
Last arrival time: 23:00
➦ A830 to point 2 miles W of Arisaig. Turn left at signpost "Back of Keppoch", continue ¾ mile to road end across cattle grid.

ARROCHAR Strathclyde   12C1

Forestry Commission Ardgartan Campsite
Ardgartan, Arrochar G83 7AR
☎ 013012-293
Open end March-end October
Size 17 acres, 200 touring pitches, 46 with electric hookup, 100 level pitches, 9 🚿, 25 WCs, 3 CWPs
£ car/tent £5.80-£7, car/caravan £5.80-£7, motorhome £5.80-£7, motorbike/tent £5.80-£7
C MasterCard Visa
Calor Gaz WS
Last arrival time: 22:00
➦ 2 miles West of Arrochar on A83 Glasgow - Inverary road.

SCOTLAND

APPLECROSS
Campsite

Peaceful park in an area of outstanding natural beauty.
Electric hookups and water points.
Well equipped toilet blocks
with showers, launderette.
Shop, bakery and licensed restaurant.
Static vans.

**APPLECROSS,
STRATHCARRON IV54 8ND
Tel: (015204) 268 & 284**

Hints & Tips

Tyres are your only contact with the road. Look after them and you will improve the safety and behaviour of your unit. Never mix cross ply and radials on the same axis.

Aviemore

AVIEMORE Inverness-shire 15D3

Aviemore Mountain Resort Caravan Park
Aviemore PH22 1PF
☎ 01479-810751 Fax 01479-810862
Open 1 December-31 October
Size 6 acres, 90 touring pitches, 72 with electric hookup, 90 level pitches, 4 ♿, 18 WCs, 1 CWP
£ car/tent £5-£6, car/caravan £6.50-£8, motorhome £6.50-£8, children £1
℅ MasterCard Visa
Last arrival time: 22:00
→ Off A9 in Aviemore village next to Tourist Information office.

Forestry Commission Glenmore C & C Site
Aviemore PH22 1QU
☎ 01479-861271
Open December-end October
Size 20 acres, 220 touring pitches, 122 with electric hookup, 200 level pitches, 21 ♿, 26 WCs, 2 CWPs
£ car/tent £7.70-£8.70, car/caravan £7.70-£8.70, motorhome £7.70-£8.70, motorbike/tent £7.70-£8.70
℅ MasterCard Visa
Calor Gaz
Last arrival time: 22:00
→ A9, B9152 (S of Aviemore), at Aviemore turn right onto B970. Site is 5 miles further on right.

AYR Ayrshire 12C3

Middlemuir Holiday Park
Tarbolton, Mauchline, Ayr KA5 5NR
☎ 01292-541647 Fax 01292-541649
Open 1 March-31 October
Size 18 acres, 35 touring pitches, 18 with electric hookup, 64 static caravans, 4 ♿, 8 WCs, 1 CWP
£ car/caravan £7-£13.50, motorhome £7-£13.50
Rental £140-£300
Gaz
→ 5 miles E of Ayr on B743 Mauchline road.

Sundrum Castle Holiday Park
Coylton, Ayr KA6 6HX
☎ 01292-570057
Open 26 March-31 October

Well-organised site with games room, adventure playground, nightclub. Suitable for families. 103 caravans for hire (own WCs). All-male or female parties with management's prior consent.
Size 23 acres, 52 touring pitches, 30 with electric hookup, 52 level pitches, 252 static caravans, 8 ♿, 16 WCs, 1 CWP
£ car/tent £10-£16, car/caravan £10-£16, motorhome £10-£16, motorbike/tent £10-£16
Rental
℅ MasterCard Visa
Calor
Last arrival time: 00:00
→ 4 miles E of Ayr A70, turn N, site signed.

BALMACARA Ross-shire 14B3

Forestry Commission Balmacara C & C Site
Balmacara Square, Balmacara IV40 8DN
☎ 01599-566374
Open Easter-end September
Size 7.5 acres, 120 touring pitches, 8 with electric hookup, 60 level pitches, 12 WCs, 1 CWP
£ car/tent £4.20-£5.30, car/caravan £4.20-£5.30, motorhome £4.20-£5.30, motorbike/tent £4.20-£5.30
℅ MasterCard Visa
Last arrival time: 22:00
→ From the E on A87, take second on right after Reraig village.

BALMAHA Stirlingshire 12C2

Forestry Commission Cashel C & C Site
Rowardennan G63 0AW
☎ 01360-870234
Open end March-end October
Size 11 acres, 250 touring pitches, 36 with electric hookup, 200 level pitches, 8 ♿, 26 WCs, 2 CWPs
£ car/tent £7.50-£8.60, car/caravan £7.50-£8.60, motorhome £7.50-£8.60, motorbike/tent £7.50-£8.60, children £1.50-£1.75
℅ MasterCard Visa
Calor Gaz WS
Last arrival time: 22:00
→ On B837 Drymen to Rowardennan road, 3 miles N of Balmaha.

BANFF Banffshire 15F3

Wester Bonnyton Farm Site
Gamrie, Banff AB45 3EP
☎ 01261-832470 Fax 01261-832470
Open March-October

Blairgowrie

Size 3 acres, 30 touring pitches, 8 with electric hookup, 10 level pitches, 18 static caravans, 4 ⓘ, 4 WCs, 1 CWP
£ car/tent £5-£6, car/caravan £6-£7, motorhome £6-£7, motorbike/tent £5-£6
Rental Chalet. Caravans £150-£310.
⚂ ▣ ⒼⓇ ⓠ ⛿ Calor ♿ ⚞ WS

BLAIR ATHOLL Perthshire   15D4

Blair Castle Caravan Park
Blair Atholl, Pitlochry PH18 5SR
☎ 01796-481263 Fax 01796-481587
Open 1 April-26 October ⛺ 🚐 🚙
Size 35 acres, 283 touring pitches, 191 with electric hookup, 112 static caravans, 29 ⓘ, 97 WCs, 3 CWPs
£ car/tent £8-£9.50, car/caravan £8-£9.50, motorhome £8-£9.50, children £0.50
₡ MasterCard Visa
⚂ ✕ ⓟ ▣ ☎ ⒼⓇ ⓉⓋ ⛿ Calor Gaz ♿ ⚞
Last arrival time: 21:30
➜ Turn off A9, 6 miles N of Pitlochry. Follow signs to Blair Atholl.
See advert on this page

The River Tilt Park
Bridge of Tilt, Blair Atholl PH18 5TE
☎ 01796-481467 Fax 01796-481511
Open March-November ⛺ 🚐 🚙

Situated on the banks of the River Tilt, next to the golf course and overlooking the castle entrance. Panoramic views over the river.
Size 14 acres, 35 touring pitches, 35 with electric hookup, 35 level pitches, 45 static caravans, 4 ⓘ, 6 WCs, 1 CWP
£ car/tent £6-£9, car/caravan £9-£14, motorhome £9-£13, motorbike/tent £6-£7
Rental £265-£325, chalets £225-£510.
₡ MasterCard Visa
⚂¼ ✕ ⓟ ▣ ☎ ⒼⓇ ⓉⓋ ▤ ⓟ ⓠ ⓙ ⛿ Calor Gaz ⚞ WS
Last arrival time: 23:00
➜ A9 N of Pitlochry onto B8079 signed Blair Atholl. On entering village turn left before hotel and follow sign.

Blair Castle
CARAVAN PARK
BLAIR ATHOLL, PERTHSHIRE PH18 5SR
Tel: 01796 481263 Fax: 01796 481587

- 32 acre Park set amidst spectacular mountain scenery
- Grass and hard-standing mains serviced pitches
- 'Roll-On, Roll-Off' pitches • Heated amenity blocks
- Spacious park and recreation areas
- Extensive woodland, hill and riverside walks
- General Store and Coffee Shop
- Indoor Games Room and Television Lounge
- Situated in the grounds of Blair Castle (open to the public)
- Voted 'Readers' Choice' for Scotland by Practical Caravan in 1995, 1996, 1997 and 1998
- Pony trekking, golf, fishing, bowling, mountain bikes all available from the village of Blair Atholl

PLEASE WRITE OR TELEPHONE FOR OUR FREE COLOUR BROCHURE

BLAIRGOWRIE Perthshire   13D1

Nether Craig Caravan Park
Alyth, Blairgowrie PH11 8HN
☎ 01575-560204 Fax 01575-560315
Open mid March-end October ⛺ 🚐 🚙

Enjoy the peace of rural Angus at this award winning, family run touring park, convenient for country pursuits and near much of historic interest.
Size 4 acres, 40 touring pitches, 40 with electric hookup, 40 level pitches, 5 ⓘ, 7 WCs, 1 CWP
£ car/tent £5, car/caravan £7.50-£9.50, motorhome £7.50-£9.50, motorbike/tent £5, children £1
⚂ ▣ ☎ ▣ ⓙ ⛿ Calor Gaz ♿ ⚞ WS
Last arrival time: 21:00
➜ At roundabout S of Alyth join B954 signposted Glenisla. Follow caravan signs for 4 miles. Do not go into Alyth.

SCOTLAND

Boat of Garten

BOAT OF GARTEN Inverness-shire   15D3

Boat of Garten Caravan & Camping Park
Boat of Garten PH24 3BN
☎ 01479-831652 Fax 01479-831652
Open all year
Size 11 acres, 37 touring pitches, 37 with electric hookup, 37 level pitches, 30 static caravans, 8 ♺, 15 WCs, 1 CWP
£ car/tent £5-£8.50, car/caravan £6.50-£11, motorhome £6.50-£11, motorbike/tent £8
Rental £169-£365
CC MasterCard Visa
Calor Gaz WS
Last arrival time: 22:00
➡ From A9 take A95 towards Grantown-on-Spey, then follow signs for Boat of Garten. Park is situated in centre of village. Signposted. See advert on this page.

Croft Na-Carn Caravan Park
Loch Garten, Boat of Garten
☎ 01343-830880 Fax 01343-830880
Open all year

Located on the 'Road to the Ospreys' and surrounded by beautiful scenery; fishing, golf, a whisky trail and walking are just some of the attractions.
Size 4.5 acres, 15 touring pitches, 10 with electric hookup, 15 level pitches, 10 static caravans, 2 ♺, 4 WCs, 1 CWP
£ car/tent £4.50-£8.50, car/caravan £6.50-£8.50, motorhome £6.50-£8.50, motorbike/tent £4.50-£8.50, children £1
Rental Chalet. £70-£350
Calor Gaz WS
Last arrival time: 20:30
➡ Leave A9 immediately N of Aviemore onto A95 heading for Grantown on Spey, turn right for Boat of Garten. Through village, cross River Spey at road junction of B970, turn left towards Nethybridge. In ½ mile turn right for Loch Garten, the park is 100 yards on the left. Alternatively follow RSPB roadsigns for osprey.

Boat of Garten
CARAVAN & CAMPING PARK

This Thistle Award winning Holiday Park is set in a traditional Highland Village. Nearby there is the Strathspey Steam Railway and the famous Ospreys. Fishing on the River Spey, an 18 hole golf course and tennis are all within walking distance. The Park offers an ideal base for exploring the Spey Valley and the Highlands.

**BOAT OF GARTEN,
INVERNESS-SHIRE PH24 3BN
Tel: 01479 831 652 Fax: 01479 831 652**

BRIDGE OF CALLY Perthshire   15E4

Corriefodly Holiday Park
Bridge of Cally PH10 7JG
☎ 01250-886236
Open December-October

Situated in central Perthshire six miles north of Blairgowrie, the site is an ideal touring base. Open December-October, 17 acres, 55 tourers, apartments for hire.
Size 17 acres, 55 touring pitches, 55 with electric hookup, 35 level pitches, 57 static caravans, 4 ♺, 12 WCs, 1 CWP
£ car/tent £5-£7, car/caravan £8-£9, motorhome £8-£9, motorbike/tent £5-£7
Rental Apartments £135-£260
Calor
Last arrival time: 23:00
➡ A93 N from Blairgowrie for 6 miles. At junction of A93 and A924 fork onto A924. Site is 300 yards on left.

Comrie

CALLANDER Perthshire   12C1

Keltie Bridge Caravan Park
Keltie Bridge, Callander FK17 8LQ
01877-330811 Fax 01877-330075
Open 1 April-31 October
Size 12 acres, 40 touring pitches, 30 with electric hookup, 40 level pitches, 40 static caravans, 5, 7 WCs, 1 CWP
£ car/tent £7.50-£9.50, car/caravan £7.50-£9.50, motorhome £7.50-£9.50, motorbike/tent £6-£8
WS
➜ Signposted from A84 between Doune and Callander.

CAMPBELTOWN Argyll   12B3

Camping & Caravanning Club Site
East Trodigal, Machrihanish, Campbeltown PA28 6PT
01586-810366
Open March-September
Size 10 acres, 89 touring pitches, 42 with electric hookup, 4, 8 WCs, 1 CWP
£ car/tent £9.60-£12.10, car/caravan £9.60-£12.10, motorhome £9.60-£12.10, motorbike/tent £9.60-£12.10, children £1.50
CC MasterCard Visa
Calor WS
Last arrival time: 23:00
➜ On A83 from Inveraray take B843 to Machrihanish, site entrance is on right, 200 yards past chimney.

CANNICH Inverness-shire   14C3

Cannich Caravan Park
Cannich by Beauly
01456-415364 Fax 01456-415263
Open Easter-31 October
Size 8 acres, 50 touring pitches, 20 with electric hookup, 50 level pitches, 9 static caravans, 8, 10 WCs, 1 CWP
£ car/tent £5.50-£8.50, car/caravan £5.50-£8.50, motorhome £5.50-£8.50, motorbike/tent £3.50-£5.50
Rental £164.50-£235
Calor Gaz WS
Last arrival time: 23:00
➜ 100 yards off A831.

CARRADALE Argyll   12B3

Carradale Bay Caravan Site
Kintyre, Carradale PA28 6QG
01583-431665
Open Easter-30 September

On safe sandy bay, beside the River Carra. Adjacent fishing, forest walks, golf course and all village amenities.
Size 12 acres, 56 touring pitches, 40 with electric hookup, 40 level pitches, 3 static caravans, 8, 16 WCs, 1 CWP
£ car/tent £7-£12.80, car/caravan £7-£12.80, motorhome £7-£12.80, motorbike/tent £7-£12.80, children £1.10-£1.20
Rental Chalet. £95-£325
¼ ¼ ¼ WS
Last arrival time: 22:00
➜ From Tarbert take A83 to Campbeltown, then B842 to Carradale. After 14 miles at T-junction, turn right onto B879 (signposted Carradale). After ½ mile turn right at Caravan Park sign and follow track to site.

CASTLE DOUGLAS Kirkcudbrightshire   12C4

Lochside Caravan Park
Castle Douglas DG7 1EZ
01556-502949 Fax 01556-504879
Open Easter-October
Size 6 acres, 160 touring pitches, 97 with electric hookup, 160 level pitches, 16, 29 WCs, 3 CWPs
£ car/tent £7.50-£9, car/caravan £7.50-£9, motorhome £7.50-£9, motorbike/tent £7.50-£9
¼ ¼ ¼
➜ Off A75 in Castle Douglas by Carlingwark Loch.

COMRIE Perthshire   12C1

Twenty Shilling Wood Caravan Park
Comrie PH6 2JY
01764-670411
Open 19 March-24 October
Size 10.5 acres, 16 touring pitches, 16 with electric hookup, 16 level pitches, 34 static caravans, 4, 16 WCs, 1 CWP
£ car/caravan £8-£10, motorhome £8-£10, children £1
Rental £130 - £315 weekly.
CC MasterCard Visa
¼ ¼ ¼ Calor Gaz
Last arrival time: 21:00
➜ On A85 (Perth to Crianlarach), ½ mile W of Comrie, opposite farm food restaurant.

SCOTLAND

Comrie

West Lodge Caravan Park
Comrie PH6 2LS
☎ 01764-670354
Open 1 April-31 October
Size 3 acres, 20 touring pitches, 20 with electric hookup, 20 level pitches, 36 static caravans, 6, 10 WCs, 1 CWP
£ car/tent £7, car/caravan £9, motorhome £9, children £0.50
Rental £19-£29 nightly. £99-£190 weekly.
Calor Gaz WS
Last arrival time: 22:00
➜ On A85, 1 mile E of Comrie.

CONNEL Argyll   12B1

Camping & Caravanning Club Site
Barcaldine, Connel PA37 1SG
☎ 01631-720348
Open March-November
Size 4 acres, 90 touring pitches, 40 with electric hookup, 4 level pitches, 6, 14 WCs, 1 CWP
£ car/tent £10.40-£13.60, car/caravan £10.40-£13.60, motorhome £10.40-£13.60, motorbike/tent £10.40-£13.60, children £1.50
CC MasterCard Visa
Calor WS
Last arrival time: 23:00
➜ Going N on A828, 7 miles from Connel bridge, turn into site at Camping Club sign on right. Opposite Marine Resource Centre proceed through large iron gates.

CONTIN Ross-shire   14C3

Riverside Chalets & Caravan Park
Strathpeffer, Contin IV14 9ES
☎ 01997-421351
Open all year
Size 2 acres, 15 touring pitches, 12 with electric hookup, 15 level pitches, 3 static caravans, 2, 5 WCs, 1 CWP
£ car/caravan £6
Rental Chalet.
Calor Gaz WS
➜ On A835 between Inverness and Ullapool at Strathpeffer Junction.

CRAIGELLACHIE Banffshire   15E3

Camping & Caravanning Club Site
Speyside, Elchies, Craigellachie AB38 9SD
☎ 01340-810414
Open January-December
Size 75 touring pitches, 34 with electric hookup, 8, 8 WCs, 1 CWP
£ car/tent £11.50-£14.60, car/caravan £11.50-£14.60, motorhome £11.50-£14.60, motorbike/tent £11.50-£14.60, children £1.60
CC MasterCard Visa

Calor WS
Last arrival time: 23:00
➜ From S leave A9 at Carrbridge, follow A95 to Grantown-on-Spey, and on to Aberlour, leaving Aberlour on A941. Do not turn right into Craigellachie, take the next left turn B9102, signposted Archiestown, site is on left (3 miles).

CREETOWN Wigtownshire   12C4

Creetown Caravan Park
Silver Street, Creetown DG8 7HU
☎ 01671-820377 Fax 01671-820377
Open 1 March-31 October
Size 3.5 acres, 21 touring pitches, 21 with electric hookup, 21 level pitches, 50 static caravans, 4, 8 WCs, 1 CWP
£ car/tent £8.80, car/caravan £8.80, motorhome £8.80, motorbike/tent £8.80
Rental
Calor
Last arrival time: 22:00
➜ Just off A75 in village of Creetown, turn down between Clock Tower and Ellangowan Hotel, sharp left into Silver Street.

CROCKETFORD Kirkcudbrightshire   13D4

Park of Brandedleys
Crocketford, Near Dumfries DG2 8RG
☎ 01556-690250 Fax 01556-690681
Open 1 March-31 October

Easily accessible landscaped park with fine views to the loch and hills. Top quality toilets with ensuite units, bath and baby/ hair care room.
Size 16 acres, 80 touring pitches, 80 with electric hookup, 50 level pitches, 28 static caravans, 13, 25 WCs, 2 CWPs
£ car/tent £9-£14, car/caravan £9-£14, motorhome £9-£14, motorbike/tent £9-£14, children £2
Rental Chalet. £140-£500
CC MasterCard Visa
Calor Gaz WS
Last arrival time: 22:00
➜ Fork left off A75 Dumfries to Stranraer in Crocketford at park sign. Site on right in 160 yards.

Drymen

175

DALBEATTIE Kirkcudbrightshire   13D4

Castle Point Caravan Park
Rockcliffe, Dalbeattie DG5 4QL
☎ 01556-630248
Open April-October

A small quiet coastal site near Rockcliffe Village in Galloway. The site and walks nearby have some of the best views along the Solway coast.
Size 3 acres, 29 touring pitches, 29 with electric hookup, 29 level pitches, 7 static caravans, 4, 10 WCs, 1 CWP
£ car/tent £7.50-£10, car/caravan £7.50-£10, motorhome £7.50-£10, motorbike/tent £7.50-£10, children £0.90-£1.50
Rental £150-£260
X¼ ¼ Calor Gaz
Last arrival time: 21:30
➔ From Dalbeattie travel S along the A710 coastal road. After 5 miles turn right to Rockcliffe (1 mile). At brow of hill just after entering Rockcliffe turn left down signposted road to site.

Islecroft Caravan & Camping Site
Dalbeattie DG5 4HE
☎ 01556-610012 Fax 01556-504879
Open Easter-September
Size 3.5 acres, 74 touring pitches, 27 with electric hookup, 60 level pitches, 4, 10 WCs, 1 CWP
£ car/tent £5.80-£6.90, car/caravan £5.80-£6.90, motorhome £5.80-£6.90, motorbike/tent £5.80-£6.90
¼ X¼ ¼
➔ In Dalbeattie, off Mill Street and adjacent to Colliston Park.

DALKEITH Midlothian   13D2

Fordel Cravan & Camping Park
Lauder Road, Dalkeith EH22 2PH
☎ 0131-660 3921 Fax 0131-663 8891
Open March-October
Size 4 acres, 45 touring pitches, 12 with electric hookup, 45 level pitches, 7, 6 WCs, 2 CWPs
£ car/tent £7.50-£8.50, car/caravan £9-£13, motorhome £9-£13, motorbike/tent £7.50-£8.50
X Calor Gaz WS
➔ 8 miles SE Edinburgh on main Edinburgh to Newcastle route, A68.

DINGWALL Ross-shire   15D3

Camping & Caravanning Club Site
Jubilee Park Road, Dingwall IV15 9QZ
☎ 01349-862236
Open March-November
Size 10 acres, 85 touring pitches, 52 with electric hookup, 6, 13 WCs, 1 CWP
£ car/tent £11.50-£14.60, car/caravan £11.50-£14.60, motorhome £11.50-£14.60, motorbike/tent £11.50-£14.60, children £1.60
CC MasterCard Visa
¼ X¼ ¼ Calor
WS
Last arrival time: 23:00
➔ From the NW, Inverness and Fort Willliam on A862 to Dingwall, take right turn down Hill Street (past Shell F.S.), turn right into High Street and first left after railway bridge, site ahead.

DORNOCH Sutherland   15D2

Grannie's Heilan' Hame
Embo, Dornoch IV25 3QP
☎ 01862-810383 Fax 01862-810368
Open April-October
Size 60 acres, 300 touring pitches, 128 with electric hookup, 300 level pitches, 103 static caravans, 9, 47 WCs, 1 CWP
Rental
CC Visa
X Calor Gaz
Last arrival time: 23:00
➔ From Inverness follow A9 Wick-Thurso road, across Dornoch Firth bridge, turn right A949. From Dornoch turn left after Dornoch Cathedral for Embo.

DRYMEN Stirlingshire   12C2

Camping & Caravanning Club Site
Milarrochy Bay, Balmaha, Drymen
☎ 01360-870236
Open March-November
Size 12 acres, 150 touring pitches, 72 with electric hookup, 6, 11 WCs, 1 CWP
£ car/tent £11.50-£14.60, car/caravan £11.50-£14.60, motorhome £11.50-£14.60, motorbike/tent £11.50-£14.60, children £1.60
CC MasterCard Visa
¼ X¼ ¼ Calor
WS
Last arrival time: 23:00
➔ From A811 Balloch to Stirling road, take Drymen turning. In Drymen turn onto B837 (junction by War Memorial) for Balmaha. In approximately 5 miles, the road turns sharp right up a steep hill from Balmaha. The site is about 1½ miles further on.

SCOTLAND

Dumfries

DUMFRIES Dumfriesshire 13D4

Southerness Holiday Village
Southerness, Dumfries DG2 8AZ
01387-880256 Fax 01387-880429
Open 1 March-31 October
Size 8 acres, 150 touring pitches, 110 with electric hookup, 150 level pitches, 350 static caravans, 35 ☔, 35 WCs.
£ car/tent £6.50-£8, car/caravan £6.50-£9, motorhome £6.50-£9, motorbike/tent £6.50-£8
Rental
CC MasterCard Visa
Calor Gaz WS
➜ Take A710 from Dumfries for 16 miles, signposted from Kirkbean.

DUNBAR East Lothian 13E2

Belhaven Bay Caravan Park
Belhaven Bay, Dunbar EH42 1TU
01620-893348 Fax 01620-895623
Open March-October

Sheltered location on the beautiful East Lothian coastline. An ideal base to explore this scenic part of Scotland.
Size 5 acres, 52 touring pitches, 25 with electric hookup, 30 static caravans, 5 ☔, 7 WCs, 1 CWP
£ car/tent £5.75-£9.50, car/caravan £5.75-£9.50, motorhome £5.75-£9.50, motorbike/tent £5.75-£9.50
Rental £125-£325 weekly.
CC MasterCard Visa
Calor WS
Last arrival time: 22:00
➜ From A1 exit at roundabout W of Dunbar. The park is approximately ½ mile down A1087 on left. From S do not take first exit onto A1087, continue to roundabout.

Camping & Caravanning Club Site
Barns Ness, Dunbar EH42 1QP
01368-863536
Open March-November
Size 10 acres, 90 touring pitches, 40 with electric hookup, 80 level pitches, 6 ☔, 10 WCs, 1 CWP
£ car/tent £9.60-£12.10, car/caravan £9.60-£12.10, motorhome £9.60-£12.10, motorbike/tent £9.60-£12.10, children £1.50
CC MasterCard Visa
Calor WS
Last arrival time: 23:00
➜ From A1, 6 miles S of Dunbar (near power station), signs for Barns Ness and Skateraw. 1 mile down road, turn right at site sign towards.

DUNOON Argyll 12B2

Stratheck Caravan Park
Loch Eck, Dunoon PA23 8SG
01369-840472 Fax 01369-840472
Open March-December

Magnificent setting amidst Argyll mountain scenery. Great location for touring the Western Highlands. Superb walking, climbing and mountain bike area with good river and loch fishing available.
Size 13 acres, 70 touring pitches, 45 with electric hookup, 70 level pitches, 80 static caravans, 8 ☔, 18 WCs, 1 CWP
£ car/tent £5-£7, car/caravan £6.50-£8.50, motorhome £6.50-£8.50, motorbike/tent £5-£7
Rental £140-£290
Calor Gaz WS
Last arrival time: 20:00
➜ 7 miles N of Dunoon on A815. 500 yards past Younger Botanic Gardens.

DURNESS Sutherland 14C1

Sango Sands Camping & Caravan Site
Sangomore, Durness IV27 4PP
01971-511262 Fax 01971-511205
Open 1 April-15 October
Size 10 acres, 82 touring pitches, 21 with electric hookup, 60 level pitches, 12 ☔, 18 WCs, 3 CWPs
£ car/tent £7.40, car/caravan £7.40, motorhome £7.40, motorbike/tent £7.40, children £1.75
Calor Gaz
Last arrival time: 18:00
➜ On A838 in centre of Durness village, overlooking Sango Bay.

Forest Holidays

Come to the heart of Britain's wonderful woodlands

for a holiday or short break. The Forestry Commission has almost 30 touring caravan and camping sites in scenic forest locations throughout the UK. From Glenmore in the Cairngorms to the New Forest, with a network of sites in between.

SCOTLAND

Brochure hotline 0131 334 0066
Quote ref: RAC

Forestry Commission

EDINBURGH	13D2

Mortonhall Caravan Park
38 Mortonhall Gate, Frogston Road East, Edinburgh EH16 6TJ
☎ 0131-664 1533   Fax 0131-6645387
Open 27 March-31 October

Country estate just 15 minutes from the city centre. Excellent amenities, restaurant and bar, games room, TV room, laundry, modern toilet and shower block.
Size 200 acres, 250 touring pitches, 150 with electric hookup, 150 level pitches, 20 static caravans, 31, 60 WCs, 2 CWPs
£ car/tent £8-£12.50, car/caravan £8-£21.50, motorhome £8-£21.50, motorbike/tent £8-£12.50, children £1
Rental holiday home 165-£415 a week, tents £5-£10 a night
CC MasterCard Visa

Calor Gaz WS
➜ From N or S, leave city bypass at Lothianburn or Straiton junctions and follow signs for Mortonhall Caravan Park. From city centre, take main road S from either E or W end of Princes Street.

ELGIN Morayshire	15E3

Red Craig Hotel & Caravan Park
Elgin IV30 2XX
☎ 01343-835663   Fax 01343-835663
Open 1 April-31 October

A family run hotel and caravan park with every facility on site. Excellent food and carryouts. Weekend entertainment. Panoramic views. Well positioned for the castle and whisky trails.

Size 4 acres, 30 touring pitches, 10 with electric hookup, 30 level pitches, 8 static caravans, 4, 6 WCs, 1 CWP
£ car/tent £6-£9, car/caravan £8-£9, motorhome £8-£9, motorbike/tent £6-£7
CC MasterCard Visa

Calor WS
Last arrival time: 22:30
➜ Take the signposted road off A96 to Burghead onto B9013, just before entering Burghead turn onto signposted B9040 Hopeman Road. Site is 300 yards on left.

ETTRICK Selkirkshire	13D3

Angecroft Caravan Park
Ettrick TD7 5HY
☎ 01750-62310   Fax 01721-730627
Open all year

Overlooking water and surrounded by woodland, Angecroft is the ideal place to get away and enjoy the peace and quiet of the Scottish Borders.
Size 5 acres, 10 touring pitches, 10 with electric hookup, 10 level pitches, 30 static caravans, 4, 8 WCs, 1 CWP
£ car/tent £5-£7.50, car/caravan £7.50-£9, motorhome £7.50, motorbike/tent £5-£7
Rental Chalet. £90-£260

Calor Gaz WS
Last arrival time: 22:00
➜ From A74/M74 enter Lockerbie and take B723 through Borland to Eskdalemuir. Turn left onto B709 and park is on left 11 miles N of Eskdalemuir. From A7 at Langholm take B709 to park (23 miles). From A7 at Hawick take B711. Park is 4 miles W of Tushielaw on B709.

Hints & Tips
In winter take your seat cushions home. Not only will they keep dry but a caravan without cushions is a less attractive prospect to thieves.

Fort William

EYEMOUTH Berwickshire   13F2

Scoutscroft Holiday Centre
St Abbs Road, Coldingham, Eyemouth
☎ 018907-71338 Fax 018907-71338
Open 1 March-31 October ▲ 🚐 🚏
Size 14 acres, 60 touring pitches, 40 with electric hookup, 60 level pitches, 120 static caravans, 12 🚿, 40 WCs, 2 CWPs
£ car/tent £6-£8, car/caravan £7-£12, motorhome £7-£10, motorbike/tent £5.50-£7.50
Rental 🚐 Chalet. Caravans £130-£270
㏄ MasterCard Visa
🛁¼ ✕ 🍴 🛒 📞 ✉ 🚽 🚿 📺 ⚠ ⛽ Calor Gaz ♿ 🐕 WS
Last arrival time: 00:00
➡ Off A1.

FOCHABERS Morayshire   15E3

Burnside Caravan Site
The Nurseries, Fochabers IV32 7ES
☎ 01343-820362 Fax 01343-820362
Open 1 April-30 October ▲ 🚐 🚏
Size 11 acres, 110 touring pitches, 40 with electric hookup, 110 level pitches, 8 🚿, 24 WCs, 2 CWPs
£ car/tent £8, car/caravan £8, motorhome £8
🛁¼ ✕¼ 🍴¼ 🛒 📞 ✉ 🚽 🚿 📺 🐕 ⚠ WS
➡ From junction on A96 and A98 travel S on A96 for ½ mile. Site on right.

FORFAR Angus   13E1

Drumshademuir Caravan Park
Roundyhill, Forfar DD8 1QT
☎ 01575-573284
Open mid March-end October ▲ 🚐 🚏
Size 7.5 acres, 80 touring pitches, 50 with electric hookup, 80 level pitches, 30 static caravans, 8 🚿, 12 WCs, 2 CWPs
£ car/tent £6.50-£7.50, car/caravan £8.50-£9.50, motorhome £8-£9, motorbike/tent £5-£6.50
Rental Chalet.
🛁 ✕ 🍴 🛒 📞 ✉ 🚽 ⚠ ⛽ Calor Gaz ♿ 🐕 WS
Last arrival time: 23:00
➡ Take A928 from A94 at Glamis for Kirriemuir, 3 miles N of Glamis Castle on Kirriemuir road.

FORT WILLIAM Inverness-shire   14C4

Glen Nevis Caravan & Camping Park
Glen Nevis, Fort William PH33 6SX
☎ 01397-702191 Fax 01397-703904
Open 15 March-31 October ▲ 🚐 🚏

Spacious park with seperate screened areas for caravans, motor caravans and tents. Good standard of facilities and 24 hour supervision in season. Magnificient location with outstanding scenery.
Size 30 acres, 380 touring pitches, 180 with electric hookup, 280 level pitches, 34 🚿, 73 WCs, 3 CWPs
£ car/tent £7-£10.30, car/caravan £7.90-£11.50, motorhome £7.60-£11.20, motorbike/tent £7-£10.30, children £1-£1.40
㏄ MasterCard Visa
🛁 ✕ 🍴 🛒 📞 ✉ 🚽 ⚠ ⛽ Calor Gaz ♿ 🐕
Last arrival time: 23:00
➡ A82 to mini roundabout at N outskirts of Fort William. Exit for Glen Nevis Park. Site is 2½ miles on right.
See advert on this page

SCOTLAND

Glen Nevis
Caravan & Camping Park

This award-winning environmental park – 1998 Best Park in Scotland and David Bellamy Gold Conservation Award – situated at the foot of Ben Nevis, Britain's highest mountain, offers modern, clean and well-equipped facilities including Motor Caravan Service Point. Many pitches are fully serviced with electricity, water and drainage. Showers, scullery, laundry, licensed shop, gas and play areas are all on park with our own spacious restaurant and lounge only a few minutes walk. Colour brochure available.

FORT WILLIAM, INVERNESS-SHIRE PH33 6SX
Tel: 01397 702191
E-mail: camping@glen-nevis.demon.co.uk
Web site: http://www.lochaber.co.uk/glenevis

Fort William

Linnhe Caravan & Chalet Park
Corpach, Fort William PH33 7NL
☎ 01397-772376 Fax 01397-772007
Open 15 December-31 October ▲ 🚐 🚏

Beautifully landscaped with magnificent views over Loch Eil. Enjoy a host of outdoor activities or simply relax in well tended surroundings. Graded "Excellent". Private beach.
Size 13.5 acres, 64 touring pitches, 64 with electric hookup, 64 level pitches, 95 static caravans, 8 🚿, 15 WCs, 1 CWP
£ car/tent £7.50-£9, car/caravan £10-£13, motorhome £10-£13, motorbike/tent £7.50-£9, children £0.50
Rental 🚐 £170-£425, chalets £300-£520
℅ MasterCard Visa
🛒 🗑 📞 🍴 🍳 Calor Gaz 🐕 WS
Last arrival time: 21:00
➔ On A830, 1½ miles W of Corpach village, signposted, 5 miles from Fort William.

FORTROSE Ross-shire	15D3

Camping & Caravanning Club Site
Well Road, Rosemarkie, Fortrose IV10 8UW
☎ 01381-621117
Open March-September ▲ 🚐 🚏
Size 5 acres, 60 touring pitches, 4 🚿, 16 WCs, 2 CWPs
£ car/tent £9.60-£12.10, car/caravan £9.60-£12.10, motorhome £9.60-£12.10, motorbike/tent £9.60-£12.10, children £1.50
℅ MasterCard Visa
🛒 🛒¼ ✕¼ 🍴¼ 🗑 📞 🍴 ▶ 🍳 GR 🔍 TV 🅿 Calor ♿ 🐕 WS
Last arrival time: 23:00
➔ Take A832 Fortrose/Cromarty from A9 at Tore roundabout. Carry on through Avoch, Fortrose, then turn right at Police House, signposted "golf course and leisure centre". Down Ness Road, take first left. Follow road 400 yards to site.

GAIRLOCH Ross-shire	14B2

Gruinard Bay Caravan Park
Laide, Gairloch IV22 2ND
☎ 01445-731225 Fax 01445-731225
Open 1 April-31 October ▲ 🚐 🚏

Level, grassy site adjacent to a sandy beach. Quiet and restful with superb views over Gruinard Bay to the islands and mountains.
Size 3.5 acres, 34 touring pitches, 18 with electric hookup, 18 level pitches, 14 static caravans, 4 🚿, 9 WCs, 1 CWP
£ car/tent £8.50, car/caravan £8.50, motorhome £8.50, motorbike/tent £8.50, children £1.50
Rental 🚐 £140-£225
🛒 🛒¼ ✕¼ 🍴¼ 🗑 📞 🍳 Calor Gaz 🐕
Last arrival time: 22:00
➔ From A835(T) Inverness to Ullapool road, at Braemore junction (near Corrieshalloch Falls), turn left onto A832 signposted to Gairloch. Park is on right.

Sands Holiday Centre
Gairloch IV21 2DL
☎ 01445-712152 Fax 01445-712518
Open 1 April-15 October ▲ 🚐 🚏
Size 50 acres, 300 touring pitches, 60 with electric hookup, 20 static caravans, 22 🚿, 54 WCs, 1 CWP
£ car/tent £7.50-£9, car/caravan £7.50-£12, motorhome £7.50-£9, motorbike/tent £7-£9
Rental 🚐
℅ MasterCard Visa
🛒 🗑 📞 🍴 🍳 🅿 Calor Gaz 🐕
Last arrival time: 22:00
➔ Follow A382 to Gairloch. At Gairloch take B8021 to Melvaig, 4 miles along this road will bring you to park.

GLASGOW	12C2

CULZEAN CASTLE & COUNTRY PARK

Spectacular Robert Adam Castle set in coastal woodland, garden and parkland. A great day out for families. **The Eisenhower Apartment** *in the top of the castle offers charming country house accommodation in six double bedrooms and the best of Scottish food.*

Maybole, Ayrshire, KA19 8LE
Tel: 01655 760274 Fax: 01655 760615

Greenlaw

181

Strathclyde Country Park
366 Hamilton Road, Motherwell ML1 3ED
☎ 01698-266155 Fax 01698-252925
Open April-October

One of Scotlands leading centres for outdoor recreation, with a wide range of activities including, land and water sports, sandy beaches, play areas and a programme of special events.
Size 14 acres, 250 touring pitches, 100 with electric hookup, 100 level pitches, 32, 24 WCs, 4 CWPs
£ car/tent £6.45, car/caravan £7.50, motorhome £7.50, motorbike/tent £6.45
Calor WS
➜ From M74 junction 5 take A725 (Belshill). Park signed off roundabout, also off motorway.
See advert on this page

STRATHCLYDE Country Park...

One of Scotland's leading Centres for outdoor recreation, with a wide range of activities to choose from, offers...

north lanarkshire leisure

Something for everyone..
Top class facilities for
Land and Water Sports,
Countryside Ranger
Service, Visitor Centre,
Sandy Beaches, Play
Areas and Caravan
& Camping Site.
Programme of Special
Events.

All enquiries are welcomed:
Strathclyde Country Park,
366 Hamilton Road,
Motherwell. ML1 4ED
Telephone: (01698) 266155

North Lanarkshire Council

GLENCOE Argyll   14C4

Invercoe Caravans
Invercoe, Glencoe PA39 4HP
☎ 01855-811210 Fax 01855-811210
Open 1 April-31 October

A family run park set on the shores of Loch Leven, surrounded by breathtaking scenery of mountain forest and loch. A wonderful base from which to explore the west coast, a warm welcome awaits you at Invercoe.
Size 5 acres, 60 touring pitches, 40 with electric hookup, 55 level pitches, 5 static caravans, 9, 14 WCs, 3 CWPs
£ car/tent £8-£9, car/caravan £9-£10, motorhome £9-£10, motorbike/tent £8-£9, children £0.50
Rental £170-£295
Calor Gaz
Last arrival time: 23:00
➜ From Glasgow follow A82 to Glencoe. At Glencoe Hotel turn right onto B863 for ¼ mile.

GREENLAW Berwickshire   13E2

Greenlaw Caravan Park
Bank Street, Greenlaw TD10 6XX
☎ 01361-810341 Fax 01361-810715
Open 1 March-30 November
Size 7 acres, 3 touring pitches, 3 with electric hookup, 65 level pitches, 55 static caravans, 8, 8 WCs, 1 CWP
£ car/tent £8.50, car/caravan £8.50, motorhome £8.50, motorbike/tent £8.50, children £8.50
Calor Gaz WS
➜ In Greenlaw Village turn N on A6105. Site is situated on left, close to nature reserve.

Hints & Tips

Tiredness can kill. If you are planning a long journey make sure you plan some breaks.

SCOTLAND

182

Gretna

GRETNA Dumfriesshire 13D4

Braids Caravan Park
Annan Road, Gretna DG16 5DQ
☎ 01461-337409 Fax 01461-337409
Open all year

Family run full facility park in an ideal touring centre. Touring advice. Open all year. Rallies welcome. Nicely placed away from motorway. B&B in owners bungalow.
Size 4 acres, 84 touring pitches, 58 with electric hookup, 50 level pitches, 5 static caravans, 8, 10 WCs, 3 CWPs
£ car/tent £6-£7, car/caravan £6.75-£7.75, motorhome £6.75-£7.75, motorbike/tent £6
Calor Gaz WS
Last arrival time: 00:00
➜ A74 N, A75, second left into Gretna.

HADDINGTON East Lothian 13E2

Monks' Muir
Haddington EH41 3SB
☎ 01620-860340 Fax 01620-861770
Open all year

A multi-award winning, friendly, sheltered site with glorious views and excellent facilities in an area of great beauty. Only 15 minutes from the fringes of Edinburgh, surrounded by fine beaches, golf courses and farmland. Short rentals tailored to suit. Winter and over-60s discounts.
Size 8 acres, 43 touring pitches, 35 with electric hookup, 43 level pitches, 25 static caravans, 6, 18 WCs, 2 CWPs
£ car/tent £8-£9.50, car/caravan £8.40-£11.50, motorhome £8.40-£11.50, motorbike/tent £8-£8.50
Rental £125-£400 weekly.
Calor Gaz WS

Last arrival time: 00:00
➜ Directly on main A1 road, north side, equidistant from Haddington and East Linton.

INVERARAY Argyll 12B1

Argyll Caravan & Camping Park
Inveraray PA32 8XT
☎ 01499-302285 Fax 01499-302421
Open 1 April-31 October

Attractively situated on the shores of Loch Fyne. 2½ miles south of Inveraray on A83. All normal modern amenities including shop, lounge bar, recreation hall and laundrette.
Size 8 acres, 60 touring pitches, 40 with electric hookup, 60 level pitches, 200 static caravans, 16, 80 WCs, 2 CWPs
£ car/tent £6.90-£8.70, car/caravan £8.50-£10, motorhome £8.50-£10, motorbike/tent £6.90-£8.70
cc MasterCard Visa
Calor Gaz WS
➜ 2 miles SW of Inveraray on A83.

INVERGARRY Inverness-shire 14C4

Faichem Park
Ardgarry Farm, Faichem, Invergarry PH35 4HG
☎ 01809-501226
Open April-October

A quiet, family run park, spotlessly clean and well maintained. Set amidst mountains and pines. A perfect location for touring the Western Highlands. B.G.H.P. graded excellent. Award for excellence in sanitation facilities and attractive environment.
Size 2 acres, 30 touring pitches, 14 with electric hookup, 11 level pitches, 2, 6 WCs, 1 CWP

Isle of Arran

£ car/tent £6.50-£7, car/caravan £6.50-£7, motorhome £6.50-£7, motorbike/tent £6.50-£7, children £0.25
Rental Chalet. £80-£405
Calor Gaz
Last arrival time: 22:00
➜ From A82 at Invergarry take A87. Continue for 1 mile and turn right at Faichem signpost. Bear left up hill and entrance is first on right.

Faichemard Farm Camping & Caravanning
Faichem, Invergarry PH35 4HG
01809-501314
Open April-October

A unique ten acre site, 40 pitches each with its own picnic table and magnificent view.
Size 10 acres, 40 touring pitches, 12 with electric hookup, 25 level pitches, 4, 8 WCs, 1 CWP
£ car/tent £6, car/caravan £6, motorhome £6, motorbike/tent £6
Rental Chalet.
Last arrival time: 22:00
➜ One mile W of Invergarry on A87, turn right and go past Ardgarry Farm and Faichem Park campsite. Turn right at sign for A & D Grant.

INVERNESS Inverness-shire   15D3

Auchnahillin Caravan Park
Daviot East, Inverness IV1 2XQ
01463-772286 Fax 01463-772282
Open Easter-mid October

Highly commended park with excellent amenities. Set amid splendid Highland scenery and nestling in a peaceful valley with views of the surrounding forests and mountains, Auchnahillin is the ideal base for touring or enjoying the multitude of activities in this lovely area.
Size 12 acres, 65 touring pitches, 35 with electric hookup, 65 level pitches, 22 static caravans, 6, 18 WCs, 1 CWP
£ car/tent £5.50-£8, car/caravan £7.50-£9, motorhome £7.50-£9, motorbike/tent £4.50-£6.50, children £0.50
Rental Chalet. £135-£295
Calor Gaz WS
Last arrival time: 22:00
➜ Turn off A9 S of Inverness onto Moy/Daviot East road (B9154). The park is just N of Moy.

Bunchrew Caravan Park
Bunchrew, Inverness IV3 6TD
01463-237802 Fax 01463-225803
Open April-December

Situated on the shore of the Beauly Firth with wonderful views of the water and hills. A perfect base for touring the Highlands.
Size 15 acres, 100 touring pitches, 50 with electric hookup, 100 level pitches, 14 static caravans, 8, 18 WCs, 1 CWP
£ car/tent £7.50-£8, car/caravan £7.50-£8.50, motorhome £7.50-£8.50, motorbike/tent £6-£6.50, children £1
Rental £145-£235
×¼ Calor Gaz WS
➜ Leave Inverness on A862, site is 3 miles W of town.

ISLE OF ARRAN   12B3

Middleton Caravan & Camping Park
Lamlash KA27 8NN
01770-600251
Open mid April-mid October
Size 7 acres, 30 touring pitches, 26 with electric hookup, 40 level pitches, 4, 9 WCs, 1 CWP
£ car/tent £7-£9, car/caravan £7.50-£9.50, motorhome £7-£9, motorbike/tent £6.50-£7.50, children £1.25
Rental from £150., £350 pw
¼ ×¼ Calor Gaz
Last arrival time: 22:00
➜ From Brodick ferry turn left 3 miles to Lamlash. Past Police Station on left, over bridge, first left and then first right.

SCOTLAND

ISLE OF SKYE	14A3

Staffin Caravan & Camping Site
Grenicle, Staffin IV51 9JX
☎ 01470-562213
Open mid April-end September ▲ 🚐 🚛

Quiet, peaceful site 1 mile from Staffin Bay. Sea, loch and river fishing, climbing and walking all available nearby. 2 static caravans and 2 chalets for hire. Shop, restaurant ¼ mile; swimming pool 15 miles. Open from the 1st of April to the 30th of September.
Size 2 acres, 50 touring pitches, 17 with electric hookup, 17 level pitches, 4 🚿, 9 WCs, 1 CWP
£ car/tent £7, car/caravan £7, motorhome £7, motorbike/tent £7, children £1.50-£2
Rental Chalet.
Calor Gaz ♿ 🐕
Last arrival time: 22:00
➔ Site is on S side of Staffin, sign at entrance.

JEDBURGH Roxburghshire	13E3

Camping & Caravanning Club Site
Elliot Park, Jedburgh TD8 6EF
☎ 01835-863393
Open March-November ▲ 🚐 🚛
Size 3 acres, 55 touring pitches, 25 with electric hookup, 8 🚿, 7 WCs, 1 CWP
£ car/tent £9.60-£12.10, car/caravan £9.60-£12.10, motorhome £9.60-£12.10, motorbike/tent £9.60-£12.10, children £1.50
㏄ MasterCard Visa
🛁 🛁¼ ✕¼ 🍴 🍴¼ 🔌 🔥 🅿 ❄ 🚿 GR 🎮 📺 ⛽ Calor ♿ 🐕
Last arrival time: 23:00
➔ Entrance directly opposite Edinburgh and Jedburgh Woolen Mills on N side of Jedburgh. On A68 Newcastle to Edinburgh road.

JOHN O'GROATS Caithness	15E1

John O'Groats Caravan Site
John O'Groats KW1 4YS
☎ 01955-611329
Open April-October ▲ 🚐 🚛
Size 4 acres, 90 touring pitches, 28 with electric hookup, 70 level pitches, 8 🚿, 10 WCs, 2 CWPs

£ car/tent £6.50-£7.50, car/caravan £6.50-£7.50, motorhome £6.50-£7.50, motorbike/tent £5-£5.50, children £0.50
🛁¼ ✕¼ 🍴¼ 🔌 🔥 ⛽ Calor Gaz ♿ 🐕
Last arrival time: 22:00
➔ Entrance on right at N end of A9 on seafront beside last house in Scotland.

KELSO Roxburghshire	13E3

Springwood Caravan Park
Springwood Estate, Kelso TD5 8LS
☎ 01573-224596   Fax 01573-224033
Open April-October ▲ 🚐 🚛

Situated in wooded parkland adjacent to River Teviot, only one mile from market town of Kelso. Riverside walks adjacent to park, short grass and clean facilities.
Size 30 acres, 46 touring pitches, 46 with electric hookup, 15 level pitches, 230 static caravans, 8 🚿, 30 WCs, 1 CWP
£ car/caravan £8-£9, motorhome £8-£9, children £0.50
㏄ MasterCard Visa
🔌 🔥 ⛽ GR 🎮 ⛽ Calor ♿ 🐕
Last arrival time: 22:00
➔ A699 from Kelso to Selkirk. Site in 1 mile.
See advert on opposite page

KENMORE Perthshire	12C1

Kenmore Caravan & Camping Park
Kenmore, Aberfeldy PH15 2HN
☎ 01887-830226   Fax 01887-830211
Open mid March-mid October ▲ 🚐 🚛

Kirkcudbright

A well located site by the River and Loch Tay in magnificent Highland Perthshire. First class facilities available, including bar, restaurant and golf course.
Size 14 acres, 160 touring pitches, 140 with electric hookup, 60 level pitches, 60 static caravans, 12 ⓕ, 20 WCs, 2 CWPs
£ car/tent £7.50-£8.50, car/caravan £8.50-£9.50, motorhome £8.50-£9.50, motorbike/tent £6-£7, children £0.50
Rental Chalet.
cc MasterCard Visa
🎿 ✕ 🏕 🍴 📞 🛒 🛁 🚻 🎣 🎾 GR 📺 🅿 ⛽ Calor Gaz ♿ 🐕 WS
Last arrival time: 22:00
➡ A9 N to Ballinluig. A837 W to Kenmore. Through village over bridge on right.

KINGHORN Fife   13D2

Pettycur Bay Caravan Park
Burntisland Road, Kinghorn KY3 9YE
📞 01592-890321 Fax 01592-891420
Open 1 March-31 October ⛺ 🚐 🚙
Size 42 acres, 50 touring pitches, 45 with electric hookup, 34 level pitches, 450 static caravans, 12 ⓕ, 20 WCs, 2 CWPs
£ car/tent £8.50-£12.50, car/caravan £8.50-£12.50, motorhome £8.50-£12.50, motorbike/tent £12.50
Rental 🚐 £100-£400
cc MasterCard Visa
🎿 ✕ 🏕 🍴 📞 🛒 🛁 🚻 🎣 🎾 GR 🔍 📺 🅿 ⛽ Calor ♿ 🐕 WS
Last arrival time: 22:00
➡ From Forth Road Bridge take junction 1, A921. Park located between Burntisland and Kinghorn.

KINLOCH RANNOCH Perthshire   15D4

Kilvrecht Camping & Caravan Site
Tay District Forestry Commission, Inver Park, Dunkeld PH8 0JR
📞 01350-727284 Fax 01350-728635
Open 26 March-25 October ⛺ 🚐 🚙
Size 7.5 acres, 60 touring pitches, 60 level pitches, 4 WCs, 1 CWP
£ car/tent £5, car/caravan £5, motorhome £5, motorbike/tent £3
🎾 🅿 🐕
➡ From Kinloch Rannoch take South Loch Rannoch road for 3½ miles to the site which is set in Birch Woods, ¾ mile from southern shore of Loch Rannoch.

KINTORE Aberdeenshire   15F3

Hillhead Caravan Park
Kintore AB51 0YX
📞 01467-632809 Fax 01467-633173

Open 29 March-31 October ⛺ 🚐 🚙
Size 1.5 acres, 24 touring pitches, 18 with electric hookup, 24 level pitches, 5 static caravans, 4 ⓕ, 6 WCs, 1 CWP
£ car/tent £5.95-£7.50, car/caravan £5.95-£7.50, motorhome £5.95-£7.50, motorbike/tent £5.95-£7.50, children £1
Rental 🚐 £110-£250
cc MasterCard Visa
🎿 📞 🛁 🚻 Calor Gaz ♿ 🐕 WS
Last arrival time: 22:00
➡ From Aberdeen go to centre of Kintore. Turn left signposted Ratch Hill, in ½ mile turn left signposted Blairs, in ½ mile caravan park is on left.

KIRKCUDBRIGHT Kirkcudbrightshire   12C4

Silvercraigs Caravan & Camping Site
Kirkcudbright DG6 4BT
📞 01557-330123 Fax 01556-504879
Open Easter-October ⛺ 🚐 🚙
Size 5 acres, 50 touring pitches, 49 with electric hookup, 40 level pitches, 4 ⓕ, 8 WCs, 1 CWP
£ car/tent £6.90-£8.50, car/caravan £6.90-£8.50, motorhome £6.90-£8.50, motorbike/tent £6.90-£8.50
🎿¼ ✕¼ 🏕¼ 📞 🛁 🚻 🐕
➡ In Kirkcudbright, off Silvercraigs Road, overlooking town.

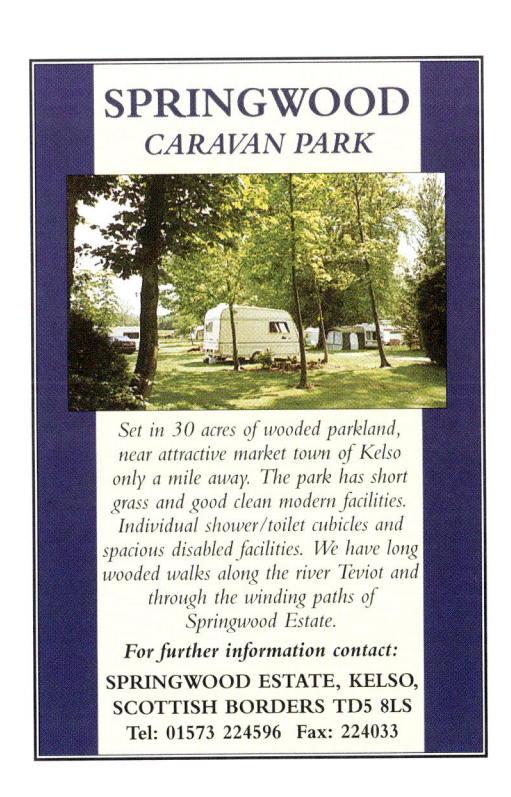

SPRINGWOOD
CARAVAN PARK

Set in 30 acres of wooded parkland, near attractive market town of Kelso only a mile away. The park has short grass and good clean modern facilities. Individual shower/toilet cubicles and spacious disabled facilities. We have long wooded walks along the river Teviot and through the winding paths of Springwood Estate.

For further information contact:
SPRINGWOOD ESTATE, KELSO, SCOTTISH BORDERS TD5 8LS
Tel: 01573 224596 Fax: 224033

SCOTLAND

185

Lairg

LAIRG Sutherland 15D2

Dunroamin Caravan & Camping Park
Main Street, Lairg IV27 4AR
☎ 01549-402447 Fax 01549-402447
Open 1 April-31 October

Situated in the village of Lairg on the south side of the A839, 300 yards from the village centre. Holiday caravans for rent. Tents, caravans and motorhomes all welcome.
Size 4 acres, 50 touring pitches, 16 with electric hookup, 50 level pitches, 10 static caravans, 2, 5 WCs, 1 CWP
£ car/tent £5-£7.50, car/caravan £5.50-£8.50, motorhome £5.50-£8.50, motorbike/tent £5-£7.50, children £0.50
 MasterCard Visa
¼ Calor Gaz
Last arrival time: 22:00
➡ S side of A839, 300 yards from Lairg village centre and Loch Shin. Immediately adjacent to Crofters restaurant.

Woodend Caravan & Camping Park
Achnairn, Lairg IV27 4DN
☎ 01549-402248
Open 1 April-30 September
Size 4 acres, 55 touring pitches, 22 with electric hookup, 5 static caravans, 4, 9 WCs, 1 CWP
£ car/tent £5.50, car/caravan £5.50-£6.50, motorhome £5.50-£6.50, motorbike/tent £5.50
Rental £130 weekly, £18 nightly.
 Calor Gaz
Last arrival time: 23:00
➡ From Lairg take A836 for 3 miles. Then take A838 and follow site signs.

LANARK Lanarkshire 13D2

Crossburn Caravan Park
Douglas, Lanark ML11 0QA
☎ 01555-851029
Open all year
Size 4 acres, 50 touring pitches, 50 with electric hookup, 50 level pitches, 6, 14 WCs, 1 CWP
£ car/tent £5.50, car/caravan £6.50, motorhome £6.50, motorbike/tent £5.50
 MasterCard Visa
¼ ¼ Calor
➡ 2 miles W of M74 on Edinburgh to Ayr road, then A70 to village of Douglas.

LAUDER Berwickshire 13E2

Thirlestane Castle Caravan & Camping
Lauder TD2 6RU
☎ 01578-722254 Fax 01578-718749
Open 1 April-1 October
Size 4 acres, 50 touring pitches, 18 with electric hookup, 30 level pitches, 8, 10 WCs, 1 CWP
£ car/tent £8, car/caravan £8, motorhome £8, motorbike/tent £7
 WS
➡ Signed off A68 and A697, ½ mile S of Lauder.

LAURENCEKIRK Kincardineshire 15F4

Dovecot Caravan Park
Northwaterbridge, Laurencekirk AB30 1QL
☎ 01674-840630 Fax 01674-840630
Open 1 April-31 October
Size 6 acres, 25 touring pitches, 25 with electric hookup, 25 level pitches, 40 static caravans, 6, 9 WCs, 1 CWP
£ car/tent £6.75-£7.75, car/caravan £6.75-£7.75, motorhome £6.75-£7.75, motorbike/tent £5.50-£6.50
Rental
 Calor WS
Last arrival time: 20:00
➡ Turn off A90 at signpost for RAF base. Site is 500 yards on left.

LEVEN Fife 13E1

Woodland Gardens Caravan & Camping Site
Lundin Links, Leven KY8 5QG
☎ 01333-360319
Open March-October
Size 1 acre, 20 touring pitches, 20 with electric hookup, 20 level pitches, 5 static caravans, 2, 7 WCs, 1 CWP
£ car/tent £7.50-£8.50, car/caravan £7.50-£8.50, motorhome £7.50-£8.50, motorbike/tent £7.50-£8.50, children £1.25
Rental £110-£270
 Calor Gaz WS
Last arrival time: 22:00
➡ Turn N off A915 at E end of Lundin Links. Site is signposted on A915 and is ½ mile from main road.

LOCKERBIE Dumfriesshire 13D4

Cressfield Caravan Park
Ecclefechan, Lockerbie DG11 3DR
☎ 01576-300702 Fax 01576-300702

Longniddry

Well kept country park, with excellent facilities, just north of the border. Ideal touring base/night halt. Finalist 'Best Park In Scotland' Calor Award '98.
Size 38 acres, 67 touring pitches, 67 with electric hookup, 67 level pitches, 48 static caravans, 8, 14 WCs, 1 CWP
£ car/tent £6-£6.50, car/caravan £6.50-£8, motorhome £6.50-£8, motorbike/tent £6-£6.50, children £1
Calor
Last arrival time: 23:00
➔ 8 miles N of Gretna. ½ mile from A74 (M) at Ecclefechan (jn 19). Park is S of village on B7076, signposted.

Halleaths Touring Camping & Caravan Park
Lochmaben, Lockerbie DG11 1NA
☎ 01387-810630 Fax 01387-810630
Open mid March-16 November
Size 8 acres, 70 touring pitches, 60 with electric hookup, 70 level pitches, 10 static caravans, 8, 12 WCs, 1 CWP
£ car/tent £5, car/caravan £7, motorhome £7, motorbike/tent £5, children £0.50
Rental £10 ppn
Calor Gaz WS
➔ From M74 Lockerbie take A709 following signs to Lochmaben and Dumfries. Site on right 3 miles W of Lockerbie.

Hoddom Castle Caravan Park
Hoddom, Lockerbie DG11 1AS
☎ 01576-300251 Fax 01576-300757
Open Easter-October
Size 24 acres, 170 touring pitches, 140 with electric hookup, 170 level pitches, 30 static caravans, 15, 60 WCs, 1 CWP
£ car/tent £6-£11.50, car/caravan £6-£11.50, motorhome £6-£11.50, motorbike/tent £5.50-£8.50
₡₡ MasterCard Visa
Calor Gaz WS
➔ From A74(M) take junction 19 at Ecclefechan. Follow signs. From A75 ½ mile W of Annan take B723 (Lockerbie), follow signs.
See advert on this page

LONGNIDDRY East Lothian   13E2

Seton Sands Holiday Park
Longniddry EM32 0QF
☎ 01875-813333
Open March-October

A family holiday park with beautiful beaches nearby and only 12 miles from the capital of Scotland - Edinburgh, the park boasts an indoor pool, kids club and a wide range of leisure facilities, restaurants and bars, excellent cabaret entertainment. A 'British Holidays Park'.
Size 60 touring pitches, 32 with electric hookup, 620 static caravans, 6, 11 WCs, 1 CWP
£ car/caravan £10-£14, motorhome £10-£14
₡₡ MasterCard Visa
Calor
➔ From Trament roundabout turn on B6371 for Cockenzie and then right on B1348. Site is 1 mile on right.

---

10 minutes from A74 and A75. Ideal stopping place or base for travelling North, South or to Ireland; exploring SW Scotland, the Borders or the Lake District. Mains toilets, showers, electric hook-ups, launderette, shop, play area, bar.

FISHING: (on our own waters) salmon, sea trout and brown trout on River Annan. Coarse fishing at Kellhead Quarry. GOLF: 9 hold golf course at Hoddon Castle, 18 hole course at Powfoot. WALKING: Woodland walks, nature trails, guided walks. Adjacent to Caravan Park.

For enquiries and bookings please contact:

Hoddom Castle Caravan Park

Hoddom, Lockerbie,
Dumfriesshire, Scotland DG11 1AS
Telephone: 01576 300251

A.A. Best Scottish Camp Site 1996/97
CC Approved
CCGBI Approved

Caravan TOP 100 FAMILY PARKS 1998

Lossiemouth

LOSSIEMOUTH Morayshire   15E2

Silver Sands Leisure Park
Covesea, West Beach, Lossiemouth IV31 6SP
☎ 01343-813262   Fax 01343-815205
Open March-October

Set next to a beautiful golden sand beach, with no roads to cross, the site has entertainment for all during the peak season. Ideally situated for fishing villages, castles and distilleries.
Size 70 acres, 140 touring pitches, 74 with electric hookup, 66 level pitches, 230 static caravans, 13, 21 WCs, 1 CWP
£ car/tent £7.55-£11.20, car/caravan £7.55-£11.20, motorhome £7.55-£11.20, motorbike/tent £7.55-£11.20
Rental £90-£485 pw, £14.80-£79.70 pn, (min 2 nights).
CC MasterCard Visa
Calor Gaz WS
Last arrival time: 22:30

➡ Follow A96 from Inverness-Aberdeen until you reach Elgin, then follow A941 to Lossiemouth. Situated beneath Covesea lighthouse.

LUSS Dunbartonshire   12C2

Camping & Caravanning Club Site
Luss, Loch Lomond, Glasgow G83 8NT
☎ 01436-860658
Open March-November
Size 10 acres, 89 touring pitches, 40 with electric hookup, 8, 10 WCs, 1 CWP
£ car/tent £11.50-£14.60, car/caravan £11.50-£14.60, motorhome £11.50-£14.60, motorbike/tent £11.50-£14.60, children £1.60
CC MasterCard Visa
Calor WS
Last arrival time: 23:00

➡ Take A82 from Erkside Bridge heading N towards Tarbet. Ignore first signpost for Luss. After bagpipe and kiltmakers workshop take next turn on right signposted 'Lodge of Loch Lomond' international camping sign. Heading S from Tarbet on A82, take first left after Camping Club site signpost and Lodge of Loch Lomond sign - approx 200 yards.

MAYBOLE Ayrshire   12C3

Camping & Caravanning Club Site
Culzean Castle, Maybole KA19 8JK
☎ 01655-760627
Open March-November
Size 10 acres, 90 touring pitches, 60 with electric hookup, 8, 9 WCs, 1 CWP

£ car/tent £11.50-£14.60, car/caravan £11.50-£14.60, motorhome £11.50-£14.60, motorbike/tent £11.50-£14.60, children £1.60
CC MasterCard Visa
Calor WS
Last arrival time: 23:00

➡ From N on A77, in Maybole turn right onto B7023 the site is on the right in 4 miles. From S on A77 turn left onto A719 (Signposted Turnbury/Maidens), site is on left in 4 miles.

MOFFAT Dumfriesshire   13D3

Camping & Caravanning Club Site
Hammerland's Farm, Moffat DG10 9QL
☎ 01683-220436
Open March-November
Size 14 acres, 200 touring pitches, 89 with electric hookup, 8, 20 WCs, 1 CWP
£ car/tent £11.50-£14.60, car/caravan £11.50-£14.60, motorhome £11.50-£14.60, motorbike/tent £11.50-£14.60, children £1.60
CC MasterCard Visa
Calor WS
Last arrival time: 23:00

➡ Take Moffat sign from A74. In 1 mile turn right by Bank of Scotland, right again in 200 yards, sign for site is on right, follow road round to site.

MUIR OF ORD Ross-shire   15D3

Druimorrin Caravan & Camping Park
Orrin Bridge, Urray, Muir Of Ord IV6 7UL
☎ 01997-433252
Open Easter-end September
Size 5.5 acres, 60 touring pitches, 24 with electric hookup, 60 level pitches, 4, 13 WCs, 1 CWP
£ car/tent £5.50-£7.50, car/caravan £6.50-£7.50, motorhome £6-£7, motorbike/tent £5-£6
Calor Gaz WS
Last arrival time: 00:00

➡ From Inverness take A9 N to Tore roundabout. A832 signposted Muir of Ord, pass through village and continue W on A832 for 2½ miles, site is on right.

MUSSELBURGH Midlothian   13D2

Drum Mohr Caravan Park
Levenhall, Musselburgh EH21 8JS
☎ 01316-656867   Fax 01316-536859
Open 1 March-31 October

Newton Stewart

Family run and set in beautiful surroundings with easy access to Edinburgh. Situated between the B1361 and B1348.
Size 10 acres, 120 touring pitches, 100 with electric hookup, 120 level pitches, 12, 20 WCs, 2 CWPs
£ car/tent £8-£10, car/caravan £8-£10, motorhome £8-£10, motorbike/tent £8-£10, children £1-£1.50
Calor Gaz
Last arrival time: 22:00
→ From the A1 follow park signs situated between the B1348 and B1361 above the mining museum.

NAIRN Nairnshire   15D3

Spindrift Caravan Park
Little Kildrummie, Nairn IV12 5QU
01667-453992
Open 1 April-31 October

Small, secluded family run park, overlooking the River Nairn. Winner of an Environmental Award 1996 and an ideal base from which to explore the Highlands.
Size 3 acres, 40 touring pitches, 28 with electric hookup, 40 level pitches, 4, 8 WCs, 2 CWPs
£ car/tent £5.50-£8.50, car/caravan £5.50-£8.50, motorhome £5.50-£8.50, motorbike/tent £5.50-£8.50
¼ ¼ ¼ Calor Gaz
Last arrival time: 22:00
→ From Nairn take B9090 Cawdor road S for 1½ miles. Turn right at sharp left hand bend onto unclassified road signposted Little Kildrummie. The entrance is 400 yards on left.

NEWTON STEWART Wigtownshire   12C4

Cock Inn Caravan Park
Auchenmalg, Glenluce, Newton Stewart DG8 0JH
01581-500227
Open 1 March-31 October

Quiet family park overlooking Luce Bay offering a full range of facilities including a shop, sauna, sunbed, laundry room, free showers and holiday caravans. Ideal for fishing, golf and hillwalking. Tourers welcome.
Size 7 acres, 30 touring pitches, 20 with electric hookup, 13 level pitches, 60 static caravans, 5, 12 WCs, 3 CWPs
£ car/tent £6.50-£8.50, car/caravan £6.50-£11, motorhome £6.50-£11, motorbike/tent £6-£8, children £0.50
Rental Chalet. £130-£235
Calor Gaz WS
Last arrival time: 22:30
→ From A75 Newton Stewart/Stranraer road take A747 to Port William for 5 miles to Auchenmalg.

Forestry Commission Caldons-Glentrool
Galloway Forest Park, Glentrool, Newton Stewart DG8 6AJ
01671 84218
Open end March-end September
Size 48 acres, 160 touring pitches, 52 with electric hookup, 100 level pitches, 12, 28 WCs, 2 CWPs
£ car/tent £6.50-£7, car/caravan £6.50-£7, motorhome £6.50-£7, motorbike/tent £6.50-£7
CC MasterCard Visa
Calor Gaz WS
Last arrival time: 22:00
→ From A714 Newton Steward to Cirian road, turn right at Barcrennan, passing Glentrool village and follow signs to site

SCOTLAND

Newton Stewart

Three Lochs Caravan Park
Balminnoch, Kirkcowan, Newton Stewart DG8 OEP
☎ 01671-830304 Fax 01671-830335
Open March-October ▲ ⚐ ⛺

Set opposite beautiful Loch Heron, with newly refurbished shower block. We are now AA four pennant and have been upgraded to Four ticks Thistle commended.
Size 22 acres, 45 touring pitches, 29 with electric hookup, 75 level pitches, 100 static caravans, 6 🛁, 7 WCs, 1 CWP
£ car/tent £6-£9, car/caravan £9-£10, motorhome £9, motorbike/tent £9
Rental ⚐ £130-£295 weekly, £26 nightly.
🛁 ♿ 🛒 🍴 ▤ ▥ ⚑ ⬜ /⚠\ Calor Gaz ♿ ✈ WS
Last arrival time: 22:00

➔ 7 miles W of Newton Stewart on A75 heading towards Stranraer turn right at crossroads signed Dirnow/Three Lochs. Then follow signs for holiday park.

NORTH BERWICK East Lothian 13E2

Tantallon Caravan Park
Dunbar Road, North Berwick EH39 5NJ
☎ 01620-893348 Fax 01620-895623
Open March-October ▲ ⚐ ⛺

Easy access to the beach and Glen golf course. Reception, games room, showers, toilets and laundry.
Size 10 acres, 147 touring pitches, 100 with electric hookup, 30 level pitches, 47 static caravans, 22 🛁, 32 WCs, 2 CWPs

£ car/tent £6.50-£10.50, car/caravan £6.50-£10.50, motorhome £6.50-£10.50, motorbike/tent £6.50-£10.50
Rental ⚐ £125-£375 per week
℄ MasterCard Visa
🛁¼ ✕¼ ♿¼ ⬜ 🛒 🍴 ▤ ▥ ⚑ ⬜ 📺 /⚠\ Calor ♿ ✈ WS
Last arrival time: 22:00

➔ On A198 immediately E of North Berwick. From Gullane take A198 through North Berwick towards Dunbar. From A198 3 miles W of Dunbar.

OBAN Argyll 12B1

Ganavan Sands Touring Caravan Park
Ganavan, Oban PA34 5TU
☎ 01631-562179
Open April-October ▲ ⚐ ⛺

Set in beautiful surroundings on the sandy seashore. Ganavan provides an ideal base for diving, hill walking and touring, and is only a short journey from Oban 'Gateway to the Highlands and Islands'.
Size 76 touring pitches, 68 with electric hookup, 62 level pitches, 6 🛁, 10 WCs, 1 CWP
£ car/tent £7-£8, car/caravan £7-£8, motorhome £7-£8, motorbike/tent £7-£8
🛁 ♿ ⬜ 🛒 🍴 ⬜ ⚑ ♿ /⚠\ WS
Last arrival time: 23:30

➔ From town centre follow Esplanade coast road keeping sea immediately adjacent on left for 2 miles.

OLDSHOREMORE Sutherland 14C1

Oldshoremore
by Lairg, Oldshoremore
☎ 0197182-281
Open April-September ▲ ⚐ ⛺

Perth

A one acre site, part grass, part hard standing. Ten minutes walk from a mile long golden sandy beach. Ideal for hill climbing, fishing, beautiful scenery.
Size 1 acre, 13 touring pitches, 3 with electric hookup, 13 level pitches, 2 static caravans, 1, 4 WCs, 1 CWP
£ car/tent £6.30-£6.80, car/caravan £6.70-£7.20, motorhome £6.80-£7.20, motorbike/tent £6.30, children £0.60-£0.85
Rental £60-£150

Last arrival time: 23:00
➜ Take A838 to Rhiconich, there join B801 in Kinlochbervie 4 miles. Then take unclassified road to Oldshoremore - 2 miles.

ORKNEY ISLANDS 15F1

Pickaquoy Caravan & Camp Site
Pickaquoy Road, Kirkwall KW15 1RR
01856-873535 Fax 01856-876327
Open May-September
Size 30 touring pitches, 6 with electric hookup, 1 CWP
£ car/tent £3.25-£4.35, car/caravan £4.85-£7.70, motorhome £4.85-£7.70, motorbike/tent £3.25-£4.35

➜ Just off main A965 road from Stromness to Kirkwall, 150 yards SW of foot of hill coming down into Kirkwall.

Point of Ness Caravan & Camping Site
Ness Road, Stromness KW16 3DN
01856-873535 Fax 01856-876327
Open May-September
Size 30 touring pitches, 6 with electric hookup, 1 CWP
£ car/tent £3.25-£4.35, car/caravan £4.85-£7.70, motorhome £4.85-£7.70, motorbike/tent £3.25-£4.35

➜ 1 mile W of pierhead.

PEEBLES Peeblesshire 13D2

Crossburn Caravan Park
Edinburgh Road, Peebles EH45 8ED
01721-720501 Fax 01721-720501

Open April-October
Size 6 acres, 40 touring pitches, 30 with electric hookup, 40 level pitches, 90 static caravans, 10, 16 WCs, 2 CWPs
£ car/tent £8, car/caravan £9, motorhome £8.50, motorbike/tent £5
Rental from £240
CC MasterCard Visa

Calor Gaz WS
Last arrival time: 23:00
➜ ½ mile N of Peebles on A703.

Rosetta Caravan Park
Rosetta Road, Peebles EH45 8PG
01721-720770 Fax 01721-720623
Open 1 April-31 October

A beautiful, family owned, wooded park, graded 5 ticks excellent. The 1990 Calor Award Winner 'Best Park in Scotland'; finalist in 1993. Licensed bar, adjacent golf course, fishing arranged.
Size 24 acres, 130 touring pitches, 130 with electric hookup, 130 level pitches, 28 static caravans, 12, 27 WCs, 3 CWPs
£ car/tent £7-£8, car/caravan £9-£9.50, motorhome £9-£9.50, motorbike/tent £7-£8
Rental £160-£190

Calor Gaz
➜ Signposted on main roads into Peebles.

PERTH Perthshire 13D1

Camping & Caravanning Club Site
Scone Palace Caravan Park, Old Scone, Perth PH2 6BB
01738-552323
Open March-November
Size 12 acres, 150 touring pitches, 86 with electric hookup, 8, 26 WCs, 1 CWP
£ car/tent £11.50-£14.60, car/caravan £11.50-£14.60, motorhome £11.50-£14.60, motorbike/tent £11.50-£14.60, children £1.60
CC MasterCard Visa

Calor WS
Last arrival time: 23:00
➜ From motorway follow signs for Scone Palace. After Scone Palace continue for 2 miles. Turn left following the camp site signs or the sign for Stormontfield. After 1 mile turn left into Racehorse Road. Site entrance from car park.

SCOTLAND

Perth

Cleeve Caravan Park
Glasgow Road, Perth PH2 0PH
📞 01738-635921 Fax 01738-475210
Open end March-end October

Quiet, well screened, wooded site with a high standard of facilities and a good reputation. Children's play area. Easy access to the centre of Perth. Off-season discount for OAPs.
Size 5 acres, 100 touring pitches, 80 with electric hookup, 80 level pitches, 11 🚿, 20 WCs, 4 CWPs
£ car/tent £7.60, car/caravan £7.80-£8.90, motorhome £7.80-£8.90, motorbike/tent £6, children £1
CC MasterCard Visa
Calor Gaz
Last arrival time: 20:00
➡ ½ mile E of A9/M90, on W side of Perth (A93).

PITLOCHRY Perthshire   15D4

Faskally Home Farm Caravan Site
Pitlochry PH16 5LA
📞 01796-472007
Open 15 March-31 October

Level grassy site. Children's play area. Fishing on Loch Faskally and rivers Tummel and Garry. Forty caravans for hire (own WCs).
Size 23 acres, 250 touring pitches, 20 with electric hookup, 60 static caravans, 18 🚿, 78 WCs,
➡ 2 miles N of Pitlochry on A924 (A9).

Milton Of Fonab Caravan Site
Pitlochry PH16 5NA
📞 01796-472882 Fax 01796-474363
Open Easter-October

A quiet family run site on the banks of the River Tummel. Spectacular scenery. Mountain bike hire and free trout fishing. Static caravans for hire.
Size 15 acres, 154 touring pitches, 130 with electric hookup, 130 level pitches, 36 static caravans, 20 🚿, 60 WCs, 1 CWP
£ car/tent £9-£9.50, car/caravan £9-£9.50, motorhome £9-£9.50, children £0.50
Rental from £43 nightly, from £200 weekly.
Calor Gaz WS
Last arrival time: 21:30
➡ ½ mile S of Pitlochry opposite Bells Distillery.

POOLEWE Ross-shire   14B2

Camping & Caravanning Club Site
Inverewe Gardens, Poolewe, Achnasheen IV22 2LF
📞 01445-781249
Open March-November
Size 3 acres, 55 touring pitches, 18 with electric hookup, 8 🚿, 10 WCs, 1 CWP
£ car/tent £11.50-£14.60, car/caravan £11.50-£14.60, motorhome £11.50-£14.60, motorbike/tent £11.50-£14.60, children £1.60
CC MasterCard Visa
Calor WS
Last arrival time: 23:00
➡ Site is on A832, just N of Poolewe.

PORTPATRICK Wigtownshire   12B4

Castle Bay Caravan Park
Portpatrick DG9 9AA
📞 01776-810462 Fax 01776-810462
Open March-October

Situated one mile from the popular and picturesque village of Portpatrick, the caravan park is set in 22 acres of rolling grassland leading to the ruins of Dunskey Castle and the cliffs overlooking the Irish Sea.
Size 22.5 acres, 26 touring pitches, 26 with electric hookup, 20 level pitches, 96 static caravans, 4 🚿, 8 WCs, 1 CWP
£ car/tent £5, car/caravan £7, motorhome £7, motorbike/tent £5
Rental £140-£215
Calor Gaz WS

St Cyrus

193

Last arrival time: 23:30
➜ Into Portpatrick on A77, left opposite Old Mill Restaurant. Continue for ¾ mile, under railway bridge, site on right.

Galloway Point Holiday Park
Portpatrick, Stranraer DG9 9AA
☎ 01776-810561 Fax 01776-810561
Open Easter-mid October ▲ ⌂ ☗
Size 18 acres, 40 touring pitches, 40 with electric hookup, 15 level pitches, 60 static caravans, 7 ℞, 20 WCs, 1 CWP
£ car/tent £7-£10, car/caravan £10-£12, motorhome £8-£10, motorbike/tent £7-£8
Rental ⌂ £175-£275
♨¼ ✕ 🍴 🏛 📞 🗄 ⚠ ⛽ Calor Gaz ⊶ WS
Last arrival time: 23:00
➜ A75 from Dumfries, A77 from Glasgow, first left opposite Old Mill, park is on right opposite Barn Inn.

Sunnymeade Caravan Park
Portpatrick, Stranraer DG9 8LN
☎ 01776-810293
Open mid March-end October ▲ ⌂ ☗
Size 8 acres, 15 touring pitches, 15 with electric hookup, 60 static caravans, 4 ℞, 9 WCs, 1 CWP
£ car/tent £7-£9, car/caravan £7-£9, motorhome £7-£9, motorbike/tent £7
Rental ⌂ from £140
♨¼ ✕¼ 🍴¼ 🏛 📞 🗄 📺 Calor ⊶ WS
➜ Take A75 to Portpatrick and turn left on entering town. Site is ¼ mile on left.

PRESTWICK Ayrshire 12C3

Prestwick Holiday Park
Prestwick KA9 1UH
☎ 01292-479261
Open March-October ▲
Size 12 acres, 40 touring pitches, 40 with electric hookup, 40 level pitches, 168 static caravans, 4 ℞, 10 WCs, 1 CWP
£ car/tent £12-£13
♨ ✕¼ 🍴 🏛 📞 🗄 📺 ⚠ ⛽ ♿ ⛲ ⊶
Last arrival time: flexible
➜ 1 mile N of Prestwick on A79, turn W opposite Prestwick Airport, for ½ mile.

ST ANDREWS Fife 13E1

Cairnsmill Caravan Site
St Andrews KY16 8NN
☎ 01334-73604
Open April-October ▲ ⌂ ☗
Ideal touring base with easy access to a range of beaches and golf courses. Games room, coffee bar, heated swimming pool.
Size 20 acres, 80 touring pitches, 185 static caravans, 10 ℞, 23 WCs, 2 CWPs
Rental ⌂
♨ 🏛 📞 🗄 🍴 📺 ⚠ ⛽ Calor Gaz ♿ ⊶ WS
Last arrival time: 22:00
➜ 1 mile S of St Andrews on A915.

Clayton Caravan Park
St Andrews KY16 9YA
☎ 01334-870242 Fax 01334-870057
Open Easter-October ▲ ⌂ ☗
Size 25 acres, 26 touring pitches, 26 with electric hookup, 26 level pitches, 170 static caravans, 5 ℞, 10 WCs, 1 CWP
£ car/tent £7.25-£8.25, car/caravan £9.75-£11.25, motorhome £8.75-£10.25, motorbike/tent £7.25-£8.25
€ Visa
♨ ✕ 🍴 🏛 📞 🗄 📄 ⚠ ⛽ Calor Gaz ♿ ⊶ WS
Last arrival time: 22:30
➜ 4½ miles W of St Andrews on A91, between Dairsie and Guardbridge.

ST CYRUS Kincardineshire 15F4

East Bowstrips Caravan Park
St Cyrus, Montrose DD10 0DE
☎ 01674-850328 Fax 01674-850328
Open 1 April-31 October ▲ ⌂ ☗

Quiet family park by the coast with excellent facilities, and a particular welcome for disabled visitors. Only one mile from the glorious sandy St Cyrus beach and nature reserve.
Size 4 acres, 30 touring pitches, 27 with electric hookup, 26 level pitches, 18 static caravans, 4 ℞, 7 WCs, 1 CWP
£ car/tent £5.50-£7.50, car/caravan £6.50-£7.50, motorhome £6.50-£7.50, motorbike/tent £5.50-£6.50
Rental ⌂ £99-£199
♨ ♨¼ ✕¼ 🍴¼ 🏛 📞 🗄 ⚠ Calor ♿ ⊶
Last arrival time: 22:00
➜ Travelling N on A92 coast road enter village of St Cyrus. Pass hotel on left, then first left, second right (signposted).

SCOTLAND

Sandhead

SANDHEAD Wigtownshire — 12B4

Sandhead Caravan Park
Sandhead DG9 9JN
☎ 01776-830296
Open April-October
Size 10 acres, 30 touring pitches, 20 with electric hookup, 30 level pitches, 80 static caravans, 5, 15 WCs, 2 CWPs
£ car/tent £7-£8, car/caravan £7-£8, motorhome £6.50-£7.50, motorbike/tent £5-£7
Rental £200-£220
Calor Gaz
Last arrival time: 22:00
→ From A75 turn S on A716 towards Drummore, site on left approaching Sandhead village.

Sands Of Luce Caravan Park
Sandhead, Stranraer DG9 9JR
☎ 01776-830456 Fax 01776-830456
Open 1 April-31 October

Peaceful, friendly park extending onto beautiful sandy beach and large dune area. Touring pitches beside the beach. New toilet blocks provide excellent facilities. A warm welcome awaits all our visitors.
Size 12 acres, 36 touring pitches, 36 with electric hookup, 36 level pitches, 34 static caravans, 8, 16 WCs, 2 CWPs
£ car/tent £6.50-£8, car/caravan £6.50-£8, motorhome £6-£7.50, motorbike/tent £5.70-£7.20, children £0.40
Rental £135-£275
Calor Gaz WS
Last arrival time: 22:00
→ From Stranraer follow A77 to turn off to Portpatrick. Keep on A716 signposted to Drummore (do not turn right to Portpatrick). Entrance to caravan park is 1 mile past village of Stoneykirk at A716/ B7084 junction.

SELKIRK Selkirkshire — 13E3

Victoria Park Caravan Site
Victoria Park, Buccleugh Road, Selkirk TD7 5DN
☎ 01750-20987 Fax 01896-757003
Open 1 April-31 October

Size 3 acres, 60 touring pitches, 26 with electric hookup, 60 level pitches, 6, 11 WCs, 1 CWP
£ car/tent £6.50-£7.50, car/caravan £6-£7, motorhome £6-£7, motorbike/tent £6-£7
¼ ¼ ¼ Calor
Last arrival time: 21:00
→ A7 N follow signs from Selkirk market place. A7 S turn at town entrance signposted A72 Peebles then A708 Moffat.

SKELMORLIE Ayrshire — 12B2

Mains Camping & Caravan Park
Skelmorlie PA17 5EU
☎ 01475-520794 Fax 01475-520794
Open March-October
Size 4 acres, 20 touring pitches, 20 with electric hookup, 20 level pitches, 70 static caravans, 13, 23 WCs, 1 CWP
£ car/tent £6-£9, car/caravan £8-£11, motorhome £7-£10, motorbike/tent £5-£6
Rental Chalet. £175-£340
Calor Gaz WS
Last arrival time: 00:00
→ Signposted off A78, 4 miles N of Largs.

SPEAN BRIDGE Inverness-shire — 14C4

Stronaba Caravan Site
Spean Bridge PH34 4DX
☎ 01397-712259
Open April-October

Stronaba Caravan and Camping Site, 2½ miles north of Spean Bridge. Entrance on main A82 road Fort William - Inverness. Central location for touring the Highlands, Loch Ness and Skye. Caledonian Canal and all outdoor activities in surrounding area.
Size 4 acres, 20 touring pitches, 4 with electric hookup, 18 level pitches, 4, 6 WCs, 1 CWP
£ car/tent £6.50-£8, car/caravan £6.50-£8, motorhome £6.50-£8, motorbike/tent £6.50-£8, children £1-£2
Last arrival time: 22:00
→ 2½ miles N of Spean Bridge on A82, gateway signposted.

Tain

STIRLING Stirlingshire　　　　　　　　12C2

Auchenbowie Caravan Site
Auchenbowie, Stirling FK7 8HE
☎ 01324-82211　Fax 01324-822950
Open April-October ▲ ⚌ ⚏
Size 3.5 acres, 60 touring pitches, 40 with electric hookup, 60 level pitches, 7 static caravans, 6 🅿, 12 WCs, 2 CWPs
£ car/tent £8-£9, car/caravan £8-£9, motorhome £8-£9, motorbike/tent £5.50
Rental ⚌ £155-£205
cc MasterCard Visa
🛢 ⚒ Calor Gaz 🐕 WS
➜ Leave M9/M80 at junction 9 and head S on A872 for ½ mile, turn right for further ½ mile.
See advert on this page

Mains Farm Camping
Thornhill, Stirling FK8 3QR
☎ 01786-850605　Fax 01786-850605
Open 1 April-31 October ▲ ⚌ ⚏

Family-run farm site near Thornhill Village, offering panoramic views to the Flintry Hills. Ideal centre for historic Stirling, Loch Lomond and the Trossachs.
Size 5 acres, 35 touring pitches, 20 with electric hookup, 35 level pitches, 2 static caravans, 3 🅿, 11 WCs, 1 CWP
£ car/tent £6, car/caravan £6-£8.50, motorhome £6-£7.50, motorbike/tent £6, children £0.50
Rental ⚌ £135-£175
🛁¼ ✗¼ 🍽¼ ⚒ Calor Gaz ♿ 🐕 WS
Last arrival time: 22:00
➜ From Stirling/M9 junction 10 and follow A84 for 5 miles. Bear left onto A873 and at crossroads in Thornhill turn left onto B822. Site 150 yards.

STRANRAER Wigtownshire　　　　　　　　12B4

Wig Bay Holiday Park
Loch Ryan, Stranraer DG9 0PS
☎ 01776-853233
Open 1 March-31 October ⚌ ⚏

On West coast of Loch Ryan, well-sheltered by a hill and woodland to West, panoramic views over Rhins Peninsula.
Size 7.75 acres, 24 touring pitches, 24 with electric hookup, 24 level pitches, 88 static caravans, 6 🅿, 19 WCs, 1 CWP
£ car/caravan £8-£10, motorhome £6-£10
Rental ⚌ Chalet. £100-£300
🛢 ⚒ 📺 ⚒ Calor 🐕 WS
Last arrival time: 22:00
➜ 4¼ miles NW of Stranraer on A718.

TAIN Ross-shire　　　　　　　　15D2

Meikle Ferry Caravan Park
Meikle Ferry, Tain IV19 1JX
☎ 01862-892292
Open 15 January-15 December ▲ ⚌ ⚏
Size 3.5 acres, 30 touring pitches, 20 with electric hookup, 30 level pitches, 15 static caravans, 4 🅿, 8 WCs, 1 CWP
£ car/tent £4.50-£7, car/caravan £6-£8, motorhome £6-£8, motorbike/tent £4.50-£5.50, children £0.50
Rental ⚌ £90-£210
🛁 ✗¼ 🛢 ⚒ 🐕 ⚒ WS
Last arrival time: 23:00
➜ 2 miles N of Tain on A9, straight on at roundabout for new Dornoch bridge. Park access is 300 yards on right.

SCOTLAND

AUCHENBOWIE
CARAVAN SITE

A peaceful site in rural surroundings in a central situation which offers an ideal base for touring. A wide range of activities and sports are available locally.
Modern, comfortable, well equipped static caravans for hire.
Please telephone or write for a copy of our brochure.
Open April to October.

AUCHENBOWIE, STIRLING, STIRLINGSHIRE, SCOTLAND FK7 8HE
Tel: 01324-822141　Fax: 01324-822950

Tarbert

TARBERT, LOCH FYNE Argyll   12B2

Point Sands Caravan Park
Tayinloan, Tarbert PA29 6XG
📞 01583-441263 Fax 01583-441216
Open 1 April-31 October 🛉 🚐 🚏

Peaceful park, superb sandy beach, magnificent scenery, set in an area of outstanding beauty. Opposite Isle of Gigha. 12 caravans for hire (own WCs).
Size 15 acres, 69 static caravans, 7 🚿, 17 WCs, 2 CWPs
£ car/tent £8-£10, car/caravan £9-£12, motorhome £8-£12, motorbike/tent £5-£9
Rental 🚐 £125-£295
💳 Visa
🚻 🚿¼ 🔲 📞 🗐 🗼 Calor Gaz ♿ 🐕 WS
➡ From Tarbert travel S on A83 for 17 miles, then right to site (in ½ mile).

TARBET Dunbartonshire   12C1

Loch Lomond Holiday Park
Inveruglas, Tarbet G83 7DW
📞 01301-704224 Fax 01301-704206
Open March-October, December-January 🚐 🚏

Beautiful lochside location, ideally situated for touring, hill walking, water sports etc.
Size 13 acres, 18 touring pitches, 18 with electric hookup, 18 level pitches, 72 static caravans, 5 🚿, 7 WCs, 2 CWPs
£ car/caravan £6.50-£12, motorhome £6.50-£12
Rental 🚐 £135-£310, chalets £180-£625

💳 MasterCard Visa
🚻 ✕¼ 🔲 📞 🍴 🗐 📺 🗼 Calor Gaz ♿ 🐕
Last arrival time: 21:00
➡ 3 miles N of Tarbet on A82.

ULLAPOOL Ross-shire   14C2

Ardmair Point Caravan Site
Ullapool IV26 2TN
📞 01854-612054 Fax 01854-612757
Open Easter-September 🛉 🚐 🚏

Beautiful quiet location with pitches having outstanding views over the Summer Isles, some sheltered pitches. Award winning facilities, boat rental, fishing all available on site.
Size 9 acres, 54 touring pitches, 54 with electric hookup, 54 level pitches, 12 🚿, 22 WCs, 1 CWP
£ car/tent £8, car/caravan £8, motorhome £8, motorbike/tent £8
Rental Chalet from £170 p.w., £100 3 nights
💳 MasterCard Visa
🚻 ✕ 🗣 🗐 🗼 🔲 Calor Gaz ♿ 🐕
Last arrival time: 22:00
➡ 3½ miles N of Ullapool on A835, enter park at beach telephone box.

Broomfield Holiday Park
Shore Street, Ullapool IV26 2SX
📞 01854-612020
Open April-September 🛉 🚐 🚏

Whithorn

Broomfield is located within Ullapool on the seafront. An ideal base for golfing, fishing, hill walking, boat cruises and pony trekking. Famous for island sunsets.
Size 11 acres, 140 touring pitches, 96 with electric hookup, 140 level pitches, 18, 40 WCs, 2 CWPs
£ car/tent £8-£10, car/caravan £8-£10, motorhome £9, motorbike/tent £6
¼ ¼ ¼ Calor Gaz
Last arrival time: flexible
➡ Drive along Shore Street, second right past harbour.

WHITHORN Wigtownshire   12C4

Burrowhead Holiday Village
Isle of Whithorn, Newton Stewart DG8 8JB
📞 01988-500252 Fax 01988-500855
Open 1 March-31 October

Ideal family park boasting indoor leisure complex, with swim, spa and sauna, outdoor pool, pitch & putt, fishing, children's play areas, plus Headland Bar with seasonal entertainment.
Size 100 acres, 40 touring pitches, 40 with electric hookup, 40 level pitches, 180 static caravans, 6, 12 WCs, 2 CWPs
£ car/tent £7.50-£9.50, car/caravan £7.50-£9.50, motorhome £7.50-£9.50, motorbike/tent £7.50-£9.50
Rental Chalet. Enquire with park
Calor
Last arrival time: flexible
➡ A746, A750, just before Isle of Whithorn village right. 2 miles to Burrow Head.

SCOTLAND

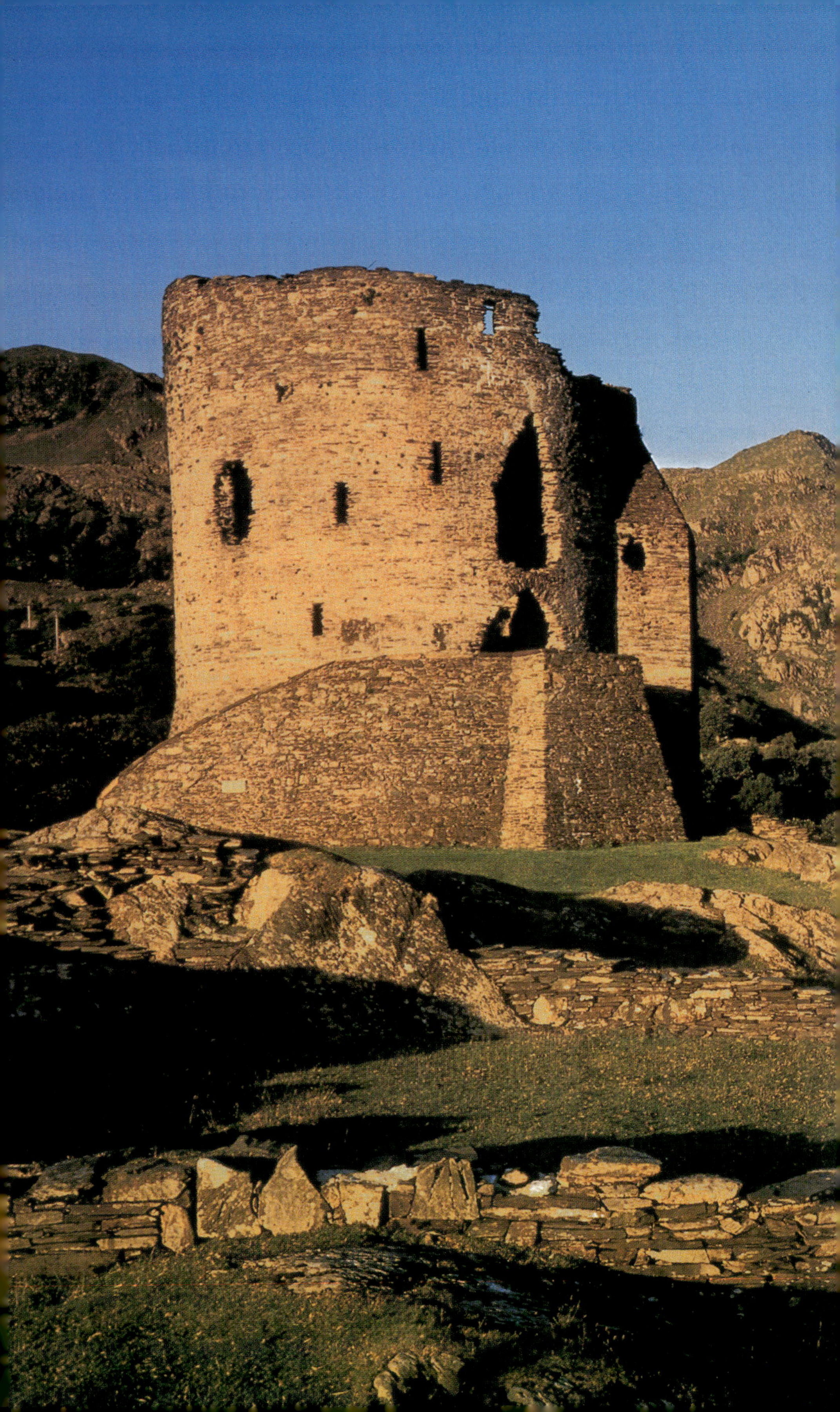

Wales

200   Abergele

ABERGELE Conwy   6C1

Henllys Farm
Towyn, Abergele
☎ 01745-351208 Fax 01745-351208
Open 1 April-15 October

A family run park overlooking open farmland, and near to the attractions of the town and Rhyl. Ideally located for touring North Wales.
Size 11 acres, 280 touring pitches, 280 with electric hookup, 280 level pitches, 19 🚿, 50 WCs, 1 CWP
£ car/tent £8.50-£9.50, car/caravan £9-£11.50
Calor Gaz
Last arrival time: 21:00
➡ Turn off A55 at Towyn, follow signs to crossroads and village. Turn off just past church.

ABERPORTH Ceredigion   6B3

Llety Caravan Park
Tresaith, Aberporth, Cardigan SA43 2ED
☎ 01239-810354 Fax 01239-811731
Open 1 March-31 October

This family run park is only five minutes walk from the beach, shop, restaurant and local inn. An ideal location with panoramic views of Cardigan Bay.
Size 12 acres, 40 touring pitches, 30 with electric hookup, 20 level pitches, 80 static caravans, 5 🚿, 18 WCs, 1 CWP
£ car/tent £7-£9.50, car/caravan £7-£9.50, motorhome £7-£9.50, motorbike/tent £7-£9.50
Calor Gaz WS
Last arrival time: 21:00
➡ Turn off A487 towards Aberporth along B4333. Take coastal road towards Tresaith where park is situated ½ mile on left.

ABERSOCH Gwynedd   6B2

Bryn Cethin Bach Caravan Park
Lon Garmon, Abersoch LL53 7UL
☎ 01758-712719
Open March-October
Size 22 acres, 15 touring pitches, 15 with electric hookup, 14 level pitches, 53 static caravans, 6 🚿, 7 WCs, 1 CWP
£ car/caravan £9-£11, motorhome £9-£11
Calor
Last arrival time: 18:00
➡ A499 to Abersoch. At Land & Sea Garage fork right - Bryn Cethin Bach ½ mile up hill on right.

Sea View Camping & Caravan Park
Sarn Bach, Abersoch LL53 7ET
☎ 01758-712052 Fax 01758-713243
Open April-October

Family site with magnificent views overlooking Abersoch harbour. Short walk down to quiet beach. Hook ups.
Size 4 acres, 60 touring pitches, 20 with electric hookup, 40 level pitches, 9 🚿, 9 WCs, 1 CWP
£ car/tent £6-£7.50, car/caravan £7.50-£9, motorhome £7.50-£9, motorbike/tent £6-£7.50
⊂⊂ MasterCard Visa
WS
➡ 1 mile from Abersoch towards Sarn Bach. Turn left at crossroads in Sarn Bach. Site is 250 yards on right.

Tyn-Y-Mur Touring & Camping Site
Lon Garmon, Abersoch LL53 7UL
☎ 01758-713223
Open Easter-end September

Aberystwyth

This elevated park has superb views and sandy beaches nearby. Shop 5 minutes. Abersoch 10 minutes. Free hot water to all facilities. Children's play area.
Size 3.5 acres, 40 touring pitches, 40 with electric hookup, 40 level pitches, 16 🚿, 16 WCs, 1 CWP
£ car/tent £9, car/caravan £11, motorhome £11, motorbike/tent £8
♨¼ ✕¼ ☕¼ 🔌 🏪 🏠 Calor Gaz 🐕
Last arrival time: 23:00
➜ Turn sharp right at the Land & Sea Garage on approach to Abersoch. Site is then ½ mile on left.

ABERYSTWYTH Ceredigion   6B3

Glan y Mor Leisure Park
Clarach Bay, Aberystwyth SY23 3DT
📞 01970-828900 Fax 01970-828890
Open March-October ⛺ 🚐

Beach front location, surrounded by wooded hillsides. Ten-pin bowling alley, indoor swimming pool, jacuzzi, sauna, sunbeds, steam room and fitness gym. Licensed clubroom with family entertainment. Children's play areas and organised activities. Easy access to Aberystwyth and Mid Wales resorts and attractions.
Size 12 acres, 100 touring pitches, 40 with electric hookup, 75 level pitches, 160 static caravans, 14 🚿, 14 WCs, 2 CWPs
£ car/tent £7-£10, car/caravan £7-£12
CC MasterCard Visa
♨ ✕ ☕ 🔌 🏪 GR 🍴 🏠 🎣 ⛽ Calor Gaz ♿ WS
Last arrival time: 00:00
➜ Leave A487 at Bow Street where Clarach Bay is signposted. Follow signs for North Beach for 2 miles. Site entrance is at beach front.

Hints & Tips
Caravans are stolen from lay-bys and motorway service stations. Even if you are just stopping for a cup of tea or to stretch your legs make sure you secure your caravan.

Midfield Caravan Park
Southgate, Aberystwyth SY23 4DX
📞 01970-612542
Open April-October ⛺ 🚐 🚗

Our small family park is situated overlooking Aberystwyth and Cardigan Bay, just 1.5 miles from the town, on the A4120. Our part of Wales offers a wealth of things to see and do.
Size 6 acres, 75 touring pitches, 28 with electric hookup, 40 level pitches, 57 static caravans, 14 🚿, 12 WCs, 1 CWP
£ car/tent £8.50-£9, car/caravan £8.50-£9, motorhome £8.50-£9, motorbike/tent £8.50-£9, children £0.60
♨¼ ✕¼ ☕¼ 🔌 🏪 🏠 Calor Gaz ♿ 🐕
Last arrival time: 22:00
➜ 1½ miles SE of Aberystwyth on A4120 and 200 yards from junction with A4817.

Pengarreg Caravan Park
Llanrhystyd, Aberystwyth SY23 5JD
📞 01974-202247
Open 1 March-31 October ⛺ 🚐 🚗

Pleasantly situated on the seafront overlooking Cardigan Bay, 9 miles south of Aberystwyth. Amenities include free showers, shop, laundry, electric hook-ups, boating ramp, restaurant/club. 9 and 18 hole golf course within 1 mile. Excellent rates, SAE for details.
Size 75 touring pitches, 20 with electric hookup, 75 level pitches, 10 🚿, 20 WCs, 1 CWP
£ car/tent £4.50-£6.50, car/caravan £4.50-£6.50, motorhome £4.50-£6.50, motorbike/tent £4.50-£6.50
♨ ✕ ☕ 🏪 🍴 GR 🏠 Calor Gaz ♿ 🐕 WS
➜ At S end of Llanrhystyd on A487, turn W opposite Lloyd Motor garage. Site signposted.

WALES

Bala

BALA Gwynedd   6C2

Camping & Caravanning Club Site
Crynierth Caravan Park, Cefn-Ddwysarn, Bala LL23 7LN
📞 01678-530324
Open March-October 🏕 🚐 🚙
Size 4 acres, 50 touring pitches, 48 with electric hookup, 6 🚿, 14 WCs, 1 CWP
£ car/tent £11.50-£14.60, car/caravan £11.50-£14.60, motorhome £11.50-£14.60, motorbike/tent £11.50-£14.60, children £1.60
((MasterCard Visa
🛒 🛒¼ ✕¼ 🍴¼ 🍺 📞 ▶ 🎱 GR 🔥 TV ⚠ Calor ♿ 🐕 WS
Last arrival time: 23:00
➜ From A5 turn off onto A494 to Bala. Continue through villages of Bethel and Sarnau. Pass the signpost "Cefn-Dowysarn" for 100 yards. Turn right up lane just before red phone box, and site is 400 yards on left. There is a brown site signpost by phone box on A494.

Pen-y-Bont Touring & Camping Park
Llangynog Road, Bala LL23 7PH
📞 01678-520549 Fax 01678-520006
Open 1 April-31 October 🏕 🚐 🚙

Only a 10 minute walk from Bala on this family run, peaceful, picturesque park in unspoilt surroundings. New quality showers, spacious private vanity cubicles, parent room and disabled facilities. Dog walk, undercover dishwash area with laundry and shop.
Size 5 acres, 35 touring pitches, 35 with electric hookup, 30 level pitches, 9 🚿, 11 WCs, 1 CWP
£ car/tent £7.45-£8.45, car/caravan £8.45-£9.45, motorhome £7.95-£8.95, motorbike/tent £7.45-£8.45
((MasterCard Visa
🛒 🛒¼ ✕ ✕¼ 🍴 🍴¼ 🍺 📞 🔥 Calor ♿ 🐕 WS
Last arrival time: 00:00
➜ From main Bala road (A494), turn onto B4391. Site ¾ mile on right.
See advert on this page.

Pen-y-Garth Caravan & Camping Park
Rhos-y-Gwaliau, Bala LL23 7ES
📞 01678-520485 Fax 01678-520485
Open 1 March-31 October 🏕 🚐 🚙

Generous pitches, acres of space and a quiet, peaceful atmosphere in beautiful surroundings. Nine acres of recreation/picnic areas overlooking lake and town. In easy reach of numerous tourist attractions, Snowdon, coast etc. Modern WC/shower blocks, games room, Dragon Award holiday homes for hire. Bar meals.
Size 20 acres, 63 touring pitches, 35 with electric hookup, 58 level pitches, 54 static caravans, 9 🚿, 12 WCs, 1 CWP
£ car/tent £6.95-£8.25, car/caravan £6.95-£8.25, motorhome £6.95-£8.25, motorbike/tent £6.95-£8.25, children £1.50
Rental 🚐 £125-£265 weekly. Short breaks available.
🛒 ✕ 🍴 🍺 GR 🔥 ⚡ Calor Gaz ♿ 🐕
Last arrival time: 22:30
➜ Take B4391 Bala to Llangynog road. 1½ mile from Bala fork right at signpost to Lake Vyrnwy and Rhos-y-Gwaliau. Site entrance 600 yards on right.

Pen y Bont
The Lovely Little Park
TOURING & CAMPING PARK
Llangynog Road, Bala, Gwynedd LL23 7PH
Tel: 01678-520549 Fax: 01678-520006

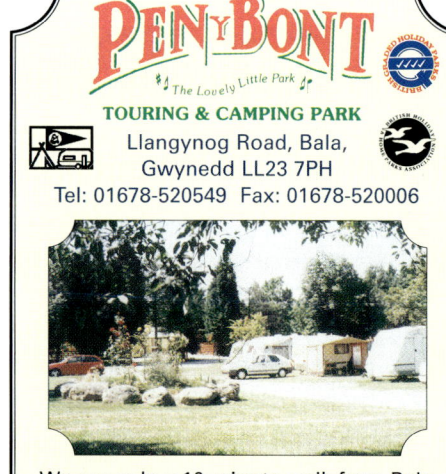

We are only a 10 minute walk from Bala on this family run, peaceful, picturesque park in unspoilt surroundings. Come and visit our **FREE NEW** quality showers, spacious private vanity cubicles, parent room and disabled facilities, dog walk, undercover dishwash area with laundry and shop.

Barmouth

BANGOR Gwynedd   6B1

Treborth Hall Farm Camping & Caravan
Trebroth Road, Bangor LL57 2RX
📞 01248-364399   Fax 01248-364333

Beautiful setting located between the Britannia Bridge and the Menai Suspension Bridge. Close to the Menai Straits. Touring site contained in old walled orchard.
Size 4 acres, 25 touring pitches, 25 with electric hookup, 100 level pitches, 4 static caravans, 8 🚿, 10 WCs, 2 CWPs
£ car/tent £4-£7, car/caravan £7, motorhome £7
Rental
¼ ¼ ¼ WS
➜ Turn off A55 dual carriageway just before crossing Britannia Bridge onto Anglesey. Turn onto A487 for Bangor, ¾ mile on left towards Bangor. Entrance to site signposted.

BARMOUTH Gwynedd   6C2

Benar Beach Camping & Touring Site
Tal-y-Bont, Barmouth LL43 2AR
📞 01341-247571   Fax 01341-247571
Open March-October

Picturesque park with spectacular scenery, within 100 yards from miles of golden sand dunes. An ideal friendly family site.
Size 9 acres, 155 touring pitches, 22 with electric hookup, 155 level pitches, 7 🚿, 8 WCs, 1 CWP
£ car/tent £4-£8, car/caravan £5-£12, motorhome £5-£12, motorbike/tent £3-£6
¼ ¼ ¼ Calor Gaz WS
Last arrival time: flexible
➜ 5 miles N of Barmouth, after Tal-y-Bont village, turn left by Llanddwywe church. Site is 100 yards from beach.

Hendre Mynach Touring Caravan & Camping
Llanaber Road, Barmouth LL42 1YR
📞 01341-280262   Fax 01341-280586
Open 1 March-30 November

Only 100 yards from a safe sandy beach, 15 minutes walk to the town centre, many mountain walks, courtesy bus to the local pub, games room, children's room
Size 10 acres, 60 touring pitches, 60 with electric hookup, 60 level pitches, 22 🚿, 22 WCs, 2 CWPs
£ car/tent £6-£8, car/caravan £7-£11, motorhome £6-£10, motorbike/tent £6-£9, children £1
⚃ MasterCard Visa
Calor Gaz
Last arrival time: 22:30
➜ ½ mile N of Barmouth on A496 Barmouth to Harlech road on seaward side.
See advert on this page

HENDRE MYNACH
CARAVAN PARK

Good clean facilities. Shop, off licence. Takeaway, café area, launderette, dishwashing, mother and baby room. Play area. Electric hookups. TV. Courtesy bus to the nearby pub with family room. Also many mountain walks. Good area for sea fishing and bird watching.

OPEN 1ST MARCH – 20TH NOVEMBER

**LLANABER, BARMOUTH,
GWYNEDD LL42 1YR
Tel: 01341 280262 Fax: 01341 280586**

WALES

Barmouth

Murmur-Yr-Afon Touring Caravan & Camping
Dyffryn Ardudwy LL44 2BE
☎ 01341-247353 Fax 01341-247353
Open March-October ▲ 🚐 🚛

Family run park set in tranquil surroundings, bordered by a trout stream and 20 minutes from the beach. Ideal base to explore the National Park. Most improved park in Wales 1997.
Size 4 acres, 37 touring pitches, 31 with electric hookup, 30 level pitches, 4 🚿, 6 WCs, 1 CWP
£ car/tent £5.50-£8.50, car/caravan £5.50-£8.50, motorhome £5.50-£8.50
♿¼ ✕¼ 🛒 🔌 📺 ⚠ Calor ♿ 🐕
Last arrival time: 23:00
➜ Take the A496 coast road from Barmouth-Harlech. Site is in Dyrffyn Village on right.

Parc Caerelwan
Talybont, Barmouth LL43 2AX
☎ 01341-247236 Fax 01341-247711
Open January-December
Size 7 acres, 150 static caravans, 3 🚿, 4 WCs
Rental 🚐 Chalet. £130-£337
℀ MasterCard Visa
♿ ✕¼ 🛒 🔌 📺 🏊 🎾 🎮 🏪 🍴 ⚠ Calor 🐕
Last arrival time: 22:00
➜ 5 miles N of Barmouth on A496 coast road. Turn left just before Talybont River bridge, down the lane, over the railway bridge, then first right.

BARRY Vale of Glamorgan	3D1

Vale Touring Caravan Park
Port Road (West), Barry
☎ 01446-719311
Open 1 March-29 December 🚐 🚛
Size 3 acres, 40 touring pitches, 15 with electric hookup, 40 level pitches, 4 🚿, 6 WCs, 1 CWP
£ car/caravan £7-£8, motorhome £7-£8, children £1-£1.50
♿¼ ✕¼ 🔌 📺 ⚠ Calor ♿ 🐕
➜ Follow A4226 Barry to St Athan. The park is on left 1½ miles out of Barry.

BEAUMARIS Anglesey	6C1

Kingsbridge Caravan Park
Llanfaes, Beaumaris LL58 8LR
☎ 01248-490636
Open March-October ▲ 🚐 🚛
Size 13 acres, 48 touring pitches, 25 with electric hookup, 40 level pitches, 29 static caravans, 6 🚿, 13 WCs, 2 CWPs
£ car/tent £5-£6, car/caravan £7.50-£10, motorhome £5-£6, motorbike/tent £5-£6, children £1.25-£1.50
Rental 🚐 £100-£260
♿ ♿¼ 🔌 📺 ⚠ Calor Gaz 🐕
➜ Through Beaumaris, past Castle for 1½ miles, turn left, park is 400 yards on right.

BEDDGELERT Gwynedd	6B1

Forestry Commission Beddgelert C & C Site
Beddgelert LL55 4UU
☎ 01766-890288
Open all year ▲ 🚐 🚛
Size 23.5 acres, 280 touring pitches, 105 with electric hookup, 100 level pitches, 17 🚿, 32 WCs, 2 CWPs
£ car/tent £7-£8, car/caravan £7-£8, motorhome £7-£8, motorbike/tent £7-£8, children £1.50-£2
℀ MasterCard Visa
♿ 🛒 🔌 📺 ⚠ Calor Gaz ♿ 🐕 WS
Last arrival time: 22:00
➜ 2 miles N of Beddgelert on A4085.

BENLLECH Anglesey	6B1

Plas Uchaf Caravan & Camping Park
Benllech Bay, Benllech LL74 8NU
☎ 01407-763012
Open March-October ▲ 🚐 🚛
Size 9 acres, 88 touring pitches, 75 with electric hookup, 75 level pitches, 25 static caravans, 6 🚿, 16 WCs, 2 CWPs
£ car/tent £6-£7, car/caravan £6-£7, motorhome £6-£7
♿¼ ✕¼ ♿¼ 🔌 🐕 ⚠ WS
Last arrival time: 22:00
➜ From A5025 take B5108. Site is signposted and is ½ mile from Benllech.

Ty Newydd Leisure Park
Llanbedrgoch, Benllech LL76 8TZ
☎ 01248-450677 Fax 01248-450711
Open March-October ▲ 🚐 🚛
Size 9 acres, 40 touring pitches, 40 with electric hookup, 40 level pitches, 61 static caravans, 4 🚿, 8 WCs, 1 CWP
£ car/tent £7-£18, car/caravan £7-£18, motorhome £7-£18, motorbike/tent £7-£18
Rental 🚐 £220-£350
℀ MasterCard Visa
♿ ✕ 🛒 🔌 📺 🏊 🎾 🎮 🏪 🍴 ⚠ 🍺 Calor Gaz ♿ 🐕 WS
Last arrival time: 00:00
➜ Take A5025 from Pentraeth. After ½ mile turn left at layby. Site is 1 mile on right.

Brecon

205

BORTH Ceredigion   6C3

Cambrian Coast Holiday Park
Ynyslas, Borth SY24 5JU
📞 01970-871233 Fax 01970-871124
Open March-October ▲ 🚐 🚍

'Excellence' graded park close to sandy beaches. Licensed clubroom with family entertainment. Children's activities include go-karts, bouncy castle and fun pool with water chute. Concessionary use of indoor swimming pool.
Size 12 acres, 75 touring pitches, 48 with electric hookup, 75 level pitches, 144 static caravans, 9 🚿, 9 WCs, 1 CWP
£ car/tent £7-£10, car/caravan £7-£12
Rental 🚐 £99-£419
ᴄᴄ MasterCard Visa
♨ ✕ 🍴 🛒 🔌 🎣 ⚡ 🛢 Calor Gaz ♿ WS
Last arrival time: 00:00
➡ From A487 N of Aberystwyth to Borth. Park entrance is on seafront road, 1 mile N of Borth village.

Glanlerry Caravan Park
Borth
📞 01970-871413
Open Easter-October ▲ 🚐 🚍

A small family-owned site, well sheltered with level pitches. The site is within easy walking distance of Borth, with its 3 miles of unspoilt sand.
Size 40 touring pitches, 40 with electric hookup, 40 level pitches, 6 🚿, 11 WCs, 1 CWP
£ car/tent £6.50-£6.75, car/caravan £7-£9, motorhome £6.50-£8
♨¼ ✕¼ 🍴¼ 🛒 🔌 ⚡ 🛢 Calor Gaz 🐕 WS
➡ 5 miles NE of Aberystwyth (A487), turn N on B4353. Site 2 miles.

Mill House Caravan & Camping Park
Dol-y-Bont, Borth SY24 5LX
📞 01970-871481
Open Easter-mid October ▲ 🚐 🚍

Select sheltered site beside a trout stream, with modern amenities. One mile from the seaside village of Borth, with sandy beaches, safe bathing and rock pools.
Size 8 acres, 16 touring pitches, 16 with electric hookup, 16 level pitches, 15 static caravans, 2 🚿, 5 WCs, 1 CWP
£ car/tent £8, car/caravan £8, motorhome £8
📞 🔌 Calor Gaz 🐕 WS
Last arrival time: 20:00
➡ From Borth to Aberyswyth B4353, 1 mile from Borth fork left by railway bridge and white railings into Dol-y-Bont village and follow signs.

BRECON Powys   7D4

Brynich Caravan Park
Brecon LD3 7SH
📞 01874-623325 Fax 01874-623325
Open Easter-October ▲ 🚐 🚍

Family-run site with panoramic views of Brecon Beacons. Well maintained, flat site with short grass, large pitches. Clean, modern shower facilities, free hot water, disabled & baby rooms. Adventure playground & dog exercise field.
Size 20 acres, 130 touring pitches, 106 with electric hookup, 120 level pitches, 18 🚿, 24 WCs, 3 CWPs
£ car/tent £8-£9, car/caravan £8-£9, motorhome £8-£9, motorbike/tent £8-£9, children £1.25
ᴄᴄ MasterCard Visa
♨ 🛒 🔌 ⚡ Calor Gaz ♿ 🐕 WS
➡ 1 mile E of Brecon on A470 (Builth Wells), 200 yards from roundabout with A40 (Abergavenny).

WALES

Brecon

Llynfi Holiday Park
Llangorse Lake, Llangorse, Brecon LD3 7TR
01874-658283 Fax 01874-658575
Open April-October
Size 17 acres, 60 touring pitches, 40 with electric hookup, 60 level pitches, 100 static caravans, 8, 12 WCs, 2 CWPs
£ car/tent £7-£9, car/caravan £7-£9, motorhome £7-£9, motorbike/tent £7-£9, children £1.50-£2
¼ X¼ Calor Gaz WS
Last arrival time: 23:00
➜ Follow A40 via Bwlch to Llangorse Lake via B4560. From A438 via Talgarth on B4560.
See advert on this page

BRONLLYS Powys   7D4

Anchorage Caravan Park
Bronllys, near Brecon LD3 0LD
01874-711246
Open all year

A park with high standards and panoramic views of the Brecon National Park. Ideally situated for touring and walking in south and mid Wales.
Size 13 acres, 60 touring pitches, 40 with electric hookup, 25 level pitches, 8, 20 WCs, 1 CWP
£ car/tent £7, car/caravan £7, motorhome £7, motorbike/tent £7
¼ X¼ ¼ Calor Gaz WS
Last arrival time: 23:00
➜ On A438, 8 miles N of Brecon on the W side of Bronllys village.

Riverside International C & C Site
Talgarth, Bronllys, Near Brecon LD3 0HL
01874-711320 Fax 01874-712064
Open Easter-October

Well maintained, clean and friendly family run site, situated in the heart of Wales with panoramic views of the Black Mountains. Warm welcome assured.
Size 10 acres, 84 touring pitches, 78 with electric hookup, 84 level pitches, 12, 32 WCs, 2 CWPs
£ car/tent £8-£9, car/caravan £8-£9, motorhome £8-£9, motorbike/tent £8-£9, children £1-£1.20
¼ X Calor Gaz WS
Last arrival time: 23:00
➜ Situated on A479 between Bronllys and Talgarth, directly opposite Bronllys Castle.

BRYNSIENCYN Anglesey   6B1

Fron Caravan & Camping Site
Brynsiencyn, Llanfairpwllgwyngyll LL61 6TX
01248-430310 Fax 01248-430310
Open Easter-end September
Size 5 acres, 70 touring pitches, 50 with electric hookup, 60 level pitches, 8, 9 WCs, 1 CWP
£ car/tent £8, car/caravan £9, motorhome £8, motorbike/tent £7
Calor Gaz
Last arrival time: 23:00
➜ Leave Britannia Bridge at first sliproad signed A4080 Llanfairpwllgwynn, after 400 yards turn left again signed Brynsiencyn. Site is ½ mile on right after village.

LLYNFI HOLIDAY PARK

Llynfi is close to Llangorse Lake in the Valley between the Brecon Beacons and the Black Mountains. All facilities plus heated pool, club and slipway. Llynfi is an ideal place to stay when visiting either south or mid Wales.

**LLANGORSE LAKE,
BRECON, POWYS LD3 7TR
Tel: 01874 658 283
Fax: 01874 658 575**

Builth Wells

BRYNTEG Anglesey 6B1

Ad Astra Caravan Park
Brynteg, Nr Benllech LL78 7JH
☎ 01248-853283
Open 1 March-31 October

Quiet, secluded family run park with first class facilities. Best park in Wales runner up. Tourist board grade 5. Ideal for a quiet and peaceful holiday.
Size 3.5 acres, 12 touring pitches, 12 with electric hookup, 12 level pitches, 38 static caravans, 4 🚿, 8 WCs, 1 CWP
£ car/tent £5-£6, car/caravan £7.50-£10, motorhome £7.50-£9, motorbike/tent £6
Rental £175-£255
Calor WS
➜ 2 miles W of Benllech off B5108 (Brynteg), on B5110 (Llangefni) road.

Nant Newydd Caravan Park
Brynteg LL78 8JH
☎ 01248-852842
Open 1 March-31 October
Size 4 acres, 30 touring pitches, 30 with electric hookup, 30 level pitches, 83 static caravans, 8 🚿, 14 WCs, 3 CWPs
Calor Gaz WS
➜ After leaving Britannia Bridge take A5025 Amlwch-Benllech. Turn left at square, take B5108 towards Llangefni for 2 miles. At crossroads turn left on to B5110. Site 1 mile on right.

BUILTH WELLS Powys 6C3

FForest Fields Caravan & Camping Park
Hundred House, Builth Wells LD1 5RT
☎ 01982-570406 Fax 01982-570444
Open Easter-October

A beautiful, tranquil, family run site with no clubhouse or statics. Immaculately maintained facilities. Hill and farm walks direct from the site. Graded 4 ticks. Award for environmental excellence. 'A rare gem of a site'.
Size 7 acres, 60 touring pitches, 40 with electric hookup, 40 level pitches, 6 🚿, 8 WCs, 1 CWP
£ car/tent £5-£6.50, car/caravan £7.50, motorhome £6.50, motorbike/tent £5.50-£6.50
Calor Gaz WS
➜ 4 miles E of Builth Wells on A481.

Llewelyn Leisure Park
Cilmery, Builth Wells LD2 3NU
☎ 01982-552838 Fax 01982-551090
Open Easter-31 October

Customer comments - 'treated like royalty', 'friendly and relaxed atmosphere', 'comfortable and clean', 'peaceful with wonderful views'. Nearby fishing, golf, and theatre. Adjacent inn with meals. Bus and train services 100 yards.
Size 2.16 acres, 25 touring pitches, 18 with electric hookup, 10 level pitches, 30 static caravans, 2 🚿, 3 WCs, 2 CWPs
£ car/tent £5-£8, car/caravan £5-£9, motorhome £5-£9, motorbike/tent £4-£8
Rental Chalet. £49-£299.
℃ MasterCard Visa
Calor Gaz WS
Last arrival time: 22:30
➜ 2 miles W of Builth Wells on S side of A483 in Cilmery Village, adjacent to Prince Llewelyn inn/restaurant.

WALES

Caernarfon

CAERNARFON Gwynedd　　　　　　　　6B1

Bryn Gloch Caravan & Camping Park
Betws Garmon, Caernarfon LL54 7YY
☎ 01286-650216　Fax 01286-650216
Open all year

Clean and quiet award-winning site, just in Snowdonia National Park and on the banks of the River Gwyrcai. Splendid facilities in the area overlooked by the Snowdonia mountain ranges.
Size 12 acres, 150 touring pitches, 110 with electric hookup, 100 level pitches, 15 static caravans, 22, 31 WCs, 3 CWPs
£ car/tent £7.50-£8.50, car/caravan £7.50-£8.50, motorhome £7.50-£8.50, motorbike/tent £7.50-£8.50, children £1.50
Rental £100-£260
Calor Gaz
➜ On A4085 Caernarfon to Beddgelert road, 7 miles from Beddgelert on left, 5 miles from Caernarfon on right. Site entrance on main road.
See advert on this page

Dinlle Caravan Park
Dinas Dinlle, Caernarfon LL54 5TW
☎ 01286-830324　Fax 01286-831526
Open 1 March-31 October

With extremely good and well maintained facilities and touring pitches, particularly well spaced out on large areas of open grassland, this is an ideal site for discerning tourers.
Size 22 acres, 250 touring pitches, 150 with electric hookup, 250 level pitches, 138 static caravans, 25, 50 WCs, 2 CWPs
£ car/tent £5-£11, car/caravan £5-£11, motorhome £5-£11, motorbike/tent £5-£11
Rental £100-£500
CC MasterCard Visa
Calor Gaz WS
Last arrival time: 22:00
➜ A499 out of Caernarfon towards Pwhelli (4 miles), right for Dinas Dinlle & Caernarfon airport. Park on right.

Glan Gwna Holiday Park
Caeathro, Caernarfon LL55 2SG
☎ 01286-673456　Fax 01286-672322
Open Easter-September
Size 200 acres, 100 touring pitches, 80 with electric hookup, 120 static caravans, 7, 15 WCs, 1 CWP
£ car/tent £7-£14, car/caravan £7-£14, motorhome £7-£14, motorbike/tent £7
Rental Chalet.
Calor
Last arrival time: 23:00
➜ 1½ miles S of Caernarfon, off A4085.
See advert on opposite page

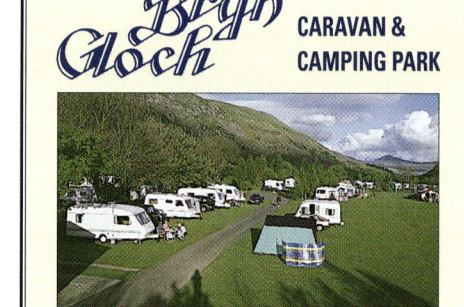

Bryn Gloch CARAVAN & CAMPING PARK

On A4085 Beddgelert to Caernarfon Road our 28 acre picturesque park is bounded partly by the river Gwyrfai in the Vale of Betws and is overlooked by the Welsh mountains of Myndd Mawr and Moel Eilio.
• LICENSED BAR & RESTAURANT • CHILDREN'S PLAY AREA • LUXURY TOILET & SHOWER BLOCKS • MOTHER/BABY ROOM • ELECTRIC HOOK-UPS • LAUNDERETTE • SHOP/OFF-LICENCE • GAMES ROOM • FISHING
Campsite of the year awards '91 & '92.
For further details send S.A.E. for brochure.
OPEN ALL YEAR (limited facilities in winter)

BETWS GARMON, NR. CAERNARFON, GWYNEDD LL54 7YY
Tel/Fax: (01286) 650216

Hints & Tips

Tiredness can kill. If you are planning a long journey make sure you plan some breaks.

GLAN GWNA
HOLIDAY PARK

Welcomes you to Snowdonia

Glan Gwna is an enchanting holiday village hidden amongst the woods and meadows of an old country estate. Within easy reach of historic castles, golden beaches, lakes, and breath-taking mountain walks.

Glan Gwna has many amenities including excellent Coarse and Game fishing on four lakes and the river Seiont, horse-riding on site, tennis court, heated (outdoor) swimming pool, clubhouse with live entertainment, and poolside bar with meals and takeaway.

SHOP • HAIRDRESSING SALON • LAUNDERETTE • GAMES ARCADE • COACH EXCURSIONS.

Excellent touring facilities for caravans, tents and motor homes, full time warden on site – dogs welcome. Super pitches available.

BOOKING ESSENTIAL BANK HOLIDAYS AND SUMMER MONTHS.

Directions to site:
1½ miles from Caernarfon on A4085.

For brochure and bookings phone or fax
CAEATHRO, NR. CAERNARFON, GWYNEDD, NORTH WALES LL55 2SG
Tel/Fax: Caernarfon (01286) 673456   Site Wardens: 676402

210

Caernarfon

Llyn-y-Gele Farm Caravan Park
Pontllyfni, Caernarfon LL54 5EL
☎ 01286-660283
Open Easter-31 October ▲ 🚐 🚙
Size 5 acres, 24 touring pitches, 6 with electric hookup, 6 level pitches, 24 static caravans, 2 ⛴, 7 WCs, 2 CWPs
£ car/tent £5-£6.50, car/caravan £7-£8, motorhome £5-£7.50, motorbike/tent £5-£6.50, children £1
¼ ⬜ ⛽ Calor ⚓ WS
➜ On A449, 7½ miles SW of Caernarfon.

Riverside Camping
Caer Glyddyn, Pontrug, Caernarfon LL5 2BB
☎ 01286-678781 Fax 01286-677223
Open Easter-October ▲ 🚐 🚙
Size 4.5 acres, 60 touring pitches, 8 with electric hookup, 60 level pitches, 4 ⛴, 8 WCs, 1 CWP
£ car/tent £5-£8, car/caravan £9-£12, motorhome £8-£11, motorbike/tent £5
¼ ✕¼ ¼ ⬜ ⛽ Gaz ♿ ⚓
➜ 2 miles E of Caernarfon on right side of Llanberis road A4086.

Tyn-yr-Onnen Mountain Farm C&C Park
Waunfawr, Caernarfon LL55 4AX
☎ 01286-650281 Fax 01286-650043
Open April-October ▲ 🚐 🚙

Welcome to a traditional upland farm, secluded and off the beaten track. Freedom to roam our beautiful hills, interesting walks, friendly animals. Immaculate facilities, free showers, toddlers bathroom, games and TV lounge. SAE for brochure.
Size 4 acres, 30 touring pitches, 30 with electric hookup, 20 level pitches, 3 static caravans, 6 ⛴, 6 WCs, 1 CWP
£ car/tent £7-£8, car/caravan £8-£9, motorhome £7-£8, motorbike/tent £6, children £1
Rental 🚐 Chalet.
㏄ MasterCard Visa
¼ ✕¼ ¼ ⬜ ⛽ 🅿 🎣 🎵 🎰 📺 ⛽ Calor Gaz ♿ ⚓ WS
Last arrival time: 22:00
➜ 4 miles from Caernarfon on A4085 turn left at Fish & Chip shop/Church. Site is signposted from there.

CARDIFF	3D1

Pontcanna Caravan Site
Pontcanna Fields, Cardiff CF1 9JL
☎ 01222-398362
Open March-October ▲ 🚐 🚙
Size 20 acres, 43 touring pitches, 43 with electric hookup, 43 level pitches, 8 ⛴, 10 WCs, 2 CWPs
£ car/tent £11.25, car/caravan £13.75
¼ ✕¼ ¼ ⬜ ⛽ Calor Gaz ♿ ⚓
➜ W of Cardiff city centre. Entrance on E side of A4119 Cathedral Road, via Sophia Close.

CARDIGAN Ceredigion	6B4

Bron Gwyn Mawr Farm Caravan & Camping
Penparc, Cardigan SA43 1SA
☎ 01239-613644 Fax 01239-613644
Open March-October ▲ 🚐 🚙

Small, select park, peacefully secluded in unspoilt countryside near the beautiful sandy beaches of Mwnt and Aberporth, and the quaint old market town of Cardigan. Ideal for walking, fishing, sight-seeing or relaxing.
Size 3 acres, 20 touring pitches, 15 with electric hookup, 20 level pitches, 3 static caravans, 1 ⛴, 4 WCs, 1 CWP
£ car/tent £5-£8, car/caravan £5-£8, motorhome £5-£8, motorbike/tent £5-£8
Rental 🚐 Chalet. £130-£320
¼ ✕¼ ⬜ ⛽ ⬜ 🅶🆁 🎰 📺 ⛽ ⚓
Last arrival time: 22:00
➜ From Cardigan take A487 towards Aberystwyth for 2½ miles. Turn left at crossroads in Penparc village signed Ferwig & Mwnt. Carry on over crossroads. Entrance is on right about ½ mile from main road.

CARMARTHEN Carmarthenshire	6B4

Pendine Sands Holiday Park
Carmarthen SA33 4NZ
☎ 01994-453398
Open March-October 🚐 🚙

A family run park adjacent to the famous Pendine beach, boasting a heated indoor pool and kids clubs in the wide range of leisure facilities. Restaurant and bar, excellent cabaret entertainment. A 'British Holidays Park'.
Size 26 touring pitches, 20 with electric hookup, 550 static caravans, 6 ☌, 16 WCs, 2 CWPs
CC MasterCard Visa
⚃ ⬤ ▦ ▣ ⅄ ▨ ⬠ ⛁ Gaz ⚹
Last arrival time: 23:45
➡ Take A40 trunk road from Carmarthen to St Clears. Pendine/Pentywyn is signposted to left along A4066, 8 miles from junction with A40. Pass through village of Laugharne and park reception is 5 miles further on right.

COLWYN BAY Conwy   6C1

Bron-Y-Wendon Caravan Park
Wern Road, Llanddulas, Colwyn Bay LL22 8HG
📞 01492-512903   Fax 01492-512903
Open 21 March-30 October ⛺ 🚐

An award winning park with truly outstanding facilities. Easily reached from the A55. All pitches have sea views. Awarded Wales Tourist Board 'Daffodil Award' for facilities and 'Welcome Host Gold Award' for excellence in customer care.
Size 8 acres, 130 touring pitches, 125 with electric hookup, 100 level pitches, 13 ☌, 31 WCs, 2 CWPs
£ car/caravan £8-£9, motorhome £8-£9, children £0.50
CC Visa
⚃¼ ✕¼ ⬤¼ ▣ 📞 ▦ ▣ ▣ TV ⛁ Calor ♿ ⚹
➡ Follow the A55 into North Wales and take the Llanddulas junction (A547). Then follow the tourist information signs to the park.

CONWY Conwy   6C1

Conwy Touring Park
Trefriw Road, Conwy LL32 8UX
📞 01492-592856   Fax 01492-580024
Open Easter-October ⚐ ⛺ 🚐

Set in spectacular scenery, the perfect location for touring Snowdonia and coastal resorts. Pitches from £4.85 per night. Special offers available.
Size 70 acres, 319 touring pitches, 270 with electric hookup, 300 level pitches, 50 ☌, 72 WCs, 7 CWPs
£ car/tent £4-£10.25, car/caravan £4.85-£10.25, motorhome £4.85-£10.25, motorbike/tent £4-£10.25
CC MasterCard Visa
⚃ ⬤¼ ▣ 📞 ▣ GR ⛁ ⬠ Calor Gaz ♿ ⚹
Last arrival time: 19:00
➡ Follow A55 to Conwy. Turn left at mini roundabout in front of Conwy Castle. Follow B5106 for 1½ miles. Look for sign on left.

CRICCIETH Gwynedd   6B2

Camping & Caravanning Club Site
Tyddyn Sianel, Llanystumdwy, Criccieth LL52 OLS
📞 01766-522855
Open March-November ⚐ ⛺ 🚐
Size 4 acres, 60 touring pitches, 45 with electric hookup, 6 ☌, 9 WCs, 1 CWP
£ car/tent £11.50-£14.60, car/caravan £11.50-£14.60, motorhome £11.50-£14.60, motorbike/tent £11.50-£14.60, children £1.60
CC MasterCard Visa
⚃ ⚃¼ ✕¼ ⬤¼ ▣ 📞 ▶ ▣ GR ▣ TV ⛁ Calor ♿ ⚹ WS
Last arrival time: 23:00
➡ From Criccieth take A497 W, take second on right.

Hints & Tips
In winter take your seat cushions home. Not only will they keep dry but a caravan without cushions is a less attractive prospect to thieves.

WALES

Llwyn Bugeilydd Farm
Criccieth LL52 0PN
☎ 01766-522235
Open March-31 October
Size 6 acres, 30 touring pitches, 30 with electric hookup, 30 level pitches, 6 🚿, 6 WCs, 1 CWP
£ car/tent £5-£6.50, car/caravan £7-£8.50, motorhome £7-£8.50, motorbike/tent £5-£6.50
Calor Gaz
➡ From A55 take A487 through Caernarfon, then just after Bryncir turn right onto B4411. Site 3½ miles on left. From Porthmadog along A497, turn right in Criccieth onto B4411, site 1 mile on right.

| CROSSKEYS Caerphilly | 3E1 |

Cwmcarn Forest Drive Campsite
Nant Carn Valley, Cwmcarn, Crosskeys NP1 7FA
☎ 01495-272001
Open March-November

Nestling on the banks of a stream and at the foot of a seven mile scenic drive, stands this picturesque campsite. Only 15 minutes from the M4.
Size 3 acres, 40 touring pitches, 30 with electric hookup, 30 level pitches, 6 🚿, 8 WCs, 1 CWP
£ car/tent £4.20-£6.70, car/caravan £6.60-£7.70, motorhome £6.60-£7.70
Last arrival time: 18:00

| FISHGUARD Pembrokeshire | 6A4 |

Fishguard Bay Caravan Park
Dinas Cross, Fishguard SA42 0YD
☎ 01348-811415 Fax 01348-811425
Open 1 March-10 January

Beautiful views and walks available from this secluded park on Pembrokeshire's Heritage Coast. Modern caravans equipped to a high standard.
Size 6 acres, 20 touring pitches, 20 with electric hookup, 20 level pitches, 50 static caravans, 4 🚿, 10 WCs, 1 CWP
£ car/tent £6.75-£8.75, car/caravan £7.75-£9.75, motorhome £7.75-£9.75, motorbike/tent £6-£7
Rental £125-£320
cc MasterCard Visa
Calor Gaz WS
➡ Take A487 out of Fishguard towards Cardigan, clearly signposted on right hand side. Take the turning on the left hand side.

| HAVERFORDWEST Pembrokeshire | 6A4 |

Redlands Touring Caravan Park
Little Haven, Haverfordwest SA62 3SJ
☎ 01437-781300 Fax 01437-781093
Open Easter-end October

Park set in six, mainly level, acres with lush grass and trees. Pitches are spacious, some with sea views. Beautifully kept utility block and grounds.
Size 5 acres, 64 touring pitches, 53 with electric hookup, 64 level pitches, 4 🚿, 10 WCs, 1 CWP
£ car/tent £5-£6, car/caravan £7-£8, motorhome £7-£8
cc MasterCard Visa
➡ 6½ miles W of Haverfordwest take B4327 Dale road. Site on right. Do not approach via Broad Haven.

South Cockett Caravan & Camping Park
Broadway, Little Haven, Haverfordwest SA62 3TU
☎ 01437-781296 Fax 01437-781296
Open Easter-October
Size 6 acres, 70 touring pitches, 60 with electric hookup, 70 level pitches, 6 🚿, 12 WCs, 3 CWPs
£ car/tent £5-£5.50, car/caravan £5.25-£7.20, motorhome £4.75-£6.70, motorbike/tent £4.50-£5.50
Rental price on application
Calor Gaz WS
Last arrival time: 23:00
➡ From Haverfordwest take B4341 signed Broad Haven for 4¼ miles, then left signposted Milford Haven to site after 300 yards.

Llandovery

LAUGHARNE Carmarthenshire   6B4

Ants Hill Caravan & Camping Park
Laugharne, Carmarthen SA33 4QN
📞 01994-427293   Fax 01994-427293
Open Easter-31 October ▲ 🚐 🚛

Situated in Dylan Thomas country and ideal for inland and coastal touring. Near the famous Pendine sands.
Size 9 acres, 60 touring pitches, 50 with electric hookup, 60 level pitches, 60 static caravans, 8 🚿, 20 WCs, 1 CWP
£ car/tent £6-£10, car/caravan £8-£15, motorhome £8-£11, motorbike/tent £6-£10
Rental 🚐 £120-£300
♨ ♨¼ ✕¼ 🍴 🍴¼ 🔥 📞 📅 ⚡ GR ⚠ ⛽ Calor WS
Last arrival time: 22:30
➡ M4 to Carmarthen, A40 towards St Clears. A4066 for Laugharne. Take first left turning before signpost of Laugharne.

LLANBRYNMAIR Powys   6C2

Cringoed Caravan and Camping Park
Llanbrynmair SY19 7DR
📞 01650-521237
Open 1st April-31 October ▲ 🚐 🚛

Cringoed is a quiet site on the river with beautiful views of the soft mid Wales countryside. Ideal for walks, bird-watching, lakes and coasts.
Size 10 acres, 50 touring pitches, 30 with electric hookup, 20 static caravans, 4 🚿, 6 WCs, 1 CWP
£ car/tent £6.50, car/caravan £6.50, motorhome £6.50, motorbike/tent £6.50, children £0.50
Rental 🚐
🔥 📞 Calor ♿ 🐕 WS
Last arrival time: 24 hours
➡ Turn off A470 at Llanbrynmair on B4518 for 1 mile.

LLANDOVERY Carmarthenshire   6C4

Camping & Caravanning Club Site
Rhandirmwyn, Llandovery SA20 0NT
📞 01550-760257
Open March-November ▲ 🚐 🚛
Size 11 acres, 90 touring pitches, 49 with electric hookup, 6 🚿, 9 WCs, 1 CWP
£ car/tent £11.50-£14.60, car/caravan £11.50-£14.60, motorhome £11.50-£14.60, motorbike/tent £11.50-£14.60, children £1.60
CC MasterCard Visa
♨ ♨¼ ✕¼ 🍴¼ 🔥 📞 📅 ⚡ GR ⚠ ⛽ Calor ♿ 🐕 WS
Last arrival time: 23:00
➡ From Llandovery take the A483 left signposted Rhandirmwyn, left at post office, site is on left before river.

Erwlon Caravan & Camping Park
Llandovery SA20 0RD
📞 01550-720330
Open all year ▲ 🚐 🚛
Size 8 acres, 40 touring pitches, 15 with electric hookup, 40 level pitches, 4 static caravans, 6 🚿, 14 WCs, 2 CWPs
£ car/tent £5-£9, car/caravan £5-£9, motorhome £5-£9, motorbike/tent £5-£9
♨¼ ✕¼ 🍴¼ 🔥 📞 📅 ⛽ Calor ♿ 🐕 WS
Last arrival time: 23:30
➡ Beside A40 between Brecon and Llandovery, ½ mile from Llandovery.

Maesbach Caravan Park
Ffarmers, Llanwrda SA19 8EX
📞 01558-650650
Open March-October ▲ 🚐 🚛

Open views of rural Wales. Ideal centre for bird watching, pony trekking and visit to local gold mine. Good pub foor nearby.
Size 4.5 acres, 20 touring pitches, 20 with electric hookup, 10 level pitches, 3 static caravans, 2 🚿, 5 WCs, 1 CWP
£ car/tent £5.50-£9, car/caravan £5.50-£9, motorhome £5.50-£9, motorbike/tent £5.50-£9
Rental 🚐 £80-£150
♨ 🔥 📅 Calor ♿ 🐕
➡ 1¾ miles NW of Pumpsaint (A482), turn N for 1½ miles to Farmers. Turn right opposite Drovers Arms. Site ¾ mile.

WALES

Llandrindod Wells

LLANDRINDOD WELLS Powys	6C3

Disserth Caravan Park
Disserth, Howey, Llandrindod Wells LD1 6NL
01597-860277 Fax 01597-860277
Open March-October
Size 3.5 acres, 40 touring pitches, 40 with electric hookup, 40 level pitches, 19 static caravans, 6, 8 WCs, 1 CWP
£ car/tent £6.50-£7.75, car/caravan £6.50-£7.75, motorhome £6.50-£7.75, motorbike/tent £6.50-£7.75, children £0.95
Rental £100-£275
cc MasterCard Visa
Calor Gaz WS
Last arrival time: 22:30
→ Just 1 mile off A483 (Llandrindod Wells-Builth Wells road), follow signs for Disserth. Park alongside 13th century church and River Ithon.

Park Motel Caravan & Camping Park
Rhayader Road, Crossgates, Llandrindod Wells LD1 6RF
01597-851201 Fax 01597-851201
Open 1 March-31 October
Size 3 acres, 15 touring pitches, 5 with electric hookup, 15 level pitches, 15 static caravans, 2, 4 WCs, 1 CWP
£ car/tent £6-£7.50, car/caravan £6-£7.50, motorhome £6-£7.50, motorbike/tent £5-£7, children £1
Rental Chalet.
Calor Gaz WS
Last arrival time: 22:00
→ Situated on A44, ½ mile W of Crossgates (Rhayader) roundabout towards Rhayader, 3 miles N of Llandrindod Wells (A483).

LLANDYSUL Carmarthenshire	6B4

Camping & Caravanning Club Site
Llwynhelyg, Cross Inn, Llandysul SA44 6LW
01545-560029
Open March-November
Size 13.5 acres, 90 touring pitches, 57 with electric hookup, 6, 10 WCs, 1 CWP
£ car/tent £10.40-£13.60, car/caravan £10.40-£13.60, motorhome £10.40-£13.60, motorbike/tent £10.40-£13.60, children £1.50
cc MasterCard Visa
Calor WS
Last arrival time: 22:00
→ Turn left from A487 onto A486. After 2 miles, in village of Cross Inn, turn left after Penrhiwgated Arms Pub. Site is on right, in ¾ mile.

Rhydygalfe Caravan Park
Pontwelli, Llandysul SA44 5AP
01559-362738
Open all year

Size 3 acres, 30 touring pitches, 18 with electric hookup, 30 level pitches, 15 static caravans, 8, 6 WCs, 1 CWP
£ car/tent £4, car/caravan £6, motorhome £6, motorbike/tent £4
Rental
¼ ¼ ¼ Calor WS
→ On right of A486 (from Llandysul to Cardigan), ¼ mile SW of Llandysul.

LLANGADOG Carmarthenshire	6C4

Abermarlais Caravan Park
Llangadog SA19 9NG
01550-777868
Open 15 March-1 November
Size 16 acres, 88 touring pitches, 43 with electric hookup, 80 level pitches, 8, 14 WCs, 1 CWP
£ car/tent £7, car/caravan £7, motorhome £7, motorbike/tent £6.50, children £1
Calor Gaz WS
Last arrival time: 23:00
→ 7 miles W of Llandovery on A40 - site on right, or 7 miles E of Llandfield on A40 - site on left.

Cross Inn & Black Mountain Caravan Park
Llanddeusant, Llangadog SA19 9YG
01550-740621
Open all year

Small family site set in the beautiful Brecon Beacons National Park with glorious views. Great walking, fishing. Lots of history and wildlife.
Size 9 acres, 30 touring pitches, 22 with electric hookup, 10 static caravans, 2, 5 WCs, 1 CWP
£ car/tent £4-£6, car/caravan £6-£8, motorhome £6-£8, motorbike/tent £6-£8
Rental £120-£255 weekly. Short stays available.
Calor Gaz
→ Take A40 from Brecon towards Llandovery. At Trecastle turn left and carry on over open countryside for 9 miles to site on the left.

LLANGORSE Powys	7D4

Lakeside Caravan Park
Llangorse Lake, Llangorse LD3 7TR
01874-658226 Fax 01874-658430
Open April-October

Lligwy Bay

Size 14 acres, 50 touring pitches, 19 with electric hookup, 50 level pitches, 80 static caravans, 10 ⚿, 19 WCs, 2 CWPs
£ car/tent £6.50-£8.50, car/caravan £6.50-£8.50, motorhome £6.50-£8.50, motorbike/tent £6.50-£8.50, children £2
Rental £140-£190 per week
₢ MasterCard Visa
🚻 ✗ 🚿 🅿 🔌 ♿ Calor Gaz 🐕
Last arrival time: 21:00
➜ B4560 from A40 from S, B4560 from A438 from N.

LLANRWST Conwy 6C1

Bodnant Caravan Park
Nebo Road, Llanrwst LL26 0SD
☎ 01492-640248
Open 1 March-31 October ⛺ 🚐 🚍

A small quiet landscaped site for touring caravans and tents, and a winner of "Wales in Bloom" for 24 years. Centrally situated, near Llanrwst, for exploring the mountains and beaches of North Wales.
Size 4 acres, 54 touring pitches, 44 with electric hookup, 54 level pitches, 2 static caravans, 6 ⚿, 9 WCs, 1 CWP
£ car/tent £7.50-£9, car/caravan £7.50-£9, motorhome £7.50-£9, motorbike/tent £7.50-£9, children £1
Rental £175-£240, cottage £175-£240
🚻¼ ✗¼ 🚿¼ 🔌 Calor Gaz ♿ 🐕
Last arrival time: 23:00
➜ S of Llanrwst turn off A470 opposite Birmingham garage onto B5427, signposted Nebo. Site is by 30 mph sign.

Maenan Abbey Caravan Park
Maenan, Llanrwst
☎ 01492-660630
Open 1 March-31 October 🚐 🚍
Plenty of trees and shrubs at this pleasant site, children's play area. 7 chalets for hire (own WCs). Good touring centre within easy reach of all attractions. No motorcycles.

Size 7 acres, 36 touring pitches, 25 with electric hookup, 36 level pitches, 71 static caravans, 4 ⚿, 7 WCs, 1 CWP
£ car/caravan £4.50-£9, motorhome £4.50-£9
Rental Chalet from £100-£250
🔌 Calor
Last arrival time: 22:00
➜ 3 miles N of Llanrwst on A470, by Maenan Abbey Hotel.

Plas Meirion Caravan Park
Gower Road, Trefriw LL27 0RZ
☎ 01492-640247 Fax 01492-640247
Open March-October 🚐 🚍
Size 2 acres, 5 touring pitches, 5 with electric hookup, 5 level pitches, 26 static caravans, 2 ⚿, 5 WCs, 1 CWP
£ car/caravan £6.50-£9.50, motorhome £6.50-£9.50
Rental £100-£260
🚻¼ ✗¼ 🚿¼ 🅿 🔌 WS
Last arrival time: 22:30
➜ Site is in Trefriw, 1.5 miles from Llanrwst on B5106. Turn right directly opposite Trefriw woollen mill down Gower Road. Site is 200 yards on left.

LLIGWY BAY Anglesey 6B1

Tyddyn Isaf Camping & Caravan Site
Dulas, Lligwy Bay LL70 9PQ
☎ 01248-410203 Fax 01248-410667
Open March-October ⛺ 🚐 🚍
Size 16 acres, 80 touring pitches, 40 with electric hookup, 50 static caravans, 8 ⚿, 14 WCs, 2 CWPs
£ car/tent £8-£10, car/caravan £10-£11.50, motorhome £8-£10, motorbike/tent £8-£10, children £1
Rental £150-£320
🚻 ✗ 🚿 🅿 🔌 🏪 📺 ♿ Calor Gaz 🐕 WS
Last arrival time: 22:00
➜ Travel over Britannia Bridge onto Anglesey and take A5025 to Moelfre. Left at roundabout onto A5025 for 2 miles. At phonebox/craft shop at Brynrefail turn right and site is ½ mile on right.

Hints & Tips

If you have any information concerning caravan theft contact the confidential freephone Crimestoppers Line on 0800 555111.
You may be entitled to a reward and there is no need to give your name if you don't want to.

WALES

215

Manorbier

MANORBIER Pembrokeshire 2B1

Tudor Glen Caravan Park
Jameston, Manorbier SA70 7SS
01834-871417 Fax 01834-871832
Open March-October

A family run site in the Pembrokeshire National Park, midway between Tenby and Pembroke. Manorbier Beach is less than 1 mile away.
Size 6 acres, 30 touring pitches, 30 with electric hookup, 30 level pitches, 20 static caravans, 7 ⛌, 14 WCs, 1 CWP
£ car/tent £4.50-£7.50, car/caravan £5.50-£8.50, motorhome £5.50-£8.50, motorbike/tent £4.50-£7.50, children £1-£1.25
Rental £60-£365
Calor WS
Last arrival time: 22:00
➜ Off Tenby to Pembroke road (A4239). Entrance is as you enter village of Jameston on right side from Tenby direction.

MERTHYR TYDFIL Merthyr Tydfil 6C4

Grawen Farm Camping & Caravan Site
Cwm Taff, Cefn Coed, Merthyr Tydfil CF48 2HS
01685-723740 Fax 01685-723740
Open April-October
Size 4 acres, 50 touring pitches, 8 with electric hookup, 30 level pitches, 3 ⛌, 7 WCs, 1 CWP
£ car/tent £6-£7, car/caravan £7-£8, motorhome £6-£7, motorbike/tent £6-£6.50, children £0.50
CC MasterCard Visa
Calor WS
Last arrival time: 00:00
➜ Site on A470, ½ mile from village of Cefn Coed y-Cymmer.

NARBERTH Pembrokeshire 6B4

Noble Court Caravan Park
Redstone Road, Narberth SA67 7ES
01834-861191 Fax 01834-861484
Open March-November

A small, friendly site with touring, motorhomes and tent pitches, with electric hookup. Ideal touring centre - 6 miles from beaches and mountains, 4 miles from Oakwood Park.
Size 8 acres, 92 touring pitches, 92 with electric hookup, 92 level pitches, 60 static caravans, 12 ⛌, 15 WCs, 2 CWPs
£ car/tent £6-£8, car/caravan £6-£13.50, motorhome £8-£13.50, motorbike/tent £8-£13.50
CC MasterCard Visa
Calor Gaz WS
➜ ½ mile off A40 trunk road on B4313, within ½ mile of Narbeth.

NEW QUAY Ceredigion 6B3

Cei Bach Country Club
New Quay SA45 9SL
01545-580237 Fax 01545-580237
Open Easter-end September

Award winning site set in Cei Bach Bay. All modern facilities including bar, take-away, games room, ball and play park, launderette and shop (100 yards). New Quay 1½ miles.
Size 3.1 acres, 60 touring pitches, 50 with electric hookup, 20 level pitches, 6 ⛌, 12 WCs, 1 CWP
£ car/tent £6-£12.50, car/caravan £6-£12.50, motorhome £6-£12.50, motorbike/tent £6-£12.50
CC MasterCard Visa
Calor Gaz
Last arrival time: 22:00
➜ From Aberystwyth S on A487 for 25 miles, then right onto B4342 signed New Quay. Turn right at Cambrian Hotel and follow signs.

Oakdale

NEWCASTLE EMLYN Carmarthenshire 6B4

Afon Teifi Caravan & Camping Park
Pentre Cagal, Newcastle Emlyn SA38 9HT
☎ 01559-370532
Open all year
Size 23 acres, 110 touring pitches, 95 with electric hookup, 110 level pitches, 9, 16 WCs, 1 CWP
£ car/tent £6-£7, car/caravan £6-£7, motorhome £6-£7, motorbike/tent £5-£6
¼ ¼ ¼ Calor Gaz WS
➜ On A484 Carmarthen to Cardigan road, 2 miles E of Newcastle Emlyn. From M4 take A484.

NEWPORT Pembrokeshire 6A4

Llwyngwair Manor Holiday Park
Newport SA42 0LX
☎ 01239-820498
Open April-October

Set in 55 acres of beautiful parkland bounded by the River Nevern, renowned for fishing, in Pembrokeshire National Park. One mile from the Coastal Path.
Size 55 acres, 80 touring pitches, 54 with electric hookup, 80 level pitches, 100 static caravans, 6, 10 WCs, 1 CWP
£ car/tent £8-£10, car/caravan £9-£12, motorhome £9-£12, motorbike/tent £8-£10
Rental £90-£240, chalet £120-£270
CC MasterCard Visa
¼ Calor WS
Last arrival time: 22:00
➜ On main A487 coast road between Fishguard and Cardigan; 1 mile N of Newport.

OAKDALE Caerphilly 3D1

Pen-y-fan Caravan & Leisure Park
Manmoel Road, Oakdale NP2 0HY
☎ 01495-226636 Fax 01495-227778
Open all year

Size 42 acres, 50 touring pitches, 50 with electric hookup, 50 level pitches, 10 static caravans, 8, 14 WCs, 2 CWPs
£ car/tent £7, car/caravan £7, motorhome £7, motorbike/tent £7, children £2
CC MasterCard Visa
WS
➜ Leave M4 at junction 28 and take A467 to Crumlin, where left at traffic lights onto B4251 towards Oakdale. In 1¼ miles turn right and follow signs to Penyfan Pond. Fork left to site. This site is signposted.
See advert on this page

PEN-Y-FAN
CARAVAN & LEISURE PARK

A quiet level park with magnificent views of the surrounding countryside. An ideal base to visit the Welsh coastline, Brecon Beacons and Cardiff. All facilities of a very high standard. Warm welcome guaranteed.

MANMOEL ROAD, OAKDALE, CAERPHILLY NP2 0HY
Tel: 01495 226636 Fax: 01495 227778

Hints & Tips

Watch your speed. With a load on your back, acceleration will be slower. You will need more time and space for overtaking. Your combination is longer and wider than your car so you will need to take this into consideration before pulling out. Stopping distances will be longer so allow more space between the car in front as your speed increases.

WALES

Penmaenmawr

PENMAENMAWR Gwynedd 6C1

Woodlands Camping Park
Pendyffrnn Hall, Penmaenmawr LL34 6UF
☎ 01492-623219
Open Easter-end October

Situated in 96 acres of parkland/woodlands, a few minutes walk to the beach. Level sites, licensed club, launderette, hookups, showers, toilets. Central for touring North Wales.
Size 96 acres, 100 touring pitches, 40 with electric hookup, 100 level pitches, 16 WCs, 1 CWP
£ car/tent £6-£9, car/caravan £6-£11, motorhome £6-£9

Last arrival time: 21:00

➜ Off A55 between Conway-Penmaenmawr. Bypass Conway under river tunnel - approx. 1½ miles, further on A55 pass through another road tunnel, 100yds after the tunnel take first turn left, entrance fourth on left, signposted.

PENTRAETH Anglesey 6B1

Rhos Caravan Park
Pentraeth LL75 8DZ
☎ 01248-450214 Fax 01248-450214
Open March-October
Size 15 acres, 92 touring pitches, 70 with electric hookup, 92 level pitches, 66 static caravans, 12, 24 WCs, 2 CWPs
£ car/tent £5.50, car/caravan £6, motorhome £5.50, motorbike/tent £5.50, children £0.50
Rental

Calor Gaz

➜ 1 mile N of Penreath on A5025 - pass Bull Hotel, park on left.

PORT EYNON Swansea 2C1

Carreglwyd Camping & Caravan Park
Port Eynon, Swansea SA3 1NN
☎ 01792-390795 Fax 01792-390796
Open March-October

Beautifully situated alongside the sandy bay of Port Eynon, and an ideal base for exploring the magnificent Gower peninsula. Particularly suitable for families with young children.
Size 20 acres, 180 touring pitches, 16 with electric hookup, 100 level pitches, 16, 24 WCs, 1 CWP
£ car/tent £9, car/caravan £13, motorhome £9, motorbike/tent £9, children £0.50
cc MasterCard Visa

Calor Gaz

Last arrival time: 22:00

➜ Follow A4118 from Swansea to village of Port-Eynon (16 miles). Drive through car park to site entrance.

See advert on this page

Carreglwyd
CAMPING AND CARAVAN PARK

Carreglwyd is located in an idyllic position alongside the safe, sandy beach of Port-Eynon on the beautiful Gower peninsula. Campers have the freedom to choose their own pitch, whilst touring caravans are parked together in their own area with electrical hook-up points.
Facilities include hygienic toilet blocks, hot showers, full laundry equipment and a chemical disposal point. There is also a small shop at Reception.
OPEN – March to December.
180 touring pitches, 16 electrical hook-ups, 100 level pitches.
CAR & CARAVAN £12.00 (inc. awning & hook-up).
CAR & TENT from £7.50.

Port-Eynon, Gower, Swansea SA3 1NN
Tel: 01792 390795 Fax: 390796

Don't forget to mention the guide
When booking, please remember to tell the site that you chose it from RAC Camping & Caravanning 1999

219

Newpark Holiday Park
Port Eynon SA3 1NL
☎ 01792-390292 Fax 01792-391245
Open April-October

Striking scenic views overlooking the Bristol Channel. Camping on level plateaux, luxury bungalows for six with superb views.
Size 14 acres, 112 touring pitches, 112 with electric hookup, 80 level pitches, 10 ☗, 20 WCs, 2 CWPs
£ car/tent £8-£11, car/caravan £8-£15, motorhome £8-£15
Rental Chalets £130 - £310
CC MasterCard Visa
Calor Gaz WS
➡ M4 (jn 47), A4118 to Gower, turn left as the hill starts to descent into Port Eynon.
See advert on this page

PORTHCAWL Bridgend   3D1

Happy Valley Caravan Park
Wig Fach, Porthcawl CF32 0NG
☎ 01656-782144 Fax 01656-782146
Open 1 April-30 September

Licensed club with entertainment/shops. All facilities. Electric hook-ups for tourers. Situated on the Heritage Coast overlooking Newton Bay and Ogmore by Sea with panoramic views of the Bristol Channel coastline.
Size 100 touring pitches, 60 with electric hookup, 60 level pitches, 12 ☗, 18 WCs, 1 CWP
£ car/tent £6-£7, car/caravan £6-£7, motorhome £6-£7, motorbike/tent £6-£7
Rental
CC MasterCard Visa
Calor Gaz WS
Last arrival time: 21:00
➡ From A48 take A4106 Bridgend/Porthcawl road 1 mile to Wigfach, turning immediately on right.

PORTHMADOG Gwynedd   6B2

Black Rock Touring & Camping Park
Morfa Bychan, Porthmadog LL53 9LD
☎ 01766-513919
Open March-October

An ideal family park situated behind the dunes of Black Rock beach. The site offers high class facilities including showers and toilets.
Size 9 acres, 150 touring pitches, 40 with electric hookup, 150 level pitches, 18 ☗, 16 WCs, 1 CWP
£ car/tent £9.50, car/caravan £11.50, motorhome £9.50, motorbike/tent £9.50
Calor Gaz
Last arrival time: 22:30
➡ Cross tollgate at Porthmadog, turn left at Woolworths in High Street, and follow Morfa Bychan road to end. At beach entrance bear right to park.

WALES

NEWPARK
• HOLIDAY PARK •

Striking scenic views overlooking Bristol Channel.
Camping on level plateaux, luxury bungalows for 6 with superb views.

OPEN APRIL – OCTOBER

PORT-EYNON SA3 1NL
Tel: 01792-390292
Fax: 01792-391245

220

Porthmadog

Greenacres Holiday Park
Blackrock Sands, Morfa Bychan, Porthmadog LL49 9YB
☎ 01442-248668 Fax 01442-232459
Open March-October

A family holiday park with direct access to a lovely sandy beach, indoor pool, kids clubs, great live entertainment, bars and hot food. A 'British Holidays Park'.
Size 80 acres, 71 touring pitches, 61 with electric hookup, 71 level pitches, 180 static caravans, 10, 8 WCs, 1 CWP
£ car/caravan £6.50-£17, motorhome £6.50-£17, children £1.50
Rental
cc MasterCard Visa
Calor
Last arrival time: 23:00
➡ After arriving at toll bridge at Porthmadog, go along High Street and turn between Post Office and Woolworths towards Black Rock Sands, Greenacres is on road, the other side of small village of Morfa Bychan.

Tyddyn Llwyn Caravan Park & Camp Site
Morfa Bychan Road, Porthmadog LL49 9UR
☎ 01766-512205 Fax 01766-512205
Open 1 March-31 October

Situated in a delightful saucer-shaped valley with beautiful views across rural countryside. Within twenty minutes walk from town and close to beach, golf club and water sports.
Size 12 acres, 153 touring pitches, 65 with electric hookup, 50 level pitches, 53 static caravans, 14, 24 WCs, 3 CWPs
£ car/tent £6-£10, car/caravan £8-£12, motorhome £8-£12, motorbike/tent £6-£8, children £1
Calor Gaz
Last arrival time: 23:00
➡ From Porthmadog High Street turn by Woolworths towards Morfa Bychan. After passing sign to Borth-y-Gest only, signs for site on roadside at bottom of hill. Drive for park on right immediately opposite signs.

PRESTATYN Denbighshire	6C1

Nant Mill Touring Caravan Park
Nant Mill Farm, Prestatyn LL199L4
☎ 01745-852360
Open 1 April-15 October
Size 5 acres, 150 touring pitches, 92 with electric hookup, 150 level pitches, 4, 15 WCs, 1 CWP
£ car/tent £8.50-£10.50, car/caravan £8.50-£10.50, motorhome £8.50-£10.50, motorbike/tent £8.50, children £0.30
Calor Gaz
Last arrival time: 22:30
➡ ½ mile E of Prestatyn on A548 coast road. Site is close to junction with A547.

PWLLHELI Gwynedd	6B2

Henllys Newydd Farm Touring C & C Site
Llanbedrog, Pwllheli LL53 7RE
☎ 01758-740398 Fax 01758-740398
Open 1 March-31 October
Size 1 acre, 10 touring pitches, 10 with electric hookup, 6 level pitches, 2, 2 WCs, 1 CWP
£ car/tent £4-£6, car/caravan £7, motorhome £7, motorbike/tent £4-£6
Last arrival time: 21:00
➡ Take first on right after Ship Inn to Llanbedrog. Map ref. is E316 N317.

Refail Caravan & Camping Site
Refail, Llanbedrog, Pwllheli LL53 7NP
☎ 01758-740511
Open Easter-end September
Size 2 acres, 33 touring pitches, 27 with electric hookup, 27 level pitches, 6, 6 WCs, 1 CWP
£ car/tent £6-£9, car/caravan £8-£9, motorhome £8-£9, motorbike/tent £6-£7
Calor Gaz WS
➡ Take A499 from Pwllheli. Turn right in Llanbedrog onto B4413 (signposted Llanbedrog Village & Aberdaron). Park is 200 yards on right.

RHOSSILI West Glamorgan	2C1

Pitton Cross Caravan Park
Swansea SA3 1PH
☎ 01792-390573 Fax 01792-391010
Open 1 April-31 October

Swansea

Size 6 acres, 100 touring pitches, 50 with electric hookup, 100 level pitches, 8, 12 WCs, 2 CWPs
£ car/tent £7.50, car/caravan £8-£10, motorhome £8-£9, motorbike/tent £7-£7.50
cc MasterCard Visa
Calor Gaz WS
Last arrival time: 21:00
➜ From A4118 turn right at Scurlage (from Swansea 16miles) onto B4247 signposted Rhossilli. Park is 2 miles on left.

ST DAVID'S Pembrokeshire 6A4

Caerfai Bay Caravan & Tent Park
Caerfai Bay, St David's SA62 6QT
01437-720274 Fax 01437-720274
Open 1 April-31 October

A quiet family run park, uniquely situated within the Pembrokeshire Coast National Park and just 200 yards of the sandy Caerfai Bay bathing beach. The site offers unsurpassed panoramic sea views of coastal scenery and St David's with its magnificent cathedral is only ¾ mile away.
Size 10 acres, 85 touring pitches, 46 with electric hookup, 40 level pitches, 33 static caravans, 7, 17 WCs, 2 CWPs
£ car/tent £5-£6, car/caravan £6-£11, motorhome £5-£6, motorbike/tent £5-£6, children £1
Rental £130-£320
¼ ¼ ¼ Calor Gaz
Last arrival time: 20:00
➜ Turn off A487 near Marine Life Centre and follow signs to Caerfai Bay. Entrance to park is at end of road on right.

Camping & Caravanning Club Site
Dwr Cwmdig, St David's SA62 6DW
01348-831376
Open March-September
Size 4 acres, 40 touring pitches, 24 with electric hookup, 4, 7 WCs, 1 CWP
£ car/tent £10.40-£13.60, car/caravan £10.40-£13.60, motorhome £10.40-£13.60, motorbike/tent £10.40-£13.60, children £1.50
cc MasterCard Visa
¼ ¼ ¼ Calor WS
Last arrival time: 23:00
➜ 4 miles N of St David's, off the coast road (A487) signposted to Fishguard.

Rhos-Y-Cribed
St David's SA62 6RR
01437-720336
Open all year
Size 6 acres, 5 touring pitches, 2, 4 WCs, 1 CWP
£ car/tent £3.50-£5, car/caravan £5.50-£6.50, motorhome £4-£5, motorbike/tent £3-£4, children £1.50
Last arrival time: 22:30
➜ Follow Porthclais road from St David's via Porthclais Harbour. Site signed.

SWANSEA 2C1

Riverside Caravan Park
Ynysforgan Farm, Morriston, Swansea SA6 6QL
01792-775587
Open all year

Flat, level, grassy site with hardstandings, alongside the River Tawe. Ideal base for touring all of Gower, the Mumbles, Swansea and the attractions of the Vale of Neath.
Size 7 acres, 120 touring pitches, 100 with electric hookup, 120 level pitches, 13, 15 WCs, 1 CWP
£ car/tent £7-£14, car/caravan £9-£14, motorhome £9-£14
cc MasterCard Visa
Calor Gaz WS
Last arrival time: 22:00
➜ 200 yards from junction 45 of M4 motorway.

Hints & Tips

If you have any information concerning caravan theft contact the confidential freephone Crimestoppers Line on 0800 555111.
You may be entitled to a reward and there is no need to give your name if you don't want to.

WALES

Tenby

TREFALUN PARK

Ideally situated between Tenby and Saundersfoot, Trefalun is a family-run park with excellent facilities, offering peace and tranquility in glorious countryside, yet only minutes drive from nearby resorts. Dragon award fully-serviced caravans for hire. Grassy level paddocks for tourers and tents with electric hookups and super pitches. Pets welcome.

Ring now for free colour brochure
FREEPHONE: 0500 655314

ST. FLORENCE, TENBY SA70 8RD
Tel: 01646 651514

TENBY Pembrokeshire   2B1

Kiln Park Holiday Park
Marsh Road, Tenby SA70 7RB
☎ 01834-844121 Fax 01834-845159
Open March-October

A family holiday park set amidst the beauty of the Pembrokeshire Coast National Park. Indoor/outdoor heated pools, kids clubs, tennis and bowling included in the wide range of leisure facilities, restaurants and bars, excellent cabaret entertainment. A 'British Holidays Park'.
Size 95 acres, 490 touring pitches, 115 with electric hookup, 490 level pitches, 620 static caravans, 20 ⚲, 47 WCs, 2 CWPs
£ car/tent £7-£10.50, car/caravan £7-£14, motorhome £7-£14
Rental
⊂⊂ MasterCard Visa
Calor Gaz

Last arrival time: 22:00
➡ Approaching Tenby, arrive at Kilgetty roundabout and follow A478 to Tenby for 6 miles. Follow signs to Penally/Pembrune. The park is ½ mile on left.

Trefalun Park
Devonshire Drive, Florence, Tenby SA70 8RH
☎ 01646-651514 Fax 01646-651746
Open March-October
Size 11 acres, 60 touring pitches, 40 with electric hookup, 60 level pitches, 10 static caravans, 6 ⚲, 9 WCs, 1 CWP
£ car/tent £5-£8, car/caravan £6-£10, motorhome £6-£10, motorbike/tent £5-£8, children £0.50
Rental £100-£330
⊂⊂ MasterCard Visa
Calor Gaz
Last arrival time: 20:00
➡ A477 Kilgetty to Sageston, turn left onto B4318. After 2 miles turn left opposite wildlife park, Trefalun second entrance on left.
See advert on this page

Well Park
Tenby SA70 8TL
☎ 01834-842179
Open 1 March-31 October
Size 11 acres, 80 touring pitches, 50 with electric hookup, 80 level pitches, 42 static caravans, 10 ⚲, 20 WCs, 1 CWP
£ car/tent £5-£9, car/caravan £6-£11, motorhome £6-£11, motorbike/tent £5-£9
Rental Chalet. £95-£360
Calor Gaz
Last arrival time: 22:30
➡ 1 mile before Tenby, on right side of A478.

Wood Park Caravans
New Hedges, Tenby SA70 8TL
☎ 01834-843414
Open April-September
Size 10 acres, 60 touring pitches, 30 with electric hookup, 24 level pitches, 90 static caravans, 6 ⚲, 14 WCs, 1 CWP
£ car/tent £4-£8.50, car/caravan £5-£10, motorhome £5-£10, motorbike/tent £4-£8.50
Rental £100-£355
Calor Gaz
Last arrival time:
➡ At roundabout 2 miles N of Tenby follow A478 towards Tenby. Take second right and right again.

TOWYN Clwyd   6C1

Ty Mawr Holiday Park
Towyn Road, Towyn LL22 9HG
☎ 01442-230300 Fax 01442-230368
Open April-October
Size 50 acres, 282 touring pitches, 162 with electric hookup, 282 level pitches, 464 static caravans, 28 ⚲, 56 WCs, 3 CWPs
Rental

Wrexham

CC MasterCard Visa
♀ ✕ ▼ ⊡ ⚙ ⊡ ⊠ ⊞ ⚠ ⚑ Calor ♿ ✈
Last arrival time: 24 hours
➤ Situated on the A548 between Rhyl and Abergele, ¼ mile W of Towyn.

TYWYN Gwynedd   6B2

Woodlands Holiday Park

Bryncrug, Tywyn LL36 9UH
☏ 01654-710471 Fax 01654-710100
Open Easter-end September 🚐 🚍

Within the Snowdonia National Park and now offering the latest hookup services including electric, water, TV and sewage disposal. On site country club.
Size 25 acres, 20 touring pitches, 20 with electric hookup, 20 level pitches, 122 static caravans, 2 ⚿, 4 WCs, 1 CWP
£ car/caravan £6–£7.50
Rental 🚐 Chalet. £90–£235 p.w.
✕ ▼ ⊡ ⚙ ⚘ ⊞ ⚙ ⊠ ⚠ ⚑ Calor ✈
➤ At Bryncrug, 18 miles S of Dolgellau and 2 miles N of Tywyn, turn E on B4405 for 1 mile to site on left.
See advert on this page

WREXHAM Wrexham   7D1

Camping & Caravanning Club Site

c/o the Racecourse, Bangor-Is-Y-Coed, Wrexham LL13 0DA
☏ 01978-781009
Open March-November 🅰 🚐 🚍
Size 6 acres, 100 touring pitches, 29 with electric hookup, 9 ⚿, 10 WCs, 1 CWP
£ car/tent £9.60–£12.10, car/caravan £9.60–£12.10, motorhome £9.60–£12.10, motorbike/tent £9.60–£12.10, children £1.50
CC MasterCard Visa
♀ ♀¼ ✕¼ ▼ ▼¼ ⊡ ⚙ ⊞ ⊠ ⊞ ⚙ ⊠ ⚠ ⚑ Calor ♿ ✈ WS
Last arrival time: 23:00
➤ From A525 follow the race course camping signs through village, looking out for Buck Hotel, turn left immediately opposite hotel (signposted race course), the site is approximately 1 mile along road on right.

Plassey Touring Caravan & Leisure Park

Eyton, Wrexham LL13 0SP
☏ 01978-780277 Fax 01978-780019
Open March-November 🅰 🚐 🚍

Set in beautiful countryside with level, grassy pitches and many amenities on site. Ideal for walking, fishing, golfing and touring North Wales.
Size 9 acres, 120 touring pitches, 80 with electric hookup, 120 level pitches, 10 ⚿, 20 WCs, 8 CWPs
£ car/tent £10.50–£12.50, car/caravan £10.50–£12.50, motorhome £10.50–£12.50
CC MasterCard Visa
♀ ✕ ▼ ⊡ ⚙ ⊡ ⊠ 🔊 ⊞ ⊞ ⊠ ⚙ ⊠ ⚠ ⚑ Calor Gaz ♿ ✈ WS
Last arrival time: 21:00
➤ Take A483 S of Wrexham. Follow brown and cream signs to Plassey at exit to B5426. Site 2½ miles on left.

WALES

WOODLANDS
Holiday Park & Country Club

Situated within the Snowdonia National Park, Woodlands offers good clean facilities on this well established site. Country Club, outdoor swimming pool, launderette, play area, amusements and high-season entertainment.

New in 1996 – full service hook-up points for electric, water, T.V. and mains sewage.

Three miles from the sandy beaches of Tywyn and surrounded by beautiful countryside.

Telephone for colour brochure: 01654 710471
Bryncrug, Tywyn, Gwynedd LL36 9UH

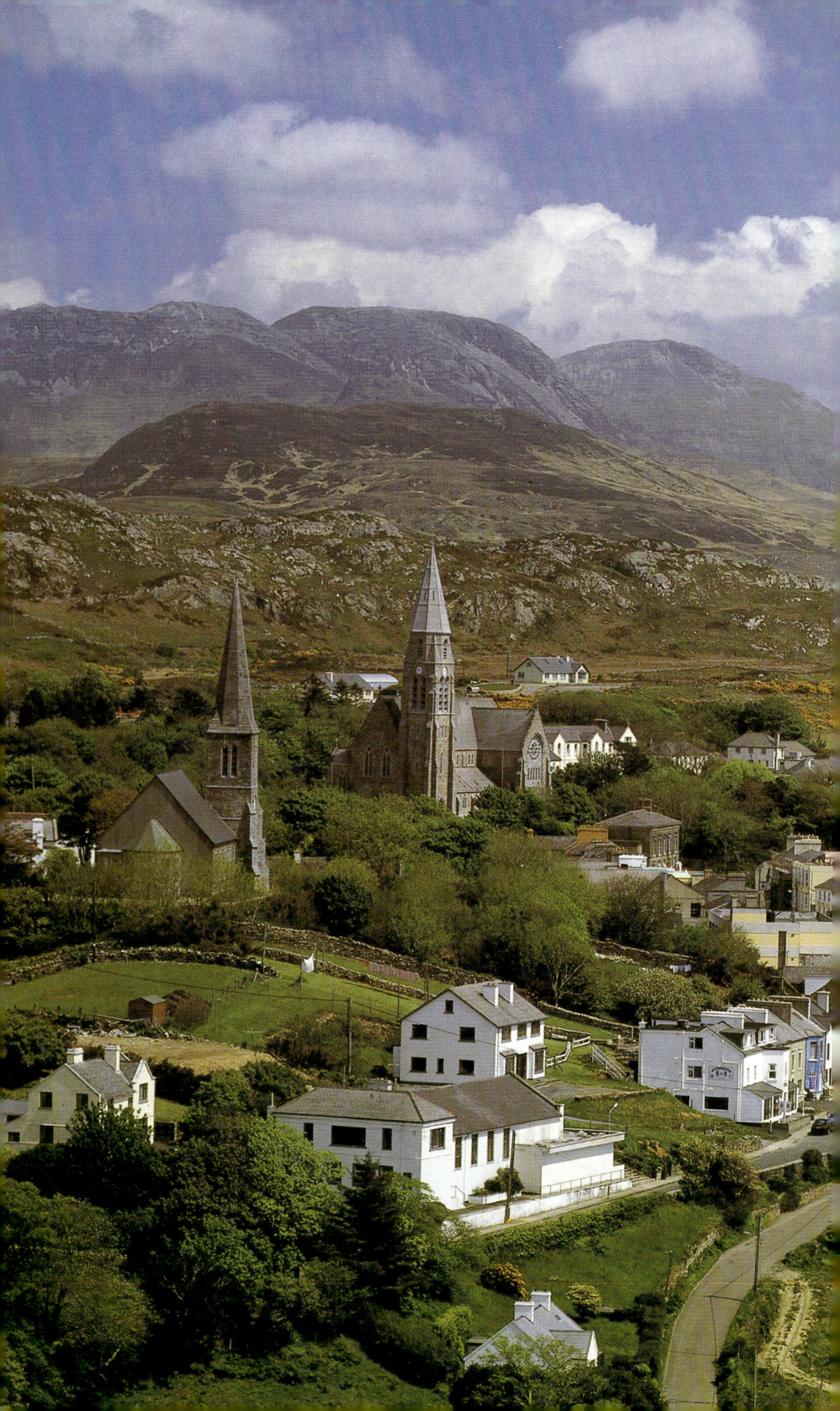

Northern Ireland and the Republic of Ireland

Northern Ireland

BALLYCASTLE Co. Antrim	17E1

Silvercliffs Holiday Village
Clare Road, Ballycastle
☎ 012657-62550
Open March-October 🅰 🚐 🚍
Size 2 acres, 50 touring pitches
⚃ ✕ 🍽 ♿
➡ Site is ½ mile to the NW of Ballycastle on B15.

CASTLEROCK Co. Londonderry	17E1

Castlerock Holiday Park
24 Sea Road, Castlerock
☎ 01265-848381
Open Easter-October 🅰 🚐 🚍
Size 13 acres, 15 touring pitches, 15 with electric hookup, 15 level pitches, 250 static caravans, 4 🚿, 14 WCs, 2 CWPs
£ car/tent £8-£10, car/caravan £8-£10, motorhome £8-£10, motorbike/tent £8-£10
Rental 🚐 £150-£300
⚃¼ ✕¼ 🍽 ☕¼ 📞 GR TV ⚠ Calor Gaz 🐕 WS
Last arrival time: 19:30
➡ 5 miles NW of Coleraine on B1119. Turn right at Thatched Cottage.

MAGHERY Co. Armagh	17E2

Maghery Caravan Park
Maghery
☎ 01762-322205 Fax 01762-347438
Open April-September 🅰 🚐 🚍

Situated on the southern shore of Lough Neagh, in the heart of Northern Ireland, the tranquil park offers wonderful views of Coney Island and Lough Neagh.
Size 30 acres, 9 touring pitches, 9 with electric hookup, 4 🚿, 7 WCs, 1 CWP
£ car/tent £5, car/caravan £6, motorhome £6
⚃¼ ✕ 📞 🔲 ♿ 🐕
Last arrival time: 17:00
➡ From M1 (junction 12) take B196 to Maghery and follow signs.

NEWTOWNABBEY Co. Antrim	17F2

Jordanstown Loughshore Park
Shore Road, Newtownabbey BT37 0ST
☎ 01232-868751 Fax 01232-365407
Open all year 🅰 🚐 🚍
Size 0.5 acre, 6 touring pitches, 6 with electric hookup, 6 level pitches, 2 🚿, 2 WCs, 1 CWP
£ car/tent £6.50, car/caravan £6.50, motorhome £6.50, motorbike/tent £6.50
⚃¼ ✕¼ 🍽¼ 📞 ♿ ⚠ 🐕
➡ 5 miles N of Belfast on Shore Road, A2 (Belfast to Carrickfergus road). Signposted on right between Whiteabbey village and University of Ulster.

Republic of Ireland

Prices shown are in Punts £IR

ACHILL ISLAND Co. Mayo 16A3

Keel Sandybanks Caravan & Camping Park
Keel, Achill Island
094-32054 Fax 094-32351
Open 29 May-4 September

Set in beautiful surroundings alongside the Blue Flag beach at Keel. Pubs, restaurants, bicycle hire, petrol station nearby. Mobile homes for hire. Cottages for hire beside park.
Size 14 acres, 80 touring pitches, 40 with electric hookup, 40 level pitches, 17 static caravans, 7, 15 WCs, 1 CWP
£ car/tent £5-£6.50, car/caravan £6-£8.50, motorhome £6-£8.50, motorbike/tent £5-£6.50
Rental Mobile homes £185-£270, cottages £180-£350

Last arrival time: 22:00
➜ Castlebar to Newport to Mulranny to Achill Sound, then R319. At western end of Sandybanks beside Keel village and adjacent to beach. Visable from road.

ATHLONE Co. Westmeath 16C4

Hodson Bay Caravan and Camping Park
Hodson Bay, Kiltoom, Athlone
0902-92448
Open 9 May-15 September
Size 2 acres, 34 touring pitches, 20 with electric hookup, 30 level pitches, 6, 9 WCs, 1 CWP
£ car/tent £8.50, car/caravan £9, motorhome £9, motorbike/tent £8, children £1

Calor Gaz
Last arrival time: 22:30
➜ From N6 take N61 for 2½ miles. Turn right and follow signs.

Lough Ree Caravan & Camping Park
Ballykeeran, Athlone
0902-78561 Fax 0902-77017
Open May-September

Set on 5 acres of wonderful countryside on the shores of Lough Ree. Visitors may enjoy the peace and tranquillity of this park with its own jetty and boat slip. Ideal for canoeists, golfers and anglers alike. Motor boats for hire on site.
Size 5 acres, 10 touring pitches, 10 with electric hookup, 10 level pitches, 2 static caravans, 4, 8 WCs, 1 CWP
Gaz
➜ 3 miles NE of Athlone on T31 (N55).

The Glebe Caravan & Camping Park
The Glebe, Clonfanlough, Clonmacmaise
0902-30277
Open Easter-October

Located 5 kilometres from Clonmacnoise, on a family owned farm, run under the rural enviromental protection scheme, in a beautiful unspoilt rural setting.
Size 8 acres, 35 touring pitches, 15 with electric hookup, 10 level pitches, 6, 7 WCs, 1 CWP
£ car/tent £7, car/caravan £9, motorhome £9, motorbike/tent £3

Last arrival time: 22:30
➜ Located 3 miles E of Clonmacnoise off the main Clonmacnoise Road, signposted - 1 mile in.

BANDON Co. Cork 18C4

Murrays Caravan & Camping Park
Kilbrogan Farm, Bandon
023-41232
Open 1 April-30 September
Size 2 acres, 19 touring pitches, 10 with electric hookup, 19 level pitches, 2, 6 WCs, 1 CWP
£ car/tent £5, car/caravan £5, motorhome £5, motorbike/tent £5, children £1
Calor Gaz
➜ Follow official signs from town.

Bantry

BANTRY Co. Cork	18B4

Eagle Point Caravan & Camping Site
Ballylickey, Bantry
📞 027-50630
Open 24 April-30 September

Located on a peninsula with direct access to safe pebble beaches suitable for all forms of water activities. Top standard amenities and central for touring.
Size 20 acres, 200 touring pitches, 150 with electric hookup, 200 level pitches, 24, 41 WCs, 3 CWPs
£ car/tent £10-£10.50, car/caravan £10-£10.50, motorhome £10-£10.50, motorbike/tent £8
MasterCard Visa
Last arrival time: 22:00
➡ Site is 4 miles N of Bantry on N71.

BENNETTSBRIDGE Co. Kilkenny	19E2

Nore Valley Park
Bennettsbridge
📞 056-27229 fax 056-27748
Open 1 March-31 October

Situated on a working and visitor farm overlooking the scenic River Nore valley. Home baked bread, scones and pies available. Irish breakfast June - August inclusive.
Size 3 acres, 70 touring pitches, 40 with electric hookup, 40 level pitches, 4 static caravans, 5, 10 WCs, 2 CWPs
£ car/tent £6.50-£9, car/caravan £9.50-£11, motorhome £8.50-£9, motorbike/tent £5, children £0.50
MasterCard Visa
Calor Gaz WS
Last arrival time: 22:00

➡ From Kilkenny take T20 (R700) to Bennettsbridge. Just before bridge turn right at sign to park.

BLARNEY Co. Cork	18C3

Blarney Caravan & Camping Park
Stone View, Blarney
📞 021-438 5167 fax 021-438 5167
Open all year

This spacious touring park is ideally located to explore the beautiful south of Ireland. Facilities include free showers, camper's kitchen, 18 hole golf and B&B on site.
Size 3 acres, 40 touring pitches, 39 with electric hookup, 401 level pitches, 4, 7 WCs, 1 CWP
£ car/tent £7-£8, car/caravan £8-£9, motorhome £8-£9, motorbike/tent £6-£7, children £0.50
Calor Gaz WS
Last arrival time: 23:00
➡ Take N20 from Cork or Limerick or N22 from Killarney and then R617 to Blarney.

BOYLE Co. Roscommon	16C3

Lough Key Caravan & Camping Park
Boyle
📞 079-62363 fax 01-676 8598
Open April-1 September

A well landscaped site in a 350 hectare forest park on the Shannon river system. Accessible by cruiser.
Size 13 acres, 72 touring pitches, 52 with electric hookup, 52 level pitches, 4, 12 WCs, 1 CWP
£ car/tent £7-£8, car/caravan £7.50-£8.50, motorbike/tent £3
Last arrival time: 21:00
➡ 10 km W of Carrick-on-Shannon, 6 km E of Boyle on N4.

Carrick-on-Suir 229

SHANNON HERITAGE

"A COMMON CELTIC PAST"
5000 YEARS OF MAGIC AND MYSTERY

8 EXCITING HERITAGE SITES
LOUGH GUR STONE AGE CENTRE
CRAGGAUNOWEN THE LIVING PAST
KILLALOE HERITAGE CENTRE
KING JOHN'S CASTLE
BUNRATTY CASTLE AND FOLK PARK
KNAPPOGUE CASTLE
CLIFFS OF MOHER
DUNGUAIRE CASTLE

5 WORLD FAMOUS EVENING ENTERTAINMENTS
BUNRATTY CASTLE - MEDIAEVAL BANQUET
KNAPPOGUE CASTLE - MEDIAEVAL BANQUET
BUNRATTY CEILI (TRADITIONAL IRISH NIGHT)
DUNGUAIRE CASTLE - MEDIAEVAL BANQUET
THE OFFICER'S CLUB - CASTLE LANE TAVERN
(CONTEMPORARY IRISH ENTERTAINMENT)

CENTRAL RESERVATIONS
BUNRATTY CASTLE & FOLK PARK
BUNRATTY, CO. CLARE IRELAND
TEL: 00353 61 360788 FAX: 00353 61 361020

CAHERDANIEL Co. Kerry 18A4

Wave Crest Caravan & Camping Park
Caherdaniel
📞 066-947 5188 Fax 066-947 5188
Open March-October
Size 4.5 acres, 45 touring pitches, 45 with electric hookup, 30 level pitches, 4 static caravans, 10, 11 WCs, 1 CWP
£ car/tent £8.50, car/caravan £8.50-£10.50, motorhome £8.50, motorbike/tent £7, children £0.50
MasterCard Visa
Calor Gaz WS
Last arrival time: 23:00
➤ From Kenmare take N70 SW for 30 miles. Site is on left just before Caherdaniel village.

CAPE CLEAR ISLAND Co. Cork 18B4

Cuas An Uisce
Cape Clear Island
📞 028-39119
Open June-end September
Size 4 acres, 20 touring pitches, 4, 4 WCs

➤ Take ferry from Baltimore to South Harbour, Cape Clear.

CARRICK-ON-SUIR Co. Waterford 19D3

Carrick-on-Suir C & C Park
Ballyrichard, Kilkenny Road, Carrick-on-Suir
📞 051-640461 Fax 051-640204

Town centre a 5 minute walk. Musical pubs, Tudor manor, river walks, the Magical Road. A fully-serviced site, central for the south east tour.
Size 2.5 acres, 30 touring pitches, 23 with electric hookup, 6 static caravans, 2, 5 WCs, 1 CWP
£ car/tent £6, car/caravan £9, motorhome £9, motorbike/tent £6, children £0.50
Rental £200-280, chalets £250-£300
Calor Gaz
Last arrival time: 23:00
➤ From Rosslare to Carrick. Through traffic lights, second turn right, under railway bridge sharp right, 200m on left to reception - Lonergans shop. Or: From Conmel to Carrick. First left after fire station, straight through next junction via Mart, under railway bridge, sharp right, 200m on left to reception.

REPUBLIC OF IRELAND

Clogheen

CLOGHEEN Co. Tipperary 19D3

Parsons Green Caravan & Camping Park
Clogheen
052-65290 Fax 052-65504
Open all year

Small, family run park with excellent on-site facilities. Centrally situated for touring the whole south of Ireland.
Size 3 acres, 20 touring pitches, 20 with electric hookup, 20 level pitches, 6, 9 WCs, 1 CWP
£ car/tent £8, car/caravan £8, motorhome £8, motorbike/tent £5-£7, children £1
Rental Chalet.

→ Nearest town Clogheen: take R668 from Cahir and Lismore or take R665 from Clonmel and Mitchels Town.

CLONAKILTY Co. Cork 18C4

Desert House Caravan & Camping Park
Ring Road, Clonakilty
023-33331 Fax 023-33048
Open Easter/May-October
Size 5 acres, 36 touring pitches, 14 level pitches, 5, 6 WCs, 1 CWP
£ car/tent £6, car/caravan £7, motorhome £8, motorbike/tent £6
MasterCard Visa
Last arrival time: 23:30

→ 1 mile SE of Clonakilty, off N71 Cork-Bandon-Clonakilty road, on road to Ring village.

DINGLE Co. Kerry 18A3

Ballintaggart House
Dingle
066-915 1454 Fax 066-915 2207
Open all year

Ballintaggart House, fully serviced caravan and camping site situated near Dingle town on the beautiful Dingle Peninsula. IRB approved with restaurant, hot showers, kitchen and eating area. Pets and families welcome.
Size 10 acres, 19 touring pitches, 15 with electric hookup, 19 level pitches, 5 static caravans, 8, 9 WCs, 1 CWP
£ car/tent £6-£7, car/caravan £8-£9, motorhome £8-£9, motorbike/tent £6-£7, children £1
MasterCard Visa
Last arrival time: 23:00

→ N86 Tralee to Dingle; on the right as you approach Dingle town.

Campail Theach An Aragail
Gallarus, Dingle
066-915 5143
Open 1 May-30 September
Size 2 acres, 36 touring pitches, 12 with electric hookup, 36 level pitches, 6, 10 WCs, 1 CWP
£ car/tent £7-£9, car/caravan £9, motorhome £9, motorbike/tent £7.70, children £1
Calor
Last arrival time: 21:00

→ 5 miles W of Dingle. Follow Gallarus Oratory signs.

DONARD Co. Wicklow 19F1

Moat Farm
Donard
045-404727 Fax 045-404727
Open all year

Select family run park. Secluded rural setting yet only a one minute walk from the village. Fully serviced. Ideal for relaxing or a base for touring, hill walking, mountain climbing. One hour from Dublin, 1½ hrs from Rosslare.

Dungarvan

Size 3 acres, 20 touring pitches, 20 with electric hookup, 20 level pitches, 7 🚿, 7 WCs, 1 CWP
£ car/tent £10, car/caravan £10, motorhome £10, motorbike/tent £8, children £0.50
🚐 ✕¼ 🛒¼ ▯ 📞 ▯ 📺 ⚠ Gaz ♿ 🐕 WS
Last arrival time: 00:00
➔ From Dun Laoghaire follow signs marked N4 and N7 then onto N81. 15 kms S of Blessington turn left at The Old Toll House pub. Park 2 kms from here.

DOOLIN Co. Clare   18B1

Nagle's Caravan & Camping Park
Doolin
📞 065-707 4458
Open 1 April-30 September 🅰 🚐 🚍
Size 4.5 acres, 62 touring pitches, 40 with electric hookup, 25 level pitches, 14 🚿, 13 WCs, 1 CWP
£ car/tent £7-£8, car/caravan £7-£8, motorhome £8, motorbike/tent £7, children £0.50
🚐 🚿¼ ✕¼ 🛒¼ ▯ 📞 ▯ Gaz ♿ 🐕
Last arrival time: 01:00
➔ From Lahinch take the L54.

DUBLIN Co. Dublin   19F1

Shankill Caravan & Camping Park
Shankill
📞 01-282 0011 Fax 01-282 0108
Open all year 🅰 🚐 🚍

Caravan park and camp site with lovely view of the Dublin mountains. Nearest caravan park to Stena Line and HSS fast ferry. 8 km from Dun Laoghaire car ferry terminal. 16 km south of Dublin city centre. 3 km from Bray and the sea.
Size 7 acres, 70 with electric hookup, 50 level pitches, 15 🚿, 20 WCs, 2 CWPs
£ car/tent £7-£8, car/caravan £7-£8, motorhome £7-£8, motorbike/tent £7-£8, children £0.50
Rental 🚐 Mobile homes £200 high season pw
🚐 ✕¼ 🛒¼ ▯ 📞 ▯ Gaz ♿ 🐕
➔ South on N11 Dublin/Wicklow/Wexford road. Direct bus from Dublin city centre and Dun Laoghaire car ferry terminal. Fast electric train service (DART) from Shankill station serving Dublin, Dun Laoghaire and Bray.

DUGORT Co. Mayo   16A3

Seal Caves Caravan Park
The Strand, Achill Island, Dugort
📞 098-43262
Open 1 April-30 September 🅰 🚐 🚍

Set in sheltered and scenic area beside safe bathing beach. Place of interest near by, deserted village colony settlement.
Size 1.5 acres, 30 touring pitches, 30 with electric hookup, 30 level pitches, 10 🚿, 16 WCs, 2 CWPs
£ car/tent £6.50-£7, car/caravan £6.50-£7, motorhome £6.50-£7, motorbike/tent £6.50-£7, children £0.50
🚐 ▯ 📞 ▯ 📺 ⚠ Gaz 🐕
Last arrival time: 22:30
➔ R319 from Achill Sound to Bunacurry junction, turn right on to valley crossroads, turn left, 4km to the site at Dugort Beach.

DUNGARVAN Co. Waterford   19D3

Casey's Caravan Park
Clonea, Dungarvan
📞 058-41919 Fax 058-41919
Open 2 May-7 September 🅰 🚐 🚍

Family run park adjacent to beaches and a hotel with a leisure centre. Many scenic drives are nearby.
Size 20 acres, 118 touring pitches, 83 with electric hookup, 284 level pitches, 166 static caravans, 18 🚿, 36 WCs, 2 CWPs
£ car/tent £10-£10.50, car/caravan £10-£10.50, motorhome £10-£10.50, motorbike/tent £8
🚐¼ ✕¼ 🛒¼ ▯ 📞 ▯ GR ▯ 📺 ⚠ Calor Gaz ♿ 🐕 WS
Last arrival time: 22:00
➔ 2½ miles off N25. ½ mile off R675.

REPUBLIC OF IRELAND

Kilkenny

KILKENNY Co. Kilkenny   19E2

Tree Grove Caravan & Camping Park
Danville House, Kilkenny
056-70302
Open 1st March-15th November
Size 2.5 acres, 30 touring pitches, 12 with electric hookup, 30 level pitches, 4, 6 WCs, 1 CWP
£ car/tent £7, car/caravan £8, motorhome £8, motorbike/tent £6

¼ ¼ Calor Gaz WS
→ 2 km from city centre past Kilkenny Castle on R700 after roundabout, in direction of New Ross.

KILLORGLIN Co. Kerry   18B3

West's Caravan Park
Killarney Road, Ring of Kerry, Killorglin
066-976 1240 Fax 066-976 1833
Open May-September

Family run site, where relaxing comes as naturally as the surrounding beauty. Wonderful central location. Luxury, mobile homes for hire. Ferry inclusive prices available.
Size 5 acres, 20 touring pitches, 12 with electric hookup, 20 level pitches, 40 static caravans, 4, 5 WCs,
£ car/tent £8, car/caravan £8, motorhome £8, motorbike/tent £7, children £0.50
Rental from £129
CC MasterCard Visa
Calor Gaz WS
→ On Ring of Kerry. At Killorglin bridge take Killarney road N72. Park is 1½ km from town on right.

KILRUSH Co. Clare   18B2

Aylevarroo Caravan Park
Kilrush
065-905 1102 Fax 065-905 1102
Open 1 May-12 September
Size 7.5 acres, 38 touring pitches, 24 with electric hookup, 38 level pitches, 6, 11 WCs, 1 CWP
Rental
Calor Gaz
Last arrival time: 22:00
→ Site signposted off N67 Kilrush to Killimer Road. 1½ miles from Kilrush, 4 miles from Killimer car-ferry.

KINSALE Co. Cork   18C4

Garrettstown House Holiday Park
Kinsale
021-477 8156 Fax 021-477 8156
Open May-September

Four Star AA. 4 Pennants. Park set in historic 18th century Garrettstown Estate. Ideal touring base for Cork City, Kinsale, West Cork. Top class facilities.
Size 20 acres, 80 touring pitches, 50 with electric hookup, 80 level pitches, 90 static caravans, 10, 16 WCs, 1 CWP
£ car/tent £7-£8, car/caravan £8-£9, motorhome £8-£9, motorbike/tent £7-£8, children £0.50
Rental 2 bed £130-£290, 3 bed £150-£330
CC MasterCard Visa
¼ ¼ Calor Gaz WS
Last arrival time: 23:00
→ From Cork take R600 through Kinsale for 6 miles. Go through Ballinspittle village, past school and football pitch on main road to beach.

LAHINCH Co. Clare   18B1

Lahinch Camping & Caravan Park
Lahinch
065-708 1424 Fax 065-708 1194
Open 1 May-30 September
Size 7 acres, 62 touring pitches, 36 with electric hookup, 62 level pitches, 30 static caravans, 11, 24 WCs, 2 CWPs
£ car/tent £8-£10, car/caravan £9-£10, motorhome £8-£10, motorbike/tent £8, children £1
¼ ¼ Calor WS
Last arrival time: 00:00
→ 200 yards S of village coast road.

LAURAGH VILLAGE Co. Kerry   18A4

Creveen Lodge
Healy Pass, Lauragh Village
064-83131
Open Easter-31 October

Mullingar

This small family run park, set in the heart of the beautiful scenery of south Kerry, provides a high standard of personal supervision and is fully serviced with excellent amenities.
Size 4 acres, 20 touring pitches, 7 with electric hookup, 15 level pitches, 2 ⌂, 5 WCs, 1 CWP
£ car/tent £8, car/caravan £8, motorhome £8, motorbike/tent £7-£7.50, children £0.50
Rental Chalet. £90-£105
✗ ▣ ▣ ▣ ▣ ▲ Gaz ➤ WS
Last arrival time: 00:00
➡ From Kenmare turn right at Sound Bridge onto R571. Follow signs at Lauragh for site. Site is on Healy Pass road (R574).

MIDLETON Co. Cork   18C3

Burkes Caravan & Camping Park
Shanagarry, Midleton
☎ 021-464 6796
Open 1 May-1 October ▲ ⌂ ⌂

Family run caravan park with shop, post office, laundry, walking distance of the beach (EU Blue Flag). Near Trabolgan, Fota Wild, golf clubs, fishing, heritage centre.
Size 4 acres, 10 touring pitches, 8 with electric hookup, 8 level pitches, 39 static caravans, 2 ⌂, 4 WCs,
£ car/tent £7-£8, car/caravan £7-£8, motorhome £7-£8, motorbike/tent £7-£8
Rental ⌂ mobile homes £130-£250
▣ ✗¼ ▣¼ ▣ ▣ Calor ➤
Last arrival time: 22:30
➡ Turn off N25 at Castlemartyr for Ladysbridge, Garryvoe. At Garryvoe hotel turn right for Shanagarry/Ballycotton, 1 mile from Garryvoe.

Trabolgan Holiday Village
Midleton
☎ 021-466 1551 Fax 021-466 1698
Open March-November ⌂ ⌂

Situated on the breath-taking Atlantic coastline, amid rolling meadows and majestic woodland, Trabolgan is the ideal family holiday location. Facilities include sub-tropical swimming paradise, indoor and outdoor adventure playgrounds, 18 hole par 3 golf course and sports centre.
Size 146 acres, 35 touring pitches, 35 with electric hookup, 12 ⌂, 50 WCs, 1 CWP
Rental Chalet. £125-£270 per week (Touring price)
▣ ✗ ▣ ▣ ▣ ▣ ▣ ▣ ▣ ▣ ▣ ▣ ▲ ▣ ⌂
Last arrival time: 23:00
➡ R630 from Midleton to Whitegate, continue straight through Whitegate village for 1km, site signed.

MULLINGAR Co. Westmeath   17D4

Lough Ennel Caravan & Camping
Tudenham, Mullingar
☎ 044-48101 Fax 044-48101
Open 1 April-end September ▲ ⌂ ⌂

On the shore of Lough Ennel. Children's play area. Windsurfing equipment and tuition. Some gas available. Caravans for hire.
Size 18 acres, 50 touring pitches, 50 with electric hookup, 30 level pitches, 50 static caravans, 8 ⌂, 20 WCs, 1 CWP
£ car/tent £8, car/caravan £8, motorhome £8, motorbike/tent £8
▣ ✗ ▣ ▣ ▣ ▣ ▲ Calor ➤ WS
Last arrival time: 23:00
➡ N52 from Mullingar to Kilbeggan for 5 miles, right at Lough Ennel-Tudenham to site.

REPUBLIC OF IRELAND

Omeath

| OMEATH Co. Louth | 17E3 |

Tain Holiday Village
Ballyvoonan, Omeath
042-937 5385 Fax 042-937 5417
Open 14 March-1 November

The Tain Holiday Village is a new Grade A site with all the facilities and attractions that a camper could wish for. Nestled at the foot of the Cooley Mountains, on the shores of Carlingford Lough with a beautiful view across the Mourne Mountains. Leisure facilities include steam room, jacuzzi and indoor swimming pool.
Size 10 acres, 90 touring pitches, 87 with electric hookup, 90 level pitches, 9 static caravans, 16, 16 WCs,
£ car/tent £15.50-£17.50, car/caravan £17.50-£19.50, motorhome £17.50-£19.50, motorbike/tent £15.50-£17.50, children £3.50-£4

Rental
MasterCard Visa
Calor
Last arrival time: 21:30
➡ 10km from Newry, just off main Belfast to Dublin road, on coastal road from Newry to Dundalk. Go through Omeath village 1 mile. Camp site is on left as you drive towards Carlingford village.
See advert on this page

| ROSBEG Co. Donegal | 16C2 |

Tramore Beach Caravan Park
Rosbeg
075-51491 Fax 075-51492
Open Easter-September

Set on a beautiful beach, ½ mile long, an excellent location for bathing. Surfing, golf, fishing and horse riding are all within 10 km of the park.
Size 5 acres, 20 touring pitches, 20 with electric hookup, 20 level pitches, 50 static caravans, 8, 14 WCs, 2 CWPs
£ car/tent £9-£10, car/caravan £7, motorhome £9, motorbike/tent £9, children £7
Last arrival time: 21:00
➡ Proceed N from Ardara on R261, after 4 km there is a sign for site, take this road and follow the signs to site.

| ROSSES POINT Co. Sligo | 16C3 |

Greenlands Caravan & Camping Park
Rosses Point
071-77113 Fax 071-45618
Open May-September
Size 4 acres, 78 touring pitches, 78 with electric hookup, 78 level pitches, 12 static caravans, 8, 15 WCs, 1 CWP
£ car/tent £8-£11, car/caravan £8-£11, motorhome £8-£11, motorbike/tent £8-£11, children £0.50
Rental £100-£300
¼ ¼ ¼ Calor Gaz
➡ From Sligo city, 8 km W to Rosses Point. Site is beside golf club.

TAIN
Holiday Village

Tain Holiday Village is a new Grade A site with all the facilities and attractions that a camper could wish for. Nestled at the foot of the Cooley Mountains, on the shores of Carlingford Lough with a beautiful view across to the Mourne Mountains. Leisure facilities include swimming pool, steam room and jacuzzi.

**The Tain Holiday Village,
Omeath, Co. Louth, Ireland
Tel: 042 75385**

Waterville

ROSSLARE Co. Wexford   19F3

Burrow Caravan & Camping Park
Rosslare
☎ 053-32190 Fax 053-32256
Open 15 March-10 November ▲ 🚐 🚍
Size 14 acres, 100 touring pitches, 100 with electric hookup, 100 level pitches, 150 static caravans, 6 🚿, 10 WCs, 1 CWP
£ car/tent £7-£14, car/caravan £7-£14, motorhome £7-£14, motorbike/tent £5-£12
((Visa
🛒 ✕¼ 🍺 📞 🗑 📻 GR 📺 ⚠ Calor Gaz ♿ 🐕
Last arrival time: 22:00
➡ N25 W from Rosslare Harbour to Kilrane, then turn N onto R736. Site ¾ mile N of Rosslare village.

ROUNDWOOD Co. Wicklow   19F1

Roundwood Camping & Caravanning Park
Roundwood
☎ 01-281 8163
Open April-September ▲ 🚐 🚍
Size 7 acres, 30 touring pitches, 30 with electric hookup, 55 level pitches, 6 🚿, 10 WCs, 1 CWP
£ car/tent £9-£10, car/caravan £9-£10, motorhome £9-£10, motorbike/tent £8-£9, children £1
🛒 ✕¼ 🍺¼ 📞 🗑 GR 📺 ⚠ Calor Gaz 🐕 WS
Last arrival time: 23:00
➡ From Dublin & Dun Laoghaire take N11. Turn right at Kilmacanogue, follow signs for Glendalough. From Rosslare take N11, turn left at Ashford village.

SLIGO Co. Sligo   16C3

Gateway Caravan & Camping Park
Ballinode, Sligo
☎ 071-45618 Fax 071-45618
Open all year ▲ 🚐
Size 3 acres, 24 touring pitches, 24 with electric hookup, 5 🚿, 7 WCs, 1 CWP
£ car/tent £8-£9, car/caravan £8-£10
🛒¼ ✕¼ 🍺¼ 📞 🗑 GR 📺 ⚠ Gaz ♿ 🐕
➡ ¾ mile from town centre on N16 Sligo/Belfast road at Ballinode traffic lights.

STRANDHILL Co. Sligo   16C3

Strandhill Caravan & Camping
Strandhill
☎ 071-68120
Open mid May-mid September ▲ 🚐 🚍
Size 15 acres, 48 touring pitches, 32 with electric hookup, 48 level pitches, 15 static caravans, 8 🚿, 12 WCs, 1 CWP
£ car/tent £7-£10, car/caravan £7-£10, motorhome £7-£10, motorbike/tent £7-£10, children £0.50
Rental 🚐 £120-£225
🛒¼ ✕¼ 🍺¼ 📞 🗑 GR 📺 ♿ 🐕

Last arrival time: 22:00
➡ From Sligo 6km W. Site at Strandhill on Airport road.

TRALEE Co. Kerry   18B3

Seaside Caravan & Camping Park
Camp, Tralee
☎ 066-713 0161 Fax 066-713 0331
Open Easter-November ▲ 🚐 🚍

Family run caravan & camping park next to a safe sandy beach. Children's playground and games room. Lots to do and see in an area of outstanding natural beauty. Near Tralee.
Size 7 acres, 30 touring pitches, 30 with electric hookup, 30 level pitches, 40 static caravans, 4 🚿, 9 WCs, 3 CWPs
£ car/tent £7-£8.50, car/caravan £7-£8.50, motorhome £7-£8.50, motorbike/tent £7-£8.50
Rental 🚐 Chalet. From £130 weekly.
((MasterCard Visa
🛒 ✕¼ 🗑 📞 🗑 GR 📺 ⚠ Calor Gaz 🐕 WS
➡ From Tralee take R559 SW. After 8 miles right onto R560 towards Castlegregory. Turn right towards sea in 3 miles. Site signposted.

WATERVILLE Co. Kerry   18A3

Waterville Caravan & Camping Park
Waterville
☎ 066-947 4191 Fax 066-947 4538
Open Easter-21 September ▲ 🚐 🚍
Size 5 acres, 58 touring pitches, 58 with electric hookup, 58 level pitches, 23 static caravans, 12 🚿, 15 WCs, 2 CWPs
£ car/tent £9-£9.50, car/caravan £10-£10.50, motorhome £10-£10.50, motorbike/tent £8-£9, children £0.50
Rental 🚐 £145-£375
🛒 ✕¼ 🍺 🗑 📞 🗑 ➿ GR 📺 ⚠ Gaz ♿ 🐕
Last arrival time: 22:00
➡ ½ mile N of Waterville, just off N70 'Ring of Kerry' road.

REPUBLIC OF IRELAND

Wexford

WEXFORD Co. Wexford   19F3

Carne Beach Caravan & Camping Park
Wexford
📞 053-31131 Fax 053-31131
Open May-September 🛆 🚐 🚏

Beach site with swimming, angling and riding available. Close to Rosslare ferry.
Size 30 acres, 50 touring pitches, 50 with electric hookup, 50 level pitches, 300 static caravans, 16 🚿, 30 WCs, 2 CWPs
🛁 ✕ 🍴 📞 🛒 🎲 🏪 🎯 GR 📺 ⚡ 🔥 Calor Gaz WS
Last arrival time: 23:00
➡ From Rosslare Harbour take N25 W to Kilrane, then due S to coast.

Ferrybank Caravan & Camping Park
Ferrybank, Wexford
📞 053-44378
Open Easter-end September 🛆 🚐
Size 5 acres, 53 touring pitches, 29 with electric hookup, 14 🚿, 31 WCs, 1 CWP
£ car/tent £7-£10, car/caravan £10, motorbike/tent £7-£10
🛁 ✕ 🍴 📞 🛒 🎲 🏪 GR 📺 🔥 ♿
Last arrival time: 24 hours
➡ Situated on seafront overlooking Wexford town and harbour on R741.

Republic of Ireland
When calling the Republic of Ireland dial 00 353 followed by the site number and omit the initial zero of the local code.

Channel Islands and the Isle of Man

238

Channel Islands/Isle of Man

GUERNSEY	2A2

La Bailloterie Camping
Vale GY3 5HA
☎ 01481-43636 Fax 01481-43225
Open 15 May-15 September ▲
Size 8 acres, 120 touring pitches, 4 with electric hookup, 120 level pitches, 12 ⚿, 12 WCs, 1 CWP
£ car/tent £7.10-£8.80, motorbike/tent £7.10-£8.80, children £1.75-£2.20
Rental ▲ £50-£195

⇒ Leave St Peter Port to the N. Bear left at Half Way Plantation following signs for Pembroke and L'Ancresse. At second set of traffic lights turn right, then take first left. Follow signpost.

Le Vaugrat Campsite
Route de Vaugrat, St Sampsons GY2 4TA
☎ 01481-57468 Fax 01481-51841
Open 1 May-16 September ▲

Set in the grounds of a 17th century Guernsey home, with outbuildings converted into a shop, TV room, take-away, etc. and two minutes walk from safe and sandy bays.
Size 6 acres, 150 touring pitches, 130 level pitches, 8 ⚿, 13 WCs, 1 CWP
Rental ▲ £10-£11.50 per night
₢ MasterCard Visa

JERSEY	2A2

Beuvelande Camp Site
Beuvelande, St Martins JE3 6EZ
☎ 01534-853575 Fax 01534-857788
Open 1st May-15th September ▲
Size 6 acres, 60 touring pitches, 20 with electric hookup, 60 level pitches, 30 ⚿, 20 WCs, 1 CWP
£ car/tent £10-£14, motorbike/tent £10-£14, children £2.50-£3.50
Rental ▲

⇒ A6 from St Helier to St Martin's church, then follow signs.

PEEL	10A4

Peel Camping Park
Derby Road, Peel IM5 1RG
☎ 01624-842341 Fax 01624-844010
Open mid May-late September ▲ 🚐

Situated on the edge of the town in a rural setting, just three miles from the TT course. A level site with facilities for the disabled.
Size 4 acres, 100 touring pitches, 12 with electric hookup, 100 level pitches, 8 ⚿, 10 WCs, 1 CWP
£ car/tent £7, motorhome £9, motorbike/tent £7, children £1.75

⇒ A1 from Douglas and turn right at first crossroads entering Peel. Follow signs to site on A20 on edge of town, adjacent to primary school.

France and the Benelux countries

France and the Benelux countries

Getting there

The following information is a selection of the ferry services and operators providing crossings between Great Britain and Ireland and the Continent.

Route	Company	Frequency	Crossing time
Cork–Roscoff	Brittany Ferries	1 weekly (summer)	14 hrs
Dover–Calais	P&O Stena Line	30 daily	1hr 30 mins
Dover–Calais	Hoverspeed	2 daily	35 mins
Dover–Ostend (Seacat)	Hoverspeed	4–7 daily	2 hrs
Folkestone–Boulogne	Hoverspeed	4 daily	55 mins
Harwich–Hoek	Stena Line	2 daily	3 hrs 40 mins
Hull–Rotterdam	P&O North Sea Ferries	1 daily	12 hrs 30 mins
Hull–Zeebrugge	P&O North Sea Ferries	1 daily	13 hrs 15 mins
Newcastle–Amsterdam	Scandinavian Seaways	3 weekly	14 hrs
Harwich–Hamburg	Scandinavian Seaways	3–4 weekly	19 hrs
Newhaven–Dieppe	P&O Stena Line	2 daily	2 hrs 15 mins–4 hrs
Plymouth–Roscoff	Brittany Ferries	1–3 daily (summer)	6 hrs
Plymouth–Santander	Brittany Ferries	2 weekly March–Nov	23–24 hrs
Poole–Cherbourg	Brittany Ferries	1–2 daily	4 hrs 15 mins
Portsmouth–Bilbao	P&O Euopean	2 weekly	30–35 hrs
Portsmouth–Caen	Brittany Ferries	2–3 daily	6 hrs
Portsmouth–Cherbourg	P&O European	1–4 daily	5–7 hrs
Portsmouth–Le Havre	P&O European	1–3 daily	5–7 hrs
Portsmouth–St Malo	Brittany Ferries	1 daily	8 hrs 45 mins
Poole/Ptsmth–Santander	Brittany Ferries	1 weekly	30–33 hrs
Rosslare–Cherbourg	Irish Ferries	2–3 weekly	17 hrs
Rosslare–Roscoff	Irish Ferries	2–3 weekly	16 hrs

Ferry operators

Brittany Ferries Tel: 0990 360360
Irish Ferries, Dublin Tel: 01 661 0511
P&O European Ferries Tel: 0870 242499
Scandinavian Seaways Tel: 01255 240240
Hoverspeed Tel: 0990 240241
P&O Stena Line Tel: 0990 980980
P&O North Sea Ferries Tel: 01482 377177
Stena Line Tel: 01233 647047

The Channel Tunnel

The Le Shuttle tourist service is a drive-on drive-off train operation carrying cars, caravans and motorcycles. Slip roads from the M20 near Folkestone and the A16 near Calais take vehicles direct to the terminals. Passengers pay at a toll-booth, go through frontier controls and load their vehicles on to the special carriages. Total journey time, including passing through Customs, embarkation and disembarkation is approximately 1 hour, with the Le Shuttle crossing taking only 35 minutes. At peak times the operation has up to four departures every hour but is down to one an hour in the quietest time of night. It is not possible to book space on a particular train, though you can pre-purchase a ticket. Vehicles load from the rear of Le Shuttle, and are directed to park in one of the carriages. During the journey, car passengers can stay in their cars or walk around the carriage. Each carriage is air-conditioned, sound-proofed and has access to a toilet.

Screens display journey progress information. For information and bookings contact Le Shuttle Call Centre, Tel: 0990 35 35 35

Further European travel information can be found in the publication, *RAC Motoring in Europe*. Invaluable for all motorists travelling on the Continent, this is a comprehensive guide detailing essential motoring accessories and practical motoring advice.

France in 35 minutes
and you don't even have to put your foot down

0990 35 35 35
or call your local travel agent

EURO TUNNEL

Folkestone to Calais/Coquelles in around 35 minutes, up to 4 times an hour, 24 hours a day.

Motoring in Europe 1999

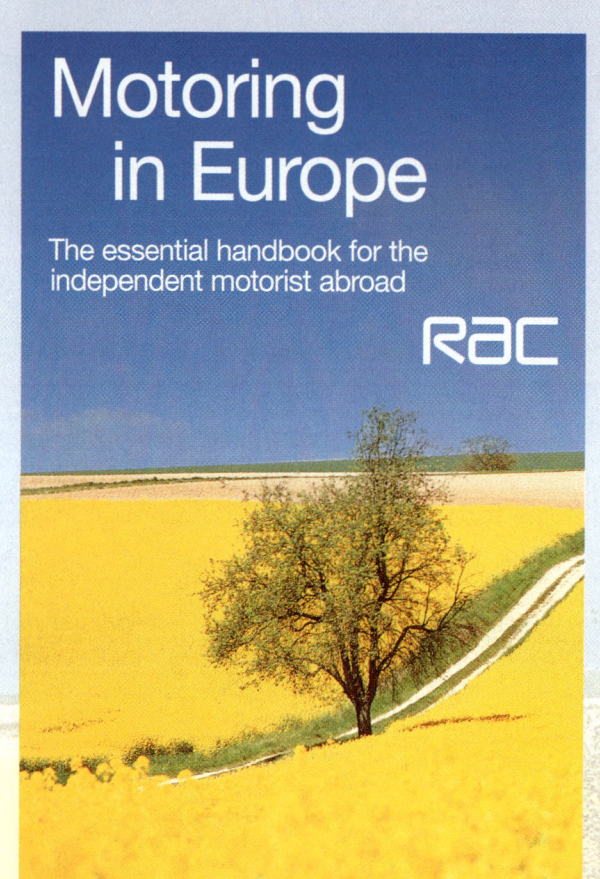

Motoring in Europe

The essential handbook for the independent motorist abroad

RAC

Quality, value
Comprehensive guide to motoring on the Continent, from the experts in European travel – the RAC.

Organised by country
Essential motoring information and practical general information.

Annually updated information on Channel crossings, toll roads, mountain passes, tunnels and Customs allowances.

Recommended for the business traveller or the independent leisure traveller.

Competitively priced

£4.99 – Available from your local bookshop

Or contact:

Trade Sales Department
West One Publishing
Portland House
4 Great Portland Street
London W1N 5AA

Telephone: 0171 580 6886
Fax: 0171 580 9788
e-mail: sales@west-one.com

Belgium

BELGIUM

Prices shown are in Belgian Francs.

BLANKENBERGE

Camping Dallas
Ruzettelaan 191, 8370 Blankenberge
050-41 81 57 Fax 050-42 94 79
Open 15 March-25 September
Size 3 hectares, 200 touring pitches, 200 with electric hookup, 60 static caravans, 14, 22 WCs, 1 CWP
£ car/tent 440-800, car/caravan 600-900, motorhome 550-900, children 75

➜ Take coast road from Blankenberge to Zeebrugge and follow signs to campsite which is on the beach.

MEMBACH

Camping Wesertal
Rue de l'Invasion 66-68, 4837 Membach
087-55 59 61 Fax 087-55 65 55
Open all year
55 touring pitches, 55 with electric hookup, 10 static caravans, 6, 8 WCs, 1 CWP
£ car/tent 430, car/caravan 450, motorhome 410, motorbike/tent 430, children 50-80
Rental 900-1950 BF per night
¼ × ¼ Calor Gaz WS
Last arrival time: 22:00

➜ From E40, exit 38 at Eupen, second on the right following signs.

MONS

Camping du Waux-Hall
Av St-Pierre 17, 7000 Mons
065-33 79 23 Fax 065-35 63 36
Open all year

A short distance from the town centre of Mons, the campsite Waux-Hall is set in a green area offering peace and quiet for your stay.
Size 1.44 hectares, 75 touring pitches, 75 with electric hookup, 6, 8 WCs, 1 CWP
£ car/tent 380, car/caravan 380, motorhome 360-380, motorbike/tent 370, children 85
Rental 2000 BF pw

Last arrival time: 22:00

➜ From Mons take inner ring road, N90 towards Binche. Site is signposted just before Waux-Hall public park.

STAVELOT

Camping L'Eau Rouge
Cheneux 25, 4970 Stavelot
080-86 30 75 Fax 080-86 30 75
Open all year
Size 4 hectares, 80 touring pitches, 40 with electric hookup, 80 static caravans, 8, 21 WCs, 1 CWP
£ car/tent 500, car/caravan 500, motorhome 500, motorbike/tent 500, children 40
Rental 1000 BF per night
Calor Gaz WS
Last arrival time: 23:00

➜ Access is from the Stavelot to Francorchamps road, close to the Francorchamps race circuit.

TURNHOUT

Baalse Hei 't Groene Caravanpark
Roodhuisstraat 10, 2300 Turnhout
014-42 19 31 Fax 014-42 08 53
Open all year

Friendly forest site, peacefully situated close to city of Turnhout. Several lakes and sports facilities. Number of walking and cycling trails in the vicinity.
Size 30 hectares, 55 touring pitches, 55 with electric hookup, 395 static caravans, 13, 16 WCs, 2 CWPs
£ car/tent 490-650, car/caravan 490-650, motorhome 490-650, motorbike/tent 350-450
Rental
× Calor Gaz

➜ From E24, take exit 24 Turnhout Centre and head towards Breda. Turn right at end of ringroad and right again after 2.5 km.

Abbeville

FRANCE

Prices shown are in French Francs.

ABBEVILLE Somme

Airotel Le Château des Tilleuls
80132 Port-le-Grand
03 22 24 07 75 Fax 03 22 24 23 80
Open 1 March-31 October ⚐ ⛺ 🚐
Size 4 hectares, 120 touring pitches, 120 with electric hookup, 10 static caravans, 13 🚿, 13 WCs, 2 CWPs
£ car/tent 84, car/caravan 99, motorhome 99, motorbike/tent 84
Rental ⚐ 900-1600 FF p.w. , Chalets 1800-2700 FF
CC MasterCard Visa

🛒 🍴 🏪 📞 ❄ 🏊 🎾 🎯 🎮 GR 📷 📺 ⛰ ⚑ Calor Gaz ♿ 🐕

➜ From Abbeville take D40 towards the bay of the Somme and camp is signposted.
See advert on this page

Camping Val de Trie
Bouillancourt-sous-Miannay, 80870 Moyenneville
03 22 31 48 88 Fax 03 22 31 35 33
Open 1 April-30 October ⚐ ⛺ 🚐

Seven miles from the bay of the Somme, a shaded, flowery campsite set in the green valley of the River Trie. Swimming pool, pond fishing facilities, bathroom for babies and animals from the farm.
Size 2.6 hectares, 50 touring pitches, 50 with electric hookup, 7 🚿, 6 WCs, 12 CWPs
£ car/tent 60-65, car/caravan 75-80, motorhome 75-80, motorbike/tent 60-65, children 11-12

🛒 ✕ ¼ 🍴 🏪 📞 ❄ 🏊 🎮 📷 ⚑ Calor Gaz ♿ 🐕
Last arrival time: 22:30
➜ From D925 to Miannay, take D86 towards Toueffles, site is in 1 km. From A28 exit Moyenville and the site is signposted.

ARCACHON Gironde

Camping de la Dune
Route de Biscarrosse, 33260 La Teste de Buch
05 56 22 72 17 Fax 05 56 22 72 17
Open 1 May-30 September ⚐ ⛺ 🚐
Size 6 hectares, 325 touring pitches, 150 with electric hookup, 34 🚿, 51 WCs, 45 CWPs
£ car/tent 75-115, car/caravan 95-135, motorhome 95-135, motorbike/tent 65-105, children 15-25
🛒 ✕ 🍴 🏪 📞 ⛰
Last arrival time: 20:00
➜ Take D218 from Arcachon to Pyla-sur-Mer.

ARGENTAT Corrèze   14B4

Camping au Soleil d'Oc
Monceaux-sur-Dordogne, 19400 Argentat
05 55 28 84 84 Fax 05 55 28 12 12
Open 9 April-1 November ⚐ ⛺ 🚐

Airotel ★★★★
Le Chateau des Tilleuls

Park of 20 ha with hundred-year-old trees. Oasis of quietness and relaxation, close to the beaches. Facilities recently created, comfort at a first-class campsite. Marked plots from 150 to 200 sq. m. Ideal site for an overnight stay or for a longer holiday. Bay of Somme: protected nature for relaxing.

Airotel Le Chateau des Tilleuls
Route D 40 A – 80132
Port-le-Grand Somme
Tel: 22 24 07 75
Fax: 22 24 23 80

Biscarosse

245

A magnificent natural site on the edge of the Dordogne featuring swimming, mini-golf, tennis, canoeing and archery. Entertainment for adults and children, mini-club, bar, creperie, regional specialities.
Size 4 hectares, 75 touring pitches, 70 with electric hookup, 5 static caravans, 13, 16 WCs, 2 CWPs
£ car/tent 76, car/caravan 76, motorhome 65, motorbike/tent 65, children 14
Rental 900-1600 FF, Chalets 1400-2900 FF p.w.
Visa
Last arrival time: 20:00
➜ From Argentat take D12 towards Beaulieu-sur-Dordogne for 4 km. Site is by bridge on left of river.

AUBENAS Ardèche

Domaine du Cros d'Auzon
07200 St-Maurice-d'Ardèche
04 75 37 75 86 Fax 04 75 37 01 02
Open March-September

A quiet and relaxing site with comfort and many activities. Open from March to September, this is an exceptional site.
Size 20 hectares, 200 touring pitches, 150 with electric hookup, 18 static caravans, 40, 20 WCs, 40 CWPs
£ car/tent 110, car/caravan 110, motorhome 110, children 16
Rental Chalet. 1900-2600 FF p.w.
MasterCard Visa
Last arrival time: 20:00
➜ 10 km S of Aubenas on road to Vallon-Pont d'Arc.

BANYULS Pyrénées-Orientales

Camping Municipal La Pinède
66650 Banyuls-sur-Mer
04 68 88 32 13 Fax 04 68 88 04 64
Open 15 May-3 November
Size 3.5 hectares, 246 touring pitches, 141 with electric hookup, 22, 36 WCs
£ car/tent 56-72, car/caravan 75-92, motorhome 70-85, motorbike/tent 56-72

MasterCard Visa
¼ Calor Gaz
Last arrival time: 20:00
➜ Turn right after the square in Banyuls and continue for 1 km until supermarket Champion. After the roundabout, site is 50 m on right.

BARFLEUR Manche

La Blanche Nef
Rue des Ecoles, 50760 Barfleur
02 33 23 15 40 Fax 02 33 23 95 14
Open all year
Size 2.5 hectares, 60 touring pitches, 40 with electric hookup, 30 static caravans, 7, 10 WCs, 1 CWP
£ car/tent 42, car/caravan 45, motorhome 40, motorbike/tent 40, children 8.50
Rental Chalet. 200-500 FF - a night; 1600-2100 FF - week
MasterCard Visa
¼ ¼ Calor Gaz WS
Last arrival time: 22:30
➜ From Cherbourg into Barfleur, turn left into rue Thomas Beckett. At the port bear left and after 100 m turn left. Site is 300 m, facing the sea.

BISCAROSSE Landes

Campotel La Réserve
Gastes, 40160 Parentis-en-Born
05 58 09 75 96 Fax 05 58 09 76 13
Open 15 May-18 September

At Campotel La Réserve you will find facilities dedicated to your pleasure. A lagoon pool, indoor heated pool, a private beachclub and a wide selection of sports equipment and installations.
Size 32 hectares, 668 touring pitches, 459 with electric hookup, 20 static caravans
£ car/tent 71.50-143, car/caravan 71.50-143, motorhome 71.50-143, motorbike/tent 71.50-143
MasterCard Visa
Calor Gaz
Last arrival time: 21:00
➜ From Biscarosse take road to Parentis-en-Born, then S round the lake to Gastes. Drive through village, site is on right and signposted.

EUROPE

Blois

BLOIS Loir-et-Cher

Le Parc du Val de Loire
41150 Mesland
02 54 70 27 18 Fax 02 54 70 21 71
Open 1 May-15 September

The site is quietly situated away from the main roads and towns, but is nevertheless well placed to visit the châteaux of the Loire. With all its equipment it's a children's paradise.
Size 15 hectares, 300 touring pitches, 300 with electric hookup, 35 static caravans, 39, 35 WCs
£ car/tent 105-155, car/caravan 105-155, motorhome 105-155, motorbike/tent 105-155, children 16-20
cc MasterCard Visa
Calor Gaz
Last arrival time: 22:00
➜ From Blois take N152 towards Tours. After 16 km turn right towards Onzain. From Onzain follow signs to Mesland.

BOISSON Gard

Castel Camping Château de Boisson
Boisson-les-Fumades, 30500 Allègre
04 66 24 82 21 Fax 04 66 24 80 14
Open 1 May-30 September

In the Cévennes - Ardèche - Provence triangle, a quiet château campsite in peaceful and tranquil surroundings. Apartments and mobile-homes for hire. Suitable for families with children under 14 years.
Size 7 hectares, 157 touring pitches, 157 with electric hookup, 29 static caravans, 16, 16 WCs, 2 CWPs

£ car/tent 99-127, car/caravan 99-127, motorhome 99-127, motorbike/tent 99-127, children 9-10
Rental Mobile home 1680-2520 FF (for 2), 2240-3360 FF (for 4)
cc MasterCard Visa
Last arrival time: 22:00
➜ From Bagnols-sur-Cèze take D6 towards Alès. After 35 km take D7 towards Fumades and Boisson is 10 km ahead on the right.

LE BOULOU Pyrénées-Orientales

Camping Caravanning Les Casteillets
66400 St-Jean-Pla-de-Corts
04 68 83 26 83 Fax 04 68 83 39 67
Open all year
Size 5.88 hectares, 100 touring pitches, 100 with electric hookup, 30 static caravans, 12, 12 WCs, 2 CWPs
£ car/tent 60-100, car/caravan 60-100, motorhome 60-100, motorbike/tent 60-100, children 12-18
Rental 990-1750 FF, Mobile home 1090-2490 FF, chalet 990-1990 FF
Last arrival time: 22:00
➜ From A9 exit Le Boulou and head towards Ceret. St-Jean-Pla-de-Corts is 2.5 km from autoroute.

LE BOURG-D'OISANS Isère   8A3

Camping Le Vernis
38520 Le Bourg-d'Oisans
04 76 80 02 68
Open 1 Dec-1 May, 20 June-15 Sept
Size 1 hectare, 54 touring pitches, 54 with electric hookup, 6, 10 WCs, 3 CWPs
£ car/tent 85, car/caravan 85, children 14
Rental
WS
Last arrival time: 19:30
➜ From Le Bourg-d'Oisans go towards Briançon. (No motorhomes in July/August)

BRAY-DUNES Nord

Club Camping Perroquet Plage
59123 Bray-Dunes
03 28 58 37 37 Fax 03 28 58 37 01
Open 1 April-30 September
Size 28 hectares, 100 touring pitches, 100 with electric hookup, 750 static caravans, 65, 95 WCs, 5 CWPs
£ car/tent 82, car/caravan 85, motorhome 75, motorbike/tent 60, children 15
Last arrival time: 22:00
➜ From A26 exit 36 - 8 km from Dunkirk.
See advert on opposite page

Cancon

247

Club Camping Perroquet ★★★ at Bray-Dunes

Passeport pour la Forme
(This means that our site offers you every opportunity to get fit – on a plate)

Camping Perroquet really does offer an 'Activity Holiday'. Set in 60 ha of wild, unspoilt dunes and beaches, just about everything you can imagine is on hand to have-a-go at. From land yachting to archery, from horse-riding to deep-sea fishing – as well as every kind of sailing.

Get your whole family off the couch and into shape.

Camping Perroquet, 59123 Bray-Dunes
Tel: 03 28 58 37 37

CALAIS Pas de Calais

Bal Parc Camping
62890 Tournehem
03 21 35 65 90 Fax 03 21 35 18 57
Open all year
Size 1.4 hectares, 63 touring pitches, 63 with electric hookup, 30 static caravans, 18, 10 WCs
£ car/tent 68-80, car/caravan 68-80, motorhome 68-80, motorbike/tent 68-80, children 12
Rental 1000 FF, Mobile homes 1600 FF
WS
Last arrival time: 23:00
➡ From A26 exit 2, or N43 exit Nordausques and follow signs for Tournehem, 10 km from Calais.
See advert on this page

CANCON Lot et Garonne

Camping des Bastides
Salles, 47150 Monflaquin
05 53 40 83 09 Fax 05 53 40 81 76
Open 15 May-15 September

A spacious terraced site situated at the southern border of the hilly and woodland scenery of the Dordogne. An environment where quiet and natural beauty are still present. Activities for children in high season.
Size 6 hectares, 80 touring pitches, 80 with electric hookup, 12, 9 WCs, 10 CWPs
£ car/tent 80-101, car/caravan 80-101, motorhome 80-101, motorbike/tent 73-91, children 15
Rental 2675 FF, Chalets 3075 FF
➡ From N21 at Cancon, take D124 through Monflanquin then D150 towards Salles and follow signs.

BAL PARC
Camping ★★★★

62890 TOURNEHEM
(2nd Exit)

Grill restaurant
63 pitches
Quiet & pleasantly situated
Caravan hire
Open all year
Also
★★ Hotel – 26 rooms

Tel: 03 21 35 65 90
Fax: 03 21 35 18 57

Telephoning the United Kingdom
When telephoning the United Kingdom from the Continent dial 00 44 and omit the initial 0 of the UK code.

EUROPE

Canet-en-Roussillon

CANET-EN-ROUSSILLON Pyrénées-Orientales

La Sainte-Marie
Chemin de la Crouste, 66470 Ste-Marie-en-Rousillon
☎ 04 68 80 48 10 Fax 04 68 73 42 22
Open 15 June-15 September ⚠ 🚐 🚍

Close to Perpignan and 1 km from the sea, the site has marked pitches, with shade, a free 25 m swimming pool, bar, snacks, entertainment and games.
Size 5 hectares, 220 touring pitches, 220 with electric hookup, 10 static caravans, 40 🚿, 40 WCs, 4 CWPs
£ car/tent 70-100, car/caravan 70-100, motorhome 70-100, motorbike/tent 70-100, children 10.50-15
Rental 🚐 Mobile homes 1100-2900 FF p.w.
🛒 ✕ 🍴 🔲 📞 🏊 🐟 🔲 GR 🔲 TV ⚠ 🔌 Gaz ♿ 🐕
➡ From Perpignan go to Canet and then N on D81 for 2 km to Sainte-Marie-la-Mer. Signposted.

CARPENTRAS Vaucluse

Domaine Naturiste de Bélézy
84410 Bédoin
☎ 04 90 65 60 18 Fax 04 90 65 94 45
Open 13 March-November ⚠ 🚐 🚍
In the heart of Provence, an exceptional site with 2 swimming pools, sauna, sports fields and archery. Activities include pottery, sculpture, chess and music with children's games, baby club, restaurant, hydrotherapy centre and a shop.
Size 25 hectares, 288 touring pitches, 288 with electric hookup, 40 🚿, 44 WCs, 5 CWPs
£ car/tent 94-188, children 18-31
Rental Chalet. 140-350 FF per night
℅ MasterCard Visa
🛒 ✕ 🍴 🔲 📞 ⚠
➡ From A7, exit at Avignon Nord or Orange, towards Carpentras and once in Bédoin take D974.

CASTELJALOUX Lot et Garonne

Camp Municipal de la Piscine
Route de Marmande, 47700 Casteljaloux
☎ 05 53 93 54 68 Fax 05 53 89 13 25
Open 25 March-30 October ⚠ 🚐 🚍
Size 1 hectare, 50 touring pitches, 50 with electric hookup, 10 🚿, 8 WCs, 1 CWP

£ car/tent 32.50, car/caravan 43, motorhome 43, motorbike/tent 32.50, children 7
✕ 🍴 🏊 ♿ 🐕
Last arrival time: 21:00
➡ Casteljaloux is on D933, S of Marmande.

CHAMBERY Savoie

Camping Les Charmilles
Lac d'Aiguebelette, 73470 Novalaise-Lac
☎ 04 79 36 04 67 Fax 04 79 36 04 67
Open 1 July-30 August ⚠ 🚐 🚍
Size 2.3 hectares, 100 touring pitches, 83 with electric hookup, 12 🚿, 15 WCs, 1 CWP
£ car/tent 60-74, car/caravan 74-90, motorhome 74-90, motorbike/tent 60-74, children 13-21
✕¼ 🍴¼ 🔲 📞 🔲 GR 🔲 TV ⚠ Calor Gaz ♿ 🐕
Last arrival time: 22:00
➡ From A43 take exit Lac d'Aiguebelette and take D921 towards St Alban de Montbel for 1.5 km.

CHATEAU-CHINON Nièvre   5E2

Manoir de Bezolle
58110 St-Péreuse-en-Morvan
☎ 03 86 84 42 55 Fax 03 86 84 43 77
Open 1 April-15 October ⚠ 🚐 🚍
Size 8 hectares, 100 touring pitches, 100 with electric hookup, 20 🚿, 22 WCs, 3 CWPs
£ car/tent 83-123, car/caravan 83-123, motorhome 83-123, children 15-20
Rental ⚠ 🚐 Mobile home 1200-2500 FF
℅ MasterCard Visa
🛒 ✕ 🍴 🔲 📞 🏊 🔲 🔲 🔲 GR 🔲 TV ⚠ 🔌 Calor Gaz ♿ 🐕 WS
Last arrival time: 20:00
➡ From Château-Chinon, W on D978 for 10 km and follow signs.

CHATEAULIN Finistère

Camping Ker-Ys
Pentrez-Plage, 29550 St-Nic
☎ 02 98 26 53 95 Fax 02 98 26 53 95
Open 1 May-11 September ⚠ 🚐 🚍

In front of a magnificent fine sandy beach, the Ker Ys is situated in the heart of a tourist area, close to Crozon peninsular, Locronan, Quimper, Pointe du Raz, etc.

Crest 249

Size 3 hectares, 190 touring pitches, 190 with electric hookup, 19 ♿, 33 WCs, 1 CWP
£ car/tent 66, car/caravan 66, motorhome 66, motorbike/tent 66, children 10
Rental 700-1000 FF, Mobile homes 1200-2400 FF
CC MasterCard Visa
⇒ On D887, W of Châteaulin

CHATELLERAULT Vienne

Le Relais du Miel
Route d'Antran, 86100 Châtellerault
📞 05 49 02 06 27 Fax 05 49 93 25 76
Open 1 May-30 September
Size 4 hectares, 80 touring pitches, 80 with electric hookup, 14 ♿, 12 WCs, 1 CWP
£ car/tent 130, car/caravan 130, motorhome 130, motorbike/tent 130
Rental
CC MasterCard Visa
⇒ From A10 exit Châtellerault Nord. From N10, N of Châtellerault, drive towards the A10 tolls.
See advert on this page

Le Relais du Miel
★★★★

☆ Halfway between Paris and Bordeaux.
☆ Close to Futuroscope (14 minutes).
☆ Beside the River Vienne.
☆ Old trees park.
☆ Bar, Restaurant, Satellite TV, Internet, Heated Pool.

**Le Relais du Miel
route d'Antran
86100 Châtellerault
Email: lrdm.chat@wanadoo.fr
Tel: 05 49 02 06 27
Fax: 05 49 93 25 76**

*Access: A10 exit 26 or N10
(follow "Antran")*

COGNAC Charente

Camping de Cognac
bd de Chatenay, Route de Ste-Sévère, 16100 Cognac
📞 05 45 32 13 32 Fax 05 45 36 55 29
Open 1 May-15 October
Size 2 hectares, 160 touring pitches, 160 with electric hookup, 20 ♿, 20 WCs
£ car/tent 61-67, car/caravan 67-78, motorhome 67-78, motorbike/tent 61-67, children 11
CC MasterCard Visa
⇒ Site is beside the river, near the town centre and well signposted.

LA COLLE-SUR-LOUP Alpes-Maritimes

Camping Les Pinèdes
Route de Pont-de-Pierre, 06480 La Colle-sur-Loup
📞 04 93 32 98 94 Fax 04 93 32 50 20
Open 1 March-15 October
Size 3.8 hectares, 150 touring pitches, 120 with electric hookup, 18 ♿, 20 WCs, 3 CWPs
£ car/tent 77-128, car/caravan 89-140, motorhome 89-140, motorbike/tent 65-88, children 11.50-15
Rental 1200-2500 FF, Mobile homes 1500-3200 FF
CC MasterCard Visa
Last arrival time: 21:00
⇒ From A8 exit Cagnes/Mer, turn right off D6 towards La Colle-sur-Loup.

CREST Drôme

Gervanne Camping
26400 Mirabel-et-Blacons
📞 04 75 40 00 20 Fax 04 75 40 03 97
Open 1 April-31 October

Set at the foot of the Vercors and Provence, the Gontard family welcome you to a 3 star site with 500 m of beach and swimming in the River Drôme. Chalets to rent, restaurant, shop. Numerous excursions and hiking trails possible.
Size 3.5 hectares, 150 touring pitches, 150 with electric hookup, 15 static caravans, 18 ♿, 25 WCs, 3 CWPs
£ car/tent 77, car/caravan 77, motorhome 77, motorbike/tent 66, children 14
Rental Chalet. 1600-2900 FF p.w.
Last arrival time: 22:00
⇒ From A7 exit Loriol, then take D104 towards Crest and D164 to site; otherwise exit Valence Sud, take D111 to Crest and then D93.

EUROPE

250

Créon

CREON Gironde

Camping-Caravanning Bel-Air
Route Départamentale 671, Lotient-Sadirac, 33670 Créon
📞 05 56 23 01 90 Fax 05 56 23 08 38
Open all year
Size 2 hectares, 92 touring pitches, 60 with electric hookup, 9 🚿, 7 WCs, 2 CWPs
£ car/tent 65, car/caravan 113
Rental
cc MasterCard Visa

➜ NW of Créon off D671. Coming from Bordeaux go E on D936 towards Bergerac, fork right onto D671 towards Créon after 11 km.

DAX Landes

Camping Les Chênes
Av Bois de Boulogne, 40100 Dax
📞 05 58 90 05 53 Fax 05 58 90 42 43
Open 1 April-1 November

The site is set in a park of oak trees, with lovely blooms, 1½ km from the centre of Dax. Our pitches are spacious and shaded and in these convivial surroundings you will spend the holiday of your dreams.
Size 5 hectares, 212 touring pitches, 212 with electric hookup, 17 static caravans, 32 🚿, 43 WCs, 4 CWPs
£ car/tent 60, car/caravan 77-105, motorhome 77-105, motorbike/tent 60, children 10
Rental Chalet 1850-2300 FF, Mobile homes 1400-1850 FF p.w.
cc MasterCard Visa

Last arrival time: 21:00

➜ Cross over the old bridge in Dax and go towards 'Bois de Boulogne'. Site is signposted near to River Adour.

LES DEUX ALPES Isère

Le Champ du Moulin
Bourg-d'Arud, 38520 Venosc
📞 04 76 80 07 38 Fax 04 76 80 24 44
Open all year

Situated at Venosc - Les Deux Alpes with walking, fishing, climbing, paragliding, white water rafting on the River Veneon and skiing in summer and in winter.... Ask for information.
Size 1.5 hectares, 51 touring pitches, 51 with electric hookup, 9 🚿, 9 WCs, 1 CWP
£ car/tent 70-102, car/caravan 70-102, motorhome 70-102, motorbike/tent 70-102, children 12-15
Rental Mobile homes 2100-2850 FF p.w.
cc MasterCard Visa

Calor Gaz WS
Last arrival time: 22:00

➜ From Grenoble heads towards Oisans, Briançon. 5 km after Bourg d'Oisans turn right towards Venosc, La Berrade. 150 m after the cable car Venosc-Les Deux Alpes turn right to site.

DOMPIERRE-LES-ORMES Saône et Loire

Le Village des Meuniers
71520 Dompierre-les-Ormes
📞 03 85 50 29 43 Fax 03 85 50 28 25
Open 7 May-2 October

Situated at the crossroads of Beaujolais, Charolais, Brionnais and Mâconnais, come and enjoy the quiet, the relaxation and the beauty of south Burgundy.
Size 4 hectares, 113 touring pitches, 113 with electric hookup, 4 level pitches, 13 🚿, 14 WCs, 2 CWPs
£ car/tent 72-105, car/caravan 87-120, motorhome 87-120, motorbike/tent 72-105, children 12-17
Rental Chalet.
cc MasterCard Visa

Calor Gaz

Fréjus

Last arrival time: 23:00
➜ From A6 exit Mâcon and take N79 towards Charolles. 35 km from Mâcon turn off towards Dompierre les-Ormes and watch for sign just before the village.

FOUESNANT Finistère

Camping La Piscine
Kerleya, Beg-Meil, 29170 Fouesnant
☎ 02 98 56 56 06 Fax 02 98 56 57 64
Open 15 May-15 September
Size 4 hectares, 160 touring pitches, 160 with electric hookup, 35 static caravans, 18 🚿, 20 WCs, 3 CWPs
£ car/tent 69.50-99.50, car/caravan 69.50-99.50, motorhome 69.50-99.50, motorbike/tent 69.50-99.50
Rental
CC MasterCard Visa

Last arrival time: 22:00
➜ From Fouesnant take D45 to Beg-Meil and follow sign to site.

La Roche Perlée
Beg-Meil, 29170 Fouesnant
☎ 02 98 94 94 15 Fax 02 98 94 48 05
Open 2 April-26 September
Size 2 hectares, 123 touring pitches, 123 with electric hookup, 49 static caravans, 17 🚿, 24 WCs, 3 CWPs
£ car/tent 81-115, car/caravan 81-115, children 8.50-12
CC MasterCard Visa

Last arrival time: 22:00
➜ From Quimper go to Fouesnant and take D45 towards Beg-Meil. Site is 1 km on left before entering Beg-Meil.

FREJUS Var

Camping Caravaning des Aubrèdes
83480 Puget-sur-Argens
☎ 04 94 45 51 46 Fax 04 94 45 28 92
Open 1 April-30 September
Size 3.8 hectares, 200 touring pitches, 120 with electric hookup, 20 static caravans, 25 🚿, 28 WCs, 3 CWPs
£ car/tent 71.40-102, children 17
Rental 1850-2000 FF, Mobile home 1350-2700 FF (6 people)
CC MasterCard Visa

Last arrival time: 22:00
➜ From A8 exit at Puget-sur-Argens and sign is well signposted just off N7, 4 km inland from Fréjus.

Solve your holiday problem at

Holiday Green

Caravans and Mobile-homes (for 2, 4, 6 pers.) in a large pinewood, Californian style swimming pool (1000 m^2), all year non-stop entertainment, tennis, restaurant, bar, discotheque, salad and ice-cream bars, supermarket and organised activities (excursions, mountain-bike trips....)

Prices and information:
Tel: 00 33 494 19 88 30
Fax: 00 33 494 19 88 31

Holiday Green, Route de Bagnois, 83600 FREJUS, France

Holiday Green
Route de Bagnols-en-Forêt, quartier de la Lègue (D4), 83600 Fréjus
☎ 04 94 19 88 30 Fax 04 94 19 88 31
Open 3 April-23 October
Size 15 hectares, 120 touring pitches, 120 with electric hookup, 200 static caravans, 16 🚿, 23 WCs
£ car/tent 101.50-145, car/caravan 133-190, motorhome 133-190, motorbike/tent 101.50-145, children 17.50-25
Rental
CC MasterCard Visa

Calor Gaz
Last arrival time: 24 hours
➜ From Fréjus take N7 and at first traffic lights take D4 on right and drive 7 km towards Bagnols-en-Forêt.
See advert on this page

Roads that are marked with the Crafty Bison (*Bison Futé*) sign are short cuts which avoid the busiest routes. Crafty Bison maps are available from Crafty Bison information centres, which are scattered along most major routes, or from tourist boards.

252

GRASSE Alpes-Maritimes

Camp Caravaning Les Gorges du Loup
Chemin des Vergers, 06620 Le Bar-sur-Loup
📞 04 93 42 45 06 Fax 04 93 42 45 06
Open 1 April-1 October

Situated within the golden triangle Cannes-Nice-Grasse, close to many sporting activities. The quiet terraced pitches are shaded by olive trees and look over the valley of the Loup.
Size 2 hectares, 64 touring pitches, 64 with electric hookup, 12, 13 WCs, 1 CWP
£ car/tent 75-125, car/caravan 90-140, motorhome 120-160, motorbike/tent 65-80, children 15-20
Rental 950-2150, Chalets 1000-2950

Last arrival time: 20:00
➡ Take D2085 from Grasse towards Châteauneuf. At Pré-du-Lac turn onto D2210.

Caravan Inn
18 Route de Cannes, 6650 Opio
📞 04 93 77 32 00 Fax 04 93 77 71 89
Open 1 June-15 September

As well as touring - ideal for your second home. Buy your own mobile home, new or second hand, on a quiet wooded hill site.
Size 5 hectares, 43 touring pitches, 43 with electric hookup, 70 static caravans, 18, 15 WCs, 2 CWPs
£ car/tent 97-166, car/caravan 97-166, motorhome 97-166, children 9.50
Rental Chalet. 2000-3100 FF per week

Calor Gaz WS
➡ Situated 6 km from Grasse and 14 km from A8.

GUINES Pas-de-Calais

La Bien-Assise
62340 Guînes
📞 03 21 35 20 77 Fax 03 21 36 79 20
Open 20 April-25 September

Whether by chunnel or funnel, it's right on England's doorstep. Situated 20 minutes drive from Calais port and Eurotunnel in a quiet country setting. Recommended by major camping and caravanning associations.
Size 12 hectares, 180 touring pitches, 130 with electric hookup, 8 static caravans, 28, 27 WCs, 3 CWPs
£ car/tent 100-128, car/caravan 100-128, motorhome 100-128, motorbike/tent 80-100, children 15-17
Rental Chalet.
CC MasterCard Visa

Calor Gaz

Last arrival time: 00:00
➡ 10 km SW of Calais and 5 km from Eurotunnel. On D231, signposted in Guînes.

HAUTEFORT Dordogne

Le Moulin des Loisirs
Nailhac, 24390 Hautefort
📞 05 53 50 46 55 Fax 05 53 50 46 55
Open 15 April-30 September
Size 5 hectares, 62 touring pitches, 48 with electric hookup, 12 static caravans, 7, 8 WCs, 12 CWPs
£ car/tent 56-72, car/caravan 56-72, motorhome 56-72, motorbike/tent 56-72
Rental Chalet. 950-2400 FF
CC MasterCard Visa

➡ Near the Etang du Coucou, on D71 between St-Agnan and Badefols.

LUNEL Hérault

Les Amandiers
Chemin de Cafoulin, 30660 Gallargues-le-Montueux
📞 04 66 35 28 02 Fax 04 66 35 28 02
Open 1 May-13 September

Meyrueis

253

Size 3 hectares, 150 touring pitches, 150 with electric hookup, 20 static caravans, 15 🚿, 15 WCs, 1 CWP
£ car/tent 50.40-72, car/caravan 63-90, motorhome 63-90, motorbike/tent 50.40-72
Rental 🛏 🚐 Mobile homes (with WC)
℀ MasterCard Visa
Last arrival time: 22:00
➜ From A9, 20 km from Nîmes, exit Gallargues, or from N113, 3 km from Lunel, take direction Gallargues-le-Montueux.
See advert on this page

LES MATHES Charente-Maritime

Les Charmettes
av de la Palmyre, 17570 Les Mathes
📞 05 46 22 50 96 Fax 05 46 23 69 70
Open 27 March-2 October 🛏 🚐 🚚
Size 24 hectares, 40 touring pitches, 14 with electric hookup, 260 static caravans, 10 🚿, 8 WCs, 2 CWPs
£ car/tent 15-26.50, car/caravan 15-26.50, motorhome 15-26.50
Rental 🚐
℀ Visa
➜ From La Palmyre follow signs to Les Mathes. Take first exit at roundabout and site is on left. Well signposted.
See advert on this page

MEYRUEIS Lozère

Camping de Capelan
48150 Meyrueis
📞 04 66 45 60 50 Fax 04 66 45 60 50
Open 30 April-20 September 🛏 🚐 🚚
Size 2 hectares, 120 touring pitches, 100 with electric hookup, 34 static caravans, 16 🚿, 26 WCs, 1 CWP
£ car/tent 58-79, car/caravan 58-79, motorhome 58-79, motorbike/tent 58-79, children 10-14
Rental 🚐 Chalet.
℀ MasterCard Visa
Calor Gaz
Last arrival time: 22:00
➜ From A75 at Aguessac take road to Le Rozier, then site is signposted on D996.

Electrical voltages

Standard mains voltage is 220 AC at 50 HZ. Generally, the two rather than the three-pin plug is in use - so you will need a travel adaptor for most electrical items you will be carrying.

CAMPING LES AMANDIERS

Ideally situated for exploring the Cévennes, the Camargue and Provence, 15 mins from the beach and 800 m from the river (fishing).

Swimming pools, tennis, entertainment, shops.

Tent, caravan and mobile-home hire.

20 to 50% reductions low-season.

For information and reservations contact:

**30660 Gallargue-le-Montueux France
Tel/Fax: 66 35 28 02**

Les Charmettes
★★★
La Palmyre

With spacious pitches measuring at least 120m², Les Charmettes is an ideal base from which to explore this part of the Atlantic Riviera. Glorious beaches are just 3 miles away.

Facilities include:
Fabulous pool complex with waterslides & bubblepool, tennis, all weather multi-sport pitch, bar, restaurant & takeaway.
Free Tiger Club for 5 - 12 year olds.
Open 27th March – 2nd October.
Ferry inclusive packages available.

To obtain a brochure
call 0870 242 6666
quoting FMA01.

Haven Europe

EUROPE

254

Montaigu

MONTAIGU Vendée	7D3

Domaine de L'Eden
44119 La Boisière de Montaigu
☎ 02 51 41 62 32 Fax 02 51 41 56 07
Open 1 March-31 November
Size 15 hectares, 100 touring pitches, 100 with electric hookup, 10 static caravans, 14 🚿, 20 WCs,
£ car/tent 60-87, car/caravan 60-87, motorhome 60-87, motorbike/tent 60-87, children 10
Rental Chalets 1200-2900 FF
MasterCard Visa

➔ From Nantes take autoroute towards Bordeaux and exit at Montaigu. Take D23 from Montaigu for 2.2 km and site is signposted.
See advert on this page

MONTPELLIER Hérault	15F4

Le Lac des Rêves
Rue de Pérole, 34970 Latres
☎ 04 67 40 26 07 Fax 04 67 40 33 26
Open 22 March-26 September
Size 33 hectares, 20 touring pitches, 20 with electric hookup, 300 static caravans, 10 🚿, 10 WCs
£ car/tent 17.50-24.50, car/caravan 17.50-24.50, motorhome 17.50-24.50
Rental
MasterCard Visa

➔ From A9 take Montpellier-Sud exit and follow signs for Palavas, then Lattes. After bridge, continue straight on until roundabout, then heads towards Péroule on D132. Site is about 2 km and well signposted.
See advert on this page

Le Lac Des Reves
★★★★
Montpellier

With spacious pitches measuring at least 120m², Le Lac Des Reves is an ideal base from which to explore the beauties of Languedoc and the Camargue.

Facilities include:
Outdoor pools, waterslides, crazy golf, tennis, volleyball, BMX bicycle track, boules, bar, restaurant & takeaway.
Free Tiger Club for 5 - 12 year olds.
Open 15th April – 15th September.
Ferry inclusive packages available.

To obtain a brochure
call 0870 242 6666
quoting FMA01.

Haven Europe

DOMAINE DE L'Eden ★★★

*Superb open site
Large pitches
Mobilehomes from 100 to 300m²
Open all year*

- 15 hectare green field site
- Close to Puy de Fou
- Lake – fishing – beach
- 200 m² swimming pool – 2 tennis courts
- Mini-golf – ponies
- Dam with artificial lake 3 kms
- Sailboarding
- Bar, restaurant, shop
- Games room – discotheque

La Raillière – 85600 LA BOISIÈRE DE MONTAIGU
Tel: 02 51 41 62 32 – Fax: 02 51 41 56 07

La-Plaine-sur-Mer

LE RELAIS DE LA NAUTIQUE

The site stands close to the 'Etang de Bages' lake, ideal for sailing and windsurfing, but also offering the extensive sport and leisure facilities that you expect from quality sites in the south of France.

All pitches now have their own private sanitary block.

Reservations are strongly advised …which tells its own story.

**Le Relais de la Nautique
La Nautique
11100 Narbonne
Tel: 04 68 90 48 19
Fax: 04 68 90 73 39**

NANTES Loire-Atlantique

Camping Municipal Les Grenettes
La Varenne, 49270 St-Laurent-des-Autels
02 40 98 58 92 Fax 02 40 98 53 06
Open 1 June-15 September
Size 1 hectare, 35 touring pitches, 16 with electric hookup, 2 static caravans, 2, 6 WCs, 1 CWP
£ car/tent 29, car/caravan 38.30, motorhome 38.30, motorbike/tent 29, children 4.70

Last arrival time: 22:00
➜ From Nantes E on S bank of Loire (D751) for 17 km towards Champtoceaux. Site is on banks of Loire, well signposted in La Varenne.

NARBONNE Aude

Le Relais de la Nautique
La Nautique, 11100 Narbonne
04 68 90 48 19 Fax 04 68 90 73 39
Open 27 February-14 November
Size 16 hectares, 390 touring pitches, 390 with electric hookup, 50 static caravans, 390, 390 WCs
£ car/tent 82-130, car/caravan 82-130, motorhome 82-130, motorbike/tent 82-130, children 10-28
Rental Caravan 1001-1820 FF, Mobile homes 1365-3360 FF
CC MasterCard Visa

Last arrival time: 22:00

➜ From Narbonne take Narbonne-Sud exit off motorway and follow signs to La Nautique. After toll turn left at roundabout and campsite is 2.5 km on right.
See advert on this page

LES PIEUX Manche

Le Grand Large
Anse de Sciotot, 50340 Les Pieux
02 33 52 40 75 Fax 02 33 52 58 20
Open 3 April-19 September

A four star camping site, 25 km from Cherbourg and set by a superb long sandy beach. Well placed for visiting Bayeux tapestry, D Day beaches and Mont St Michel.
Size 4 hectares, 220 touring pitches, 220 with electric hookup, 50 static caravans, 23, 18 WCs, 2 CWPs
£ car/tent 84-105, car/caravan 84-105, motorhome 84-105, motorbike/tent 84-105, children 12.80-16
Rental Chalet. 1350-3000 FF
CC Visa

Calor Gaz
Last arrival time: 22:00
➜ From Cherbourg take D904 to Les Pieux/Barneville and from Les Pieux follow signs.

LA PLAINE-SUR-MER Loire-Atlantique

Camping La Renaudière
44770 La Plaine-sur-Mer
02 40 21 50 03 Fax 02 40 21 09 41
Open 1 April-30 September
Size 2.8 hectares, 82 touring pitches, 82 with electric hookup, 4 static caravans, 15, 14 WCs, 1 CWP
£ car/tent 67-93, car/caravan 67-93, motorhome 67-93, motorbike/tent 65-88, children 9-12
Rental 1030-2050 FF p.w., Chalets 920-2250 FF p.w.
CC MasterCard Visa

Calor Gaz
Last arrival time: 23:00
➜ From Pornic take D13 to La Plaine-sur-Mer and follow signs to site.

255

EUROPE

Ploërmel

Domaine de Kerlann
★★★★
Pont Aven

With spacious, secluded pitches in wooded parkland, Domaine de Kerlann is an ideal base from which to explore southern Brittany.
Children will have a great time too, with our free Tiger Club for 5-12 year olds.
Facilities include:
Indoor & outdoor swimming pool complexes, waterslides, tennis, volleyball, bar, restaurant, takeaway, Tiger Tots crèche for 2-4 year olds.
Open 27th March – 25th September.
Ferry inclusive packages available.

To obtain a brochure
call 0870 242 6666
quoting FMA01.

Haven Europe

PLOERMEL Morbihan

Camping du Lac Les Belles Rives
56800 Ploërmel
02 97 74 01 22
Open 1 April-30 September
Size 3 hectares, 135 touring pitches, 135 with electric hookup, 12, 25 WCs, 3 CWPs
£ car/tent 53, car/caravan 53, motorhome 53, motorbike/tent 53, children 9
Rental 900-1300 FF, Mobile home 1300-2000 FF
CC MasterCard Visa

➜ Leave Ploërmel beside the lake and turn right to site and beach.

PONT-AVEN Finistère   6C4

Camping du Château de Bélon
Port de Bélon, 29340 Riec-sur-Bélon
02 98 06 41 43 Fax 02 98 06 90 58
Open 1 April-15 October
Size 6 hectares, 150 touring pitches, 100 with electric hookup, 10 static caravans, 13, 14 WCs, 1 CWP
£ car/tent 57, car/caravan 57, motorhome 57, motorbike/tent 55
Rental 500 FF + camping price, Mobile homes 1300 FF + camping

Calor Gaz WS
Last arrival time: 22:00

➜ From Pont-Aven go SE on N783 for 1 km and turn right to Port of Bélon. Site is 4 km.

Domaine de Kerlann
Land Rosted, 29930 Pont-Aven
02 98 06 01 77 Fax 02 98 06 18 50
Open 27 March-25 September
Size 17 hectares, 232 touring pitches, 136 with electric hookup, 113 static caravans, 46, 50 WCs, 4 CWPs
£ car/tent 10.50-22, car/caravan 10.50-22, motorhome 10.50-22
Rental
CC MasterCard Visa

➜ From Pont-Aven take road towards Concarneau and turn left onto D77 towards Névez. Site is 1 km on right and signposted.
See advert on this page

PONT-DE-BEAUVOISIN Savoie

Camping Les Trois Lacs
Les Chaudonnes, 73330 Belmont-Tramonet
04 76 37 04 03 Fax 04 76 37 37 60
Open 1 April-15 September
Set beside two rivers, the site has large shaded pitches with a great atmosphere. It features swimming pool, paddling pool, tennis, childrens games and club and entertainment.
Size 5 hectares, 90 touring pitches, 90 with electric hookup, 12, 12 WCs, 1 CWP
£ car/tent 50-98, car/caravan 50-98, motorhome 50-98, motorbike/tent 50-98, children 10-20
Rental 1000-2000 FF 900-1800 FF Mobile home 1500-3000 FF

Calor Gaz
Last arrival time: 22:00

➜ 2 km from A43 and 3 km N of Pont-de-Beauvoisin, towards St-Genix-sur-Guiers. Follow signs in Belmont-Tramonet.

PONT-DE-VAUX Ain

Camping Les Ripettes
St-Bénigne, 01190 Pont-de-Vaux
03 85 30 66 58
Open 15 April-15 October
Size 2.5 hectares, 50 touring pitches, 47 with electric hookup, 6, 6 WCs,
£ car/tent 60, car/caravan 70, motorhome 70, motorbike/tent 70, children 10
Rental Mobile home

Last arrival time: 22:00

➜ Take A6/N6 to Tournus, D975 to Cuisery and D933 towards Pont-de-Vaux. Turn onto D2 (Pizzeria on corner) and site is 4 km on left at St Bénigne.

To convert kilometres to miles divide by 8 and multiply by 5

Campazur
CAMPING & CARAVAN

A few minutes from the most famous village of the Côte d'Azur.

**PRAIRIES DE LA MER
KON-TIKI
TOISON D'OR**

3 sites by the sea on the most beautiful beaches of the Gulf of St Tropez.

Special rates for families and pensioners for tent and caravan pitches.

A park of luxury Mobile-Homes.

Information and bookings:
Tel: 04 94 79 09 09 Fax: 04 94 79 09 10
Internet: http://www.campazur.com

PONTCHATEAU Loire-Atlantique

Castel Campingfay
Château du Deffay, Ste-Reine de Bretagne, 44160 Pontchâteau
02 40 88 00 57 Fax 02 40 01 66 55
Open 5 May-25 September
Size 8 hectares, 120 touring pitches, 100 with electric hookup, 22, 19 WCs, 2 CWPs
£ car/tent 71-122, car/caravan 71-122, motorhome 71-122, motorbike/tent 71-122, children 11-15
Rental Chalet. 800-3400 FF per week
CC MasterCard Visa

➡ From N165 take D33 W of Pontchâteau and go towards Ste Reine. The site is 1.5 km after the Calvaire on the right.

PORT GRIMAUD Var

Les Prairies de la Mer
83310 Port Grimaud
04 94 79 09 09 Fax 04 94 79 09 10
Open 1 April-5 October
Size 22 hectares, 700 touring pitches, 700 with electric hookup, 400 static caravans, 250 WCs, 15 CWPs
£ car/tent 119-140, car/caravan 119-140, motorhome 119-140, motorbike/tent 119-140, children 14
CC MasterCard Visa

Last arrival time: 00:00
➡ Leave Autoroute at Le Muy, towards Ste Maxime. Once there, take the road to St Tropez. Camp entrance right on N98, 6 km from Ste Maxime.
See advert on previous page

LE POULDU Finistère   8A3

Camping Les Grands Sables
Rue du Philosophe Alain, Le Pouldu, 29360 Clohars-Carnoët
02 98 39 94 43
Open 3 April-19 September
Size 2.4 hectares, 147 touring pitches, 110 with electric hookup, 12, 24 WCs, 1 CWP
£ car/tent 67, car/caravan 67, motorhome 67, motorbike/tent 67, children 13
Rental 800 FF, Mobile homes 950-2050 FF

Last arrival time: 22:00
➡ Off D49 from Le Pouldu.

PUY-L'EVEQUE Lot

Camping Le Ch'Timi
Touzac, 46700 Puy-l'Evêque
05 65 36 52 36 Fax 05 65 36 52 36
Open 1 April-30 September
Size 3 hectares, 70 touring pitches, 70 with electric hookup, 10 static caravans, 8, 8 WCs, 2 CWPs
£ car/tent 85, car/caravan 85, motorhome 85, motorbike/tent 85, children 15
Rental 960-1800 FF p.w. (4 people)
Gaz

➡ On D911 between Fumel and Puy-l'Evêque. Turn S on D8 following signposts and site is signed from D911.

RAMATUELLE Var

Kon Tiki
Route de Pampelonne, 83350 Ramatuelle
04 94 55 96 96 Fax 04 94 55 96 95
Open April-September
Size 9 hectares, 250 touring pitches, 250 with electric hookup, 450 static caravans, 58 WCs, 4 CWPs
£ car/tent 114-144, car/caravan 139-169, motorhome 139-169, motorbike/tent 84-109
Rental
CC MasterCard Visa
Gaz WS

Last arrival time: 24 hours
➡ Exit Autoroute at Le Muy, towards St Tropez and then take Route des Plages.
See advert on previous page

Toison d'Or
Plage de Pampelonne, 83350 Ramatuelle
04 94 79 83 54 Fax 04 94 79 85 70
Open April-September
Size 7 hectares, 100 touring pitches, 100 with electric hookup, 400 static caravans, 56 WCs, 3 CWPs
£ car/tent 114-144, car/caravan 139-169, motorhome 139-169, motorbike/tent 84-109
Rental Chalet. From 800 FF per week.
CC MasterCard Visa
Gaz WS

Last arrival time: 24 hours
➡ Exit Autoroute at Le Muy, towards St Tropez, then take Route des Plages.
See advert on previous page

RAMBOUILLET Yvelines

Camping Municipal de l'Etang d'Or
Rue du Château d'Eau, 78120 Rambouillet
01 30 41 07 34 Fax 01 30 41 00 17
Open all year

Ré, Ile de

259

Camping in the heart of a forest, on the banks of a lake. Paris is only 35 minutes by train. Numerous tourist sites close by. English spoken.
Size 5 hectares, 220 touring pitches, 180 with electric hookup, 80 static caravans, 20 ®, 22 WCs, 5 CWPs
£ car/tent 66, car/caravan 66, motorhome 66, motorbike/tent 66, children 14.50
➜ From A10 exit Rambouillet, site is on A10 NE of Chartres.

RAUZAN Gironde

Camping du Vieux Château
33420 Rauzan
05 57 84 15 38 **Fax** 05 57 84 15 38
Open 1 April-1 November

Spend your holidays in a quiet area, with good shade, in the centre of the Bordeaux vineyards. The site features swimming, table tennis, bike hire, children's games and entertainments.
Size 2.5 hectares, 50 touring pitches, 28 with electric hookup, 5 ®, 5 WCs, 1 CWP
£ car/tent 70, car/caravan 70, motorhome 70, motorbike/tent 70, children 10
Rental Mobile home Jul-Aug 2000 FF (5 people)
Calor Gaz WS
➜ At Rauzan, between Libourne and La Réole on D670.

RE, ILE DE Charente-Maritime 4A3

Camping Les Peupliers
17630 La Flotte-en-Ré
05 46 09 62 35 **Fax** 05 46 09 59 76
Open 1 May-5 September
Size 4 hectares, 200 touring pitches, 160 with electric hookup, 20 static caravans, 19 ®, 30 WCs, 1 CWP
£ car/tent 85-175, car/caravan 85-175, motorhome 85-175, motorbike/tent 85-175, children 28
Rental Chalet. 1580-3680 FF
MasterCard Visa
Calor Gaz
Last arrival time: 20:00
➜ From the bridge take D735 towards La Flotte-en-Ré. Site is before the village, on left.
See advert on this page

LES PEUPLIERS
Tel. 05 46 09 62 35 - Fax. 05 46 09 59 76
17630 LA FLOTTE EN RÉ
CAMPING ★★★ - HOTEL DE PLEIN AIR

Ile Blanche
Deviation de la Flotte, La Flotte, 17630 Ile de Ré
05 46 09 52 43 **Fax** 05 46 09 36 94
Open 1 April-11 November

Isle of Ré is an untouched island, easily reached by a bridge and motorway direct from St Malo. A paradise of nature and cycling. Quality accommodation for touring caravans with all services including indoor swimming pool and restaurant.
Size 4 hectares, 90 touring pitches, 90 with electric hookup, 80 static caravans, 18 ®, 18 WCs, 3 CWPs
£ car/tent 94-157, car/caravan 94-157, motorhome 94-157, motorbike/tent 94-157, children 17-24
Rental 1750-3450 FF
MasterCard Visa
Calor Gaz
Last arrival time: 22:00
➜ Cross bridge and follow signs for St Martin-de-Ré on D735. Bypass La Flotte and site is signed on left after several roundabouts.

EUROPE

260 Rochefort-en-Terre

ROCHEFORT-EN-TERRE Morbihan

Camping du Moulin-Neuf
56220 Rochefort-en-Terre
02 97 43 37 52 Fax 02 97 43 35 45
Open 1 April-30 September

1½ hours from St Malo. A quiet family site in a woodland setting, 10 minutes walk from a mediaval town, with fishing and a boating lake. Excellent touring centre for coast and countryside. Ideal rally site.
Size 2.5 hectares, 60 touring pitches, 44 with electric hookup, 13, 10 WCs, 3 CWPs
£ car/tent 80-95, car/caravan 80-95, motorhome 80-95, motorbike/tent 80-95, children 12-14
Last arrival time: 22:00
➔ From Rochefort-en-Terre, S on D774. Site is on right.

Le Bois Dormant/ Le Bois Masson
★★★★
St Jean de Monts

Le Bois Dormant and Le Bois Masson are adjacent parks which are both ideal for exploring the Vendée. If you're looking for a more peaceful stay, choose Le Bois Dormant; those seeking a livelier park will love Le Bois Masson. Guests can use facilities at both parks which include: Indoor and outdoor pool complexes, waterslide, jacuzzi, tennis, bar, restaurant and takeaway.
Free Tiger Club for 5 - 12 year olds.
Le Bois Masson open 27th March – 25th September.
Le Bois Dormant open 17th April - 18th September
Ferry inclusive packages available.

To obtain a brochure
call 0870 242 6666
quoting FRA01.

Haven Europe

ST-JEAN-DE-MONTS Vendée

Camping Le Bois Dormant
85160 St-Jean-de-Monts
05 51 58 62 62 Fax 05 51 58 29 97
Open 17 March-18 September
Size 10 hectares, 350 touring pitches, 350 with electric hookup, 150 static caravans
£ car/tent 11-16, car/caravan 11-16, motorhome 11-16
Rental Cabins
℃ MasterCard Visa
¼ ¼
➔ From St-Jean-des-Monts take D38 towards Les Sables d'Olonne. Site is 2 km from town centre.

Le Bois Masson
rue Sables d'Olonne, 85160 St-Jean-de-Monts
02 51 58 62 62 Fax 02 51 58 29 97
Open 27 March-25 September
Size 7.5 hectares, 250 touring pitches, 250 with electric hookup, 245 static caravans
£ car/tent 12-17, car/caravan 12-17, motorhome 12-17
Rental Cabins
℃ MasterCard Visa
➔ From St-Jean-de-Monts take D38 towards Les Sables d'Olonne. Site is 2 km from town centre.
See advert on this page

SAINTES Charente-Maritime

Camping au Fil de l'Eau
6 Rue de Courbiac, 17100 Saintes
05 46 93 08 00 Fax 05 46 93 61 88
Open 7 May-15 September

Set in Saintes, a Gallo-Roman city with 2000 years of history and rich in monuments. Only 30 minutes from the Atlantic and its fine sand beaches. A magnificent park on the banks of the River Charente.
Size 6 hectares, 214 touring pitches, 132 with electric hookup, 22, 27 WCs, 2 CWPs
£ car/tent 71, car/caravan 71, motorhome 71, motorbike/tent 71, children 11.50
Rental 1400-1800 FF per week
℃ MasterCard Visa
Calor Gaz

Vallon-Pont-d'Arc

Last arrival time: 22:00
➜ From A10 exit 35 and head for town centre. From town centre only 1 km via Quai de l'Yser to Rue de Courbiac.

SANTENAY-LES-BAINS Côte d'Or

Camping des Sources
Av des Sources, 21590 Santenay-les-Bains
☏ 03 80 20 66 55 Fax 03 80 20 67 36
Open 1 April-30 October ▲ ⛺ 🚐
Size 2.3 hectares, 130 touring pitches, 130 with electric hookup, 16 ⚿, 15 WCs, 2 CWPs
£ car/tent 83.50, car/caravan 83.50, motorhome 84.50, motorbike/tent 65, children 11.50
cc MasterCard Visa
▣ ✕ ▣ ▣ ▣ ▣ ▣ ▣ ▣ Calor Gaz ⚓ 🐕
Last arrival time: 22:30
➜ From N, exit A6 Beaune Sud and take N74, then D974. From S, exit Chalon Nord, then N6 and D974 to site.

SARLAT Dordogne

Aqua Viva
Carsac, 24200 Sarlat
☏ 05 53 31 46 00 Fax 05 53 29 36 37
Open Easter-30 September ▲ ⛺ 🚐
Size 10 hectares, 186 touring pitches, 160 with electric hookup, 26 ⚿, 22 WCs, 3 CWPs
£ car/tent 58-113, car/caravan 58-113, motorhome 58-113, motorbike/tent 58-113, children 10-22
Rental Chalet. 1100-4200 FF p.w.
▣ ✕ ▣ ▣ ▣ ▣ ▣ ▣ ▣ ▣ ▣ Calor Gaz ⚓ 🐕
Last arrival time: 22:00
➜ A20 to Souillac; then towards Sarlat. From Sarlat the site is about 6 km towards Souillac.

LA TREMBLADE Charente-Maritime

Camping La Pignade
Av des Monards, 17390 Ronce-les-Bains
☏ 05 46 36 25 25 Fax 05 46 36 34 14
Open 15 May-18 September ▲ ⛺ 🚐

At Campotel La Pignade you will find installations that are perfectly adapted to your family holiday - a swimming pool with a giant 43 metre slide, a paddling pool and a wide range of sports facilities.

261

Size 16 hectares, 448 touring pitches, 448 with electric hookup, 60 static caravans,
£ car/tent 61.50-123, car/caravan 61.50-123, motorhome 61.50-123, motorbike/tent 61.50-123
Rental 🚐 Mobile homes 1330-3815 p.w. (for 6 people)
cc MasterCard Visa
▣ ✕ ▣ ▣ ▣ ▣ ▣ ▣ ▣ Calor Gaz ⚓ 🐕
Last arrival time: 21:00
➜ From La Tremblade go N to Ronce-les-Bains. After roundabout site is signposted 200 m on left.

VALLON-PONT-D'ARC Ardèche

Camping L'Ardèchois
Route Touristique des Gorges, 07150 Vallon-Pont-d'Arc
☏ 04 75 88 06 63 Fax 04 75 37 14 97
Open 28 March-20 September ▲ ⛺ 🚐
Size 5 hectares, 244 touring pitches, 244 with electric hookup, 12 static caravans, 36 ⚿, 34 WCs, 3 CWPs
£ car/tent 103-145, car/caravan 103-145, motorhome 103-145, motorbike/tent 103-145
Rental 🚐 2190-3700 FF
cc MasterCard Visa
▣ ✕ ▣ ▣ ▣ ▣ ▣ ▣ ▣ ▣ ▣ Calor Gaz ⚓ 🐕
Last arrival time: 21:00
➜ From Vallon take D290 for 500 m. Site is signposted on right.
See advert on this page

Camping L'Ardèchois

**route Touristique des Gorges
07150 Vallon-Pont-d'Arc**

Super campsite beside the Ardèche.

A lovely pool, trees for shade, flowers to delight the eye and of course, canoes for hire.

**Tel: 04 75 88 06 63
Fax: 04 75 37 14 97**

Vannes

VANNES Morbihan

Camping Penboch
56610 Arradon
☎ 02 97 44 71 29 Fax 02 97 44 79 10
Open 5 April-20 September ▲ 🚐 🏕
Size 4 hectares, 175 touring pitches, 175 with electric hookup, 24 ☺, 20 WCs, 1 CWP
£ car/tent 85-140, car/caravan 85-140, motorhome 85-140, motorbike/tent 85-140, children 18
Rental 🏠 Chalet. 1400-3700 FF per week
℃ MasterCard Visa
🛁 🍴 🛒 📞 🏊 🎮 🎯 📺 🎾 ⛱ Gaz ♿ 🐕
➡ From N165 (E60), exit at Arradon, and follow the signs to site.

VARENNES-EN-ARGONNE Meuse

Le Paquis
Rue Saint-Jean, 55270 Varennes-en-Argonne
☎ 03 29 80 70 35 Fax 03 29 80 71 43
Open 6 April-29 September ▲ 🚐 🏕
Size 1.5 hectares, 80 touring pitches, 80 with electric hookup, 20 static caravans, 9 ☺, 9 WCs, 1 CWP
£ car/tent 32, car/caravan 32, motorhome 32, motorbike/tent 28, children 6
🛁¼ 🍴¼ 🛒¼ 📞 🎮 ⛱ ♿ 🐕
Last arrival time: 24 hours
➡ On D946 in centre of village of Varennes-en-Argonne.

VIAS Hérault

Camping Les Mimosas
Port-Cassafières, 34420 Portiragnes-Plage
☎ 04 67 90 92 92 Fax 04 67 90 85 39
Open 1 May-30 September ▲ 🚐 🏕

Situated on the banks of the Canal du Midi, 1 km from the sea (15 minutes walking) and offering a quiet relaxing stay with entertainment in the evening. Set around an aquatic centre with swimming pool, paddling pool, water slides and solarium.
Size 7 hectares, 400 touring pitches, 400 with electric hookup, 51 static caravans, 42 ☺, 50 WCs, 4 CWPs
£ car/tent 125, car/caravan 125, motorhome 125, motorbike/tent 125
Rental ▲ 🚐 Chalet.
℃ Visa
🛁 🍴 🛒 📞 ⛱

Last arrival time: 20:00
➡ Exit A9 at Beziers Est towards Vias, after 3 km turn to the beach, along the Canal du Midi.

VIELLE-ST-GIRONS Landes

Camping Le Col Vert
Léon, 40560 Vielle-St-Girons
☎ 05 58 42 94 06 Fax 05 58 42 91 88
Open 28 March-30 October ▲ 🚐 🏕
Size 30 hectares, 370 touring pitches, 370 with electric hookup, 61 static caravans, 97 ☺, 64 WCs, 8 CWPs
£ car/tent 49.50-121, car/caravan 54.50-159, motorhome 54.50-159, motorbike/tent 49.50-121, children 9-20
Rental ▲ 990-2690 FF, 🚐 1090-2790 FF, Chalet 1690-4490 FF
℃ MasterCard Visa
🛁 ✖ 🍴 🛒 📞 ⛱
Last arrival time: 20:00
➡ From N10 towards Bayonne, exit Castets towards St Girons, then head for Vielle.

VIEUX-BOUCAU-LES-BAINS Landes

Camping de Moisan
Route de la Plage, 40660 Messanges
☎ 05 58 48 92 06 Fax 05 58 48 92 06
Open 15 May-30 September ▲ 🚐 🏕
Size 7 hectares, 320 touring pitches, 220 with electric hookup, 31 ☺, 31 WCs, 12 CWPs
£ car/tent 50-72.50, car/caravan 60-88, motorhome 50-88, motorbike/tent 50-72.50, children 6-12
Rental 🚐 800-1800 FF, Mobile home 900-3000 FF
℃ MasterCard Visa
🛁 🍴 🛒 📞 ⛱
Last arrival time: 21:00
➡ In village of Messanges, 4 km N of Vieux-Boucau, follow signs to the beach.

VILLENEUVE-LOUBET Alpes-Maritimes

Camping La Vieille Ferme
296 Boulevard des Groules, 06270 Villeneuve-Loubet Plage
☎ 04 93 33 41 44 Fax 04 93 33 37 28
Open all year ▲ 🚐 🏕
Size 3 hectares, 134 touring pitches, 134 with electric hookup, 10 static caravans, 20 ☺, 16 WCs
£ car/tent 82-127, car/caravan 92-155, motorhome 92-155, motorbike/tent 76, children 13-18
Rental Chalet 1200-1900 FF (2 people), 1900-3200 FF (6 people)
℃ MasterCard Visa
🍴 🛒 📞 ⛱
Last arrival time: 21:00
➡ Leave motorway at Antibes and take N7 towards Nice for 10 km. Site is 1 km on left after Marineland. See advert on opposite page

Netherlands 263

CAMPING CARAVANING
La Vieille Ferme ★★★★
PISCINE CHAUFFÉE COUVERTE
296, Bd des Groules (par R.N.7)
F 06270 Villeneuve-Loubet Plage
Tél. 04 93 33 41 44 - Fax 04 93 33 37 28
RIVIERA COTE D'AZUR

- All-year-round camping.
- Swimming pool, heated and covered in winter.
- Long-stay reductions in winter.
- Chalets for hire.

**296, Bd des Groules (par R.N.7)
F 06270 Villeneuve-Loubet Plage
Tel: 04 93 33 41 44
Fax: 04 93 33 37 28**

Airotel Lac de Loire
★★★★

For lovers of watersports and the Loire Valley. The site lies on a wide stretch of the River Loire close to Blois.

Sail, windsurf or waterski on 140 ha of safe river… relax round the pool… or drive down the valley and take in the châteaux.
The choice is yours.

**Airotel Lac de Loire
41350 Vineuil**

VINEUIL Loir et Cher

Airotel Lac de Loire
Lac de Loire, 41350 Vineuil
 02 54 78 82 05 Fax 02 54 78 62 03
Open 1 April-15 October
Size 8 hectares, 190 touring pitches, 190 with electric hookup, 13 static caravans
Rental Chalet.
CC MasterCard Visa

➜ On D951, just outside Blois in direction of Chambord. See advert on this page

NETHERLANDS

OMMEN

Camping de Roos
Beerzerweg 10, Beerze-Ommen 7736 PJ
 052-325 1234 Fax 052-325 1903
Open 1 April-1 November

Beautifully situated campsite on the River Vecht in Overijssel. Splendid natural location with a pleasant, peaceful atmosphere. Very spacious pitches, good angling opportunities, heated toilet facilities. Ideal walking and cycling area.
Size 27 hectares, 250 touring pitches, 200 with electric hookup, 20 static caravans, 20, 36 WCs, 4 CWPs
£ car/tent 21-29, car/caravan 21-29, motorhome 21-29, motorbike/tent 21-29, children 4.50-5.50
Rental 650 NLG per week, chalets 350-950 NLG per week
CC MasterCard Visa

Last arrival time: 22:00
➜ From Zwolle (A28), take turn to Ommen (N34) and in Ommen, turn right over bridge (N347). Drive about 500 m, left towards Beerze (R103), turn right at end of road. Site on left after 7 km.

EUROPE

Discover Europe

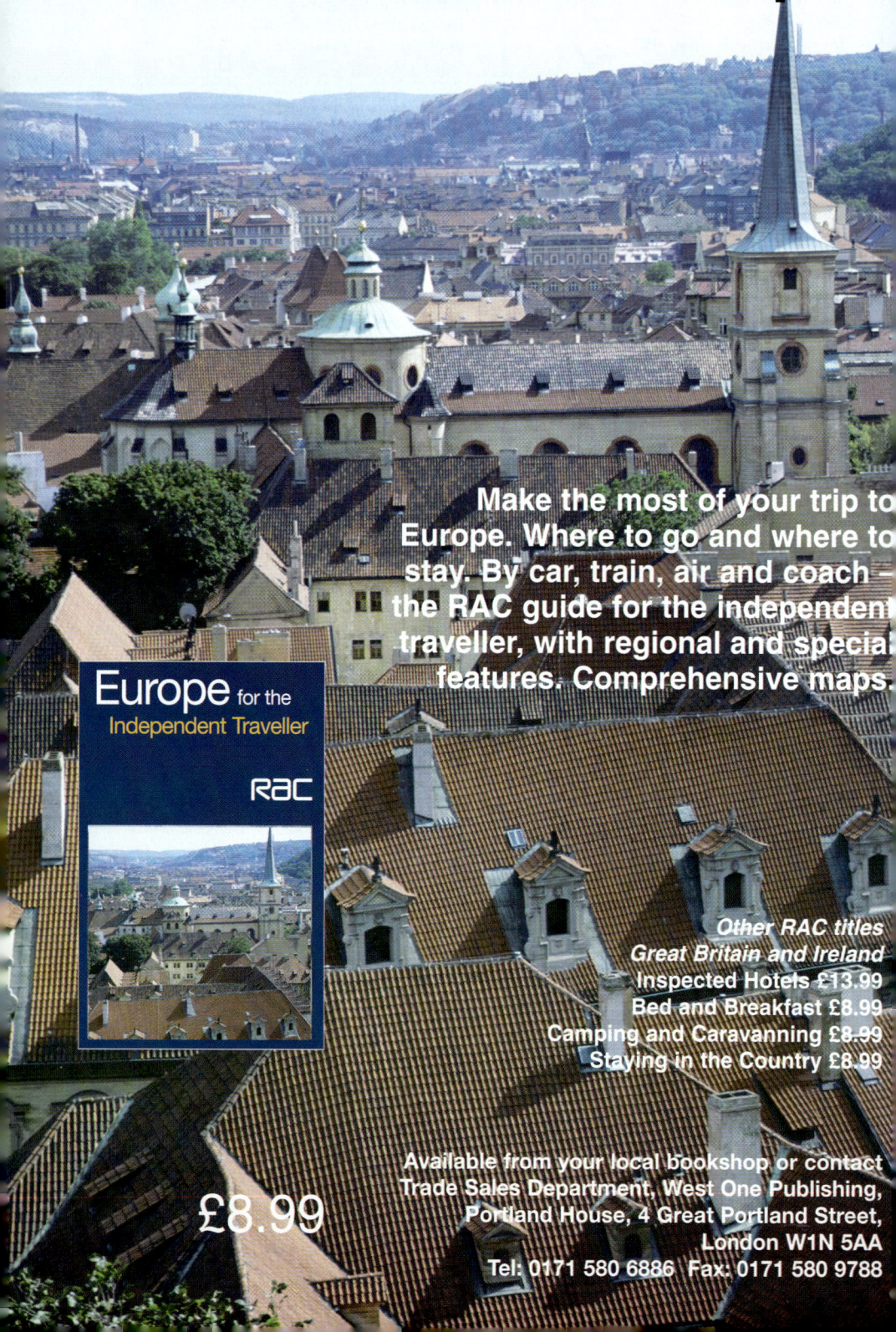

Europe for the
Independent Traveller

rac

£8.99

Make the most of your trip to Europe. Where to go and where to stay. By car, train, air and coach – the RAC guide for the independent traveller, with regional and special features. Comprehensive maps.

Other RAC titles
Great Britain and Ireland
Inspected Hotels £13.99
Bed and Breakfast £8.99
Camping and Caravanning £8.99
Staying in the Country £8.99

Available from your local bookshop or contact Trade Sales Department, West One Publishing, Portland House, 4 Great Portland Street, London W1N 5AA
Tel: 0171 580 6886 Fax: 0171 580 9788

Great Britain & Ireland Maps

Scale 1:1,185,000
19 miles to 1 inch (approx.)

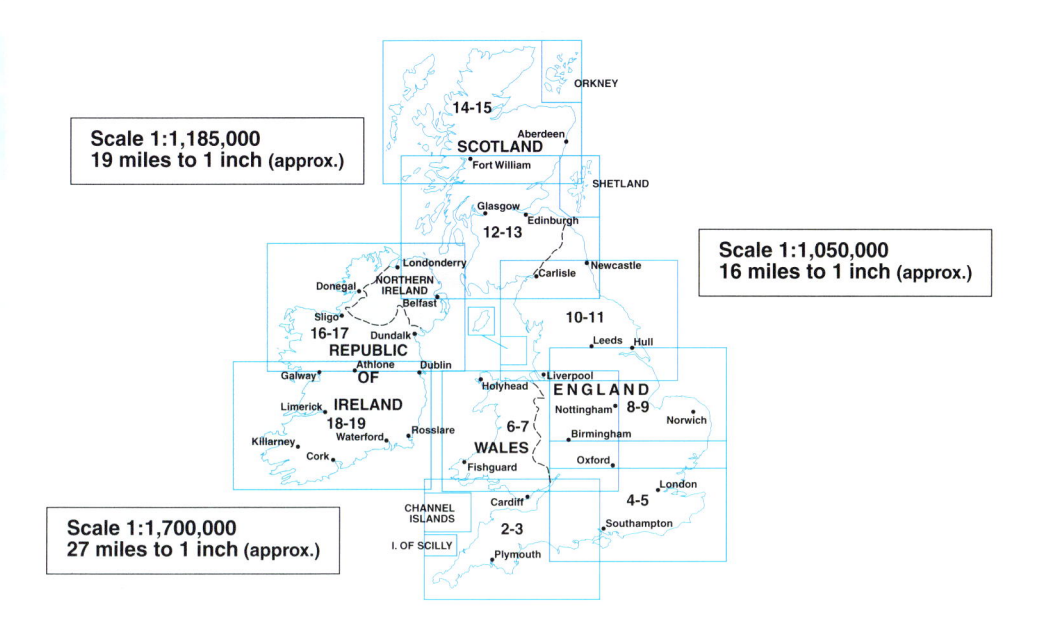

Scale 1:1,050,000
16 miles to 1 inch (approx.)

Scale 1:1,700,000
27 miles to 1 inch (approx.)

Key to Maps

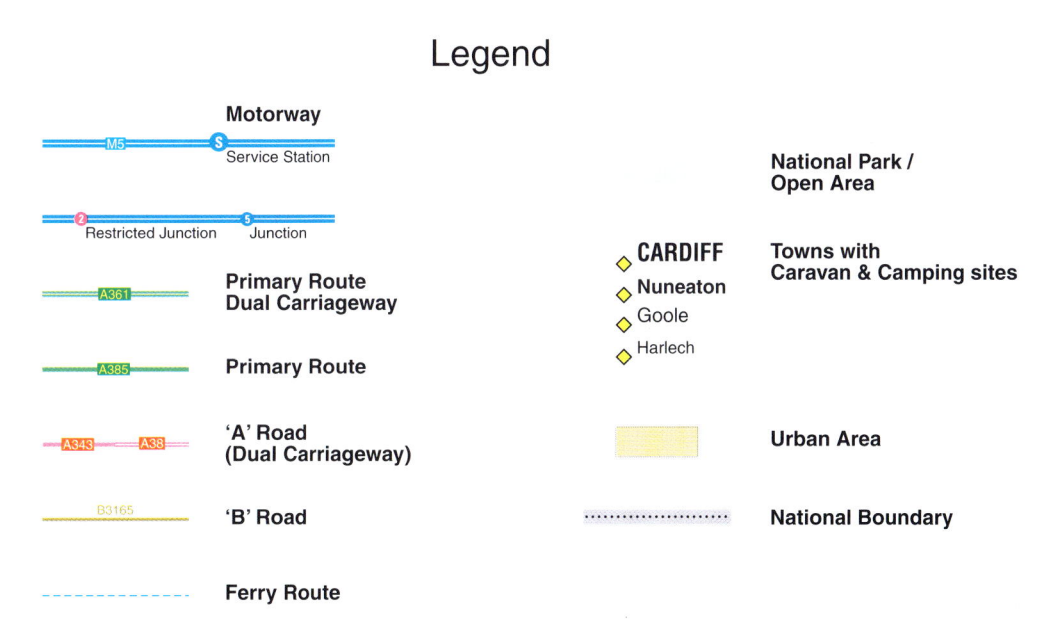

Legend

M5 — Service Station	**Motorway**
2 Restricted Junction — 5 Junction	
A361	**Primary Route Dual Carriageway**
A385	**Primary Route**
A343 — A38	**'A' Road (Dual Carriageway)**
B3165	**'B' Road**
- - - - - - - -	**Ferry Route**
	National Park / Open Area
◇ **CARDIFF** ◇ Nuneaton ◇ Goole ◇ Harlech	**Towns with Caravan & Camping sites**
	Urban Area
··············	**National Boundary**

© RAC/LOVELL JOHNS LTD.

2

Great Britain

Great Britain

3

4 Great Britain

Great Britain

5

6

Great Britain

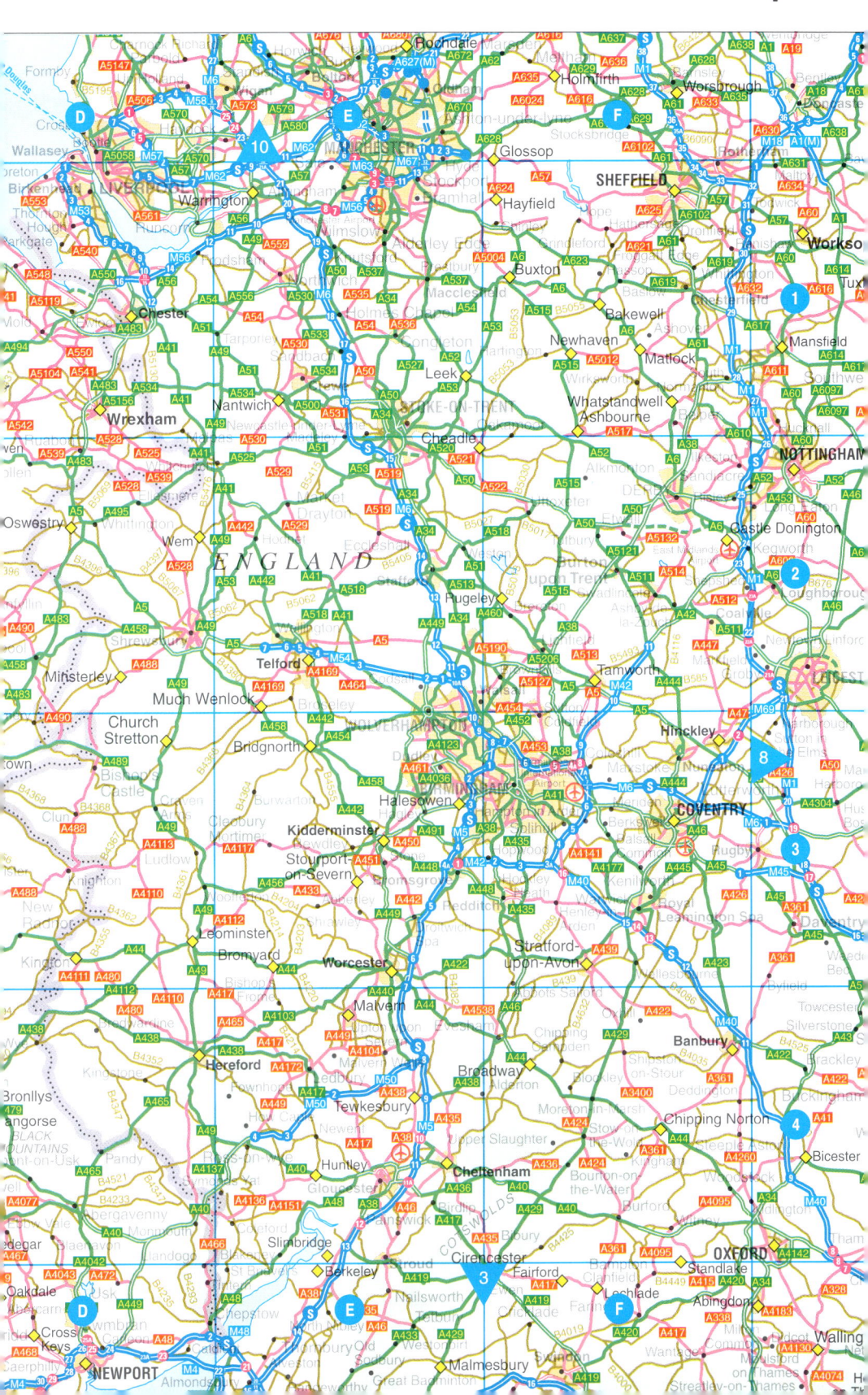

Great Britain

7

8

Great Britain

Great Britain

9

Moniaive
Parkgate
Holywood
Lochmaben
New Galloway
Dumfries
Lockerbie
Longholm
Bellingham
Otterburn
Crossmichael
New Abbey
Clarencefield
Annan
Gretna
Longtown
Castle Douglas
Dalbeattie
Gatehouse of Fleet
Kirkcudbright
Auchencairn
Haltwhistle
Haydon Bridge
Chollerford
Hexham
Carlisle
Brampton
Wetheral
Silloth
Wigton
Solway Firth
Allonby
Aspatria
Maryport
CUMBRIAN MOUNTAINS
Bassenthwaite
Mungrisdale
Penrith
Lazonby
Alston
Blanchland
Stanhope
St. John's Chapel
Workington
Cockermouth
Keswick
Thornthwaite
Braithwaite
Lamplugh
Loweswater
Whitehaven
St. Bees Head
Watermillock
Howtown
Ullswater
Patterdale
Shap
Appleby-in-Westmorland
Buttermere
Borrowdale
Egremont
Wasdale
Great Langdale
Grasmere
Rydal
Ambleside
Brough
Kirkby Stephen
Gosforth
Holmrook
Eskdale Green
Boot
Little Langdale
Elterwater
Coniston
Windermere
Tebay
Ravenstonedale
Reeth
Ravenglass
Hawkshead
Sawrey
Crosthwaite
Kendal
Sedbergh
Hawes
Askrigg
Aysgarth
Bainbridge
Broughton-in-Furness
Newby Bridge
Millom
Ulverston
Grange-over-Sands
Arnside
Milnthorpe
Burton-in-Kendal
Kirkby Lonsdale
Dalton-in-Furness
Barrow-in-furness
Isle of Walney
Carnforth
Morecambe Bay
Morecambe
Lancaster
High Bentham
Ingleton
Settle
Horton-in-Ribblesdale
Kettlewell
Malham
Grassington
Wigglesworth
Gisburn
Skipton
Barnoldswick
Earby
Lothersdale
Keighley
Fleetwood
Garstang
Thornton
Cleveleys
Clitheroe
Poulton-le-Fylde
Longridge
Haworth
Nelson
Burnley
BLACKPOOL
PRESTON
Blackburn
Lytham St. Annes
Clayton-le-Woods
Darwen
Hebden Bridge
Todmorden
Halifax
Southport
Ramsbottom
Rochdale
Bolton
Wigan
Oldham
Formby
Crosby
Bootle
Wallasey
Moreton
Birkenhead
LIVERPOOL
Warrington
MANCHESTER
Sale
Stockport
Hyde
Altrincham
Bramhall
Manchester Airport
Wilmslow
Knutsford
Northwich
Macclesfield
Holmes Chapel
Chester
Runcorn
Frodsham
Prestatyn
Rhyl
Abergele
Colwyn Bay
Llandudno
Deganwy
Conwy
Beaumaris
Penmaenmawr
Llanfairfechan
Bangor
Bethesda
Betws-yn-Rhos
St. Asaph
Holywell
Mold
Point of Ayre
ISLE OF MAN
Peel
Douglas
Newtown
Port Erin
Castletown
To Douglas
To Belfast

Great Britain

11

12

Great Britain

Great Britain

13

14

Great Britain

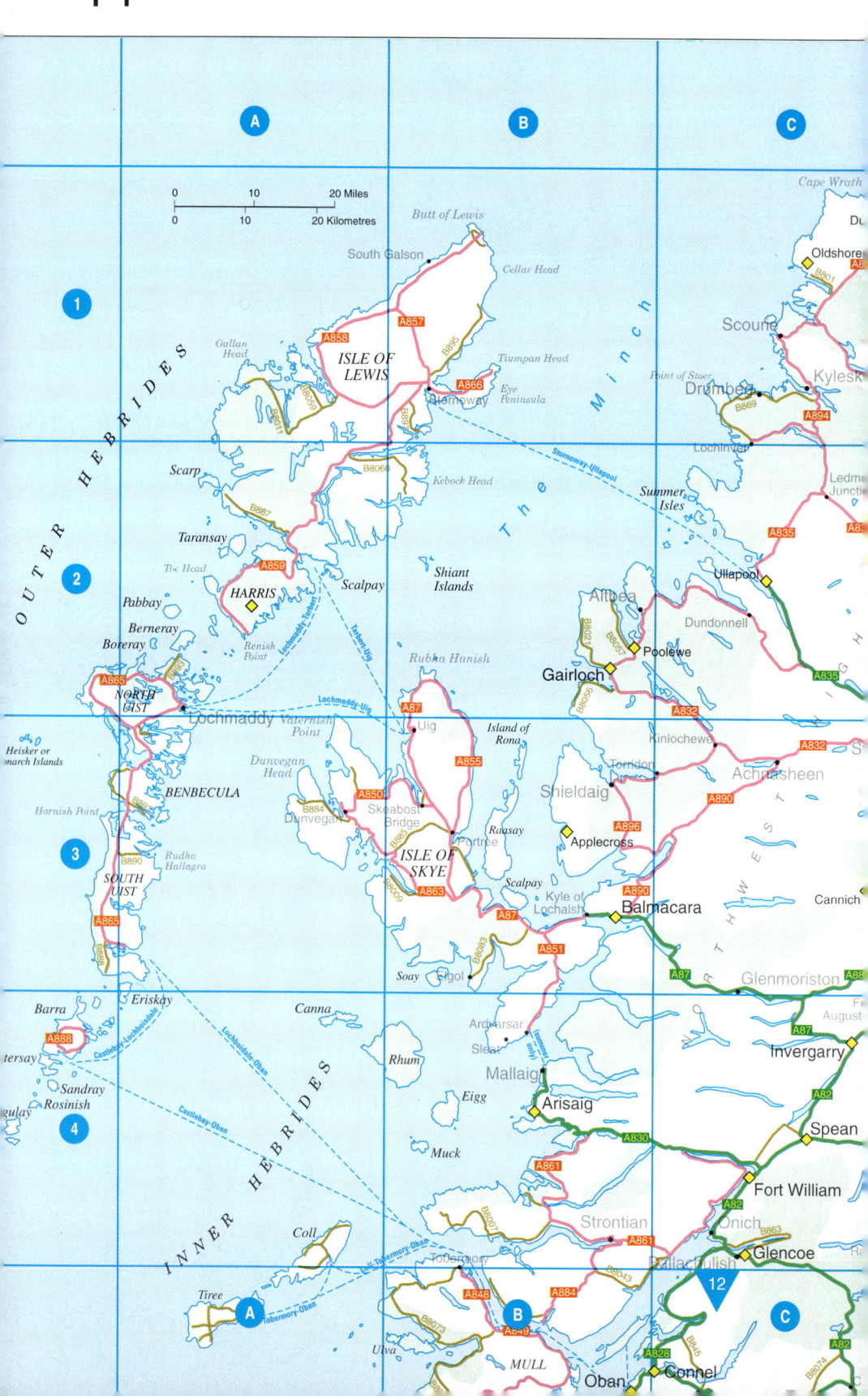

Great Britain

15

16

Ireland

A B C

1

ATLANTIC

Bloody Foreland
Falcarragh
Bunbeg
Aran Gweedore
Burtonpoint
Dunglow

Rosbeg

2

OCEAN

Rossan Point
Glencolumbkille
Ardara Glenties
Killybegs

Donegal Bay
Ballyshannon
Bundoran

3

Erris Head
Downpatrick Head
Rosses Point
Sligo
Strandhill
Belmullet
Ballycastle
Easky
Ballina
SLIEVE GAMPH MTS.
Ballysadare
Collooney
SLIGO
Bangor
Blacksod Bay
Dugort
Keel
Lough Conn
Achill Head
Mallaranny
MAYO
Charlestown
Gorteen
Boyle
Riverstown
Achill Island
Newport
Ballaghadereen
Clare
Clew Bay
Castlebar
Kiltimagh
Frenchpark
Inishturk
Louisburgh
Westport
Claremorris
Castlerea
Elphin
Strokestown
ROSCOMMON

4

Irishbofin
Lough Mask
Renvyle
Leenaun
Ballinrobe
Cashel
Roscommon
Longf
Lough Ree
CONNEMARA
Cong
Clifden
Tuam
REPUB
Slyne Head
Recess
Roundstone
Oughterard
GALWAY
Cashla
Athenry
Ballina
OF
Gorumna Islands
Lough Corrib
Galway
Salthill
Oranmore
Kilreekill
Fanore
Galway Bay
Loughrea
Aran
Kinvara

Ireland

17

18

Ireland

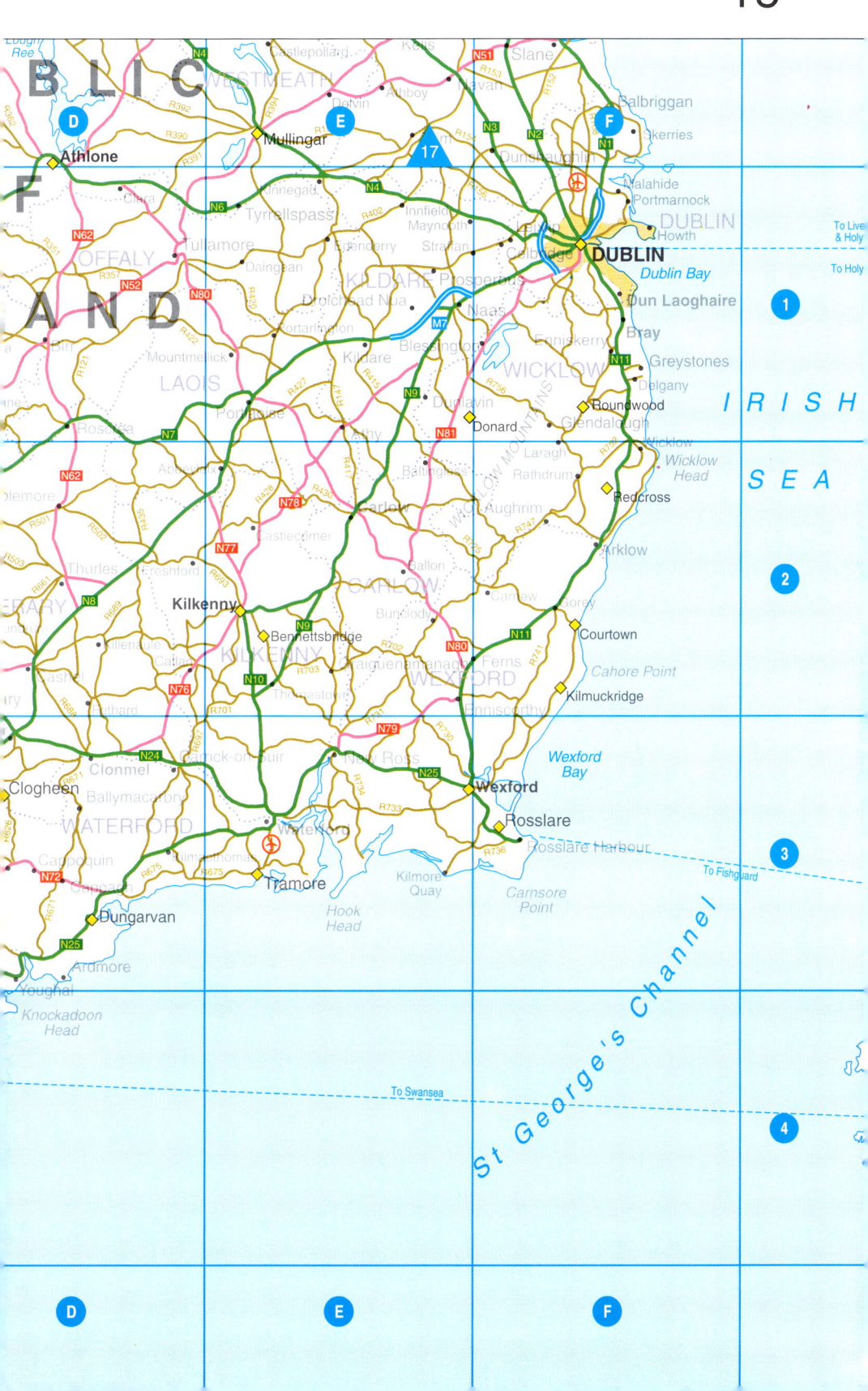

Ireland 19

Camping & Caravanning
Great Britain & Ireland 1999

Site report 1999

RAC

The publisher of this guide welcomes your comments about any sites visited that appear in this guide. Whatever your experience, good, indifferent or poor, do write to West One Publishing, Portland House, 4 Great Portland Street, London W1N 5AA, expressing your views.

Site name _____

Town _____

Dates of your stay _____

Please tick appropriate box	Yes	No
Were the staff helpful?	☐	☐
Were the washing facilities clean?	☐	☐
Was the site quiet?	☐	☐
Were the parking areas adequate?	☐	☐
Were there any problems towing your caravan to the site?	☐	☐
Did this guide accurately describe the site as it is now?	☐	☐

Site report

_____
_____
_____
_____
_____
_____

Site report continued

Name

Address

Camping & Caravanning
Great Britain & Ireland 1999

Site report 1999

RAC

The publisher of this guide welcomes your comments about any sites visited that appear in this guide. Whatever your experience, good, indifferent or poor, do write to West One Publishing, Portland House, 4 Great Portland Street, London W1N 5AA, expressing your views.

Site name _____

Town _____

Dates of your stay _____

Please tick appropriate box	Yes	No
Were the staff helpful?	☐	☐
Were the washing facilities clean?	☐	☐
Was the site quiet?	☐	☐
Were the parking areas adequate?	☐	☐
Were there any problems towing your caravan to the site?	☐	☐
Did this guide accurately describe the site as it is now?	☐	☐

Site report

_____
_____
_____
_____
_____
_____

Site report continued

Name_____

Address_____